Michigan *in* Brief: 2002–03

Michigan *in* Brief

2002–03

7TH EDITION

Michigan Nonprofit Association
Council of Michigan Foundations

*Prepared and published by
Public Sector Consultants, Inc.*

PSC
PUBLIC SECTOR
CONSULTANTS

© 1986, 1987, 1988, 1990, 1998, 1992, 2002 by Public Sector Consultants, Inc.

Published 1986, Seventh Edition 2002

Printed in the United States of America

ISBN 0-9721073-0-4

ABOUT THE SPONSORS

The Michigan Nonprofit Association (MNA) and the Council of Michigan Foundations (CMF) are co-sponsors of *Michigan in Brief: 2002–03.* This handbook and the corresponding Web site are a project of the Michigan Public Policy Initiative (MPPI), an MNA program with which the CMF is affiliated.

MICHIGAN NONPROFIT ASSOCIATION

The Michigan Nonprofit Association is the collective voice of Michigan's nonprofit organizations. The association was incorporated in 1990 and has more than 650 members. It provides a statewide network for the nonprofit sector, serves as a management-practices resource for nonprofit organizations, and acts as an advocate for the nonprofit community. The MNA's mission is to promote the awareness and effectiveness of Michigan's nonprofit sector. The goals of MNA are the following:

- *Provide services to the membership.* Examples are
  - information on fundraising, management, taxes, and technology; and
  - discounts on such items as director and officer liability insurance, long-distance telephone service, classified advertising, and office supplies.

- *Provide training and technical assistance.* Examples are
  - workshops on topics such as nonprofit management, legal issues, volunteer management, board development, and lobbying; and
  - annual statewide conferences such as the Grantmakers/Grantseekers Conference, the Volunteerism SuperConference, and a public policy day.

- *Promote nonprofit involvement in public policy.* Examples include the Michigan Public Policy Initiative, an MNA program that
  - educates policymakers and the media on issues of concern to Michigan nonprofits;
  - advocates for the Michigan nonprofit sector on public policy issues that affect all 501(c)(3) organizations and the people they serve; and
  - engages nonprofits in advocacy by providing them with the necessary tools and resources.

- *Promote and disseminate research on the nonprofit sector.* An example is
  - working with Michigan universities to develop new and promote existing research about issues of concern to the Michigan nonprofit sector and distributing it to practitioners, funders, policymakers, and the media.

For more information on the Michigan Nonprofit Association, please visit the MNA Web site at *www.mna.msu.edu* or call (517) 492-2400.

COUNCIL OF MICHIGAN FOUNDATIONS

The Council of Michigan Foundations is a 29-year-old 501(c)(3) nonprofit, membership association comprising nearly 500 independent, family, community, and corporate foundations and giving programs that make grants for charitable purposes. The CMF's mission is to enhance, improve, and increase philanthropy in Michigan.

The CMF supports both existing and developing foundations through specialized publications, educational and networking events, a Web site and listservs, consultation, and advocacy with state and federal policymakers. In addition, the CMF publishes the biennial *Michigan Foundation Directory* and assists partner organizations in sponsoring seminars for grant seekers.

The CMF has two supporting organizations, the Michigan AIDS Fund and Michigan Community Foundations' Ventures. The CMF also partners with the state—for example, through the Tobacco Settlement Partnership with community foundations.

For more information on the Council of Michigan Foundations and its services to philanthropy, please visit the Web site at *www.cmif.org* or call (616) 842-7080.

MICHIGAN PUBLIC POLICY INITIATIVE

The Michigan Public Policy Initiative is a program of the MNA and is affiliated with the Council of Michigan Foundations. The goal of the MPPI is to promote the involvement of Michigan's nonprofit community in public policy through training the community's leaders, building the capacity of its organizations, and encouraging its collaboration with public policymakers. The activities of the MPPI help to position the nonprofit sector as a partner with public and private leaders in working on pressing social issues facing Michigan residents.

The MPPI is guided by its Advisory Committee. The members are the following:

Peg Barratt *Director, Institute for Children, Youth and Families, Michigan State University*

John Chamberlin *Professor, University of Michigan Ford School of Public Policy*

Rob Collier *President and Chief Executive Officer, Council of Michigan Foundations*

David Egner *President, Hudson-Webber Foundation*

Peter Eisinger *Director, State Policy Center, Wayne State University*

Lynn Harvey *Professor, Michigan State University*

Paul Hillegonds *President, Detroit Renaissance*

Lynn Jondahl *Co-Director, Michigan Political Leadership Program*

Ann Marston *President, Michigan League for Human Services*

Chris Nelson *President, Michigan Association of United Ways*

Sharon Claytor Peters *President, Michigan's Children*

Craig Ruff *President, Public Sector Consultants, Inc.*

Earl Ryan *President, Citizens Research Council*

Sam Singh *President, Michigan Nonprofit Association*

Erin Skene *Director, Michigan Public Policy Initiative*

For more information on the Michigan Public Policy Initiative, please visit the MNA Web site at *www.mna.msu.edu* or call (517) 492-2400.

ABOUT PUBLIC SECTOR CONSULTANTS

Public Sector Consultants (PSC), Inc., is a private Michigan corporation. The firm, which was founded in 1980, strives to improve its clients' ability to meet the challenges of a changing world and communicate effectively with their constituencies. Public Sector Consultants is located in Lansing and specializes in the following:

- Nonpartisan policy research

- Health, environmental, education, human services, information technology, and economic analysis

- Strategic planning

- Program evaluation

- Survey research

- Public involvement

Public Sector Consultants' services have been commissioned by hundreds of state and local government agencies, school districts, colleges and universities, professional associations, hospitals, foundations, and private corporations. A number of its reports have attracted regional and national attention, and many have substantially affected public policy and attitudes.

Clients from the private, nonprofit, and public sectors use PSC's research, analytical, communications, and advisory capacities to develop and implement policies and strategic plans; improve internal management; identify stakeholder priorities and forge consensus among community interests; and identify political, regulatory, and economic factors influencing decisions.

The PSC staff is listed below. The firm also maintains a roster of affiliated consultants.

Craig Ruff *President and Chief Executive Officer*

William R. Rustem *Senior Vice President and Senior Consultant for Environmental Policy and Economic Development*

Jack D. Bails *Vice President and Senior Consultant for Natural Resources*

Suzanne M. Miel-Uken *Vice President and Senior Consultant for Community Health Policy*

Peter P. Pratt *Vice President and Senior Consultant for Health Policy*

Jeff D. Williams *Vice President and Senior Consultant for Technology and Public Policy*

Mark A. Coscarelli *Senior Consultant for Great Lakes and Environmental Policy*

Holly A. Madill *Senior Consultant for Natural Resources and Land Use*

Julie C. Metty *Senior Consultant for Natural Resources*

Jane E.V. Powers *Senior Consultant for Health Policy*

Dennis C. Washington *Senior Consultant*

Elisabeth T. Weston *Senior Consultant for Technology and Business Processes*

Carol A. Barish *Consultant for Health Policy*

Craig L. Garthwaite *Economist*

Amanda C. Menzies *Consultant for Health Policy*

Melissa L. Riba *Consultant for Survey Research*

Elias M. Rivers *Consultant for Technology and Public Policy*

Jeramy Donovan *Research Assistant*

Dyan Iansiti *Executive Assistant*

Janice Jackson *Administrative Assistant*

Diane W. Levy *Senior Editor*

Gerree Serrels *Network Administrator*

Linda A. Sykes *Comptroller*

Donna Van Natter *Production Assistant*

Public Sector Consultants' offices are located at 600 West St. Joseph Street, Lansing, Michigan 48933. The firm may be reached by telephone (517/484-4954), facsimile (517/484-6549), e-mail (psc@pscinc.com), or Internet (*www.publicsectorconsultants.com*).

CONTENTS

PREFACE

M ichigan in Brief: 2002–03, prepared and published by Public Sector Consultants, Inc., provides useful information about the state and an objective look at more than 40 public policy topics of current concern to Michigan residents and their elected representatives. The issues are treated in sufficient depth to be useful to the well-informed yet written plainly enough to be understood by nonexperts. Each policy topic presentation has four parts: a glossary; background information; discussion of policy options, including a balanced, nonpartisan presentation of various viewpoints; and sources of additional information, including telephone and FAX numbers as well as Web sites where available. (E-mail addresses are not included because they change too frequently.)

Chapters 1–3 of Michigan in Brief provide historical, general, and budgetary information about the state.

- "About Michigan" summarizes the economic, cultural, and political history of the state, recounting events from 1600 to the present, and presents a profile of the state's people and lifestyles in addition to a list of facts about the state.

- "About State Government" profiles the executive branch (including brief descriptions of state departments), legislative branch (with a sketch of the lawmaking process), and judicial branch (with an explanation of the various courts' jurisdictions) and also summarizes state government's checks and balances.

- "About the State Budget" outlines the process by which Michigan's annual financial plan is determined.

Chapter 4, "About Michigan's Nonprofit Sector," describes the organization, breadth, and contribution of this sector to the state's people and economy.

This is the seventh edition of Michigan in Brief, and the content is confined largely to key policy issues related to human services, the environment, health care, and the arts. In addition to the index listing the subjects treated in this edition, the tables of contents from earlier editions are presented to assist readers who are interested in topics from these publications.

This handbook is available in hard copy and on line. To order it in hard copy, please use the form on the last page of the document. On line, this edition as well the sixth may be found at www.michiganinbrief.org. For further information, please contact Public Sector Consultants, Inc., at 600 West St. Joseph Street, Lansing, Michigan 48933. The firm may be reached at 517/484-4954, 517/484-6549 (FAX), psc@pscinc.com, and www.publicsectorconsultants.com.

ACKNOWLEDGMENTS

This publication was made possible by grants to the Michigan Nonprofit Association and the Council of Michigan Foundations from the following funders:

- W.K. Kellogg Foundation
- C.S. Mott Foundation
- DaimlerChrysler Corporation Fund
- The Skillman Foundation
- Dow Chemical Company Foundation
- Frey Foundation
- Ethel and James Flinn Family Foundation

Authors for Public Sector Consultants, Inc.

Jack D. Bails *B.S., Fisheries; M.S., Aquatic Sciences (Michigan State University)*

Carol A. Barish *B.B.A., Management (Northwood University); M.S., Administration (Central Michigan University)*

Mary B. Cohen *B.A., Speech and Communication (University of Michigan); M.A., Communication (Western Michigan University)*

Mark A. Coscarelli *B.S., Environmental and Natural Resource Studies (Michigan State University)*

Laurie A. Cummings *B.A., International Relations; M.S., Agricultural Economics (Michigan State University)*

David Ellis *HNC, Business Studies (South West London College); M.S., Information and Communication Sciences (Ball State University)*

Bev Farrar Federau *B.A., French (Ohio Wesleyan University)*

Wilma L. Harrison *B.S., Education (Northwestern University)*

Christine F. Hollister *B.A., Social Science (Michigan State University); M.B.A. (University of Michigan–Flint)*

Robert J. Kleine *B.A., Economics and History (Western Maryland College); M.B.A., Finance (Michigan State University)*

Holly A. Madill *B.S., Environmental Science (University of Alabama); Master of Urban and Regional Planning (Michigan State University)*

Suzanne M. Miel-Uken *B.A., Social Science; M.S., Criminal Justice Administration (Michigan State University)*

Amanda C. Menzies *B.A., Social Science (Michigan State University)*

Julie C. Metty *B.A., Environmental Policy; M.S., Resource Development (Michigan State University)*

Jane E.V. Powers *B.S., Public Affairs Management (Michigan State University)*

Peter P. Pratt *B.A., English; M.A., English; Ph.D., English (University of Michigan)*

Melissa L. Riba *B.A., Sociology and Philosophy (California State University–Fresno); M.A., Sociology; Ph.D. program, Sociology (Michigan State University)*

Amy E. Rosewarne *B.A., Art History (University of Michigan); M.A., English Literature (California State University–Northridge); Ph.D. program, Cultural Studies (Michigan State University)*

Craig Ruff *B.A., Political Science; Master of Public Policy (University of Michigan)*

William R. Rustem *B.S., Social Science; M.S., Resource Development (Michigan State University)*

Pamela J. Sanders *B.S., Political Science (Central Michigan University)*

Alois W. Sandner *Ph.B., Philosophy (Sacred Heart Seminary)*

Paul R. Smyth *B.A., English (Kalamazoo College); M.A., English; M.S., Criminal Justice; Ph.D., English (Michigan State University)*

Dennis C. Washington *B.A., English (Oakland University); Master of Planning (University of Minnesota)*

Elisabeth T. Weston *B.A., Political Science (University of Michigan); M.B.A. (George Mason University)*

Jeff D. Williams *B.A., International Relations (Michigan State University); M.A., Public Affairs (University of Minnesota)*

Authors for the Sponsors

Rob Collier *B.A., Sociology and Political Science (Hobart College); Master of Public Administration (Central Michigan University)*

Jeri Fischer *B.A., Education (Central Michigan University); M.A., Education (Michigan State University)*

Robin Lynn Schultheiss *B.A., Liberal Arts (Central Michigan University)*

Erin Skene *B.A., Journalism; B.A., English (Michigan State University)*

Mark Wilson *B.A., Commerce; M.A., Commerce (University of Melbourne); M.A., Economics (University of Wisconsin); A.M., Regional Science; Ph.D., Regional Science (University of Pennsylvania)*

Other

All portions of the book were reviewed by at least two people other than the author and editor. These "second readers" usually were someone who has a background in the subject and another who has simply a layperson's knowledge of the topic. Many PSC authors served as second readers as did other staff members and a number of people in state government and the private sector; others assisted by providing data and other information. For their help, we are indebted to **Ari B. Adler, Rick Asher, Lance Boldrey, Craig Garthwaite, John Harrison, Howard Heideman, David Kimball, Diane Wolfe Levy, Stephen Manchester, David Murley, Randy O'Brien, Sam Singh, James Sinnamon, Sarah Slocum, Gillian Stoltman, Linda Sykes, Donald VeCasey, Tom Weston, Keith Wilson, Bradley Wittman, Jay Wortley,** and **Rhonda Oyer Zimmerman.** In addition, **Matthew Ellsworth, Brandy Barnes, Jeramy Donovan,** and **Dyan Iansiti** provided research and other assistance to the PSC authors.

Editing, Design, Production

Wilma L. Harrison *Editor*

Elisabeth T. Weston and Donna Van Natter *Format and design*

Gerree Serrels, Elias Rivers, and Jeff D. Williams *Web site*

Jeffrey Fillion *Design*

Millbrook Printing Company (Grand Ledge) *Printer*

Project Management

Jeff D. Williams for Public Sector Consultants

Erin S. Skene for the sponsors

Chapter 1

About Michigan

- Economic, Cultural, and Political History
- Profile of People and Lifestyles
- State Facts

Economic, Cultural, and Political History

ECONOMY AND CULTURE

POLITICS

1660 to 1760

About 15,000 Indians lived in Michigan when Europeans first arrived in the area in the early 1600s. The Chippewa (Ojibway) lived in the Upper Peninsula and eastern lower peninsula and the Potawatomi in the southwest. Other tribes included the Sauk, Miami, Huron, and Menominee.

The earliest European immigrants came largely from France, mainly as fur traders and missionaries. Father Jacques Marquette founded the first permanent settlement in Michigan, in Sault Ste. Marie, in 1668; three years later, he founded St. Ignace. The military posts at Mackinac Island and Mackinaw City (Fort Michilimackinac) were built to protect French influence in the region.

Southern Michigan was settled a bit later. In 1690 the French established Fort St. Joseph, near Niles. In 1701 Antoine de la Mothe Cadillac, who commanded Fort Michilimackinac, established Fort Pontchartrain in Detroit, which became a fur-trading hub, a strong defense against British exploration, and an early farming site.

In search of the mythical northwest passage to the Orient, Samuel de Champlain (founder of Quebec) sent Etienne Brulé to head west through the Georgian Bay. Brulé reached the Sault Ste. Marie area in 1618. On a later trip, in 1621, he traveled as far west as the Keweenaw Peninsula. In the 1630s Jean Nicolet explored the Lake Michigan area, reaching Green Bay.

The French settled northern Michigan first because they had made an enemy of the Iroquois Nation in southwest New York, which blocked the French path to Lake Erie and southern Michigan.

By the turn of the 18th century, the British too were interested in Michigan. The French responded by forming an alliance with various Indian tribes, as they had in the eastern areas of Canada and America. At the conclusion of the French and Indian War—which ended with a British victory on the Plains of Abraham, in Quebec—the French surrendered Detroit, in 1760, to British Maj. Robert Rogers.

1761 to 1836

Life was extraordinarily difficult in Michigan during much of this period.

Constant skirmishing occurred among the French settlers, various Indian tribes, English settlers, and—after the Revolutionary War ended, in 1783—newly independent Americans. Much of Michigan was unsettled. Control of the few forts shifted among French and British and American

The Indian tribes had found the French to be friendly and respectful, and British ascension incited nearly nonstop skirmishing among European settlers and the Indians. For example, the Ottawa leader Pontiac organized attacks against all British forts in the 1760s, and most fell.

Michigan saw little action during the Revolutionary War, and even afterward, the British settlers ignored the new U.S. government. Fort Detroit remained in British hands

▼

▼

Sponsored by the Michigan Nonprofit Association and the Council of Michigan Foundations

ECONOMY AND CULTURE

POLITICS

1761 to 1836 (cont.)

control. Indian raids, spirited by the French and British, were common.

After the War of 1812, federal surveyors dismissed Michigan as uninhabitable because of its swampland. This finding caused many easterners to settle and farm in Illinois and Missouri rather than Michigan.

Compounding problems of settlement was the lack of clearly defined property rights. Not until treaties clearing the way for titled land were signed with the Indians in 1819 through 1821 did settlers from the eastern states begin moving into the Michigan Territory.

In the 1820s and 1830s, settlement surged. New roads were built into the territory's central parts, the first public land sales were held, and the Erie Canal's completion, in 1825, spurred an influx of farmers from New England and New York. The territory grew faster than any other part of the United States.

In 1820 Michigan had 8,896 people, excluding Indians. By 1830 the population had grown to 32,000.

until 1796, and in 1812 the British and their allies, the Shawnee, led by Tecumseh, regained control of Detroit and Mackinac Island; many U.S. settlers were slaughtered at Frenchtown, in Monroe County, in 1813. It was not until 1815 that the British surrendered Mackinac Island to the United States.

The Northwest Territory was formed under the Ordinance of 1787, and the County of Wayne was defined as including most of Wisconsin, all of Michigan, and northern sections of Indiana and Ohio. Later, Minnesota, Iowa, and part of the Dakotas were added. In 1805 President Jefferson declared Michigan a separate territory, with Detroit as its capitol, and named William Hull territorial governor.

In 1833 the Michigan Territory had more than 60,000 inhabitants, sufficient to formally seek admission as a state. Voters adopted a territorial constitution in October 1835, and Michigan's acting governor, Stevens T. Mason—who, at age 19, had been appointed by President Jackson— pushed for statehood. But a skirmish with Ohio over the rightful ownership of Toledo (eventually ceded to Ohio in exchange for the Upper Peninsula) delayed statehood until 1837.

1837 to 1859

In 1840 the new state's population had reached 212,267, and settlers were pouring into Michigan, doubling the population by 1850 and again by 1860. Farming replaced fur trading as the state's primary economic activity.

The transplanted New Englanders and New Yorkers brought with them Yankee values: tolerance, a strong work ethic, and love of education. Dutch farmers settled the southwest, Germans the Saginaw Valley, Irish the southeast, and Finns and Italians the Upper Peninsula.

The Germans, in particular, strongly encouraged establishing public schools in each community. Borrowing from the Northwest Territory's policy, the property tax revenue from one section of each township in each county was dedicated to public schools.

In the 1830s oil was discovered in Macomb County, and in the 1840s rich copper and iron ore deposits were found in the Upper Peninsula.

On January 26, 1837, Michigan became the 26th state. Stevens T. Mason, a Democrat aged 24, became its first elected governor. He led the efforts to establish state-supported schools and to locate the University of Michigan in Ann Arbor. Mason left the governorship in 1840.

From 1837 to the 1850s, Michigan politics were decidedly Jacksonian and Democratic out of loyalty to President Jackson for supporting Michigan statehood. One Michigan county is named after the president and several others after members of his cabinet: Barry, Berrien, Branch, Calhoun, Eaton, Ingham, Livingston, and Van Buren.

The influx of settlers from New York and New England created a strong liberal, temperate, and abolitionist political ethos. For example, Michigan was the first government unit in the country to prohibit capital punishment, and Michigan's abolitionist sentiment gave birth to the Republican Party, uniting the Whigs and Free Soilers at a July 6, 1854, convention in Jackson.

▼

▼

Sponsored by the Michigan Nonprofit Association and the Council of Michigan Foundations

ECONOMY AND CULTURE

POLITICS

1837 to 1859 (cont.)

Rapid economic growth prompted land and money speculation fueled by an unregulated credit and banking system. Following the Panic of 1837, the boom evaporated, leaving impoverished farmers, failed banks, and abandoned projects that included several grand schemes for state-financed railways and canals. Economic stability returned during the 1850s with agricultural growth and the burgeoning lumber and mining industries.

With the exception of a single term (1840–41), when Whigs William Woodbridge and James Wright Gordon served, Democrats controlled the governorship from statehood until 1854. In 1854 the new Republican Party's standard bearer, Kingsley S. Bingham, was elected chief executive, and no Democrat managed to win the office back until 1890.

1860 to 1899

The population of the state reached 749,113 in 1860, and farming, lumbering, and early manufacturing dominated the economy in the last half of the 19th century.

Michigan's climate and fertile soil led to national leadership in wheat production. Important cash crops were fruit along the temperate Lake Michigan shoreline, sugar beets in the Thumb, and celery in the Kalamazoo area.

Lumbering became a huge industry after the Civil War. Michigan woodlands, producing about a quarter of the nation's total supply, spurred furniture manufacturing in Grand Rapids and papermaking in Kalamazoo and produced enormous capital and wealth throughout the state. Another successful industry established in this early period was the production of cereal foods, launched by W.K. Kellogg and C.W. Post.

Railroads transformed Michigan's economy by making it easier to distribute the state's timber, livestock, and food nationwide.

Between 1860 and 1890, more than 700,000 immigrants, more than half of them from Europe and Canada, migrated to Michigan.

The Civil War solidified Republican control of Michigan politics. Michigan was fiercely pro-Union, and residents revered President Lincoln.

A major force in state politics was the Grand Army of the Republic—veterans of the Civil War and staunchly Republican. Michigan's Civil War governor, Austin Blair, became one of the most prominent chief executives in America; he marshaled troops to serve in the war and raised considerable money for the effort.

Blair's successor as governor was Henry Crapo, the first of several lumber barons to serve as chief executive. One of his grandsons was William C. Durant, the founding president of General Motors.

In 1882 Josiah Begole was elected governor as a Fusionist, a political party that combined Democrats and Greenbackers (who favored paper money and populist ideals). The only other non-Republican governor in this era was Edwin Winans, a Democrat who served in 1891–92. The century ended with the election of the last person from Detroit to serve in Michigan's highest office, Hazen S. Pingree; he led property tax reform and sought unsuccessfully to make taxes progressive and shorten the workday.

1900 to 1948

By 1900 the population of the state had reached 2,402,982, and in the next few decades the major turning point in the Michigan economy occurred: Henry Ford introduced the assembly line into automobile manufacturing. Ford and such other auto pioneers as R.E. Olds, William Durant, and Walter Chrysler set in motion the 20th century's greatest wealth creator—the automobile industry.

The Republicans so dominated Michigan politics in the first half of the 20th century that the state came close to one-party control. From 1918 to 1928, not one Democrat was elected to the state Senate and only nine served in the state House of Representatives.

The Republicans, however, were torn between two factions: Progressives such as Pingree and Chase Osborn and

▼

▼

Sponsored by the Michigan Nonprofit Association and the Council of Michigan Foundations

ECONOMY AND CULTURE

POLITICS

1900 to 1948 (cont.)

Automobile manufacturing created an enormous number of jobs, attracting people to Michigan from Canada, the southern states, and Europe. Between 1900 and 1930, only Los Angeles grew faster than Detroit, the population of which soared from about 286,000 to nearly 1.6 million. Flint grew from 13,000 to more than 156,000.

During this time, new immigrants were less likely than before to be German or English, as in earlier years, and more likely to be Polish, Hungarian, Italian, Greek, and African-American. With the heterogeneous influx, the old Yankee influences—social, political, and economic— began to wane.

As the automobile industry grew, so did the labor force's unity and activism. Michigan witnessed bitter confrontations between unions and large employers. As labor organizing drives became more successful, the benefits and wages of the automobile workplace grew richer and began to spill into other segments of the economy.

The Great Depression of the 1930s took a terrible toll. By 1934, 800,000 of the state's five million residents were receiving some form of public relief. Half of the nonagricultural work force was unemployed. But by the early 1940s, World War II and the need for arms production had boosted the state's industrial capacity and ignited a new era of economic growth.

conservatives such as Albert Sleeper. In 1912 the split led to Democrat Woodbridge Ferris—the founder of Ferris Industrial School, now Ferris State University—being elected governor; he later served in the U.S. Senate.

Progressives in both parties introduced such reforms as the secret ballot, referendum and initiative, direct election of U.S. senators, women's suffrage, workers' compensation, and expanded state authority over railroads, banks, insurance companies, and the liquor industry.

Progressive support was so strong that Michigan voted for Teddy Roosevelt for president in 1912, despite his being a third-party candidate.

In the 1920s, Gov. Alexander Groesbeck served three terms and, by creating the State Administrative Board, consolidated and centralized the executive branch of state government. In 1932 and 1936, Democrats William Comstock and Frank Murphy, respectively, rode the coattails of Franklin Roosevelt into the governor's office.

Thomas Dewey, an Owosso native, carried Michigan against Democrat Harry S. Truman in the 1948 presidential election. But in the same year, Democrat G. Mennen Williams was elected governor and ushered in a new era of Michigan politics.

1949 to 1982

In 1950 the population reached 6,372,009, and in that decade the domestic vehicle industry reached its zenith.

Without serious competition from other states or countries, Michigan automobile companies spread enormous wealth among workers and employers. In 1955 Michigan's per capita income was 16 percent above the U.S. average—among the highest in the world—and by 1960 the state probably had the world's broadest middle class.

A high standard of living translated into public acceptance of considerable government intervention in the social and economic spheres, as evidenced by Michigan's highway system, construction of the Mackinac Bridge, and among the nation's most generous education and welfare programs.

Gov. "Soapy" Williams transformed the Michigan Democratic Party and state politics. He represented a new coalition of labor leaders, recent immigrants, and blacks and created a vibrant two-party system in the state.

In 1948 Republicans had controlled both U.S. Senate seats from Michigan, held all statewide elected offices, and enjoyed a 95-5 majority in the state House and a 28-4 majority in the Senate. By 1959 Democrats held both U.S. Senate seats, all statewide partisan offices, 12 of the 34 state Senate seats, and 55 of the House's 110 seats (a tie).

The *one-man, one-vote* apportioning of state legislative districts in the mid-1960s reduced the disproportionate power of out-state, rural areas and greatly strengthened Democratic representation in the state legislature. From

▼

▼

ECONOMY AND CULTURE

POLITICS

1949 to 1982 (cont.)

In 1960, however, the trickle of imported foreign cars—which later became a flood—began, and Michigan's primary reliance on the motor-vehicle industry's fortunes showed signs of becoming a serious problem. "When the nation gets a cold, Michigan gets pneumonia" was the epigram summing up the effects that national recessions had on the state.

Seeds of racial unrest emerged in the 1940s and 1950s as the black population of Detroit and other cities grew and racial segregation policies came under attack. By the 1960s, urban unrest escalated into the worst civil disturbance in the nation, as rioting cost 43 lives in Detroit.

1969 to 1993, Democrats enjoyed uninterrupted control of the state House.

From 1963 through 1982, liberal Republicans George Romney and William G. Milliken held the governorship (Milliken—in office for 14 years—is Michigan's longest serving governor).

Before he became the state's chief executive, Romney was instrumental in rewriting the state constitution and then, as governor, in winning its adoption by voters. Still in force, the 1963 constitution consolidated executive power in the office of the governor and eliminated from statewide election several positions, including treasurer, highway commissioner, superintendent of schools, and auditor.

1983 to the Present

From 1980 to 1983, the bottom seemed to have dropped out of the Michigan economy, as two serious national recessions were aggravated by fierce international competition in the automobile industry. Michigan suffered more unemployment than any other state: Some communities, such as Flint, endured an unemployment rate higher than 20 percent. The state per capita income fell to almost 7 percent below the national average.

In recent decades the Michigan economy has become less reliant on the automobile industry. Service jobs have increased dramatically, and in the 1990s Michigan led the nation in economic gains. The state unemployment rate was below the national average during most of the 1990s, and per capita income again rose above the U.S. average.

Michigan weathered the 2001 recession better than many states, but a combination of factors—a revenue slowdown associated with the recession plus phased reductions in personal income and single business taxes—created serious fiscal problems for state government in late 2001. Revenue from the largest taxes declined by 2.3 percent from 2000, and the state's "rainy day fund" was tapped heavily in 2002. The state budgets for the next few years will be among the tightest in modern history.

After 40 years of liberal domination of Michigan politics, the state has become fairly conservative. The economic anxieties of the 1980s, coupled with social unrest and racial tensions in the 1960s and 1970s, produced skepticism about government and opposition to taxes, and the Republican Party's fortunes have risen.

Democrat Gov. James J. Blanchard was upset in 1990 in his bid for a third term. The winner, Republican John Engler, instituted many conservative policies such as reforming welfare programs, eliminating the inheritance tax, and introducing competition into the state public school system.

Republicans have controlled the state Senate since 1983, but the House has shifted back and forth. At this writing, Republicans hold both chambers, enjoying a 58-52 majority in the House and a 23-15 majority in the Senate.

Voters adopted two far-reaching changes in the 1990s. In 1992 they added term limits to the constitution, restricting state representatives to three terms in office (six years) and the other major elected officials—senators, governor, lieutenant governor, secretary of state, and attorney general—to two terms (eight years). In 1994 voters approved sweeping changes in K–12 school funding by raising the sales tax and lowering and restricting the growth of the local property taxes that had supported schools.

SOURCES: Public Sector Consultants, Inc.; Legislative Service Bureau, Michigan Manual 2001–2002; George Weeks, Stewards of the State (Detroit News and Historical Society of Michigan, 1987).

Sponsored by the Michigan Nonprofit Association and the Council of Michigan Foundations

A Profile of People and Lifestyles

POPULATION

- The 2000 Census reports the Michigan population to be nearly 10 million, roughly the same as the neighboring Canadian province of Ontario, the Czech Republic, Hungary, Greece, Portugal, Senegal, or Mali.

- Michigan's population grew by 643,147, or 6.9 percent, in the 1990s. This is 19 times its growth in the previous decade but still well below the national average growth of 13.2 percent.

- Michigan is the 8th most populous state. Of the top ten, six are growing more rapidly than Michigan and three more slowly.

- Michigan's population density, averaging 174 residents per square mile, is much higher than the nation as a whole (the national average is 77). New Jersey, the most densely populated state, has 1,100 people per square mile.

- Michigan's youngest and oldest residents are roughly equal in number: about 7 percent are aged under five, while about 6 percent are over 75.

- In the percentage of population aged 65 and older, Michigan, at 12.4 percent, ranks just under the national average of 12.7 percent.

- In 2000 the 136,048 babies born in Michigan included 99,667 non-Hispanic whites, 24,003 blacks, 6,923 Hispanics, and 3,631 Asian/Pacific Islanders. One in three births was to an unmarried woman, and more than one in 10 births was to a teen. Abortions totaled 12.2 for every 1,000 women aged 15–44, lower than the 1997 national average of 22.2.

ECONOMY

- In 2001 Michigan's gross economy was nearly $298 billion. If it were a nation, Michigan would rank as the world's 16th largest economy, exceeding Argentina, Switzerland, Belgium, and Russia.

- The median household income approaches $43,000, ranking Michigan 17th in the nation. Among Michigan households, 28 percent earn less than $25,000, and about 12 percent earn more than $100,000.

- In 1998 the average household spent $28,000 on retail purchases.

- While still relying on vehicle manufacturing as a generator of high wages, Michigan is diversifying steadily. One economic diversity measure is a state's position in relation to the median of all states (100 percent): In 1970 Michigan stood at 80 percent, which meant that most states had an employment base more diverse than Michigan's; by 2001 Michigan's economic diversity score was up to 94 percent.

- Of employed Michiganians, 22 percent work in manufacturing, 40 percent in services, and 12 percent in retail.

- In 1996 Michigan firms exported $38 billion in goods to other nations, ranking the state 4th in the nation; 57 percent of the goods went to Canada.

FAMILIES

- Of Michigan households, 68 percent are family households; of these, about half are married couples, and one-third of these couples have minor children. Female householders with no husband present comprise 13 percent of the family households, and 8 percent of these women have minor children.

- The average household size is 2.6 people, and the average family size is 3.1.

- In 1998, among every 1,000 people there were seven marriages and four divorces.

- More than a fourth (27 percent) of Michigan households receive Social Security.

- Three of four Michiganians (74 percent) live in single-unit structures, 19 percent live in complexes, and 6 percent in manufactured homes.

- Among homeowners with a mortgage, the median monthly housing cost is $961; among those who have paid off their mortgage, the figure is $282. Renters pay an average of $552 a month.

- The average person in 1997 consumed 31 million British thermal units of energy, ranking Michigan 31st in the nation in energy consumption.

- In 8 percent of Michigan households, a language other than English is spoken.

- Ten percent of residents live at or below the federal poverty level (in 2002, $15,020 for a family of three); included in this group are 14 percent of the state's minors and 9 percent of those aged 65 and older. Fifteen percent of Michiganians receive some type of means-based public assistance or non-cash benefits.

- More than half of all households have a computer. Nearly two-thirds of adults have used the Internet, and nearly one-third have made an on-line purchase.

EDUCATION

- Michigan pre-primary school enrollment is 306,000, K–12 enrollment is 2.7 million (about 66,000 are in public school academies, or so-called charter schools), and 2,000 Michigan children are home schooled; 588,000 Michiganians are in college.

- Eighty-five percent of adult residents have a high school diploma. Among all adults, 15 percent have a bachelor's degree and 8 percent a graduate or professional degree.

- Among 16–19 year olds, 10 percent are not enrolled in school and have not graduated from high school.

- The average K–12 teacher's salary in 2000 was $49,044, ranking Michigan 5th in the country.

MOBILITY

- Eighty-four percent of workers drive alone to their workplace, spending, on average, 23 minutes. Nine percent carpool, 3 percent work at home, and one percent take public transportation. There are 192,000 households in metropolitan Detroit without a vehicle.

- In 2000, 15 percent of all state residents lived in a dwelling different from where they resided the previous year.

- In 1998, 14,000 foreign immigrants settled in Michigan; the countries of origin of the greatest numbers were India (1,500), Mexico (1,000), and China (560).

CRIME AND PUBLIC SAFETY

- In 1996 state and local police totaled 20,600, or 21 for every 10,000 Michigan residents; the national average is 25.

- In 1999 Michigan experienced 575 violent crimes for every 100,000 people, ranking the state 12th highest in the nation; this is an improvement over 1990, when Michigan ranked 8th with 790 crimes per 100,000 residents.

HEALTH

- Among all Michigan residents aged five and older, 16 percent report a disability.

- Compared to all Americans, Michiganians are more likely to die from heart disease, diabetes, or homicide and less likely to die from cancer, cerebrovascular diseases, a motor-vehicle accident, HIV, or suicide.

- In 1998, 27 percent of Michiganians smoked; the national figure is 23 percent.

- In 1998, 35 percent of Michigan adults were overweight (the national average is 33 percent); this is up considerably from 1989, when 26 percent were overweight.

- Roughly one in 10 Michiganians (one million) are without health insurance; 311,000 are children.

- Michigan has fewer medical doctors and more nurses than the national average. MDs number 22,000 (225 per 100,000 residents) and nurses 83,000 (830 per 100,000).

- About 25 percent of state residents are enrolled in Medicare or Medicaid. Medicare and Medicaid expenditures in Michigan total roughly $12 billion.

RECREATION

The National Sporting Goods Association surveys Americans about their recreational activities and compares participation among the states. An index is created whereby a number larger than 100 means that compared to the national average, more people in that state participate in the given activity. An index of 150, for example, means that 50 percent more than the national average say that they participate in that activity. The five highest ranking activities and their Michigan index numbers are the following:

- Boating (203)

- Darts (144)

- Golf (142)

- In-line roller skating (140)

- Camping (128)

SOURCES: Center for Educational Performance and Information; Michigan Department of Community Health; Michigan Department of Education; Michigan Information Center; National Sporting Goods Association; U.S. Bureau of the Census; U.S. Statistical Abstract; World Bank.

Sponsored by the Michigan Nonprofit Association and the Council of Michigan Foundations

State Facts

NAME

The state's name derives from *Michigama*, a Chippewa word meaning "large lake." Michigan is nicknamed the Wolverine State. Residents are referred to as Michiganians or Michiganders.

SIZE

Michigan is 456 miles long and 386 miles wide and has 56,817 square miles of land.

POPULATION

The 2000 Census reports that Michigan has 9,938,444 residents, ranking the state 8th among the 50.

CAPITAL

Lansing was named the capital city in 1847, and the current Capitol Building was built in 1879.

ADMISSION TO THE UNION

On January 26, 1837, Michigan became the 26th state to be admitted.

MOTTO

Si quaeris peninsulam amoenam circumspice, meaning "If you seek a pleasant peninsula, look about you."

SEAL

The present seal was adopted by the legislature in 1911. At the center is a shield on which a man is depicted standing on a shore with the sun at his back. His right hand is upheld, symbolizing peace, and in his left hand is a gunstock, indicating his readiness to defend his state and nation. Above him is the word *Tuebor*, meaning "I will defend." The shield is supported on the right by a moose and on the left by an elk.

Below the shield is the state motto and above is a bald eagle, representing the nation. In the bird's right talon is an olive branch with 13 olives, symbolizing a desire for peace and the 13 original states; in the left talon are three arrows, symbolizing a willingness to defend principle. Above the eagle is the national motto, *E pluribus unum*, meaning "From many, one." The seal's outer edge is encircled by the words "The Great Seal of Michigan, A.D. MDCCCXXXV."

COUNTIES

Michigan has 83 counties.

INLAND WATER

There are 11,037 inland lakes in Michigan, 36,000 miles of rivers and streams, and 1,573 square miles of inland water.

GREAT LAKES

Michigan borders on four of the five Great Lakes: Erie, Huron, Michigan, and Superior. The state's Great Lakes shoreline (including islands) is 3,288 miles.

REPRESENTATION IN CONGRESS

Michigan has two U.S. senators and is entitled (based on population) to 15 members in the U.S. House of Representatives.

LEGISLATURE

Thirty-eight senators and 110 representatives comprise the Michigan Legislature.

FLAG

The present state flag was adopted by the legislature in 1911. On a dark blue field is the state coat of arms, which is identical to the state seal but without the encircling words.

SYMBOLS

- **Bird** Robin (1931)
- **Fish** Brook trout (1987)
- **Flower** Apple blossom (1897)
- **Fossil** Mastodon (2002)
- **Game mammal** White-tailed deer (1997)
- **Gem** Chlorastrolite, commonly known as greenstone (1972)
- **Reptile** Painted turtle (1995)
- **Soil** Kalkaska soil (1990)
- **Stone** Petoskey stone (1965)
- **Tree** White pine (1955)
- **Wildflower** Dwarf lake iris (1998)

SOURCE: Legislative Service Bureau, Michigan Manual 2001–2002.

CHAPTER 2
About State Government

Michigan was the first of the post–Civil War states to model its capitol building after the Capitol in Washington. Michigan's state government likewise is patterned on the federal model. Both the state capitol and government have undergone renovations that have affected their appearance and function but not their basic structure.

Michigan state government is divided into three branches—executive, legislative and judicial—each with separate and clearly defined powers. These branches and their separate and exclusive powers have been spelled out in each of Michigan's four constitutions—those of 1835, 1850, 1908, and 1963. The most recent was adopted April 1, 1963. Presented here are brief descriptions of each branch and its subdivisions.

EXECUTIVE BRANCH

Elected Officials

Article V of the 1963 Michigan Constitution vests principal executive authority in the governor, who is elected to a four-year term. The governor oversees the departments of state government (see Exhibit 1), makes appointments to boards and commissions, delivers an annual State of the State Message in which the administration's priorities are outlined, presents the executive budget, and signs or vetoes bills passed by the legislature.

Unlike the federal government, executive authority in Michigan does not rest solely with the chief executive. The secretary of state and attorney general as well as members of the State Board of Education and the boards of control of Michigan State University, University of Michigan, and Wayne State University are elected positions having direct executive authority over their department or institution. In addition, some departments are governed by commissions appointed by the governor. The governor directly names 13 department heads, subject to the advice and consent of the Senate.

Salaries for certain elected officials are set by the State Officers Compensation Commission, a seven-member panel appointed by the governor; its recommendations stand unless overturned by a two-thirds majority in both legislative chambers. In 2000 a two-stage raise was approved that set the following 2002 salary levels:

- Governor $177,000

- Lieutenant governor $123,900

- Supreme court justices $164,610

- Legislators $79,650 plus $12,000 for expenses

Salaries for the secretary of state and attorney general are set by the legislative appropriations process as are the salaries for all other department heads.

Sponsored by the Michigan Nonprofit Association and the Council of Michigan Foundations

EXHIBIT 1. Executive Branch, State of Michigan, 2002

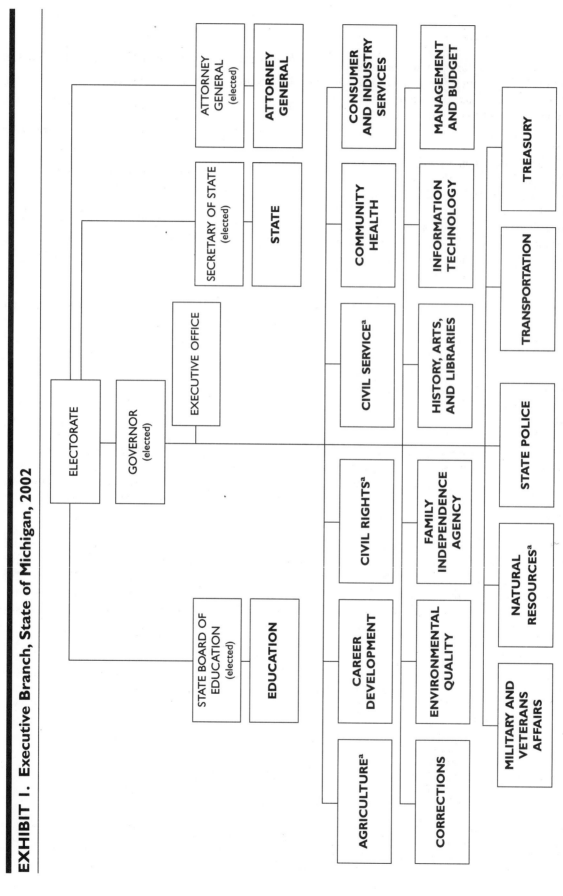

SOURCE: *Public Sector Consultants, Inc.*

NOTE: *Boldface type = departments.*

[a]*Director is appointed by the commission; all other nonelected department directors are appointed by the governor.*

Sponsored by the Michigan Nonprofit Association and the Council of Michigan Foundations

In 1992 the electorate voted to impose term limits[1] on certain elected state officials sworn into office on or after January 1, 1993. In the executive branch, the governor, lieutenant governor, secretary of state, and attorney general are limited to two terms. Terms served need not be consecutive, and if less than half a term is served in an office, it does not count toward the limitation.

Departments
The 1963 constitution dramatically reorganized the executive branch. Before that, there had been more than 100 independent agencies over which the governor had little control, making accountability difficult. The 1963 constitution decrees that all duties and functions of the executive branch (except for the governor, lieutenant governor, and university governing boards) are to be distributed by law among the 20 (or fewer) departments; today there are 20.

The constitution also permits the governor to reorganize the executive branch or reassign duties among the departments. Although previous governors used the executive reorganization power, none used it more frequently or extensively than Gov. John Engler. Since he took office in 1991, he has issued more than 100 executive orders[2] regarding reorganization.

In addition, in recent years several state functions have been turned over to the private sector—including the State Accident Fund (workers' disability insurer), liquor distribution, vaccine manufacture, business and economic development, and some state highway maintenance.

Agriculture
The Michigan Department of Agriculture (MDA) is headed by a five-member commission appointed by the governor. The commission develops policy and appoints the director. The department plays a dual role: marketer and regulator. Among its responsibilities are the following:

[1]For a full discussion of term limits, the reader is directed to *Michigan in Brief, 6th Edition*, available at *www.michiganinbrief.org*.

[2]Executive orders are the governor's official pronouncements. Executive *reorganization* orders have the force and effect of law and permit the governor to reassign functions within executive branch departments or agencies to the same extent as the legislature; they take effect in 60 days unless rejected by a majority in each legislature chamber. Other executive orders may be used to establish boards and commissions and carry out special projects appropriate to the governor's executive authority; these do not have the force of law—their purpose is to facilitate or advance policymaking. Governors also use executive orders to make budget reductions when it appears that revenue will be insufficient to support appropriations; such orders must be approved by the legislative appropriations committees.

- Promoting Michigan-grown products and animal industries at home and abroad
- Regulating the commercial handling of farm produce
- Assuring a safe, high-quality supply of dairy products
- Regulating food sanitation and labeling
- Administering the Soil Conservation Districts Act and the County Drain Code
- Supporting Michigan's county and local fairs
- Compiling weather data
- Setting rules and regulations for pari-mutuel horse racing in the state
- Developing policy on toxic substance matters
- Regulating restricted-use pesticides
- Regulating importation of plants and their movement within the state
- Assisting in establishing bargaining associations for fruit and vegetable growers
- Enforcing health standards for and humane treatment of farm animals
- Licensing pet shops and animal shelters
- Regulating the sale and quality of motor fuel

Regional offices are located in Escanaba, Grand Rapids, Lansing, Saginaw, Southfield, St. Joseph, and Traverse City.

Attorney General
The attorney general (AG) is elected by the voters every four years and is the state's chief law enforcement officer; s/he heads the Department of the Attorney General. The AG is the legal counsel for the legislature and for each office, department, board, and commission of state government; s/he is third in line of succession, after the lieutenant governor and secretary of state, should the governor be unable to fulfill gubernatorial responsibilities. The department's responsibilities are the following:

- Intervening in any lawsuit, criminal or civil, when the interests of Michigan residents require; the office has various specialized legal divisions for this purpose, such as Consumer Protection and Charitable Trusts, Social Services, and Workers' Compensation
- Representing the "public interest" in hearings before state boards and commissions, such as the Public Service Commission

Sponsored by the Michigan Nonprofit Association and the Council of Michigan Foundations

■ Investigating state departments and agencies in matters of fraud and unethical or illegal activity

To help meet the office's requirements, the attorney general appoints assistant attorneys general. Among them is the solicitor general, who supervises appeals to the Michigan Supreme Court, the U.S. Circuit Court of Appeals, and the U.S. Supreme Court.

In addition to the Lansing office, the department maintains offices in Detroit, Escanaba, Grand Rapids, and Petoskey.

Career Development

The Michigan Department of Career Development (MDCD) was created in 1999 to develop a system that will produce a workforce with the skills necessary to maintain and enhance the state economy. The 20-member Governor's Workforce Commission is housed in the MDCD and provides policy guidance and overall coordination of workforce development programs in the state. The department works with employers, K–12 schools, community colleges, and local workforce development boards to accomplish its goals. Its responsibilities include the following:

■ Providing students with opportunities to explore a variety of careers

■ Approving, administering, and evaluating career and technical education programs for secondary school students

■ Administering a variety of programs designed to help prepare workers for jobs

■ Helping Michigan residents with disabilities achieve employment and self-sufficiency

■ Providing job seekers with information on line and through local service centers

■ Developing policies and plans, through the Commission on Spanish-Speaking Affairs, to serve the needs of Michigan's Spanish-speaking residents

■ Encouraging, through the Michigan Community Service Commission, citizens to volunteer and connect with their neighbors

Local programs are administered by 25 workforce development boards (WDBs) that are appointed by local elected officials.

Civil Rights

The Michigan Department of Civil Rights (MDCR) is headed by the eight-member Civil Rights Commission, which is charged by the constitution "to investigate alleged discrimination against any person because of religion, race, color, or national origin." Since 1963 legislation has been adopted that also prohibits discrimination based on age, sex, marital status, height, weight, arrest record, or handicap. The commission sets department policy and selects the director. Commission members are appointed by the governor. Among the MDCR's duties are the following:

■ Investigating and handling complaints and issuing final orders in discrimination cases

■ Attempting through education to prevent discrimination

■ Assisting private and public entities in developing equal employment opportunity and affirmative action programs

■ Certifying the status of handicapper-owned businesses so as to increase their participation in the state-government procurement process

■ Certifying the contract-awardability status of firms seeking to do business with the state

The Michigan Women's Commission is housed in the department and makes recommendations to improve the status of women in Michigan.

The department has offices in Battle Creek, Benton Harbor, Detroit, Flint, Grand Rapids, Kalamazoo, Lansing, Marquette, Saginaw, and Traverse City.

Civil Service

The Michigan Department of Civil Service (MDCS), the principal personnel office for state government, is charged by the constitution with "regulating all conditions of employment for the state's civil service workers,"—in short, for maintaining a corps of competent career employees who carry on the work of state government regardless of change in political leadership. The MDCS is headed by the bipartisan, four-person Civil Service Commission, which is appointed by the governor. The commission appoints the state personnel director, who administers the department. Among the department's responsibilities are the following:

■ Examining candidates for state government jobs

■ Classifying positions in state government

■ Setting pay levels for state employees

■ Developing equal employment opportunity policies

■ Administering employee benefit programs

Sponsored by the Michigan Nonprofit Association and the Council of Michigan Foundations

- Providing dispute resolution services for many aspects of labor and management relations

The constitution requires that all posts in state government be classified under the civil service system except elected positions, department heads, board and commission members, court employees, the legislature, employees of institutions of higher education, Michigan National Guard members, eight positions in the governor's office, and two positions in each department if the director so requests. If approved by the Civil Service Commission, three additional positions "of a policy-making nature" also may be exempted in each department.

The department has offices in Detroit and Lansing.

Community Health

The Michigan Department of Community Health (MDCH), the largest agency in Michigan state government, is responsible for state health policy and managing public-funded health-service systems. The director is appointed by the governor, and the department's responsibilities are the following:

- Providing coverage, through the Medical Services Administration, to Medicaid recipients

- Providing mental health services, principally through contracts with 48 community mental health boards, and operating a small number of state and regional facilities for people with developmental disabilities and psychiatric illness

- Providing substance-abuse services through 15 substance-abuse coordinating agencies

- Contracting with 45 local public health departments to assess Michiganians' health needs, promote and protect their health, prevent disease, and assure their access to health care

- Assisting and promoting, through the Office of Services to the Aging, the independence and dignity of older citizens

- Addressing, through the Commission on End of Life Care, ways to improve end-of-life care

- Administering the Crime Victims Rights Fund, investigating and processing crime victim compensation, and administering federal Victims of Crime Act grants

Consumer and Industry Services

The Michigan Department of Consumer and Industry Services (MDCIS) is the state's primary licensing and regulatory agency. The director is appointed by the governor. The department's principal agencies are the following:

- Bureau of Commercial Services (licensing)

- Bureau of Construction Codes

- Bureau of Corporation and Land Development

- Bureau of Health Services

- Bureau of Health Systems

- Bureau of Regulatory Services

- Bureau of Safety and Regulation

- Bureau of Workers' and Unemployment Compensation

- Liquor Control Commission

- Michigan Employment Relations Commission

- Michigan Public Service Commission

- Michigan State Housing Development Authority

- Michigan Tax Tribunal

- Office of Contract and Grant Administration

- Office of Financial and Insurance Services

- Office of Fire Safety

Corrections

The Michigan Department of Corrections (MDOC) administers the state's adult prison, probation, and parole systems. The governor appoints the director. Among the MDOC's responsibilities are the following:

- Administering 44 adult penal facilities and 11 corrections camps (in addition, about 1,500 prisoners are in corrections centers or the electronic monitoring program)

- Supervising convicted felons who receive a sentence of probation

- Determining, through the Parole Board, whether convicted felons who have served time in prison are eligible to be placed back into the community

- Managing manufacturing and service functions in state prisons

- Delivering health care for state prisoners

The department has several regional offices across the state.

Sponsored by the Michigan Nonprofit Association and the Council of Michigan Foundations

Education

The Michigan Constitution vests leadership of and general supervision over all public education (except four-year degree-granting institutions) in an elected State Board of Education. In addition, the constitution makes the board "the general planning and coordinating body for all public education, including higher education" and requires it to advise the legislature on education's financial needs. The elected eight-member board runs the Michigan Department of Education (MDE), approves accreditation standards for school districts, sets criteria for grants awarded by the MDE, approves teacher preparation standards, approves K–12 curriculum standards, and appoints the superintendent of public instruction, who administers the department. The governor and superintendent sit on the board as nonvoting, ex officio members.

The board and department provide specialized services and outreach through the department's offices, which oversee the following:

- School excellence
- Teacher certification
- Professional preparation
- Special-education services
- Schools for the deaf and blind
- School support services
- Field services
- Education options, charters, and choice
- School aid and finance

Environmental Quality

The mission of the Michigan Department of Environmental Quality (MDEQ) is "to drive improvements in environmental quality for the protection of public health and natural resources to benefit current and future generations." The director is appointed by the governor. The department's divisions are the following:

- Air Quality
- Drinking Water and Radiological Protection
- Environmental Assistance
- Environmental Response
- Geological Survey
- Land and Water Management
- Office of Special Environmental Projects

- Office of the Great Lakes
- Surface-Water Quality
- Storage Tanks
- Waste Management

The department maintains district offices in Bay City, Cadillac, Grand Rapids, Jackson, Kalamazoo, Livonia, Marquette, and Morrice and field offices in Detroit and Gaylord.

Family Independence Agency

The Michigan Family Independence Agency (FIA) helps individuals and families to meet financial, medical, and social needs; assists people to become self-sufficient; and helps to protect children and adults from abuse, neglect, and exploitation. Among the FIA's many services are programs dealing with the following:

- Adoption
- Adult independent living
- Adult community placement
- Children's Trust Fund
- Disability determination, information, and advocacy
- Domestic violence
- Employment and training for welfare clients
- Family preservation (short-term crisis services; parenting and home-management education)
- Family support (programs to help parents successfully nurture children)
- Foster care
- HIV/AIDS
- Juvenile justice
- Delinquency/violence
- Abuse, neglect, or exploitation of children and vulnerable adults
- Foster care
- Migrant services
- Native American services
- Refugee assistance
- Runaway and homeless youth
- Teen parenting

The FIA also administers several financial assistance programs, among them the following:

- Family Independence Program (cash assistance for eligible families with children)

- Disability assistance

- Emergency assistance

- Medical program (for certain low-income adults who do not qualify for Medicaid or other medical coverage)

- Low-income energy assistance

- Child-support enforcement (to assist in establishing paternity and collecting child-support payments from noncustodial parents)

- Child care

- Such federal programs as Supplemental Security Income and food stamps

The department delivers services through more than 100 offices statewide (at least one in each of Michigan's 83 counties).

History, Arts, and Libraries

Created in 2001, the Department of History, Arts, and Libraries is responsible for coordinating state efforts to encourage the preservation of history, creation of art, and development of culture. It is headed by a director appointed by the governor and comprises the following agencies:

- Council for Arts and Cultural Affairs

- Library of Michigan

- Mackinac State Historic Parks

- Michigan Commission on Asia in the Schools, a new agency charged with furthering understanding about Asia in Michigan businesses, communities, and schools

- Michigan Film Office

- Michigan Historical Center

- Michigan Quarter Commission, a temporary agency involved in designing the state quarter, which will be coined in 2004

Information Technology

The Department of Information Technology was created in 2001 to lead efforts to reengineer the state's information technology (IT) infrastructure with the goal of achieving the use of common technology across the executive branch. A number of resources, services, and technology-management functions were transferred to the department. The director is appointed by the governor. Among the department's responsibilities are the following:

- Coordinating a unified, executive-branch strategic IT plan

- Identifying "best practices" from executive branch agencies and other public- and private-sector entities

- Developing and implementing processes to replicate IT best practices and standards throughout the executive branch

- Serving as a general contractor between the state's IT users and private-sector providers of IT products and services

- Developing standards for IT application development

Housed in the department is the e-Michigan Office, created in 2000 to lead all state agencies in electronic-government initiatives and policy development. The office is headed by a director appointed by the governor and receives advice from the five-member e-Michigan Advisory Council.

Management and Budget

The Michigan Department of Management and Budget (MDMB) is an interdepartmental service-and-management agency. The department director and the state budget director are appointed by the governor, and the department is organized into budget and management units.

The budget unit, headed by the state budget director, prepares, presents, and executes the state budget on behalf of the governor. The management units carry out the following responsibilities:

- Financial management

- Property management

- Capital facility development

- Procurement

- Retirement and related benefits

- Employee benefits programs

- Accounting and payroll functions

- Demographic functions

- Geographic information

- Systems development

- Office support to state agencies

The department also includes the Office of Children's Ombudsman, an independent agency authorized to investigate complaints about children in Michigan's child-welfare system. The ombudsman is appointed by the gover-

Sponsored by the Michigan Nonprofit Association and the Council of Michigan Foundations

nor and recommends changes in child-welfare laws, rules, and policies.

Also housed in the MDMB is the Michigan Economic Development Corporation (MEDC), which assumed the economic development functions of the former Michigan Jobs Commission. The MEDC is not a traditional state agency but rather a partnership between the state and local communities. A 15-member MEDC Executive Committee hires the president and chief executive officer of the corporation. The MEDC's responsibilities are the following:

- Attracting new business to Michigan

- Keeping business in Michigan and helping them grow

- Providing information on Michigan and its industries

- Providing site location and financial assistance

- Assisting in employee recruitment and training

- Providing permit assistance

- Coordinating site development, resources, and services

The department also provides clerical, management, and other general services support to the State Administrative Board. The board approves contracts and leases, oversees the state capital-outlay process, and settles small claims against the state. Its members are the governor, lieutenant governor, secretary of state, attorney general, superintendent of public instruction, and state treasurer.

Military and Veterans Affairs
The Michigan Department of Military and Veterans Affairs (DMVA) is directed by the adjutant general of Michigan, who is appointed by the governor. The Michigan Army and Air National Guard constitute the armed forces of the state; the commander-in-chief is the governor. Major responsibilities of the department are the following:

- Recruiting, training, and maintaining the Michigan Army National Guard and the Michigan Air National Guard as reserve components of the U.S. Army and Air Force, respectively

- Protecting lives and property in times of disaster and promoting peace, order, and public safety at the governor's direction

- Administering state-supported veterans' programs, including the Michigan Veterans Trust Fund and veterans' homes in Grand Rapids and Marquette

Approximately 11,000 guard members are based in 51 armories and trained at five sites (Alpena, Battle Creek, and Selfridge Air National Guard bases and Camp Grayling and Fort Custer Army National Guard facilities).

Natural Resources
The mission of the Michigan Department of Natural Resources (MDNR) is to conserve, protect, manage, and develop the state's natural resources. The department director is appointed by the seven-member Natural Resources Commission, which is appointed by the governor. The department has jurisdiction over most of the 4.5 million acres of state-owned land and is organized into the following six resource-management offices:

- Fisheries Division

- Forest Management

- Land and Mineral Services

- Law Enforcement

- Parks and Recreation

- Wildlife Division

The department has two regional offices (Marquette for the Upper Peninsula and Roscommon for the lower) and 10 field offices.

State
The oldest department in state government, the Michigan Department of State (MDS) is headed by the secretary of state, who is elected every four years and is second in line (after the lieutenant governor) to succeed the governor. The department is responsible for services and programs in the following areas:

- Traffic safety and motor vehicles (driver and vehicle licensing, licensing automobile-related businesses)

- Elections (election supervision, voter registration, campaign finance oversight, lobbyist registration)

- Record keeping (maintains many important state and local documents, administers the notary public program, and operates the Office of the Great Seal, which provides the highest level of document certification)

The four-member bipartisan Board of State Canvassers certifies election results for state offices and other races that may be referred to it.

The department has four regional offices (Gaylord, Inkster, Lansing, and Oak Park), 15 district offices, and 173 local branch offices.

State Police

The mission of the Michigan State Police (MSP) is to "provide leadership, coordination, and delivery of law enforcement and support services in order to preserve, protect, and defend people and property, while respecting the rights and dignity of all persons." The governor appoints the director, traditionally a state police officer, who holds the rank of colonel and has the powers of a peace officer in enforcing the state's criminal laws. The department's primary responsibilities are the following:

- Providing investigative services, conducting arson investigations, and operating regional crime labs

- Developing and setting employment and training standards for police officers

- Coordinating traffic safety in the state

- Regulating safety and weight of commercial vehicles using state highways

- Providing emergency-management services that deal with preventing, mitigating, and helping with disaster recovery

- Maintaining all criminal and noncriminal records, freedom-of-information requests, firearm and licensing information, and uniform crime reporting

- Developing plans, through the Michigan Automobile Theft Prevention Authority, to combat automobile theft

The department also provides personal protection for the governor and his/her immediate family. It operates from 64 state police posts as well as district offices, laboratories, and motor-carrier scale houses.

Transportation

The Michigan Department of Transportation (MDOT) is headed by a six-member bipartisan commission and the director, all appointed by the governor. The department is charged with the following:

- Overseeing state highway design, construction, improvement, and maintenance

- Administering grants to local governments for local road projects

- Promoting aviation in the state

- Managing the International Bridge at Sault Ste. Marie (connecting Michigan and Canada), the Mackinac Bridge (connecting Michigan's peninsulas), and half of the Blue Water Bridge at Port Huron (connecting Michigan and Canada)

- Providing financial and technical support for inter-city bus services, passenger services, and freight transportation services

- Operating freeway rest areas and roadside parks

Treasury

The Michigan Department of Treasury (MDT) is headed by the state treasurer, who is appointed by the governor and acts as financial advisor to him/her. The department's responsibilities include the following:

- Collecting state taxes (e.g., income, sales and use, motor-vehicle fuel, cigarette, alcoholic beverages, intangibles, estate, single business)

- Estimating revenue for the state budget, analyzing tax proposals, and preparing the governor's annual economic and tax-expenditures reports

- Managing the State of Michigan's short-term borrowing and long-term bond debt

- Managing and investing funds deposited in state accounts (common cash fund, retirement funds, Michigan Education Trust, and various trust and agency funds)

- Auditing local governments and providing fiscal-management training to local officials

- Administering the local government revenue-sharing program

Also housed in the department are the following:

- Bureau of State Lottery

- Higher Education Facilities Commission

- Michigan Broadband Development Authority

- Michigan Higher Education Assistance Authority

- Michigan Higher Education Facilities Authority

- Michigan Higher Education Student Loan Authority

- Michigan Public Educational Facilities Authority

- State Hospital Finance Authority

LEGISLATIVE BRANCH

Article IV of the 1963 Michigan Constitution vests the state's legislative power in a House of Representatives (110 members) and a Senate (38 members). Representatives are elected to two-year terms, and senators are elected to four-year terms coterminous with the governor's. The House currently comprises 51 Democrats and 58 Republi-

Sponsored by the Michigan Nonprofit Association and the Council of Michigan Foundations

cans, with one seat vacant. The Senate has 23 Republicans and 15 Democrats.

Unless convicted of certain crimes, any person aged 21 or older who is a U.S. citizen and a registered voter in the district to be represented may be elected to the legislature. Legislators may hold no other public office except notary public, and they are subject to term limits: three terms for House members and two for senators (terms served need not be consecutive, and if less than half a term is served in an office, it does not count toward the limitation).[3]

House districts range in population from 77,000 to 91,000 residents, Senate districts from 225,000 to 265,000. Districts are redrawn every 10 years, to assure that the population in each is roughly equal (the U.S. Supreme Court has permitted variances up to 16.4 percent).

Legislative salaries and expense allowances are recommended by the State Officers Compensation Commission.[4] Currently, the annual legislative salary is $79,650 plus $12,000 for expenses. Those serving in the 10 leadership positions receive supplemental salaries ranging from $27,000 annually for the Speaker of the House to $7,000 for the Appropriations Committee chair in each chamber.

Organization
The presiding officer of the House of Representatives is the Speaker, who is elected by the controlling party. The Speaker's primary responsibilities are to appoint committee members and chairs (the House minority leader nominates minority members, who traditionally are approved by the Speaker), assign bills to the appropriate committees, manage floor debate, and serve as the chief legislative spokesperson for the majority party.

The state constitution provides that the president of the Senate shall be the lieutenant governor, but s/he does not vote except to break a tie. The controlling party elects the Senate majority leader, whose responsibilities are similar to those of the Speaker of the House.

To conduct its business, the legislature is organized into committees. There are 23 *standing* (permanent) commit-

tees in the House and 21 in the Senate, and the Appropriations Committee in each chamber has several subcommittees that specialize in various sections of the budget. Standing committees generally have 5–29 members, and each legislator sits on at least one. Exhibit 2 lists the chambers' standing committees.

A *joint* committee is composed of members from both chambers. The following are permanent:

- Legislative Council (runs such joint administrative offices as the Legislative Service Bureau)

- Legislative Retirement Board of Trustees (administers the legislative retirement system)

- Michigan Capitol Committee (manages the Capitol Building and its grounds)

- Joint Committee on Administrative Rules (reviews administrative rules promulgated by the executive branch)

In addition, *special purpose* and *conference* committees often are established. The former do not consider legislation but study and investigate topics of special interest; the latter try to resolve differences in versions of the same bill passed by the two chambers.

Legislators are assisted by their personal staffs as well as the staffs of the committees on which they serve and that of their party caucus. The lawmakers rely on the nonpartisan Legislative Service Bureau for drafting and editing bills, research, printing, and similar tasks. The nonpartisan House and Senate fiscal agencies provide the lawmakers with economic and fiscal analyses and research.

Passing Legislation
During an average two-year session, approximately 6,000 bills are introduced in the House and Senate; usually, 600–800 become law. Exhibit 3 summarizes the bill-enactment process. Legislation may be introduced in either chamber; sometimes, identical bills are introduced simultaneously in both. After introduction, a bill is read (not literally; only the title is read aloud), and then the Senate majority leader or the Speaker of the House refers the bill to an appropriate standing committee.

The committee debates the bill, then may (1) report it, with or without change, to the floor with a favorable recommendation, (2) report a substitute bill in place of the original, or (3) recommend that the bill be referred to another committee. A committee also may "kill" a bill by simply refusing to act on it unless the full chamber votes to discharge it from the committee. If a discharge motion is approved by a majority of the chamber's members, the

---

[3]Term limit opponents are pushing for a November 2002 Michigan ballot question to amend the state constitution to allow House and Senate members to serve 12 years each, up from the current limits of six and eight years, respectively.

[4]A question on the 2002 primary ballot would require legislators to approve by majority vote the commission's recommendations. Currently, a reject/accept vote is not required, but if one is held, two-thirds in each chamber are needed to reject the recommendations.

Sponsored by the Michigan Nonprofit Association and the Council of Michigan Foundations

EXHIBIT 2. Legislative Standing Committees, 2002

Michigan House of Representatives
Agriculture and Resource Management
Appropriations
Civil Law and the Judiciary
Commerce
Conservation and Outdoor Recreation
Criminal Justice
Education
Employment Relations, Training and Safety
Energy and Technology
Family and Children Services
Gaming and Casino Oversight
Health Policy
House Oversight and Operations
House Television and Oversight
Insurance and Financial Services
Land Use and Environment
Local Government and Urban Policy
Redistricting and Elections
Regulatory Reform
Senior Health, Security and Retirement
Tax Policy
Transportation
Veterans Affairs

Michigan Senate
Appropriations
Banking and Financial Institutions
Detroit Metro Airport Review
Economic Development, International Trade and Regulatory Affairs
Education
Families, Mental Health and Human Services
Farming, Agribusiness and Food Systems
Finance
Financial Services
Gaming and Casino Oversight
Government Operations
Health Policy
Human Resources and Labor
Hunting, Fishing and Forestry
Judiciary
Local, Urban and State Affairs
Natural Resources and Environmental Affairs
Reapportionment
Senior Citizens and Veterans Affairs
Technology and Energy
Transportation and Tourism

SOURCE: *Michigan Legislature.*

bill goes to the floor for consideration by the full body. Discharge motions, though frequently made, rarely succeed. Under the state Open Meetings Act, all committee business must be conducted during public meetings of which notice has been given.

A bill reported from committee moves to the floor, where it receives *general orders* status in the Senate or *second-reading* status in the House. In this phase, committee recommendations are considered, and amendments may be offered by any member of the body. The bill then advances to *third reading*, where it again may be debated and amended. At the conclusion, the bill may be

- passed or defeated by a recorded roll-call vote (which is reported in the chamber's journal of proceedings) of the majority of members elected and serving (56 members comprise a majority in the House and 20 in the Senate);

- referred back to committee for further consideration;

- postponed indefinitely; or

- tabled.

If a bill passes in one chamber, it goes to the other, where the same procedure is followed. If the bill passes in the same form by both chambers, it is ordered "enrolled" in the chamber in which it originated. It then goes to the governor for signature or veto.

If the bill is passed in a different form by the second chamber, it is returned to its house of origin for a vote of concurrence on the changes. If the changes are accepted, the bill is enrolled and sent to the governor. If they are rejected, the bill is sent to a conference committee, composed of three members from each chamber, to iron out the differences. If there is no agreement, a second conference committee may be appointed. When a compromise is reached, a conference report is sent to the floor of each chamber for acceptance or rejection—not amendment—by the respective bodies.

Once the legislature has passed a bill, it is printed and presented to the governor, who has 14 calendar days in which to act. The governor may (1) sign the bill, (2) veto the bill, (3) veto a "line" (a specific expenditure) in a budget bill, or (4) do nothing, in which case the bill becomes law without signature.

If the governor vetoes a bill or line-item expenditure, the legislature may override the veto by a two-thirds vote of the members elected and serving in each chamber (74 votes in the House of Representatives and 26 in the Senate).

Sponsored by the Michigan Nonprofit Association and the Council of Michigan Foundations

EXHIBIT 3. Michigan's Legislation Enactment Process

PROCESS IN THE CHAMBER OF ORIGIN

First Reading
A bill is introduced by a representative or senator. The title of the bill is read, constituting the first reading. The Speaker (in the House) or the majority leader (in the Senate) refers the bill to a standing committee.

Committee
Committees hold public meetings to receive testimony and debate a bill. Committees may report a bill to the floor with favorable recommendation, may report a substitute bill, or may recommend a bill be referred to another committee. Committees also may reject or take no action on a bill, and the chamber may discharge a bill from committee by a majority vote of members "elected and serving." A bill dies if it remains in committee at the end of the legislative session.

Second Reading
Bills reported out of committee receive a second reading (again, just the title). The full chamber considers the committee's recommendations, debates the bill, and may offer amendments.

Third Reading and Vote
On the third reading bills are open for debate by the full chamber. A bill may be tabled, postponed indefinitely, referred back to committee, or brought to a roll-call vote. Passage requires a "yes" vote from a majority of members elected and serving (normally, 56 members in the House and 20 in the Senate). A bill may be given immediate effect if two-thirds of the members serving support such a motion.

PROCESS IN THE SECOND CHAMBER

First Reading
A bill receives a first reading and is referred to a committee by the Speaker (in the House) or the majority leader (in the Senate).

Committee
Committees hold public meetings to receive testimony and debate a bill. The process and possible actions are the same in both chambers.

Second Reading
Bills recommended by committee receive a second reading. The full chamber considers the committee's recommendations, debates the bill, and may offer amendments.

Third Reading and Vote
Bills are read for a third time and undergo the same process as in the other chamber. If a bill passes without amendment in the second chamber, it is sent to the governor. If a bill passes but has been amended in the second chamber, it is returned for concurrence to the chamber of origin.

PROCESS IF THE TWO CHAMBERS DIFFER

Concurrence
If the chamber of origin approves the second chamber's amendments, the bill is sent to the governor. If the amendments are rejected, the bill is assigned to a conference committee composed of three senators and three representatives.

Conference Committee
If agreement is reached, the conference committee presents a conference report to each chamber. The chamber may accept or reject but not amend the conference report.

ROLE OF THE GOVERNOR

A bill becomes law if the governor signs it or fails to sign or veto it within 14 days after officially receiving it. In the event of veto, a bill becomes law if both chambers vote to override the veto by a two-thirds majority; if one or the other does not override, the bill dies.

SOURCE: Public Sector Consultants, Inc.
NOTE: Acts ordinarily take effect on the 91st day after the end of the legislative year; as the legislature usually ends its year in late December, the effective date of most legislation is approximately April 1 of the following year. An earlier or later effective date may be written into the bill, however, or, after a bill has been passed, "immediate effect" may be granted by a two-thirds vote of the membership both chambers.

Sometimes a bill is "tie-barred" to another bill, which means that even if it passes, it cannot take effect unless the other also is enacted.

Acts ordinarily take effect on the 91st day after the end of the legislative year; as the legislature usually ends its year in late December, the effective date of most legislation is approximately April 1 of the following year. An earlier or later effective date may be written into the bill, however, or, after a bill has been passed, *immediate effect* may be granted by a two-thirds vote of the membership both chambers.

Other Responsibilities
Advice and Consent
In addition to its principal responsibility to pass laws, the legislature has other important functions. One is the Senate's power of advice and consent on many gubernatorial appointments. The Senate has 60 days to reject an appointment. If it does not act within that time, the appointment is confirmed.

Auditor General
Michigan is one of 25 states in addition to the federal government in which the audit function is vested in the legislative branch. The Michigan Office of the Auditor General (OAG) was established by state constitution to conduct post-financial (end of fiscal year), compliance, and performance (measuring efficiency and effectiveness) audits of state government operations. The OAG's reports provide a continuing information flow that assists the legislature in overseeing approximately 83 individual state funds and an annual budget of $45 billion. The OAG's overall goal is to improve accounting and financial reporting practices and promote effectiveness, efficiency, and economy in state government.

Audit activities are performed in accordance with generally accepted auditing standards of the American Institute of Certified Public Accountants and with government auditing standards issued by the U.S. comptroller general.

State Budget
Finally, each year the legislature adopts the state budget, a process discussed in detail in Chapter 3 of this book.

Citizen Involvement
State residents may participate directly in the lawmaking process, and they also may propose and vote on amendments to the state constitution. In addition, questions of long-term borrowing must be submitted to the electorate.

Initiative
The Michigan Constitution of 1963 defines the right of initiative as "the power to propose laws and to enact and reject laws." To initiate legislation, a person or group must obtain a number of signatures of registered voters equal to 8 percent of the total vote cast for all candidates for governor in the previous election. In 1998, 3,027,104 such votes were cast, which means that currently, 242,168 valid signatures must be obtained for an initiative. Public Act 116 of 1954 specifies the procedure that must be followed for an initiative petition to become a question on the ballot (usually referred to as a ballot proposal). First, the petitions proposing the measure are filed with the secretary of state, and the Board of State Canvassers determines whether they carry a sufficient number of valid signatures. If so, the initiative goes to the legislature, which has 40 days to enact the measure, reject it, or propose a different measure on the same question. The legislature makes the initiative law if both chambers adopt it without change. If not enacted, the initiative proposal and any alternative passed by the legislature go before the voters as a ballot question.

If an initiated ballot proposal that has been rejected or changed by the legislature is approved by the voters, it becomes effective 10 days from the date of the secretary of state's official declaration of the vote. An initiated law may not be vetoed by the governor and may be amended or repealed only by a subsequent vote of the electors or a three-fourths vote of the members elected and serving in both legislative chambers.

Referendum
The 1963 constitution defines the right of referendum as "the power to approve or reject laws enacted by the legislature." Currently, the signatures of 151,355 registered voters (equal to 5 percent of the total vote for governor in the last election) are required for a referendum by the voters on a law passed by the legislature. The petitions are filed with the secretary of state, and if the Board of State Canvassers declares them valid, the proposal appears on the ballot in the next general election. If a majority of the voters approve, the action takes effect 10 days after the date of the official declaration of the vote. The legislature may amend a law approved by the referendum process.

Constitutional Amendment
The petition also may be used to propose amendments to the state constitution. Signatures of registered voters must number at least 10 percent of the number of votes cast for all candidates in the previous gubernatorial election, currently 302,710. After petitions are filed with the secretary of state, they are examined by the Board of State Canvassers. If the petitions qualify, the proposed amendment

Sponsored by the Michigan Nonprofit Association and the Council of Michigan Foundations

goes on the ballot. If a majority of voters approve, the measure becomes part of the constitution, taking effect in 45 days.

If the legislature wishes to have the state constitution amended, either chamber may introduce a joint resolution describing the proposed change. To qualify the proposal for the ballot in the next general or special election, the resolution must pass both legislative bodies by two-thirds or more. If a majority of the voters approve, the measure becomes effective in 45 days.

Other
Ordinarily, a bill becomes a law when passed by both legislative chambers and signed by the governor. Sometimes, however, the legislature also wishes voter concurrence and inserts into the bill a provision requiring such approval. (Bills that appropriate money cannot include such a provision.)

If the legislature seeks to have the state borrow money long term (more than one year), a two-thirds majority in each chamber must approve legislation authorizing the action and then put the question before the voters. The proposal must state the amount to be borrowed, the specific purpose to which the funds are to be devoted, and the repayment method.

JUDICIAL BRANCH

Article VI of the 1963 Michigan Constitution provides that "the judicial power of the state is vested exclusively in one court of justice which shall be divided into one supreme court, one court of appeals, one trial court of general jurisdiction known as the circuit court, one probate court, and courts of limited jurisdiction that the legislature may establish by two-thirds vote of the members elected to and serving in each house." Exhibit 4 presents the current state judicial structure.

Judicial compensation is based on the salary of a supreme court justice (currently, $164,610). Circuit and probate judges receive a salary equivalent to 85 percent of that of a justice, and district judges receive 84 percent.

All Michigan judges are elected, although the governor is empowered to make appointments (not subject to the Senate's advice and consent) to fill vacancies until the end of the term in question. A candidate for any judgeship must be an attorney, aged under 70 on the date of appointment or election, and a qualified elector. Candidates for the appeals, circuit, district, and probate benches must reside in the jurisdiction in which they will serve.

Judges are prohibited from holding any other elective office during their term and for one year thereafter.

Judges are disciplined by the supreme court on recommendation from the Judicial Tenure Commission, which consists of nine members: two attorneys and one judge elected by the State Bar of Michigan, four judges elected by their peers, and two lay members appointed by the governor. The commission investigates complaints and recommends disciplinary action when necessary.

Supreme Court
The Michigan Supreme Court is the highest court in the state, hearing cases appealed to it from other state courts. In addition to its judicial duties, the court is charged with general administration of all courts in the state. The court is composed of seven justices (chief justice and six associate justices) chosen in nonpartisan elections (they are nominated by political parties, however) to serve eight-year terms. For continuity, the terms are staggered; no more than two seats are on the ballot in any one election year except to fill vacancies.

The supreme court, which sits in Lansing and does much of its work in conference, hears only cases on appeal from lower courts. A party wishing to have its case heard files an "application for leave to appeal." If the application is denied, the lower court's decision stands. A decision of the court is written and must be approved by a majority of the justices. If a justice disagrees with the majority opinion in whole or in part, s/he may write a dissenting opinion. The court issues 2,400 to 3,000 decisions a year.

Court of Appeals
The Michigan Court of Appeals has jurisdiction in civil and criminal cases appealed from lower courts. The 28 appeals court judges are elected to six-year terms in nonpartisan elections, seven from each of the four districts in the state, which have roughly equal population. To change the number of judges or alter the districts, state law must be amended.

Panels of at least three of any of the appeals court judges hear cases in Detroit, Grand Rapids, Lansing, and Marquette; the panels are rotated among these locations. Cases are decided in a procedure similar to that followed by the supreme court, and decisions are final unless the supreme court agrees to review a case.

Appeals court opinions may be published or unpublished. Published opinions are binding on all lower courts and may be used by lawyers to argue cases authoritatively. Unpublished opinions are not binding and may be used to argue cases only persuasively. Generally, unpublished opin-

EXHIBIT 4. Michigan Judicial Branch (arrows indicate route of appeal)

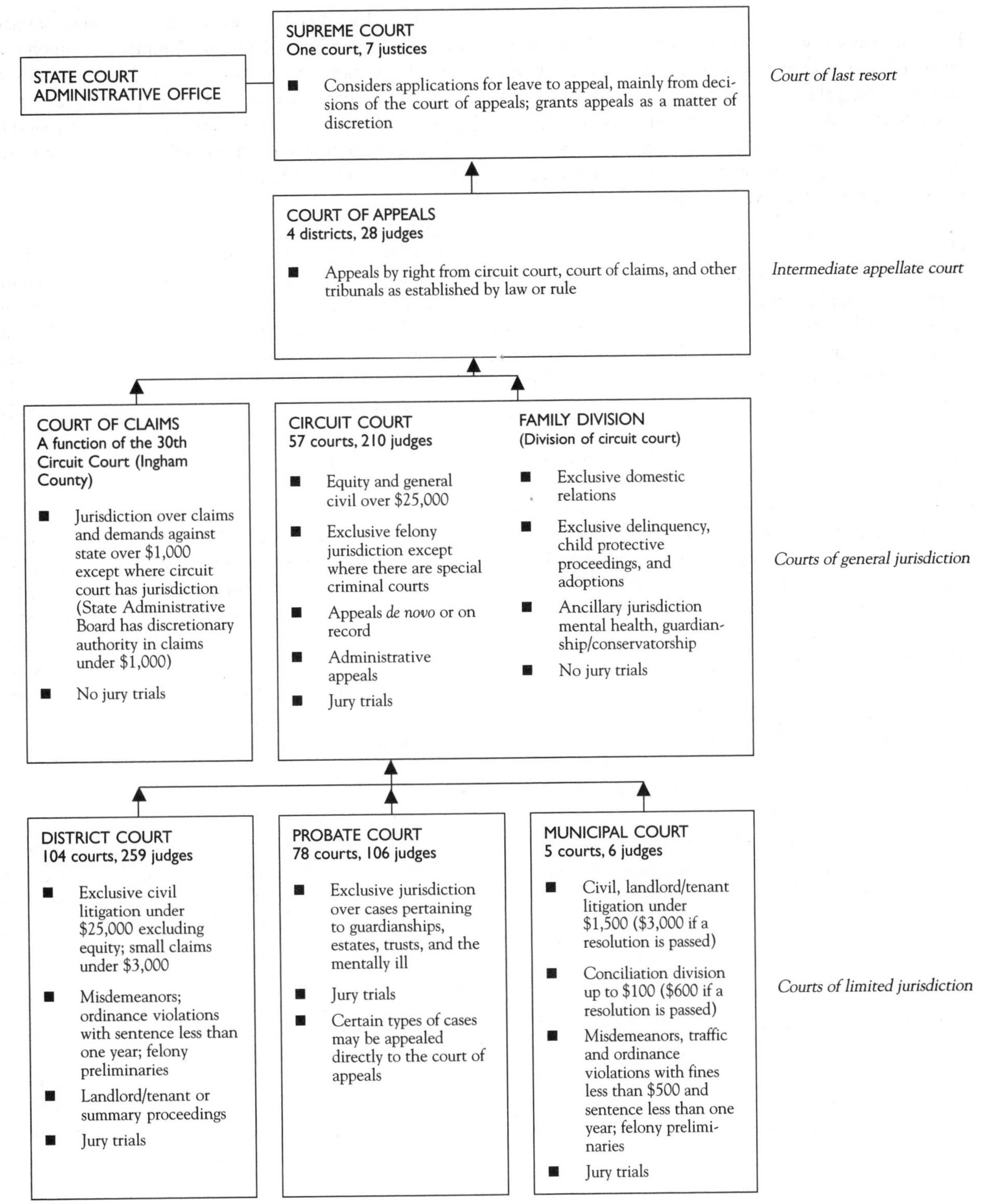

STATE COURT ADMINISTRATIVE OFFICE

SUPREME COURT
One court, 7 justices

- Considers applications for leave to appeal, mainly from decisions of the court of appeals; grants appeals as a matter of discretion

Court of last resort

COURT OF APPEALS
4 districts, 28 judges

- Appeals by right from circuit court, court of claims, and other tribunals as established by law or rule

Intermediate appellate court

COURT OF CLAIMS
A function of the 30th Circuit Court (Ingham County)

- Jurisdiction over claims and demands against state over $1,000 except where circuit court has jurisdiction (State Administrative Board has discretionary authority in claims under $1,000)
- No jury trials

CIRCUIT COURT
57 courts, 210 judges

- Equity and general civil over $25,000
- Exclusive felony jurisdiction except where there are special criminal courts
- Appeals *de novo* or on record
- Administrative appeals
- Jury trials

FAMILY DIVISION
(Division of circuit court)

- Exclusive domestic relations
- Exclusive delinquency, child protective proceedings, and adoptions
- Ancillary jurisdiction mental health, guardianship/conservatorship
- No jury trials

Courts of general jurisdiction

DISTRICT COURT
104 courts, 259 judges

- Exclusive civil litigation under $25,000 excluding equity; small claims under $3,000
- Misdemeanors; ordinance violations with sentence less than one year; felony preliminaries
- Landlord/tenant or summary proceedings
- Jury trials

PROBATE COURT
78 courts, 106 judges

- Exclusive jurisdiction over cases pertaining to guardianships, estates, trusts, and the mentally ill
- Jury trials
- Certain types of cases may be appealed directly to the court of appeals

MUNICIPAL COURT
5 courts, 6 judges

- Civil, landlord/tenant litigation under $1,500 ($3,000 if a resolution is passed)
- Conciliation division up to $100 ($600 if a resolution is passed)
- Misdemeanors, traffic and ordinance violations with fines less than $500 and sentence less than one year; felony preliminaries
- Jury trials

Courts of limited jurisdiction

SOURCE: State Court Administrative Office, 2001.
NOTE: A "cyber court," expected to be in operation in late 2002, has been created to conduct electronic hearings and proceedings in commercial litigation involving more than $25,000. All matters heard in the court will be via electronic communication. Use of the court will be voluntary, and proceedings will be similar to those of the circuit court. The supreme court will determine where the court will be located and assign circuit court judges to serve as cyber court judges for terms of at least three years.

Sponsored by the Michigan Nonprofit Association and the Council of Michigan Foundations

ions are issued in cases that either raise no unusual legal issue or have narrow application.

Circuit Court

As Michigan's trial court of general jurisdiction, the circuit court operates statewide in 57 circuits, staffed by 210 judges. It has original jurisdiction in all civil cases involving more than $25,000, in all criminal cases involving a felony or certain serious misdemeanors, and in all domestic-relations cases, including divorce and paternity actions. The court also hears cases appealed from lower courts and from some state-government administrative agencies. Circuit judges are elected every six years on a nonpartisan ballot.

Cyber Court

To accommodate parties located outside the state, a "cyber court" is being created to conduct electronic hearings and proceedings in commercial litigation involving more than $25,000; the court is expected to be in operation in the fall of 2002. All matters heard in the court will be via electronic communication, including but not limited to video and audio conferencing and Internet conferencing. Use of the court will be voluntary, and proceedings will be similar to those of the circuit court. The supreme court will determine the court's location and assign circuit court judges to serve as cyber court judges for terms lasting at least three years.

Family Division of Circuit Court

The Family Court Division of circuit court has exclusive jurisdiction over all family matters—divorce, custody, parenting time, support, paternity, adoption, name change, juvenile proceedings, emancipation of minors, parental consent, and personal protection proceedings. The division also has jurisdiction over guardianship and conservatorship and proceedings involving the mentally ill and developmentally disabled when they arise from a case already being heard in family court. (Otherwise, estate, guardianship cases, and those involving the mentally ill and developmentally disabled continue to be heard in probate court.)

Court of Claims

The court of claims, part of the 30th Circuit Court of Ingham County (Lansing), is limited to hearing claims against the State of Michigan. It has jurisdiction over claims of more than $1,000. (The State Administrative Board is vested with discretionary authority in claims against the state under $1,000.)

District Court

The district court has exclusive jurisdiction in all civil litigation up to $25,000 and handles garnishments, evic-

tion proceedings, land contract and mortgage foreclosures, and certain other proceedings. In criminal cases, it handles misdemeanors punishable by not more than one year of punishment, including arraignment, bail hearings, trial and sentencing, and preliminary examination of accused felons.

District courts have a Small Claims Division for civil actions up to $3,000. A case may be heard in small claims court if both parties agree to waive their right to a trial by jury, rules of evidence, representation by a lawyer, and appeal. If either party objects, the case will be heard in general district court.

District judges may appoint magistrates, who need not be a lawyer, whose duties generally are limited to setting bail for criminal offenses, accepting guilty pleas, and issuing sentences for violations of traffic, motor carrier, snowmobile, dog, game, and marine law. A magistrate also may issue arrest warrants or search warrants authorized by the prosecutor or municipal attorney. Attorney magistrates may hear small claims cases and, at the direction of the chief judge, perform other duties allowed by statute.

District judges are chosen in nonpartisan elections every six years.

Probate Court

The probate court has limited jurisdiction. It supervises "probation" of wills and the administration of deceased persons' estates and trusts, guardianships, conservatorships, and the treatment of mentally ill and developmentally disabled persons.

There is a probate court in 73 Michigan counties; the remaining 10 have formed five two-county probate districts. Each county or two-county district has one or more judges, depending on population and caseload. Probate judges are elected for a six-year term on a nonpartisan ballot.

Municipal Court

Municipal courts have jurisdiction over local ordinances, civil actions up to $1,500 (unless the city in which the court is located increases the jurisdictional amount to $3,000), and all criminal cases within the municipality. Five municipalities have chosen to retain a municipal court rather than change to district court. Municipal judges are elected to four-year terms as provided by city charter. They are part-time judges and may practice law.

DIVISION AND BALANCE OF POWER

Just as the framers of the U.S. Constitution divided government into branches, to provide checks and balances against the tyranny or supremacy of any one individual or group, the writers of Michigan's four constitutions balanced state power among legislative, executive, and judicial branches. It is said that the legislature makes policy, the executive implements it, and the judiciary interprets it.

One characteristic of a government built on checks and balances is that it is guarded against an individual public official or branch having excessive authority. Another characteristic is that the division of power and the checks against intrusion by one branch into the authority of another means that the governing process proceeds at a pace more deliberate than is appreciated by those who would like to "just get it done." Checks and balances also sometimes give rise to jurisdictional disputes, and this can slow—even paralyze—policymaking.

The most frequent inter-branch conflicts occur between the legislature and governor, usually over policy or budget. (Partisan and ideological differences typically are the basis of disagreement, but sometimes personality clashes or geographic focus—Detroit versus out state and so forth—trigger a problem.) Disputes generally are resolved by negotiation, but each branch has the means to frustrate another's intentions: For example, the legislature may decline to pass legislation that the governor wants, or the governor may veto legislation s/he doesn't like (the legislature, in turn, may overturn a veto if there are sufficient votes).

In Michigan, as in most states, the governor possesses the line-item veto, which is a device that gives the chief executive considerable power in the appropriation of funds. Although only the legislature may appropriate funds, the governor may reject specific spending (the "lines" in a budget bill).

The third branch, the judiciary, may determine that a state law (passed by the legislature and signed into law by the governor) violates the state constitution, which is the highest written authority. Such a decision is binding on the legislature and governor.

Examples of Checks and Balances in Action

Occasionally, disputes go beyond policy and budget differences, to jurisdiction. For example, the state supreme court cannot raise taxes and appropriate monies to special education, but its decision in the 1997 *Durant* v. *State of Michigan* case essentially ordered the legislature to appropriate more money to local school districts (in partial compensation for programs the state had mandated but not fully funded). And the governor cannot write a law that establishes a new executive department, but through an executive order, s/he may move agencies from one de-

partment to another, rename an old one, or create a new one. And the legislature does not administer the judicial branch, but in 1996 lawmakers passed a statute reorganizing the way in which local courts are configured. The legislature cannot administer the executive branch, either, but at the end of an appropriation bill, lawmakers may put language (so-called boilerplate) that clearly conveys to the governor how lawmakers desire the funding to be administered.

Balance of Power Today

Since Gov. John Engler first was inaugurated, in 1991, the executive branch has gained a good deal of power relative to the legislative branch. Governor Engler has used executive reorganization orders to end various commissions' power to appoint department directors, move agencies from one department to another, eliminate several departments, rename and change the duties of others, and create new ones.

Governor Engler also stripped the legislature of its pre-promulgation involvement in the rules that executive agencies make to implement legislation; although the legislature may take action to change rules *after* they have been issued, that branch's power in regard to rule writing has been reduced significantly.

Some political observers believe that term limits will allow future governors to gain and exercise even greater power over the legislature. So many legislators will come and go that the governor—even though s/he, too, is limited to only two terms—will wield enormous clout. Likewise, some believe that the nonelected officials in the executive branch—career civil servants—will come to greatly influence policy because they will be the repository of institutional memory and expertise; the check on their power will be lost when governors and legislators are forced to give up their offices.

Sponsored by the Michigan Nonprofit Association and the Council of Michigan Foundations

CHAPTER 3
About the State Budget

The state budget is the spending plan for state government; it reflects the program priorities of the governor and the legislature. The budget is a complete financial plan; it encompasses all revenue and expenditures (both operating and capital outlay) of the General Fund and special revenue funds for the 12-month period, the *fiscal year,* extending from October 1 of one calendar year through September 30 of the next.

GLOSSARY

Consensus Revenue Sharing Conference
A twice-yearly meeting of officials from the Senate and House fiscal agencies and the Michigan Department of Treasury at which they agree on the amount of revenue they expect the state to collect in the current and next fiscal year.

Executive order
In a budget context, a document the governor issues that will cut spending; must be approved by the appropriations committees in both legislative chambers.

Fiscal year (FY)
In Michigan, October 1 through September 30.

General Fund/General Purpose (GF/GP) Fund
Monies not "earmarked," or dedicated, to a specific purpose; available for appropriation for any purpose specified by the legislature.

Line-item veto
The governor's authority to veto individual items ("lines") in a budget bill.

Special revenue fund
Holds revenue "earmarked" for a special purpose; e.g., the School Aid Fund.

Supplemental appropriation
Legislation passed after the budget has been enacted that appropriates additional money to an agency or program.

PROCESS

In the case of state government, "budget" also refers to the document submitted by the governor to the legislature. This document—formally, the *Executive Budget,* and informally, the "governor's budget message"—sets forth the governor's spending recommendations for each department and function of state government. The requirement for budget preparation is set out in Article V, section 18, of the Michigan Constitution.

> The governor shall submit to the legislature at a time fixed by law, a budget for the ensuing fiscal period setting forth in detail for all operating funds, the proposed expenditures and estimated revenue of the state. Proposed expenditures from any fund shall not exceed the estimated revenue thereof. On the same date, the governor shall submit to the legislature general appropriation bills to embody the proposed expenditures and any necessary bill or bills to provide new or additional revenues to meet proposed expenditures. The amount of any surplus created or deficit incurred in any fund during the last preceding fiscal period shall be entered as an item in the budget and in one of the appropriation bills. The governor may submit amendments to appropriation bills to be offered in either house during consideration of the bill by that house and shall submit bills to meet deficiencies in current appropriations.

Exhibit 1 summarizes the budget process, which begins 13–14 months prior to a new fiscal year, when the various departments submit their spending requests to the Michigan Department of Management and Budget (MDMB). The requests include program descriptions, financial needs, program alternatives, and performance data. These requests are reviewed by MDMB analysts, hearings are held with the departments and the governor, and final recommendations are presented by the governor to the legislature, usually in February. By law, the governor must present the budget to the legislature within 30 days after it convenes in regular session on the second Wednesday in January. (In a governor's first year in office, the presentation deadline is extended to 60 days.) Half of the several appropriation bills are introduced ("originated") in the House and the other half in the Senate.

The governor's budget recommendations are considered first by the appropriations committees of the House and Senate. These each have subcommittees that specialize in various sections of the budget; for example, the Higher Education Subcommittee reviews the recommendations made for public colleges and universities. The governor's proposals may be accepted as presented, changed by a committee, or changed by either

Sponsored by the Michigan Nonprofit Association and the Council of Michigan Foundations

EXHIBIT 1. State Budget Process, Step-by-Step Summary

I. Preparation and Presentation

Several months in advance of a new fiscal year, departments review current operations, program objectives, issues, and future plans relative to their budget. The departments submit management plans to the Office of the Budget in the Michigan Department of Management and Budget (MDMB) along with supporting material for their funding requests, analytical studies of major issues, alternatives for resolving issues, and comparisons of costs and effectiveness.

Briefings and hearings occur among department officials, budget analysts, and the governor, to prepare funding recommendations for the upcoming fiscal year.

In February the Consensus Revenue Estimating Conference (budget officials from the executive and legislative branches) meet and agree on a revenue forecast to be used for budget; the forecast is updated in May.

In February the governor presents the recommended budget to the legislature. Bills are submitted containing the governor's recommended appropriations.

II. Consideration

An appropriation bill is "read" (the title only, not the text) in the chamber in which it is being considered. Because there are several appropriation bills, half are introduced (originated) in the House and half in the Senate.

The bill is referred to the chambers' respective appropriations committees.

The bill is deliberated by a subcommittee.

The full appropriations committee holds a hearing on the subcommittee's recommendations.

The full appropriations committee adopts or amends the subcommittee recommendations and reports the bill with amendments or as a substitute to the floor.

Floor debate, amendment, and passage of the bill occur in the chamber of origin.

The bill is transmitted to the other chamber, where the process is repeated.

III. Enrollment and Enactment

If the bill passes both chambers in identical form, it is ordered enrolled by the originating chamber and printed. Upon enrollment, the bill is sent to the governor.

If the bill is passed in a different form by the second chamber, it must be returned to the originating chamber for concurrence. If that chamber accepts the amendments or the substitute bill of the other, the bill is enrolled and sent to the governor.

If the originating chamber rejects the amendments or substitute bill of the other, the bill is sent to a special conference committee composed of legislators from both bodies who attempt to make compromises between the two versions. The conference committee does not consider any matters other than the differences between the two versions. If the agreement reached affects other parts of the bill, the conferees may recommend amendments to conform with the agreement. They also may recommend correction of any errors in the bill or in the title. When the conference committee reaches a compromise, it submits a report to both chambers. If the report is approved by both, the bill is enrolled and sent to the governor. If the conference committee cannot reach a compromise, or if the legislature does not accept the conference report, a second conference committee may be appointed.

When the governor receives the bill, s/he may sign it into law, veto the entire bill, or veto only specific "line items." To override a veto, a two-thirds vote by the full membership of each chamber is required.

IV. Implementation and Adjustments

During the fiscal year each department may request allotment revisions, transfers, or supplemental appropriations. The MDMB submits revised allotments to the State Administrative Board for approval. Transfers of funds within a department are submitted by the MDMB to the House and Senate appropriations committees for approval before being sent on to the State Administrative Board. Action by the legislature and the governor on supplemental appropriation bills is similar to that taken on an appropriation bill.

The MDMB reviews appropriations, prepares allocations, and estimates revenue (in cooperation with the legislature and Consensus Revenue Estimating Conference). If there is insufficient revenue, the MDMB prepares an executive order by which the governor makes recommendations to reduce the budget.

The governor transmits the executive order to the legislature. It is not necessary that the full legislature act, but the approval of both appropriations committees is required within 10 days after the recommendation is made.

SOURCE: Public Sector Consultants, Inc.

Sponsored by the Michigan Nonprofit Association and the Council of Michigan Foundations

legislative chamber. The budget bills must be approved by both chambers (differences between the two are resolved in conference committees comprising three members from each chamber) and signed by the governor before becoming law. The governor may veto any item in the budget (this is called a *line-item* veto). The legislature may override a veto by a two-thirds vote of the full membership in both chambers.

After the governor submits the budget recommendations in February, the appropriation bills usually are considered and passed in the spring by the chamber in which they were introduced and in early June by the other; conference reports or final action usually is completed around July 4. If legislative passage of a budget bill is not accomplished by October 1, the beginning of a new fiscal year, a *continuing resolution* is passed, keeping spending for that section of the budget at the level of the prior year.

The process is not complete with the budget's final enactment. At any time during the year *supplemental spending* bills may be enacted, or the governor may submit an *executive order* cutting spending; the latter must be approved by both appropriations committees but not by the full legislative bodies. In roughly the last 25 years there have been 16 executive orders to reduce expenditures; on five occasions they were not approved by the appropriations committees, but in each instance the governor issued a subsequent executive order that was.

SIZE AND COMPOSITION

State government (including public colleges and universities) is a major industry in Michigan, spending more than $36 billion in FY 2000–01 and employing 170,000 workers. If higher education and other nonagency employees (e.g., university and state hospital workers) are excluded from the number of state employees, the current figure is about 64,000.

A major share of the budget is allocated to local units of government; spending on local programs has been increasing faster than spending on state programs for several years. The largest local-program categories are school aid, revenue sharing, transportation, community mental health, and community colleges. As a result of the so-called Headlee amendment (1978), the constitution (Article IX, section 30) requires that no less than 41.6 percent of the state budget (not including federal aid) be allocated to local units of government. If this percentage is not met, make-up payments must be made in the following fiscal year; this has occurred twice. Because of school finance reform (1994), which shifted most K–12 funding to the state level and therefore increased state payments to local

school districts, the share of state spending allocated to local units of government now is about 60 percent, effectively eliminating the relevance of this provision.

Exhibit 2 displays total FY 2000–01 state spending by major category. The largest are school aid and community health, accounting for 30 percent and 23 percent, respectively, of total state spending.

Exhibit 3 shows the FY 2000–01 figures for the three major fund categories into which the state budget is divided; these are the revenues that support state spending.

- General Fund/General Purpose (GF/GP), commonly, the "General Fund"

- General Fund/Special Purpose (GF/SP), commonly, "special purpose" funds

- Special revenue

The major share of transactions occurs in GF/GP funds. The budget process is concerned mainly with the *general purpose* portion, as only these monies are subject to the complete control of the governor and the legislature (special purpose funds may be expended only for designated programs).

- In FY 1999–2000 the GF/GP budget totaled $9.40 billion.

- In FY 2000–01 the GF/GP budget totaled $9.74 billion.

- For FY 2001–02 the governor's recommended GF/GP spending (after executive order reductions) is $9.27 billion.

- For FY 2002–03 the governor's recommended spending is $9.24 billion.

As mentioned, the uses to which *special purpose* revenue may be put are restricted. By constitution, statute, contract, or agreement, such revenue is reserved ("earmarked") for specific purposes, and its expenditure is limited by how much revenue there is. The major categories—which account for about 86 percent of special purpose revenue and spending—are

- tax revenue that is allocated to local governments ($1.47 billion in FY 1999–2000), and

- federal aid ($8.5 billion in FY 1999–2000).

Special revenue funds are used to finance particular activities from the receipts of specific taxes or other revenue. Such funds are created by the constitution or statute to provide certain activities with definite and con-

EXHIBIT 2. Total State Spending by Major Category, FY 2000–01 ($ millions)

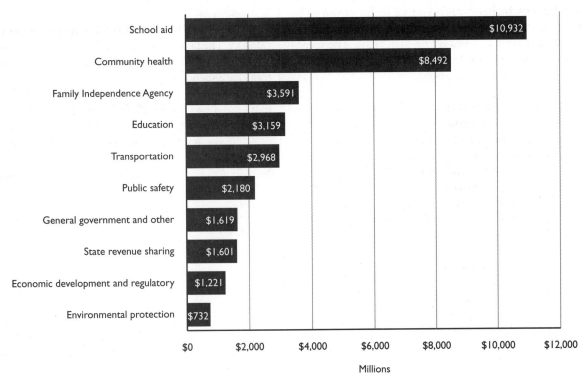

SOURCE: Senate Fiscal Agency, 2000 Statistical Report

NOTES: (1) Higher education = higher education and Department of Education. (2) Public safety = departments of Corrections, State Police, and Military Affairs. (3) Economic development and regulatory = departments of Career Development and Consumer and Industry Services and the Strategic Fund Agency. (4) Environmental protection = departments of Agriculture, Environmental Quality, and Natural Resources.

EXHIBIT 3. Major State Funds, FY 2000–01 ($ millions)

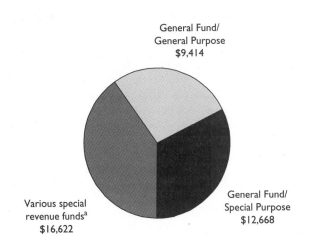

SOURCE: State of Michigan, Comprehensive Annual Financial Report, FY 2000–01.

aIncludes the School Aid, Lottery, and Transportation funds.

tinuing revenue. The largest special revenue funds—which together account for more than 90 percent of total special fund revenue ($16.62 billion in FY 2001–01)—are the School Aid and Transportation funds; another is the Lottery Fund.

- The School Aid Fund is financed by restricted taxes, lottery revenue, and a grant from the General Fund.

- The Transportation Fund is financed mainly by motor fuel and weight taxes and federal aid.

- The Lottery Fund receives all revenue from lottery ticket sales; after deductions for prizes and administrative expenses, the remainder is transferred to the School Aid Fund.

The Budget and Economic Stabilization Fund (BSF, usually called the "budget stabilization" or "rainy day" fund) is among the most important budget tools available to state government. It was established in 1977 to smooth out the peaks and valleys in state spending. During years of economic health or malaise, monies are deposited or withdrawn according to a formula: Deposits are made when

Sponsored by the Michigan Nonprofit Association and the Council of Michigan Foundations

real (adjusted for inflation) Michigan personal income increases more than 2 percent, and withdrawals are made when that income declines from the previous year. The law also provides for withdrawals when the Michigan unemployment rate averages more than 8 percent for a quarter; these monies are to be used for economic stabilization purposes, such as job retraining or summer youth employment. Major withdrawals from the BSF, ranging from $170 million to $530 million, to cover budget shortfalls were made in FYs 1979–80, 1990–91, 1991–92, 2000–01, and 2001–02. Smaller withdrawals have been made several times to fund such programs as school aid, prison construction, road construction, and court judgments. Large payments were made from the General Fund to the BSF in FYs 1992–93, 1993–94, 1994–95, 1995–96, 1998–99, and 1999–2000. The balance in the BSF as of September 30, 2001, was about $995 million. The balance as of September 30, 2002 is expected to be about $740 million.

CHANGES IN STATE SPENDING

Spending priorities change over time because economic, social, and political conditions change. This certainly has been the case in Michigan during the last 25 years. Tracking these changes has been complicated by school finance reform and government reorganization.

As may be seen in Exhibit 4, school aid (and two smaller programs) increased from about 20 percent of the state budget in FY 1990–91 to nearly 33 percent 10 years later, in FY 2000–01. This resulted from the transfer of most K–12 funding from the local to the state level and the accompanying increase—from about $3.5 billion to more than $10.5 billion—in state payments to school districts. School finance reform vastly increased total state spending, which means that the share of the total attributed to other programs has diminished.

REVENUE SOURCES

Exhibit 5 compares state revenue sources over the past 10 years. The three largest sources are federal aid, the personal income tax, and sales and use taxes.

■ Federal aid accounted for about 24 percent of total state revenue in FY 1999–2000. This is down from 25.5 percent in FY 1990–91.

■ The personal income tax accounted for about 22 percent of total revenue in FY 1999–2000. This source also is down due to Proposal A's enactment in 1994 and the subsequent cuts in the income tax rate and addition of new and increased state revenue sources to replace school property taxes.

■ Sales and use tax collections accounted for nearly 22 percent in FY 1999–2000. This is up due to Proposal A's increase in the rate of both taxes from 4 percent to 6 percent.

The decline over the last decade in business tax revenue is due largely to reductions in the rate and base of the single business tax, which is being phased out over 20 years.

The increase in other taxes, to almost 6 percent in FY 1999–2000, is due to Proposal A, which replaced most school property taxes with new and increased state revenue sources, the most important of which are the 6-mill state education property tax, real estate transfer tax, and 50-cent-per-pack cigarette-tax hike.

EXHIBIT 4. Selected Expenditure Categories as a Share of the Total State Budget, Selected Fiscal Years

Category	FY 1982–83	FY 1990–91	FY 2000–01
School aid (K–12), Department of Education, and State Library	19.4%	20.1%	32.6%
Family Independence Agency[a]	33.5	30.5	9.8
Transportation	9.4	8.5	8.1
Higher education	8.1	8.4	6.1
Community Health[a]	7.9	9.1	23.3
Grants to locals (revenue sharing)[b]	6.1	5.6	4.4
Safety and corrections	3.9	5.7	6.0
General government and other	15.6	12.1	9.7

SOURCES: Senate Fiscal Agency, 2000 Statistical Report; State of Michigan Executive Budget, 2001–02 Fiscal Year. Calculations by Public Sector Consultants, Inc.

[a]In FY 1990 the departments of Mental Health and Public Health were merged, creating the Department of Community Health, and the Medicaid program was transferred to the new department from the Department of Social Services. The latter was renamed the Family Independence Agency.

[b]In 1994 school finance reform shifted most K–12 funding to the state level and therefore increased state payments to local school districts.

EXHIBIT 5. State Government Revenue Sources, FY 1990–91 and FY 1999–2000

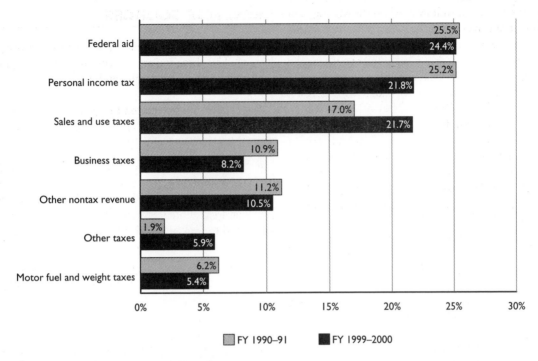

SOURCE: Senate Fiscal Agency, 2000 Statistical Report. Calculations by Public Sector Consultants, Inc.

SPENDING TRENDS

State Government Spending Growth

As indicated in Exhibit 6, the rate of state government spending growth has slowed markedly in recent years. In the 1960s and 1970s state government spending increased faster than the national average. Since 1975 Michigan spending growth has been below the national average. Spending growth slowed even more in the last two years and, due to the economic slowdown and the phased reduction of the income and single business tax rates, declined sharply in FY 2001–02.

Limits on State Spending

Partly in response to large increases in spending and taxes, in 1978 the voters approved a constitutional limit on state spending—the so-called Headlee amendment, which requires that

- total state spending (excluding federal aid) not exceed 9.49 percent of Michigan personal income (the ratio in the fiscal year in which the amendment was approved) and

- any excess revenue be refunded to the taxpayers.

As a result of the 1994 school finance reform, which replaced local property taxes with state taxes (mainly on sales, use, and property), revenue approached the limit in FY 1994–95 and would have exceeded it except for enacted tax cuts—one of which was a 2 percent income tax credit enacted specifically to keep revenue below the Headlee limit. Revenue is expected to be about $3.84 bil-

EXHIBIT 6. Growth in Total State General Fund Spending, Michigan and All States, FY 1959–60 to FY 2001–02 (average annual rates)

Time Period	Growth, Michigan	Growth, All States
FYs 1960–70	11.1%	10.5%
FYs 1970–75	13.4	12.4
FYs 1975–80	10.6	10.7
FYs 1980–90	5.9	8.7
FYs 1990–00	3.1	5.4
FYs 2000–01	1.1	8.1
FYs 2001–02	–6.4	3.6

SOURCE: National Association of State Budget Officers, Washington, D.C.

Sponsored by the Michigan Nonprofit Association and the Council of Michigan Foundations

lion below the limit in FY 2001–02 and $4.26 billion below in FY 2002–03.

COMPARISONS WITH OTHER STATES

Expenditures

State-local spending (direct general-government expenditures) in Michigan is $5,125 per capita—almost exactly the U.S. average (FY 1998–99 data, the latest available). As a share of personal income, state-local spending is 19.3 percent; the U.S. average is 18.9 percent.

Exhibit 7 shows state-local spending in various categories for all states. Michigan ranks high in education, sanitation, and corrections but low in public welfare, highways, interest payments, parks and recreation, and government administration and other. The low ranking in highway spending is somewhat misleading because that category is largely a function of population density: States with a small population and many miles of highways (e.g., Alaska, Wyoming) have high per capita spending, and states with a large population and few miles of highway (e.g., Massachusetts, Rhode Island) have low per capita expenditures. Michigan's low rank on interest payments reflects its "pay-as-you-go" philosophy for financing capital projects.

Revenue

One criterion for a good state-local tax system is the balanced use of the major revenue sources—income, sales, and property taxes. A rule of thumb is that each should contribute 20–30 percent of total state-local taxes. Prior to school finance reform in 1994, it could be said that for many years the Michigan tax system was unbalanced because it relied too much on property taxes and too little on the sales tax. The 1994 reforms corrected this imbal-

EXHIBIT 7. Per Capita State-Local Direct General Spending, by Category, Michigan and the United States, 1998–99

Category	Michigan	United States	Michigan as a Percentage of U.S. Average
Education	$2,150.54	$1,772.19	1.21%
K–12	1,463.33	1,246.36	1.17
Higher education	631.78	450.02	1.40
Public welfare	654.10	789.13	0.83
Health and hospitals	429.30	437.72	0.98
Highways	308.50	341.11	0.90
Police and fire	232.84	273.67	0.85
Corrections	185.08	167.22	1.11
Parks and recreation	66.65	85.87	0.78
Sanitation and sewerage	189.32	157.86	1.20
Interest on general debt	226.04	246.78	0.92
Govt. admin. and other	683.09	857.09	0.80
TOTAL	$5,125.46	$5,128.64	1.00%

SOURCE: U.S. Department of Commerce, Bureau of the Census, Government Finances: 1998–99.

ance by reducing property taxes by about one-third and increasing the sales tax rate by 50 percent.

Michigan's total tax burden is slightly above average. Total state-local own-source revenue is 16.3 percent of personal income (down from 17.3 percent in FY 1993–94), or $4,362 per capita; this compares with the U.S. average of 15.8 percent and $4,268 per capita. Michigan ranks 22d and 15th, respectively, in these categories (FY 1998–99 data).

Sponsored by the Michigan Nonprofit Association and the Council of Michigan Foundations

CHAPTER 4
About Michigan's Nonprofit Sector

■ Giving and Volunteering for the Common Good

INTRODUCTION

Michigan's nonprofit sector involves a wide range of services and activities that make a significant difference in the quality of life in the state. The sector commonly is recognized for its public spirit, service to others, altruism, and ideals. Nonprofit action can occur unobtrusively, among individuals, or very publicly and visibly through the work of statewide, national, or international organizations that meet complex health, education, or cultural needs. This chapter examines the scale and scope of nonprofit action in Michigan, with emphasis on the contribution it makes to daily life, and the significance of giving and volunteering in Michigan.

Formal Entities
Nonprofits operate under the Internal Revenue Service (IRS) definitions that classify tax-exempt organizations under section 501(c) of the Internal Revenue Code. A group deemed tax-exempt may operate for a purpose outlined in one of the 27 section 501(c) categories (see Exhibit 1). A group also may choose to incorporate as a nonprofit in Michigan by submitting a formal document of organization, such as articles of incorporation and bylaws, to the Michigan Department of Consumer and Industry Services. Any group that holds assets in Michigan or solicits funds in the state must register with the Charitable Trust Section of the state attorney general's office.

An organization recognized as nonprofit under 501(c) is exempt from federal income tax. Depending on state and local laws, these nonprofits also may be exempt from sales, use, income, and property taxes. The largest percentage of the sector is comprised of 501(c)(3) nonprofits, which must operate for charitable, religious, scientific, literary, or educational purposes. Also referred to as *charities*, these organizations may benefit from national, state, and/or local tax deductions/credits that provide an incentive for people to engage in charitable giving: federal income-tax deductions for donations and, in Michigan, an income-tax credit for gifts to certain types of charities.

Informal Entities
The legal and tax definitions tend to capture only the largest and most active nonprofit organizations, but Michigan's nonprofit sector far exceeds the officially recognized organizations. There are thousands of local and informal groups undertaking nonprofit action that neither have nor need legal recognition. Any formal analysis of the sector relies on valid data, which can be gathered only for formally organized organizations, and this means that much of the nonprofit sector—the informal component—is statistically invisible. Nevertheless, there are some data that provide insight into the scale, structure, and character of the Michigan nonprofit sector as a whole.

By Mark Wilson, MSU Institute for Public Policy and Social Research; Rob Collier and Jeri Fischer, Council of Michigan Foundations; and Robin Lynn Schultheiss and Erin Skene, Michigan Nonprofit Association

EXHIBIT 1. Tax-Exempt Organizations as Defined by the IRS

Subsection	Description
501(c)(1)	Corporations organized under an act of Congress
501(c)(2)	Title-holding corporations
501(c)(3)	Charitable and religious organizations
501(c)(4)	Social welfare organizations
501(c)(5)	Labor and agricultural organizations
501(c)(6)	Business leagues
501(c)(7)	Social and recreational clubs
501(c)(8)	Fraternal beneficiary associations
501(c)(9)	Voluntary employees' beneficiary associations
501(c)(10)	Domestic fraternal beneficiary associations
501(c)(11)	Teacher's retirement fund associations
501(c)(12)	Benevolent life insurance associations
501(c)(13)	Cemetery companies
501(c)(14)	State chartered credit unions
501(c)(15)	Mutual insurance companies
501(c)(16)	Corporations organized to finance crop operations
501(c)(17)	Supplemental unemployment benefit trusts
501(c)(18)	Employee funded pension trusts
501(c)(19)	War veterans' organizations
501(c)(20)	Legal service organizations
501(c)(21)	Black lung trusts
501(c)(22)	Withdrawal liability payment funds
501(c)(23)	Veteran's associations funded prior to 1880
501(c)(24)	Trusts described in section 4049 of ERISA
501(c)(25)	Title-holding corporations or trusts with multiple parents
501(c)(26)	State-sponsored high-risk health coverage organizations
501(c)(27)	State-sponsored workers' compensation reinsurance organizations

SOURCES: Michigan Nonprofit Association and Internal Revenue Service.

Range and Location of Nonprofits

Michigan nonprofit organizations provide a wide range of services; most may be grouped into six major categories.

- *Arts and amusement* nonprofits include radio and television broadcasting, dance education, orchestras, amusement services, museums, and art galleries.

- *Recreation* nonprofits include camps and membership hotels.

- *Health* nonprofits include medical instruments producers, doctors and other health practitioners, nursing and personal-care facilities, hospitals, medical laboratories, and home health care services; health nonprofits employ more people than any other component of the state's nonprofit sector.

- *Education* nonprofits include elementary and secondary schools, colleges and universities, libraries, and vocational schools.

- *Social services* nonprofits include individual and family services, job training, child daycare services, and residential-care programs; social service nonprofits are the second largest employer in Michigan's nonprofit sector.

- *Membership* nonprofits include business associations; professional, labor, civic, and social organizations; and religious groups.

The number and activity level of nonprofits varies from place to place. Where one lives determines the type and range of services that are available. Southeastern Michigan and major metropolitan areas host the full range of nonprofit services, while less populous and more remote areas have more a limited range.

AN ECONOMIC FORCE

Nonprofit organizations, through employment and spending, are important to the Michigan economy. At the state level, an economic-benefits study of the nonprofit sector (Public Sector Consultants, 1999) finds that

- the assets of Michigan nonprofits exceed $60 billion;

- the nonprofit community spends about $28 billion annually, of which nearly all (95 percent) remains in the state; and

- the sector directly provides about 380,000 jobs for Michiganians and nearly $10 billion in personal income annually (only durable manufacturing, services, government, and the retail-trade sectors provide more Michigan jobs).

The National Center for Charitable Statistics (Washington) finds that in 1999 there were 23,640 registered 501(c)(3) organizations in Michigan, but only 7,498 meet the financial threshold that requires that they regularly report to the IRS. (The wide difference in the numbers illustrates the absence of common definitions for and data collection on the nonprofit sector.) The counties having the most reporting nonprofits are Wayne (1,254 organizations), Oakland (1,081), Kent (653), Ingham (436), Washtenaw (415), Kalamazoo (282), Genesee (256), and Macomb (233).

MICHIGAN GIVES

Nonprofit finances derive from many sources—for example, service fees, grants, and donations from the public, corporations, and foundations. Donated resources often allow nonprofits to reduce the cost of their services, permitting more people at all income levels to benefit. Details about household giving in Michigan are available from public opinion surveys, most recently, *Giving and Volunteering 2001*, which was commissioned by ConnectMichigan Alliance, the Council of Michigan Foundations, Michigan Association of United Ways, Michigan Community Service Commission, and the Michigan Nonprofit Association and conducted in October and November 2001.

■ Almost 90 percent of Michigan adults made a charitable contribution during the 12 months preceding the survey.

■ Men and women are equally likely to make a charitable contribution.

■ Giving rates are similar across all major religions.

■ Giving is strong across all age groups, with the 60–64 group having the highest rate (96 percent).

■ Giving tends to increase with income, but there also is high participation among people in the lowest income groups: Of people with annual household income under $10,000, 78 percent reported making a charitable contribution during the year preceding the survey, and of those with annual household income of $10,000–19,999, the figure is 74 percent.

■ Most survey respondents (64 percent) say that in 2002 they plan to give about the same amount they gave in 2002, 27 percent plan to give more, and 10 percent believe they will give less.

■ Government financial support (e.g., contracting for services with faith-based organizations) is supported by 59 percent of Michigan residents.

■ Of the respondents who are Internet users, 25 percent said they have gone on line to learn more about a charitable organization, and 6 percent have made a charitable donation on line.

MICHIGAN'S COMMITMENT TO VOLUNTEERISM

Michigan has a long history and strong commitment to volunteerism and frequently is cited as one of the leading states in the nation in this regard. This proud distinction reflects Michiganians' high degree of collaboration and innovation in their approach to volunteer service. The distinction is no accident—it grew from many years of effort and innovation and a willingness to put aside the partisan political agenda to serve the common good.

Although the greatest strides in volunteerism have come in the last decade, the foundation of the modern volunteer movement was laid more than 30 years ago when George W. Romney was elected governor. He lived the concept of citizen service and championed its cause throughout Michigan and the nation. Governor Romney saw volunteering as vital and necessary to community problem solving and considered it to be the responsibility of every individual. Few who met him failed to be moved by his passion for service or challenged by his conviction. Among his permanent contributions to the field of service are establishment of the Volunteer National Center (1970) and the Points of Light Foundation (1990). He also receives credit for conceiving and kindling the Presidents' Summit for America's Future (1997). Although the summit occurred after Governor Romney died, it is testament to his legacy that the event marked the first time in U.S. history that all the living presidents joined forces to address a volunteer issue.

Today Michigan has an extensive network of public and private organizations that support volunteer service, and these are supplemented by the work of national, regional, and local affiliates. To name but a few, statewide organizations include the ConnectMichigan Alliance, Council of Michigan Foundations (CMF), Michigan Association of United Ways, Michigan Campus Compact, Michigan Community Service Commission, Michigan League for Human Services, Michigan Nonprofit Association (MNA), and Volunteer Centers of Michigan. Although each serves a particular constituency (with some small overlap), all work closely at the state level to coordinate their efforts and foster community collaboration. As other state networks and organizations evolve to promote volunteerism, they inevitably become part of this growing circle of support.

Voluntary action is popular in Michigan, but its nature is difficult to formally capture. Many volunteer activities are so central to daily life—such as helping in a school—that they are seen not as volunteering but as routine. Whether a given activity is seen as "volunteering" is a matter of personal interpretation, and such designation varies by culture, religious affiliation, and socioeconomic group. Volunteering also is affected by a number of societal phenomena, including single-parent families, dual-income households, family and corporate volunteer programs, national service, and changing lifestyles.

Sometimes there is confusion about the difference between *volunteerism* (something one does because s/he wishes to) and *community service* (something one does because it is mandated, usually by a school or court). Often, however, the terms are used interchangeably, and there certainly

Sponsored by the Michigan Nonprofit Association and the Council of Michigan Foundations

are no boundaries restricting what may be considered "volunteering." The tasks one may volunteer to do are unlimited, ranging from raking a local park to helping organizations raise funds to advocating for a cause to serving on a community organization's board. Moreover, people become involved in volunteerism in any number of ways: at their own initiative, as part of an elective group (e.g., family, youth organization, service club), or as part of a prescribed group (e.g., classroom, workplace). However people come to volunteer, their efforts generally fall into one of three categories: service learning, service corps, or mandatory/compulsory service.

- *Service learning* is tied to an education curriculum or has a specific education component. Not only is a service rendered for the greater good, but the volunteer gains from the personal development that comes from helping others.

- A *service corps* is a team of volunteers organized to perform service over an extended period. Full-time corps members may receive living allowances and/or education awards; examples are AmeriCorps, AmeriCorps*VISTA, National Civilian Community Corps, and the Peace Corps. Programs involving a shorter commitment, such as the Youth Volunteer Corps, may offer no financial support.

- *Mandatory or compulsory* service is carried out when an authoritative body, such as a school or court, requires such service as a way to earn credit or discharge an obligation.

Volunteering is a popular way to make a difference in one's community. It is promoted through such large-scale national events as Make A Difference Day (annually, in October) and National Volunteer Week (annually, in April) and through such individual organization and local efforts as Day of Caring, Alternative Spring Break, and Nickelodeon's Big Help Day. As the nonprofit sector takes on new and expanded functions, the role of volunteers is likely to increase. In addition, welfare reform and other initiatives are drawing volunteers from nontraditional sectors, and this will increase the frequency of volunteering. All indicators point to volunteerism continuing to have a strong presence in Michigan, with volunteers becoming more active, vocal, and selective (that is, they look for opportunities through which they may help to meet real community needs) in their efforts.

MICHIGAN VOLUNTEERS

A number of surveys have been conducted to ascertain the extent of volunteerism in Michigan and gain information about the people who do it. The 2001 survey on giving and volunteering in Michigan reveals the scale of volunteering in the state.

- Fifty percent of the adult Michigan population volunteered during 12 months prior to the survey, with men and women volunteering at the same rate.

- The age groups most likely to volunteer are 40–49 years (55 percent volunteer), 18–24 years (54 percent) and 50–59 years (54 percent); the age group least likely to volunteer is 25–29 years (41 percent).

- Volunteering occurs most in the northern lower peninsula (57 percent of residents) and least in the southwest (47 percent).

- Among survey respondents who are Internet users, 19 percent have searched on line for volunteering information or opportunities.

- Almost two-thirds of volunteers seek out volunteer work on their own.

- Common ways of learning about volunteer opportunities include friends and family (55 percent) and advertising (29 percent).

- Almost 15 percent of volunteers use a referral organization, such as a volunteer center, to locate their volunteer position.

- The most common reasons for volunteering are to give back to the community (96 percent of volunteers) and to express compassion for those in need (98 percent).

- There is a strong association between volunteering and giving: 96 percent of volunteers also make charitable donations.

NONPROFITS AND GOVERNMENT

The nonprofit sector is heavily influenced by local, state and federal public policy. Government affects the daily activities of charities through regulation, contracting, tax breaks, incentives for charitable giving, in-kind donations, and more. This interdependence is most evident in four categories.

- *Regulation* As mentioned earlier, the federal and state government regulates charities' finances and operations, ensuring accountability through IRS Form 990, and state requirements for financial and operation reports, lobbying registration, and solicitation licenses.

- *Client* Government often contracts with nonprofits to provide training, housing, food, medical care, and much more to state and local residents.

- *Funding*   Public funding is important to nonprofits; contributions from government currently comprise 32 percent of nonprofit support.

- *Partnership*   To solve today's most pressing social needs, government, nonprofits, and also the business sector must work together. As partners, these sectors can provide the legal, financial, and "people power" necessary to keep a civil society running.

Today and throughout history, charities have acted as a voice for sustaining their own work and as a voice for those who do not have one—children, the elderly, the sick, and so on. The Michigan Nonprofit Association represents the interests of nonprofits across the state in enhancing the relationships listed above. The public policy priorities of the MNA and its members are federal, state, and local government actions that will serve to

- encourage tax incentives for charitable giving to Michigan nonprofit organizations;

- permit nonprofits to continue to communicate and interact with elected or appointed officials;

- continue funding for national service programs;

- maintain and extend sales, use, and property tax exemptions;

- increase volunteerism;

- eliminate fraudulent nonprofit fundraising; and

- monitor government activity that regulates the activities of nonprofits.

MICHIGAN FOUNDATIONS

A *foundation* is a nongovernment, nonprofit organization established to aid social, education, charitable, religious, or other activities serving the common welfare, primarily through making grants. Foundation funds and programs are managed by the foundation's trustees or directors.

There are over 50,000 grant-making foundations in the United States; 1,980 are located in Michigan.

- Michigan foundations have total assets of $22 billion and in their last reporting year made annual grants totaling $1.2 billion.

- Over a third of Michigan foundations have assets under $200,000.

- The great bulk of the assets held and grants awarded in Michigan are by the 720 foundations that have assets exceeding $1 million.

Foundations are characterized both by flexibility and diversity in their giving. Requests to foundations vastly exceed their funding capability, obliging trustees to define specific programmatic and geographic areas to which funding will be directed. Exhibit 2 presents the findings of a recent sample of the annual giving of 46 of Michigan's nearly 2,000 foundations: a total of $787 million during 2000. Because the sample is based on only one year's grants, the figures may not accurately represent the continuing pattern of giving by Michigan foundations, but they do give an idea of the foundations' major areas of interest.

EXHIBIT 2. Grant Distribution in Major Subject Categories, Selected Michigan Foundations, 2000

Subject	Amount	Percentage of Total Amount	Number of Grants	Percentage of Total Number of Grants
Arts, culture and humanities	$93,710,609	11.90%	549	10.1%
Education	178,193,084	22.6	1,282	23.6
Environment/animals	48,635,034	6.2	249	4.6
Health	73,309,190	9.3	488	9.0
Human services	153,942,757	19.5	1,170	21.6
International/foreign affairs	14,380,278	1.8	115	2.1
Public affairs/society benefit	193,680,932	24.6	1,321	24.4
Religion	27,633,641	3.5	244	4.5
Mutual/membership benefit	3,955,000	0.5	5	0.1
Nonclassifiable entities	10,000	0.0	1	0.0
TOTAL	$787,450,525	100.0%	5,424	100.0%

SOURCE: The Foundation Center, New York.
NOTE: The Foundation Center's sample includes grants of $10,000 or more for community foundations; only discretionary and donor-advised grants are included. Grants to individuals are not included. Grants by the 46 Michigan foundations in the sample account for nearly 70 percent of total giving reported by all Michigan foundations in 2000.

Sponsored by the Michigan Nonprofit Association and the Council of Michigan Foundations

Council of Michigan Foundations

The Council of Michigan Foundations is a membership association of more than 490 private, family, community, and corporate foundations and giving programs. The CMF's mission is to improve, increase, and enhance philanthropy in Michigan. For more than 30 years, the organization has offered one-on-one, on-site consultation to individuals, families, corporations, and communities interested in establishing a foundation and setting up grant programs. The council's publication, *Establishing a Charitable Foundation in Michigan*, explains the laws and regulations pertaining to foundations and presents the advantages of each type of foundation.

People desiring information about a specific foundation or corporate-giving program may communicate directly with the foundation or corporation or visit a Michigan Foundation Center cooperating collection library. Foundations and corporate-giving programs will be pleased to send an annual report or an informational statement if one is available. In addition, the CMF, in association with the Foundation Center (New York), publishes *The Michigan Foundation Directory*.

The Michigan Foundation Center Cooperating Collections are an excellent resource for grant seekers. The Foundation Center gathers information on philanthropy nationwide and disseminates it through its publications and through cooperating libraries. The library reference collections are available to the public without charge and offer a wide range of materials, including books and periodicals about foundations and philanthropy as well as foundation annual reports, newsletters, and press clippings. The 11 Michigan libraries listed at the end of this chapter have Michigan Foundation Center reference collections.

Types of Foundations

There are different types of foundations. Although they have different structures and intent, all serve the common interest. The leading forms of foundation organization are private, community, and corporate.

Private/Independent Foundations

A private foundation (also may be called an *independent* foundation) is a fund or endowment so designated by law that has grant making as its primary function. Such foundations' assets most commonly are derived from a gift by an individual or family. Many function under the voluntary direction of family members and are known as *family* foundations. Others, which may bear a family name, have an independent board of trustees and are managed by professional staff.

Typically, private/independent foundations have a broad charter but in practice limit their giving to a few fields of interest, although they may move into new fields in response to changing priorities. Depending on their range of giving, they also may be known as *general purpose* or *special purpose* foundations. Some private foundations are *operating* foundations, which means their primary purpose is to operate research, social welfare, or other programs determined by their governing body. Such foundations may make some external grants, but the number generally is small relative to the funds directed into the foundation's own programs.

In the United States, of the 50 largest private foundations having assets of over $1 billion, four originated in Michigan, including the nation's third largest, the Ford Foundation, now headquartered in New York.

Community Foundations

Community foundations receive and administer endowment and other funds received from private sources; funds are managed under community control and directed to charitable purposes that focus primarily on local needs. Community foundations are characterized by multiple funding sources, and their expenditures benefit a specified geographic area.

Internal Revenue Service regulations (1) require a community foundation's governing body to represent broad community interests and (2) classify the foundations not as private foundations but as *public charities*, the same category into which it places churches, schools and colleges, hospitals, and certain other nonprofit organizations.

Community foundations are growing in importance not only as professional grant-making organizations but as a flexible means to administer many kinds of charitable funds for local benefit.

Michigan is fortunate to have 65 community foundations and 34 affiliate funds (subfunds established by community foundations to serve specific locales within their service areas), and in total they cover all 83 counties. For a listing of the community foundations and their service areas, see the CMF website, *www.cmif.org*. This statewide coverage is due largely to a major challenge grant from the W.K. Kellogg Foundation to give every state resident access to benefits and services of a community foundation. The same challenge grant resulted in the endowment of 86 community foundation youth funds statewide; these funds are directed toward the needs of youth and are overseen by youth advisory committees, annually involving more than 1,500 high schoolers as grant makers.

The statewide growth of community foundations and the involvement of youth as grant makers has led the state, through the Michigan Community Service Commission, to contract with the CMF to distribute a portion of the interest earned on Michigan's share of the national tobacco settlement. These funds go to community foundations, based on the population of youth and seniors in their service areas, to be used for Healthy Youth and Healthy Seniors programs. To date, the 65 community foundations have received more than $20 million, and 50 percent of the funds have been permanently endowed. The governor's proposed FY 2002–03 budget recommends an allocation of $4 million to continue this unique partnership.

The state provides a tax credit to individuals and businesses that make a gift to an endowment held by a community foundation. Michigan is one of only three states to offer this incentive to charitable giving, which rewards thousands of state taxpayers annually for helping to build the nonprofit endowment funds held by their local or regional community foundation. The maximum tax credit allowed is

- $100 for individuals,
- $200 for families, or
- $5,000 or 10 percent of single business tax liability, whichever is less.

Company/Corporate Foundations
A company-sponsored or corporate foundation is classified as a private foundation under the tax law and derives its funds from a for-profit company or corporation. It is independently constituted, and its purpose is to make grants, often on a broad basis. Company officials as well as people not affiliated with the company may serve on the board. It is not uncommon for a company-sponsored foundation to assume responsibility for the parent company's giving in locales where offices, production or service facilities, or distribution outlets are located. Such a foundation makes it possible for a company to set aside funds for use in years when company earnings may be lower than normal, which may coincide with a general economic downturn that generates a greater-than-usual need for charitable spending.

Company-sponsored foundations are different from "corporate-giving" programs, which are administered within a corporation and may make grants for limited purposes closely associated with the corporation's interests, although this is not always the case. In some instances, the two types of giving are coordinated by a company under one general policy; in others, there may be a private foundation that bears a name associated with the corporation but has few if any ties with the original source of its funds.

In Michigan there are 29 company-sponsored foundations that have assets exceeding $1 million. The largest, in terms of annual grant making, is the Ford Motor Company Fund (nearly $1 million).

State/CMF Collaboration
The CMF first partnered with the state in the late 1980s, on the distribution of Exxon settlement funds. In addition to the tobacco-settlement partnership mentioned above, the CMF also works with the Michigan Department of Community Health through the Michigan AIDS Fund, a collaborative response by foundations and corporate givers to prevent the spread of HIV/AIDS and help those affected. The CMF also assists the Michigan State Housing Development Authority in partnering with 20 community foundations to help create permanent endowments to support homelessness emergency programs.

The most recent collaboration, the Michigan IDA Partnership, is with the Family Independence Agency. This five-year, public-private effort matches the contributions that up to 2,000 low-income working families make to their individual development account (IDA), a savings account that they may use toward buying a home, obtaining advanced education, or starting a small business. In 51 program sites, participating families complete financial-literacy training as they save up to $1,000, which will be matched, to put into their IDA.

CONCLUSION

The nonprofit sector is an important vehicle in delivering services that people and communities see as important to themselves and others. Michigan's nonprofit sector is a vital force in meeting the social, spiritual, and service needs of the community, but the sector is more than just a collection of organizations. Nonprofit action takes many forms, from simple acts of kindness to informal networks and associations to the formal world of nonprofit organizations. The continuing growth of the sector is testimony to its dynamism in the face of changing economic, social, and political conditions.

Sponsored by the Michigan Nonprofit Association and the Council of Michigan Foundations

NONPROFIT RESOURCES

National Organizations

Aspen Institute
Nonprofit Sector Research Fund
One Dupont Circle, N.W.
Washington, DC 20036
(202) 736-5800
www.aspeninst.org

BoardSource (National Center for Nonprofit Boards)
1828 L Street, N.W., Suite 900
Washington, DC 20036
(800) 883-6262
(202) 452-6262
www.boardsource.org

Center on Nonprofits and Philanthropy
The Urban Institute
2100 M Street, N.W.
Washington, DC 20037
(202) 833-7200
www.urban.org/centers/cnp.html

Charity Lobbying in the Public Interest
2040 S Street, N.W.
Washington, DC 20009
(202) 387-5048
www.clpi.org

Independent Sector
1200 18th Street, N.W., Suite 200
Washington, DC 20036
(202) 467-6100
www.independentsector.org

National Center for Charitable Statistics
The Urban Institute
2100 M Street, N.W.
Washington, DC 20037
(202) 833-7200
www.nccs.urban.org

National Council for Nonprofit Associations
1030 15th Street, N.W.
Washington, DC 20005
(202) 962-0322
www.ncna.org

Michigan Organizations

ConnectMichigan Alliance
1048 Pierpont, Suite 3
Lansing, MI 48911
(517) 492-2440
(517) 492-2444 FAX

Council of Michigan Foundations
One South Harbor Avenue, Suite 3
Grand Haven, Michigan 49417
(616) 842-7080
(616) 842-1760 FAX
www.cmif.org

Michigan League for Human Services
1115 South Pennsylvania Avenue, Suite 202
Lansing, MI 48912
(517) 487-5436
(517) 371-4546 FAX
www.milhs.org

Michigan Nonprofit Association
1048 Pierpont, Suite 3
Lansing, MI 48911
(888) 242-7075 (Michigan only)
(517) 492-2400
(517) 492-2410 FAX
www.mna.msu.edu

Michigan Association of United Ways
1627 Lake Lansing Road, Suite B
Lansing, MI 48912
(517) 371-4360
(517) 371-1801 FAX
www.uwmich.org

Sponsored by the Michigan Nonprofit Association and the Council of Michigan Foundations

Volunteerism Resources

Association of Volunteer Administrators
P.O. Box 32092
Richmond, VA 23294
www.avaintl.org

Corporation for National and Community Service
1201 New York Avenue, N.W.
Washington, DC 20525
(202) 606-5000
www.nationalservice.org

Michigan Campus Compact
1048 Pierpont, Suite 3
Lansing, MI 48911
(517) 492-2430
(517) 492-2444 FAX

Michigan Community Service Commission
1048 Pierpont, Suite 4
Lansing, MI 48913
(517) 335-4295
(517) 373-4977 FAX
www.michigan.gov/career/mcsc

Points of Light Foundation
1400 Street, N.W., Suite 800
Washington, DC 20005
(202) 729-8000
www.pointsoflight.org

Volunteer Centers of Michigan
1048 Pierpont, Suite 3
Lansing, MI 48911
(517) 492-2424
(517) 492-2444 FAX

Michigan Foundation Center Cooperating Collections

Alpena County Library
Reference Room, 2d Floor
211 North First Avenue
Alpena, MI 49707
(989) 356-6188
www.alpenalib.org

Farmington Community Library
32737 West 12 Mile Road
Farmington Hills, MI 48334
(248) 553-0300
www.farmlib.org

Grand Rapids Public Library
1100 Hynes Avenue, S.W., Suite B
Grand Rapids, MI 49507
(616) 988-5400
www.grpl.org

Henry Ford Centennial Library
Adult Services, 2d Floor
16301 Michigan Avenue
Dearborn, MI 48126
(313) 943-2330
www.dearborn.lib.mi.us/centenni.htm

Michigan State University Library
Social Science and Humanities Reference
Michigan State University
100 Library
East Lansing, MI 48824
(517) 353-8700
www.lib.msu.edu/harris23

Michigan Technological University
J. Robert Van Pelt Library
1400 Townsend Drive
Houghton, MI 49931
(906) 487-2507
www.lib.mtu.edu

Northwestern Michigan College
Mark & Helen Osterlin Library
1701 East Front Street
Traverse City, MI 49684
(231) 955-1540
www.nmc.edu/-library/res/net/grants.htm

University of Michigan–Ann Arbor
209 Hatcher Graduate Library
Ann Arbor, MI 48109
(734) 764-9373
www.lib.umich.edu

Sponsored by the Michigan Nonprofit Association and the Council of Michigan Foundations

University of Michigan–Flint
Frances Wilson Thompson Library
303 East Kearsley Street
Flint, MI 48502
(810) 762-3408
http://lib.umflint/edu

Wayne State University
Purdy/Kresge Library
5265 Cass Avenue
Detroit, MI 48202
(313) 577-6424
www.lib.wayne.edu/purdy

Willard Library
Funding Resource Center
7 West Van Buren Street
Battle Creek, MI 49017
(616) 968-8166
www.willard.lib.mi.us

Sponsored by the Michigan Nonprofit Association and the Council of Michigan Foundations

CHAPTER 5: ABOUT THE ISSUES

Abortion

BACKGROUND

According to the federal Centers for Disease Control and Prevention (CDC), an estimated 1.33 million abortions were performed in the United States in 1997 (latest available national data); this is down from the peak of 1.6 million in 1990. The 1997 national rates were

- 22.2 per 1,000 women aged 15–44, down from 27.4 in 1990; and

- 27.5 per 1,000 woman aged 15–19, down from 40.3 in 1990.

Michigan Data

The latest data available from the Michigan Department of Community Health show that 26,807 abortions were performed in Michigan in 2000, an increase of 2.3 percent from the previous year but a 45.4 percent decrease since 1987, the year with the highest number of reported abortions. The rate is 12.2 per 1,000 for Michigan women aged 15–44. Data from the state may not reflect the true prevalence of abortion because, while reporting is required, abortion providers may not report all the procedures they perform.

The reasons for the abortion decline are intensely debated by pro-life and pro-choice advocates. The following reasons are most frequently cited, but the decrease probably is attributable to a combination of factors rather than a single one:

- Wider and more effective contraception use

- Changing attitudes toward premarital sexual activity

- Diminished access to abortion because of the ban on paying for abortions with Medicaid funds

- Enactment of parental and informed-consent laws

- A decrease in the number of abortion providers

- Increased teaching of abstinence and/or sex education in schools

- Changing age distribution of females in their reproductive years

Of the abortions reported in Michigan in 2000,

- 87 percent occurred during the first 12 weeks of pregnancy;

- 98 percent occurred within the first 20 weeks of pregnancy;

- women aged under 20 accounted for 19 percent (down from 31 percent in 1980);

- women aged 20–24 accounted for 32 percent;

- women aged 25–29 accounted for 23 percent;

- women aged 30 and older accounted for 25 percent;

Sponsored by the Michigan Nonprofit Association and the Council of Michigan Foundations

- unmarried women accounted for 84 percent; and

- among those who had an abortion that year, 48 percent had previously had one.

In 2000, physical complications—most frequently, shock—immediately following an abortion were reported in 26 cases, or about one in 1,000 procedures. Information on subsequent complications (within seven days) was collected for the first time in 2000. Any physician providing care to a woman suffering from such a complication must report it to the state. Seven incidents of subsequent complications were reported.

In 2000, 76 percent of reported abortions were performed in a physician's office, 23 percent in a freestanding, outpatient surgical facility, and the remainder in a hospital or satellite clinic.

Since 1988 Michigan has prohibited payment for abortions through the Medicaid program unless the procedure is necessary to save a woman's life. (In 1987 about 18,000 Medicaid-funded abortions had been performed in the state.) The federal government subsequently (in 1994) required states also to pay for abortions desired by Medicaid recipients to terminate a pregnancy resulting from rape or incest. Information on the source of payment for non-Medicaid abortions was collected for the first time in 2000; where source of payment was reported, self-pay was most frequently indicated.

Legal History

In 1973 the U.S. Supreme Court, in *Roe* v. *Wade*, ruled that the Constitutional right to privacy extends to a woman's decision, in consultation with her physician, to terminate her pregnancy. The same ruling says that states may prohibit abortion in the third trimester unless a woman's life or health is endangered ("health" has not been defined precisely). In 1989, in *Webster* v. *Reproductive Health Services*, the Court reopened the door to state regulation of pre-third-trimester abortion by upholding Missouri's 1986 law (1) declaring that life begins at conception and (2) prohibiting public facilities from being used for abortions not necessary to save a woman's life. The Court allowed the declaration that life begins at conception because it believed there was insufficient evidence that the declaration would restrict protected activities such as abortion.

Following *Webster*, many state legislatures imposed new restrictions on abortion. In fact, while debate continues as to whether abortion should be permitted at all or only in very limited circumstances, most recent judicial decisions and legislative activity have focused on restrictions

to abortion (or access to abortion providers) that fall short of an outright ban.

DISCUSSION

Few issues engender more controversy than abortion. The main and opposing camps on the issue are "pro-life," which includes people who oppose abortion in all (or almost all) circumstances, and "pro-choice," which includes people who believe a woman has the right to choose whether she will have an abortion in all (or almost all) circumstances. These camps disagree on most aspects of the issue, including how they refer to themselves and the others.

- Pro-life advocates often call pro-choice advocates "pro-abortion." But pro-choice supporters argue that they do not prefer abortion to childbirth or adoption, but they do favor a woman's right to choose for herself, which is why they call themselves pro-choice.

- Pro-choice supporters often call pro-life supporters "anti-abortion." This reflects the pro-choice belief that life does not begin at conception. But pro-life advocates counter that it does, and therefore "pro-life" is more accurate than "anti-abortion." (In this piece, we use "pro-choice" and "pro-life.")

To cite just one more example of the many disagreements between the two camps, pro-choice advocates call a "fetus" that which pro-life advocates call an "unborn child" or "baby."

Many see abortion as a black-and-white issue—that is, one either favors a woman's right to choose to terminate her pregnancy, or one does not—but the issue's complexity allows for shades of gray. Some believe that abortion should not be allowed under any circumstance, while others would permit it to save the mother's life or in cases when the pregnant woman is a rape or incest victim. In addition, some believe that abortion should not be permitted after viability (that is, the point at which the fetus/unborn child can live a sustained life outside the mother's uterus). Pro-choice advocates view this as restricting a woman's legal right to abortion; pro-life advocates view it as saving lives. The debate about viability is complicated because advances in medical science may continue to reduce the number of weeks of pregnancy before viability is achieved.

"Partial-Birth" or "Dilation and Extraction" Abortion

Related to the viability debate is the ongoing battle over "partial-birth" abortion. Again, the nomenclature itself is controversial. Pro-life supporters define the procedure as partial birth because the fetus/unborn child is partially delivered, usually feet-first, through the vagina before the abortion is performed. Such abortions usually are performed after 20 weeks gestation, and pro-life advocates contend that these abortions are particularly objectionable because the fetus/unborn child is viable; they add that such a procedure rarely is needed to save the mother's life or even preserve her health.

Pro-choice supporters respond by defining this procedure as "dilation and extraction" abortion, arguing that partial birth is a political construct and misnomer with no equivalent in real-world medical practice; that is, the fetus is not partially born. They further contend that these abortions rarely are performed, and when they are, it is only to save a woman's life when no other method will suffice.

A 1996 Michigan law, Public Act 273, bans partial-birth abortions, allowing an exception when the mother's life is in danger. The law, which subsequently was permanently enjoined (prohibited from being in effect) by federal court, defines the procedure broadly and refers to a vaginally delivered "living fetus," which is defined vaguely and may mean from the moment of conception.

In 1999 two partial-birth abortion laws were enacted in Michigan, but the U.S. District Court permanently enjoined the first and temporarily enjoined the other.

- P.A. 107 of 1999 added the Infant Protection Act to the Michigan Penal Code. Pro-life supporters say the measure bans partial-birth abortions; pro-choice supporters say it could ban all abortions.

- P.A. 192 of 1999 amended the Michigan Code of Criminal Procedure, imposing a maximum sentence of life imprisonment for performing a procedure on a live infant with intent to cause death.

The State of Michigan is not appealing the decisions to enjoin, which were based on rulings by the U.S. Supreme Court in *Stenberg* v. *Carhart*, 2000. The Court (1) upheld a lower court decision invalidating Nebraska's ban on "partial-birth" abortion, (2) ruled that the language in the Nebraska law covered a broad range of abortion procedures, thus resulting in an undue burden on a woman's right to make an abortion decision, and (3) ruled that every abortion regulation must provide for an exception when necessary to preserve the mother's life or health.

Access to Abortion

Three major Michigan laws enacted in the last decade relate to a woman's access to abortion; one pertains to parental consent and two to informed consent. The 1992 U.S. Supreme Court ruling in *Planned Parenthood of Southeastern Pennsylvania* v. *Casey* was a key factor in

the implementation of the first measure and the genesis of the second and third. The Court upheld a Pennsylvania law's provisions requiring a woman to wait 24 hours before an abortion, read state-authored materials about abortion and fetal development, and, if a minor, obtain parental consent or a judicial waiver. The Court reaffirmed the right of a woman to an abortion under *Roe* v. *Wade* but revoked the definition of that right as "fundamental." The Court instead offers a standard of review that allows restrictions on abortion prior to viability if the restrictions do not constitute an undue burden on the woman. The Court held that the Pennsylvania law's provisions are not unduly burdensome merely because they attempt to discourage a woman from obtaining an abortion.

Parental Consent

Michigan P.A. 211 of 1990 requires parental consent to abortion for minors (aged 17 and younger) unless the minor obtains a waiver from a judge. This law has been in effect since 1993.

Pro-life supporters argue that the law restores parental and familial rights. They argue that many other less momentous procedures (e.g., ear piercing) require parental consent.

Pro-choice supporters believe that the law violates a female's right to decide for herself about childbearing options; they further contend that the judicial waiver may be an undue burden for females who may not be able to prove (or dare not try) that they have been a victim of abuse or incest in their own home.

Informed Consent

Public Act 133 of 1993 requires any woman seeking an abortion to (1) be given state-prepared information about the procedure, (2) wait 24 hours before undergoing the procedure, and (3) sign a state-prepared informed-consent form immediately prior to the abortion. The information includes depictions of the fetus at the stage corresponding to the woman's pregnancy, a description of the abortion procedure, information on the risks and complications of abortion and live birth, information on pregnancy-related services, and a prenatal care and parenting information pamphlet. The law was temporarily enjoined and then implemented in 1999.

P. A. 345 of 2000 amends the above law and imposes limits on how a woman may receive the required information; it specifies that she may obtain it only in person, by registered mail, by fax, or from a state government Web site. The effective date of the law was delayed while the state completed court-directed changes in the Web site; the site was posted in March 2002, and the law may take effect on May 1, 2002. On March 4, 2002, the federal

Sponsored by the Michigan Nonprofit Association and the Council of Michigan Foundations

district court in Detroit struck down the provision in the law that prohibits a physician from obtaining payment for "abortion related" services until the 24-hour waiting period expires.

Pro-choice advocates claim that informed-consent laws are unnecessary at best and, at worst, prevent women from exercising their right to make private decisions about reproductive choices. They argue that evidence demonstrates that women already carefully consider their options before choosing abortion, adding that established medical standards ensure that women are given accurate and unbiased information about their health care options. Moreover, they note, clinics routinely refer women who are ambivalent about their decision for additional counseling.

Pro-life advocates counter that such legislation enables women to make informed choices about abortion. They believe that the information on fetal development balances what they consider biased information already offered to women considering abortion.

More recent legislation pertaining to access includes language in the budget for community colleges that prohibits the schools from providing insurance to their employees that covers abortion services (P.A. 52 of 2001). There also is a requirement that a physician's office in which abortions are annually performed on 50 percent or more patients must be licensed to operate as a freestanding, surgical, outpatient facility (P.A. 206 of 1999); pro-choice advocates maintain that the additional money and time needed to obtain licensure will discourage providers from offering abortion services, thus making it harder for women to obtain them.

Family Planning

Controversy about abortion extends to federal support for family planning services, which are funded largely through Title X of the Social Security Act. Title X provides subsidized, affordable contraceptives and other reproductive health services (Pap smears, breast exams, HIV testing, and screening and treatment for sexually transmitted diseases) to more than four million low-income women each year.

While Title X funds cannot be used for abortions themselves, clinics receiving the funds must offer "nondirective counseling" on women's options, which include carrying a child to term, adoption, and abortion. Pro-life proponents argue that the clear purpose of Title X, enacted in 1970, is to provide *pre*-pregnancy services. The title's authorizing language states that funds shall not be used in programs in which abortion is a method of family planning. Pro-choice proponents counter that denying a woman information about the full range of options vio-

lates the principle of informed consent and her right to reproductive choice. Arguing that pro-life advocates wish to eliminate or cut funding for Title X, pro-choice advocates add that the program does not fund abortions but rather, by providing contraceptives and pre-pregnancy counseling, prevents unwanted pregnancies and abortions.

In Michigan, pregnancy prevention programs funded by state dollars are precluded from counseling women about abortion. House Bill 4655, under consideration by the legislature at this writing, would give family-planning or reproductive-health services funding priority to entities that do not (1) perform elective abortions, (2) refer women to abortion providers, (3) advocate for the legality or accessibility of elective abortion, or (4) have a written policy that abortion is part of a continuum of family planning or reproductive health services. Pro-choice supporters contend that enacting the measure will preclude Planned Parenthood Affiliates of Michigan from receiving state and federal funding for family-planning and reproductive-health programs and result in an increase in unwanted pregnancies and abortions. Pro-life supporters counter that Planned Parenthood Affiliates of Michigan will lose funds only if another agency is available to provide the services being funded.

Other Matters of Controversy

The "morning after" contraceptive pill, if taken within 72 hours after unprotected intercourse, can prevent a fertilized egg from becoming implanted on the uterus wall. Some pro-life supporters oppose the drug's use on the ground that it is a form of abortion. Pro-choice supporters see the drug as a means to prevent unwanted pregnancies and an alternative to abortion.

More controversial still are *abortifacients*, drugs that induce abortion weeks into pregnancy. The U.S. Food and Drug Administration (FDA) has approved mifepristone—the generic name for RU-486, the French brand name—for use as an abortifacient for use in pregnancies of 49 days or less duration. Pro-life supporters contend that using mifepristone, in addition to inducing abortion, leads to such complications as prolonged bleeding, severe cramping, and nausea, and its long-term effects are unknown. Pro-choice supporters point out that mifepristone was rigorously tested and thoroughly reviewed before receiving FDA approval, and, while there are some side effects, it offers women a safe and effective non-surgical, private option.

Since FDA approval of mifepristone, bills restricting access to the drug have been introduced in Congress and several state legislatures.

New Reproductive Technology

The rapid advances in reproductive technology and medical research are raising new legal, moral, and ethical questions for policymakers and courts. Emerging issues related to assisted reproductive technologies—including *in vitro* fertilization; donation and storage of sperm, eggs and embryos; posthumous fertilization; and surrogate parenting arrangements—are forcing courts to rule, often in the absence of guiding legislation, on the rights of mothers, fathers, and fetuses.

Another emerging issue fraught with controversy is stem cell research, which involves human embryos and fetal tissue. The research raises hope for development of ways to treat such diseases as diabetes, but it also intensifies debate about the point at which life begins.

See also Genetic Cloning, Testing, and Research.

FOR ADDITIONAL INFORMATION

Alan Guttmacher Institute
1120 Connecticut Avenue, N.W., Suite 460
Washington, DC 20036
(202) 296-4012
(202) 223-5756 FAX
www.agi-usa.org

Data Development Section
Michigan Department of Community Health
P.O. Box 30195
Lansing, MI 48909
(517) 335-8705
(517) 335-8711 FAX
www.michigan.gov/mdch

Planned Parenthood Affiliates of Michigan
P.O. Box 19104
Lansing, MI 48901
(517) 482-1080
(517) 482-4876 FAX
www.miplannedparenthood.org

Right to Life of Michigan
2340 Porter Street, S.W.
P.O. Box 901
Grand Rapids, MI 49509
(616) 532-2300
(616) 532-3461 FAX
www.rtl.org

Sponsored by the Michigan Nonprofit Association and the Council of Michigan Foundations

Aging

BACKGROUND

The generation born following the end of World War II—the babyboomers (born roughly between 1946 and 1964)—now is aged 38–57. This is the largest generation of U.S. residents ever born. As this group has grown from childhood to adulthood, its size has affected all aspects of American life, from housing to education to health care, and now it is affecting retirement and other aging issues.

At the same time that babyboomers are nearing senior status, health care advances are reducing the mortality rate for several diseases that once took the lives of people at an earlier age. According to preliminary figures from the Health and Human Services (HHS) Centers for Disease Control and Prevention (CDC), U.S. life expectancy is 76.9 years and mortality rates are increasing for conditions that disproportionately affect the aging population, such as Alzheimer's disease, influenza and pneumonia, kidney disease, and hypertension.

The population aged 65 and older comprises 12.7 percent of the U.S. population, and Michigan and other states are preparing for the challenges and opportunities that policymakers face as this population increases. Currently,

- 1.2 million Michigan residents (12.3 percent of the total state population) are *seniors* (aged 65 and older);

- an additional 863,000 (8.7 percent of Michigan's population) are *near seniors*, (aged 55–64); and

- over the next 30 years, both the number of Americans aged 65 and over and the number aged 85 and over are expected to double.

DISCUSSION

Long-Term Care Insurance and Retirement Income

Recent studies indicate that the adequacy of retirement planning among babyboomers differs significantly by socioeconomic group. As a group, however, life expectancy for men at age 65 is approximately 9 years, for women 15 years. If people do not prepare adequately for retirement (that is, have sufficient means to meet their needs and withstand inflation), dependency on government programs (Medicaid in particular) will increase. A critical public policy question is how to encourage and enable middle- and lower-income Americans to prepare for a long retirement. Another is how to help those who already have arrived at retirement with inadequate or diminishing means.

The federal Health Insurance Portability and Accountability Act of 1996 provides favorable tax treatment for payment of long-term-care (LTC) insurance premiums. Eighteen states now offer small tax incentives to individuals or employers to purchase LTC insurance, and federal employees may purchase LTC insurance through the Federal Employee Health Benefits Program.

Although the Michigan Legislature has not enacted a tax break for LTC premium payments, it has taken steps to protect LTC purchasers. Public Act 4 of 2001 requires LTC

GLOSSARY

Alzheimer's disease
A progressive, neurodegenerative disease characterized by loss of function and death of nerve cells in the brain, leading to loss of mental functions such as memory and learning.

Dementia
The loss of intellectual functions (such as thinking, remembering, and reasoning) of sufficient severity to interfere with a person's daily functioning. Dementia is not a disease itself but rather a group of symptoms that may accompany certain diseases or conditions. Alzheimer's disease is the most common cause of dementia.

Near seniors
Generally, people aged 55–64.

Senior citizen; senior
Generally, a person aged 65 or older.

Sponsored by the Michigan Nonprofit Association and the Council of Michigan Foundations

insurers for home health care and assisted living to define and provide a detailed explanation—in plain English—of what the coverage entails. Pending legislation (HB 4797) would require the state commissioner of financial and insurance services to prepare and publish annually a consumer guide to LTC, available to the public on request.

As people live longer, retirement plans must address the needs of a longer life span. To help people anticipate their needs and plan for their retirement years, the Social Security Administration and some states offer workers the use of on-line benefit calculators to help them realistically assess how much money they will need. Michigan does not offer such retirement and financial planning services, but the U.S. Department of Health and Human Services's Administration on Aging (AOA) has several planning sites listed on its Web site. The AOA identifies resources, including government and other booklets and brochures about retirement planning, calculators of future financial needs and asset values, and general information about personal financial planning. Despite these efforts, access to—and use of—such retirement-planning tools is low, as is the purchase of LTC insurance.

Without LTC insurance, many seniors will be unable to afford assisted living or nursing care. One effort to address this is the state's Homecare Options for Michigan's Elders (HOME) program, which began in 2000 and is administered by the Michigan Office of Services to the Aging (OSA). This program helps to defray the cost of services that the frail elderly need to remain in their home and community. HOME provides a variety of services to seniors who cannot afford in-home care on their own but are ineligible for other state assistance because their income is above the poverty level. Among the services are

- home-delivered meals,
- chore services,
- respite care (temporarily relieves caregivers),
- personal-care supervision, and
- private-duty nursing.

Funding for HOME will expire on October 1, 2002. Those working for its continuation support HB 5161, which would add the program to the public health code and establish and fund it through the Michigan Department of Community Health (MDCH).

Older Workers

The traditional retirement age is 65, when people are eligible for Medicare and full Social Security (SS) benefits. (This will rise in future years because the SS-eligible age is being raised, eventually to 67.) Although only about 3 percent of people over 65 currently still are working either part or full time, more babyboomers probably will work beyond their retirement age to (1) obtain additional income to ensure financial security and (2) retain the sense of well-being that they associate with meaningful employment. According to the AARP, 80 percent of babyboomers say they plan to work at least part-time during their retirement.

In 2000 the Social Security "test" (outside-earnings limit) for people over age 65 was eliminated, which means that people over this age may earn any amount of money without their SS payments being reduced. Permitting seniors to work if they need or wish to, without loss of pension or SS monies, can benefit society in a number of ways. For example, some states, to address teacher shortages, have adopted policies that allow retired teachers to return to work without losing their pension benefits. Other labor shortages are expected as babyboomers begin to retire, and policymakers may wish to consider how pension and employment policies may be adapted to encourage older workers to remain in or rejoin the work force.

Elder-Friendly Communities

Surveys show that most people prefer to retire and stay in the community in which they have lived, remaining close to friends and possibly family. For communities and states, there are economic, political, and community-involvement advantages to having retirees stay rather than migrate elsewhere. Among the several key characteristics that senior-friendly communities have are

- adequate public transportation and para-transit (wheelchair-accessible) systems,
- driver-safety amenities such as classes to inform seniors about the effects of medication on one's ability to drive,
- pedestrian-safety amenities such as wide sidewalks,
- affordable housing and home-modification programs,
- neighborhood shops and services, and
- a variety of municipal features (e.g., senior centers, public library branches, parks), services, and leisure facilities.

Many planners believe that achieving senior-friendly communities will require a combination of public, private, and philanthropic community investment. Currently, planning for this is occurring through the State Plan for Services to the Elderly, administered by OSA, which has developed the following nine goals to be used by the various area agencies on aging in developing and implementing local plans:

Sponsored by the Michigan Nonprofit Association and the Council of Michigan Foundations

- Improve accessibility, availability, and affordability of a continuum of health and long-term care
- Improve the nutritional condition of older people
- Improve elders' access to services and programs
- Improve the mobility of older persons
- Improve employment opportunities for older persons
- Improve volunteer opportunities for older persons
- Develop a continuum of housing options that address seniors' special needs
- Protect and promote the rights and independence of older persons
- Foster positive public understanding of the contributions, needs and problems of the aging population

Local services offered may vary from area to area, but preference will be given to seniors who have the greatest economic or social need. Funding for these efforts includes federal, state, and private monies as well as some funding from the state's share of the tobacco settlement. The state appropriation is for three years, fiscal years 2001–03.

Work-Force Needs

According to a recent Alliance for Aging Research report, by 2030 the United States will need about 36,000 physicians with geriatric training to manage the complex health and social needs of an aging population—currently, there are 9,000 certified practicing geriatricians in the country. In addition, the demand for home-health, hospice, and nursing home aides will be immense. Developing an LTC work force is difficult because the pool for the aide jobs can find other work that is less demanding and pays equal or higher wages. Moreover, complexities of health care reimbursement and regulation affect the ease with which the market niche for LTC services can be filled.

Health aides care for vulnerable people, and the quality of care received by this population is of great concern to everyone. A good deal of legislation has been enacted to address this, and more is pending. For example, SB 1120 and HB 5603 would allow electronic monitoring of residents in Michigan nursing homes.

Mental health problems are expected to increase as the population reaches ages at which the risk of cognitive disorder (Alzheimer's disease and dementia) is high. According to the Alzheimer's Association, four million Americans suffer from the disease, and the number is expected to more than double in the next 50 years. The MDCH estimates that more than 166,000 Michigan residents currently are afflicted. This adds to the demand for facilities (nursing homes, outpatient dementia care, daycare centers) and specially trained staff.

Paralleling the shortage of geriatricians and aides is a nursing shortage. The current shortage in part is because of short-term, cyclical changes in the supply and demand for nurses but also because the nursing work force itself is aging—more than 60 percent of registered nurses have been on the job for more than 16 years, and many are eligible for retirement in the next few years. Of real concern is that there are fewer nurses coming along to take their place: The percentage of nurses under 30 years old dropped from 26 percent in 1980 to 9 percent in 2000. Michigan is trying to address the nursing shortage issue through legislation. Two pending bills, SBs 792–3, would use money from the tobacco settlement for a nursing scholarship program.

Technology

Studies show that seniors already are among the most prolific users of the Internet. Babyboomers, already accustomed to an electronic workplace, will be even more inclined to engage in telecommuting, e-mail, cell phone use, and the electronic shopping services that will help them reduce social isolation and maintain their independence as they grow older.

Economic and Poll Power

Senior citizens are a driving force in the state and national economies. Census Bureau data show that seniors are the wealthiest consumer segment and have the largest disposable income of any population group. The average per capita *discretionary* income for Americans aged 50 and older is almost $8,500 a year, compared with $6,500 for Americans of all ages. Studies show that the 50+ age group

- eats out an average of three times a week,
- owns 77 percent of all assets in the United States,
- purchases 43 percent of all cars, and
- accounts for 90 percent of all travel.

Voter complacency may be prevalent in younger people but not so among their elders. Voter turnout among senior citizens is steadily increasing. Census data show that voting participation is highest among those aged 65–74: Nationally, 72 percent of this age group voted in the 2000 presidential election, compared with 55 percent of all age groups. The elderly lobby is strong and has the capacity to keep aging issues on the public policy agenda and exercise its approval or disapproval at the ballot box.

See also Consumer Protection; Domestic Violence; Health Care Access, Medicaid, and Medicare; Health Care Costs and Managed Care; Housing Affordability; Long-Term and Related Care.

FOR ADDITIONAL INFORMATION

Administration on Aging
U.S. Department of Health and Human Services
300 Independence Avenue, S.W.
Washington, DC 20201
(800) 677-1116 [Eldercare Locator, to find local services]
(202) 619-7501 [AOA National Aging Information Center]
(202) 260-1012 FAX
www.aoa.gov

American Association of Retired Persons
309 North Washington Square, Suite 110
Lansing, MI 48933
(517) 482-2772
(517) 482-2794 FAX
www.aarp.org

Michigan State Housing Development Authority
735 East Michigan Avenue
P.O. Box 30044
Lansing, Michigan 48912
(517) 373-8370
(517) 335-4797 FAX
www.michigan.gov/mshda

Office of Financial and Insurance Services
Michigan Department of Consumer and Industry Services
611 West Ottawa Street, 2d Floor
P.O. Box 30220
Lansing, MI 48909
(517) 335-3167
(517) 335-4978 FAX
www.michigan.gov/cis

Office of Services to the Aging
Michigan Department of Community Health
611 West Ottawa Street, 3d Floor
P.O. Box 30676
Lansing, MI 48909
(517) 373-8230
(517) 373-4092 FAX
www.miseniors.net

Sponsored by the Michigan Nonprofit Association and the Council of Michigan Foundations

Air Quality

BACKGROUND

Air quality is affected in many ways by the wide variety of pollutants that are emitted from numerous sources. Air pollution comes from such stationary sources as factories, power plants, smelters, and dry cleaners; from such mobile sources as automobiles, buses, planes, trucks, and trains; and from such naturally occurring sources as windblown dust and volcanic eruptions. These pollutants can impair the health of people and wildlife; reduce visibility; corrode cars, buildings, and historical monuments; produce unpleasant odors; and damage agriculture and forests.

Clean Air Act

Since 1970 the federal Clean Air Act (CAA) has provided the principal framework for national, state, and local efforts to protect air quality. The CAA underwent major revisions in 1977 and again in 1990. Central to the 1990 amendments are

- revisions to the *permit system* that allows entities to emit certain substances into the air,

- additional specifications to reduce *urban smog* and reduce pollutants in ambient (surrounding) air,

- a change from using primarily health-based standards to using *technology-based standards* to regulate air pollution,

- more restrictive *mobile-source emission standards*, requiring automobile manufacturers to further reduce tail pipe emissions and refineries to reformulate fuel,

- *acid rain* emission caps and air-particle restrictions to address long-range transport of sulfur and nitrogen pollutants, and

- more stringent *enforcement*.

To comply with the federal amendments, Michigan enacted enabling legislation amending the state Air Pollution and Motor Fuels Quality acts and created four new statutes that (1) provide the basis for the Michigan Department of Environmental Quality (MDEQ) pollution-emission permit program; (2) authorize fees mandated by the federal legislation; (3) create a program to help small businesses comply with requirements; and (4) increase the state's enforcement authority. In 1996 all state air pollution and control laws were codified into the already-existing Public Act 451 of 1994, the Natural Resources and Environment Protection Act (NREPA).

Stationary Sources: Permits and Fees

For stationary facilities that wish to emit pollutants, including toxics, the NREPA establishes three types of air-pollution permit:

- Permit to install (or construct, reconstruct, relocate, alter, or modify) any process or equipment that may emit a pollutant into the air

- Nonrenewable permit to operate

- Renewable permit to operate (renewal is required every five years)

GLOSSARY

Ambient
Surrounding, encircling.

Attainment area
A geographic area in which criteria pollutant concentrations do not exceed national ambient air quality standards.

Criteria pollutants
Six pollutants for which there are national ambient air quality standards to protect public health.

Ground-level ozone
A gas formed in the atmosphere near the earth's surface by a chemical reaction, on hot, humid days, between volatile (vaporizes readily) organic compounds and oxides of nitrogen; it is smog's primary component.

Hazardous air pollutant (HAP)
One of 188 substances known or suspected to cause, from even relatively low exposure, cancer, genetic mutation, birth defects, or other serious illness in people.

National ambient air quality standards (NAAQS)
The level above which the presence in the air of any of the six criteria pollutants is considered harmful to the public health.

The cost of the permit program is paid for largely through annual facility and emission fees that are established by the legislature (most recently in 2001) and based on the type of facility and the type and tons of pollutant(s) emitted. Facility fees range from $250 to $24,816, and emission fees are $45.25 per ton of pollutant unless fewer than 10 tons are emitted, in which case no emission fee is assessed.

Criteria Pollutants

For certain air pollutants, the U.S. Environmental Protection Agency (EPA) sets ambient air concentration limits called national ambient air quality standards (NAAQS). The EPA has set standards for six common pollutants.

Particulate matter
Solid particles or fine liquid droplets in the air as a result of industrial processes; the chemical composition depends on the emission source.

Smog
A harmful concentration of ground-level ozone.

State implementation plan (SIP)
A plan required by the federal Clean Air Act that provides for the way in which a state will implement, maintain, and enforce the national ambient air quality standards.

- *Carbon monoxide* (CO) is a colorless, odorless gas formed when carbon in fuel from motor vehicles and other combustion processes is not burned completely; CO can harm one's health by reducing oxygen delivery to the body's organs (e.g., heart and brain) and tissues.

- *Nitrogen dioxide* (NO_2) is a reddish-brown gas with a pungent and unpleasant odor that can irritate one's lungs and lower one's resistance to respiratory infection. It transforms in the air to form gaseous nitric acid, which, when deposited, contributes to lake acidification, corrodes metals, degrades rubber, damages trees and crops, and fades fabrics. NO_2, along with other oxides of nitrogen (NO_x), plays a major role in atmospheric reactions that produce ground-level ozone, a major component of smog.

- *Ozone* is created by a chemical reaction between NO_x (the primary sources are motor vehicles, electric utilities, and other industrial, commercial, and residential sources that burn fuel) and volatile organic compounds (VOCs) in the presence of heat and sunlight. Motor-vehicle exhaust and industrial emissions, gasoline vapors, and chemical solvents are among the major sources of NO_x and VOCs that help to form ozone. Even at very low levels, this pollutant triggers a variety of health problems—e.g., long-term exposure may cause permanent lung injury—and damages plants and ecosystems.

- *Lead* is a metal found naturally in the environment as well as in manufactured products. The major sources of lead emissions historically have been motor vehicles and industrial facilities. Because lead primarily affects the brain and nervous system, children under age six are at the greatest risk because they then are undergoing rapid neurological and physical development.

- *Particulate matter* is the term for particles found in the air—including dust, dirt, soot, smoke, and droplets—that arise from such activities as combustion, incineration, construction, mining, metal processing, motor-vehicle exhaust, road dust, forest fires, and volcanic activity. Particulate matter causes a wide variety of health and environmental problems, including aggravated asthma, chronic bronchitis, and impaired visibility.

- *Sulfur dioxide* is released to the air primarily from coal-burning electric power plants and contributes to respiratory illness (particularly in children and the elderly), aggravates existing heart and lung diseases, and adds to the formation of acid rain.

These pollutants are referred to as *criteria* pollutants because health-based criteria are used as the basis for setting permissible ambient air levels.

Periodically, ambient air concentrations of the six criteria pollutants are measured at several locations within a region to determine its NAAQS attainment/nonattainment status. In Michigan, the MDEQ operates monitors that collect pollutant data. Air-quality levels must not exceed standards over various averaging times. Short averaging times

Sponsored by the Michigan Nonprofit Association and the Council of Michigan Foundations

(e.g., one hour) are used to measure acute, or short-term, health effects. Longer averaging times (e.g., one year) are used to gauge chronic effects.

Although the entire state of Michigan is in attainment for all six criteria pollutants, this may change when the EPA's revised standards for ozone and particulate matter (smog and soot) are implemented. The revisions, issued in 1997, were tied up in court until early 2002 due to legal challenges by industry groups and three states (including Michigan), but the EPA's authority to set NAAQS was upheld. The new standards, which the EPA expects to take effect in summer 2002, will reduce the allowed amount of ozone and small (2.5 micrometers) particulate matter (PM).

Existing MDEQ monitoring information suggests that the new ozone standard may not be met in ten counties: Allegan, Benzie, Berrien, Cass, Genesee, Mason, Muskegon, Macomb, St. Clair, and Wayne. The new particulate-matter emission limits are expected to affect only Wayne County.

In the last few years, a major effort has been made by the EPA to address ozone pollution (smog) in the northeast United States by reducing nitrogen oxide emissions from "upwind" states. In 1998 the EPA published a rule, referred to as the "NO_x SIP Call," requiring 22 midwest states and the District of Columbia to reduce their nitrogen oxide emissions by 85 percent, a significant amount. In 1999 the EPA also granted petitions filed under section 126 of the Clean Air Act by four northeast states seeking to reduce ozone pollution through NO_x reductions in emissions from other states. The State of Michigan, with seven other states, challenged the section 126 rule and the NO_x SIP Call, but the U.S. Court of Appeals issued decisions largely upholding both. The MDEQ currently is drafting its NO_x SIP, which must be adopted by the state and approved by the EPA by mid-2002.

Hazardous Air Pollutants

There currently are 188 substances that qualify as a hazardous air pollutant (HAP); that is, they are known or suspected to cause (1) cancer or such other serious health problems as reproductive effects or birth defects or (2) adverse environmental effects. Among the substances are benzene, dioxin, vinyl chloride, mercury, and polychlorinated biphenyls (PCBs).

Prior to the 1990 federal amendments to the Clean Air Act, HAPs were regulated, as criteria pollutants currently are, according to the risk each poses to human health. But because of the legal, political, and scientific complexity of this approach, the EPA had issued only eight standards

in 20 years. The 1990 amendments shifted HAPs from health-based to technology-based regulation, moving the focus from the individual *pollutants* to the pollution *sources*. The EPA now develops regulations called *maximum achievable control technology* (MACT) standards, which require a source to meet specific emissions limits that are based on levels already being achieved by similar sources in the country. The health-risk-based approach has not been abandoned but remains as a residual option.

As of August 2000, the EPA had issued MACT standards for 90 categories of industrial air-pollution sources, such as chemical plants, oil refineries, steel mills, and dry cleaners. These standards are expected to reduce air toxics emissions by about 1.5 million tons annually. In addition, the EPA has announced that by 2003 it will regulate mercury and other air toxics emitted from oil- and coal-fired power plants, the nation's largest sources of human-caused mercury emissions. Mercury is linked with several serious health problems, including both neurological and developmental problems; humans and wildlife are exposed to mercury primarily through consuming contaminated fish.

Although the federal government is responsible for regulating 188 specific hazardous air pollutants, it may delegate this responsibility to the states, and Michigan has received such "delegated authority." Michigan rules 230–32 are the "air toxic rules" and set out the state's role in this regard. Michigan law does not list specific air contaminants as toxic; instead, it defines as toxic—and thus subject to state regulation—"any air contaminant for which there is no national ambient air quality standard and is or may become harmful to public health or the environment when present in the outdoor atmosphere in sufficient quantity and duration." Michigan's air-toxic regulation rests on two basic requirements.

- Each new emission source must manage its toxics by using the best available control technology (referred to as T-BACT).

- A toxic emission cannot result in a maximum ambient concentration that exceeds the health-based screening level defined for each substance.

Mobile-Source Emissions

The federal Clean Air Act requires the EPA to prescribe standards for any class of vehicle causing or contributing to air pollution that may reasonably be anticipated to endanger public health or welfare. Recently, the EPA proposed new standards for NO_x, hydrocarbon (HC), and CO emissions from several types of currently unregulated nonroad engines and vehicles. Only newly manufactured products will be affected, among them forklifts, some diesel marine engines, off-highway motorcycles, all-terrain-vehicles (ATVs), snowmobiles, electric generators, airport baggage-transport vehicles, and various other construction, farm, and industrial equipment.

The EPA also established a national program regulating, as a group, heavy-duty vehicles and their fuel. New emission standards will begin to take effect in model year 2007 and are based on the use of high-efficiency, catalytic exhaust emission-control devices or comparably effective advanced technologies.

Because these catalytic devices are damaged by sulfur, the EPA also is reducing, by 97 percent, the level of sulfur permitted in highway diesel fuel; the effective date is mid-2006. The program gives substantial flexibility to refiners, especially small operations, and engine/vehicle manufacturers, to help them implement the new requirements in the most cost-efficient manner.

DISCUSSION

Regional Ozone Transport

The EPA's latest effort to reduce nitrogen oxide emissions is opposed by the State of Michigan, business groups such as the Michigan Chamber of Commerce, and the electric utility industry. Opponents believe that (1) the proposed reductions are unnecessary in "downwind" states, and (2) the growth projections on which the emissions limits are based will not accommodate Michigan's energy needs. In support of the latter position, the Michigan House of Representatives adopted a resolution urging the EPA to reevaluate and adjust Michigan's cap on NO_x emissions, using more realistic energy-growth rates.

The NO_x rules supporters, including the Michigan Environmental Council and the American Lung Association, believe that a decrease in smog is necessary to diminish asthma, bronchitis, and other respiratory ailment incidences. These organizations point to the health effects caused by ground-level ozone pollution, including aggravated asthma, reduced lung capacity, and increased susceptibility to respiratory illnesses such as pneumonia and bronchitis. In addition, a recent study links smog to low birth weight, premature birth, stillbirth, and infant death.

Ozone and Fine Particulate Matter

In Michigan, the new federal ozone and particulate matter air standards are being met with considerable criticism by the regulated community, the governor, and state administrators. The manufacturing and industry sectors claim that (1) air-quality laws already are too complicated and expensive, and (2) Michigan's air quality is greatly affected by pollutants coming from the Chicago area, which is in serious nonattainment for ozone and other criteria pol-

lutants. The governor further claims that the additional regulatory burden will outweigh any further benefit to human health.

The new standards' supporters, such as the American Lung Association and the Michigan Environmental Council, believe it is crucial that the EPA revise the ozone-standard implementation process quickly in order to minimize any further delay in protecting the public from ozone pollution. These organizations point to EPA research that indicates that the new particulate standard, along with other clean-air programs, will reduce premature deaths by about 15,000 a year and serious respiratory problems in children by about 250,000 cases a year.

See also Great Lakes Concerns; Water Quality.

FOR ADDITIONAL INFORMATION

Air Quality Division
Michigan Department of Environmental Quality
Constitution Hall, 3d Floor
525 West Allegan Street
P.O. Box 30260
Lansing, MI 48909
(517) 373-7023
(517) 335-6993 FAX
www.michigan.gov/deq

Capital Region Office
American Lung Association of Michigan
403 Seymour Avenue
Lansing, MI 48933
(800) 678-LUNG
(517) 484-4541
(517) 484-2118 FAX
www.alam.org

Director of Environmental and Regulatory Affairs
Michigan Chamber of Commerce
600 South Walnut Street
Lansing, MI 48933
(517) 371-2100
(517) 371-7224 FAX
www.michamber.com

Michigan Environmental Council
119 Pere Marquette Street
Lansing, MI 48912
(517) 487-9539
(517) 487-9541 FAX
www.mecprotects.org

Sponsored by the Michigan Nonprofit Association and the Council of Michigan Foundations

Arts Funding

BACKGROUND

The term "the arts" means different things to different people. Over the past few years, the Michigan Council for Arts and Cultural Affairs (MCACA)—the entity that promotes and distributes state funds for art and culture—has used a widely inclusive definition: "[any] unique human creation that allows society to view itself." This includes the fine arts (e.g., classical music, ballet), folk arts and crafts, commercial art and design, and popular art (e.g., motion pictures, popular music).

Commercial arts (for example, decorating, advertising, landscaping) and popular arts (for example, movies, television, comic books, recordings) are profit-making ventures and thus ineligible for federal and state funds or charitable gifts. They contribute substantially to the state economy: According to a 1997 MCACA report, in Michigan the for-profit commercial arts and cultural sector—roughly 8,200 radio stations, publishers, dance schools, film production companies, and so on—accounted for approximately $7.8 billion in direct expenditures.

The fine arts and folk arts and crafts traditionally are not-for-profit enterprises and rely on public and private help. There are 485 nonprofit "arts and cultural" organizations in the state, with $681 million in assets (Michigan Nonprofit Association, 2000). Most are quite small: Only 30 of the state's nearly 500 "arts and humanities" nonprofit organizations (radio and television stations, orchestras and theatres, and museums, botanical gardens, and zoological gardens) spend $1 million or more annually (report funded by the Aspen Institute, 1999).

Data from the National Center for Charitable Statistics (1997) show that in Michigan, nonprofit arts rely more on government funding than do most other nonprofits. Michigan's nonprofit *arts and humanities* organizations received almost 49 percent of their revenue from federal, state, and local government; 30 percent from private support by individuals, foundations, and corporations; and the balance from investment returns, sales and admission fees, and other sources. On average, *all* charitable organizations in the state derive only 14 percent of their income from public sources.

State government's support for the arts goes back more than 40 years.

- In 1960 the Michigan Cultural Commission was created.

- This body was replaced in 1963 by the Michigan Council for the Arts, charged with stimulating creative and performing arts, encouraging public interest in the state's cultural heritage, and promoting freedom of artistic expression.

- In 1991 a successor agency was created: the Michigan Council for Arts and Cultural Affairs. The MCACA, then housed in the Department of Consumer and Industry Services, was charged to ". . . encourage, develop and facilitate an enriched environment of artistic, creative, cultural activity in Michigan."

- In 2001 the MCACA was moved to the newly created Michigan Department of History, Arts, and Libraries. This was accomplished through an executive order that consolidated the MCACA, Mackinac Island Park Service Commission, Michi-

Sponsored by the Michigan Nonprofit Association and the Council of Michigan Foundations

gan Office of Film and Television Services, Michigan Historical Commission and Center, and, slightly later, the Library of Michigan.

In FY 2001–02 state arts funding was nearly $28.8 million. These funds are used for grants to orchestras, museums, jazz/blues programs, film festivals, schools, theaters, dance companies, film/video programs, zoos, and arts/crafts programs. For FY 2002–03 the governor has recommended about $24 million for arts funding.

DISCUSSION

Why Fund the Arts?

The nineteenth century British education reformer, Matthew Arnold, professed that the job of the arts is to "instruct and delight," that is, not to only entertain and provide pleasure but to educate and enlighten the public. Similarly, in the twenty-first century, arts supporters believe that because the arts are essential to a vibrant and educated and moral culture, they must be supported by government. The Wayne State University Commission on Arts and Public Policy (CAPP) conducted a study for the MCACA in 1997 entitled, *Arts and the Quality of Life in Michigan, Part I*. The findings illustrate how the arts significantly affect society in several specific and important areas:

- Education
- Cultural preservation
- Crime reduction
- Benefits to at-risk youth
- Economic development
- Social cohesion

The report suggests that the arts can and do contribute measurably to improving the quality of life in the state. In addition, educators cite persuasive data showing that children who participate in the arts do better in "core" areas of education. For example, it is suggested that children who are exposed to music, particularly at a very young age, do better in math. Finally, skills fostered through creativity are in high demand in the workplace.

Conversely, some people question whether the arts should be publicly funded at all, arguing that the government should not collect taxes to support institutions that many taxpayers do not use. They believe that the arts are properly supported by devoted consumers, as sports are, or by private philanthropy. Even so, over the last decade, Michigan has consistently ranked among the top states in the amount of arts funding disbursed, indicating that the state, in general, is dedicated to supporting the arts, although

some citizens and policymakers occasionally may be ambivalent or divided over which kind and where.

In the last few years a new argument in support of the arts has emerged: The arts—especially when defined as arts *and* culture (and sometimes recreation)—are important because they are a vibrant sector of the state economy. In September 2001 CAPP, using the broad category of "arts and culture *industry*,"—which includes such products as mass-produced jewelry, clothing, and furniture as well as amusement parks and toys and product packaging—estimated that in 2001 the sector would contribute nearly $46 billion to the state economy (data are based on the U.S. Census Bureau's 1997 *Census of Service Industries*). Thus, for some, art has value not only for its own sake but for the state economy as well.

Where Should the Funding Go?

Given the widely divergent notions of what constitutes "the arts" and the differing opinions on what kind of art is valuable and what is not, it is not surprising that people disagree on the who, what, and where of arts funding. Ultimately, the arts that are funded (or not) in Michigan make a statement about who we are as a state and what our cultural values are.

During the last decade, there has been a nationwide push to support arts and culture projects that address the background and tastes of an increasingly diverse citizenry, and this trend is evident in Michigan. For example, many fine-arts museums showcase what traditionally were considered to be regional or "craft" arts, such as quilting, and permanent Native American museums have been established. Some fear that public and private funding for these arts comes at the expense of the traditional fine arts. For example, some complained that the funding directed toward Detroit's relatively new Dr. Charles H. Wright Museum of African-American History would cause the large and internationally known but financially strapped Detroit Institute of Arts (DIA) to suffer. Others believe that funding the museum was appropriate and that recognition and support of the city's African-American heritage was overdue. (Some observers assert that the controversy was constructive and, in the end, strengthened the DIA, which, in 2000, established the General Motors Center for African American Art as a new curatorial department and resource center at the museum.) The state officially supports culturally diverse arts through MCACA's Cultural Projects program, which aims to create a greater understanding and appreciation for differing heritages and cultures.

Even more controversial than *how* state arts funding is distributed is *where* it goes. Throughout the 1970s, 1980s,

Sponsored by the Michigan Nonprofit Association and the Council of Michigan Foundations

and early 1990s, a majority of state arts funding supported Detroit organizations, primarily the DIA and the Detroit Symphony. The spending (1) reflected state policy that the financially fragile institutions in the state's biggest city should be assisted and (2) recognized the size, overall budget, large audience, and international reputation of the organizations. Legislators from elsewhere in Michigan, however, have complained almost from the beginning of state arts funding that the money is unevenly distributed geographically.

Statewide, MCACA funding averages $2.29 per person. There are two ways to look at the data.

■ If one visualizes the state as divided into four tiers going from south to north, the southern 18 counties (including the three-county metropolitan Detroit area) fare best: the per capita figures are $3.11 if the legislative special grants to the DIA, Detroit Symphony, and Detroit Zoo are included, and $1.17 if they are excluded. The central tier fares worst ($0.98 per capita), and the northern tier and Upper Peninsula fall in the middle ($1.08 and $1.06, respectively).

■ If one views the state as divided into MCACA's 13 service regions (see the exhibit), it may be seen that state arts funding follows a rough "L," from the Traverse City area through the Grand Rapids and Lansing areas to the southeast counties. This covers the major population concentrations with the excep-

Michigan Council for Arts and Cultural Affairs Funding, per Person, by Region, 1997

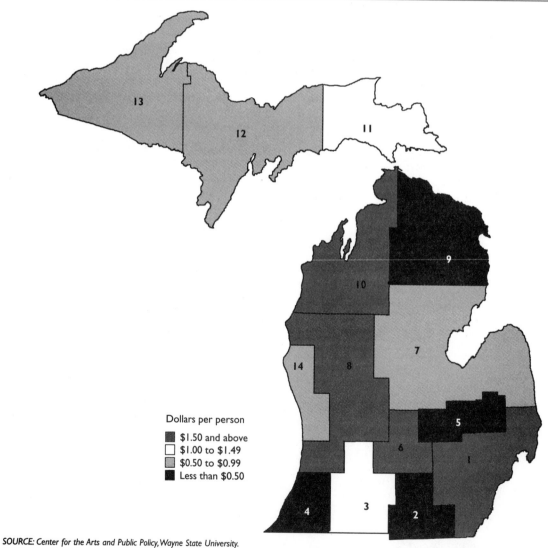

Dollars per person
■ $1.50 and above
□ $1.00 to $1.49
▨ $0.50 to $0.99
■ Less than $0.50

SOURCE: Center for the Arts and Public Policy, Wayne State University.
NOTE: Statewide funding/person is $2.29.

tion of the Flint area. In some of the more sparsely populated areas, the arts grants are fewer and sometimes far between.

For the last several years state public policymakers have been trying to ensure that funding is distributed in such a way that all Michigan residents have access to state-sponsored arts. The MCACA's Rural Arts and Culture Program, launched in 2001, is designed to reach communities and organizations in 39 rural Michigan counties. The program's objectives are to strengthen and showcase the unique arts and culture of Michigan's rural communities; this is being accomplished through community-based collaborations relating to local or regional arts, history, and culture. The MCACA also is trying to fund more regional arts programs, which, because they serve a wider geographic area, reach more people than do local programs.

Finally, for more than a decade, the nation has witnessed fierce debate about public funding for controversial art. Some argue that policymakers are not qualified nor is it appropriate for them to judge the content of art, and that a work of art should not be regulated or limited by its funding sources. Other, more traditional voices insist that public funding should not support art that many Americans find offensive. While this debate has been primarily about *federal* funding, Michigan lawmakers, residents, and institutions also have questioned whether certain kinds of art are appropriate for a public audience: For example, in 1999, the Detroit Institute of Arts sponsored but ultimately decided not to open a controversial exhibition by a Michigan artist because the work was deemed "offensive to large parts of our communities."

FOR ADDITIONAL INFORMATION

Americans for the Arts
1 East 53d Street
New York, NY 10022
(212) 223-2787
(212) 980-4857 FAX
www.americansforthearts.org

ArtServe Michigan
17515 West Nine Mile Road, Suite 1025
Southfield, MI 48075
(248) 557-8288
(248) 557-8581 FAX
        and
913 West Holmes Road, Suite 160
Lansing, MI 48910
(517) 272-2336
(517) 272-3013 FAX
www.ArtServeMichigan.org

Center for Arts and Public Policy
College of Fine, Performing, and Communications Arts
192 Manoogian Hall
Wayne State University
Detroit, MI 48202
(313) 577-9257
(313) 577-6300 FAX
www.capp-wsu.org

Michigan Council for Arts and Cultural Affairs
525 West Ottawa Street
P.O. Box 30705
Lansing, MI 48909
(517) 241-4011
(517) 241-3979 FAX
www.michigan.gov/hal

Michigan Humanities Council
119 Pere Marquette Drive, Suite 3B
Lansing, MI 48912
(517) 372-7770
(517) 372-0027 FAX
        and
E4624 State Highway M-35
Escanaba, MI 49829
(906) 789-9471
(906) 789-2568 FAX
www.michiganhumanities.org/index.html

National Endowment for the Arts
1100 Pennsylvania Avenue, N.W.
Washington, DC 20506
(202) 682-5400
www.arts.gov

Sponsored by the Michigan Nonprofit Association and the Council of Michigan Foundations

Career Development

BACKGROUND

In the past decade Michigan government has taken several major steps to address businesses' need for a skilled workforce and residents' need for good jobs.

- In 1993 the Governor's Workforce Commission was created, which, among its other tasks, assessed the extent to which federal, state, and local programs were meeting the state's workforce needs.

- In 1994 the Michigan Jobs Commission was created, and many economic- and job-development programs from various state agencies were consolidated into the new agency.

- In 1996 workforce development boards (WDBs) were established around the state to administer career-development programs in their service areas.

- In 1999 the governor split the Jobs Commission into the Michigan Economic Development Corporation (MEDC) and the Michigan Department of Career Development (MDCD). The MEDC assumed the commission's economic-development functions, and the MDCD was assigned responsibility for workforce development, the subject of this piece.

- In 2002 the Workforce Commission was replaced with a 53-member Workforce Investment Board (27 members from business groups and the balance from the legislature, local government, youth programs, education, and unions) and charged with reviewing the state's workforce-investment system, designating local workforce-investment areas, developing formulae to distribute federal and state workforce funds, and developing a statewide employment-statistics system.

The MDCD's mission is "to develop and continuously improve a system to produce a workforce with the skills needed to maintain and enhance the Michigan economy."

The department first consisted of three agencies: Office of Workforce Development, Michigan Rehabilitation Services, and Employment Service Agency. A later executive order shifted the offices of Career and Technical Education Services, Postsecondary Services, and Adult Education into the MDCD. The department now employs 1,100 and oversees the distribution and use of $200 million in education funds, $500 million in federal funds, and $35 million from the state General Fund.

State government's career-related activities are grouped in this one department, which has wide authority and is responsible for

- helping Michiganians choose careers and providing education and training to equip them for those careers;

- helping schools give students a solid foundation in core subjects of reading, writing, mathematics, science, and social studies;

- informing Michiganians about the workplace and how to acquire academic and career skills through career academies, technical-education centers and programs,

GLOSSARY

Baldrige quality criteria
Criteria, administered by the National Institute of Standards and Technology, that an organization may use to improve overall performance in leadership, strategic planning, customer and market focus, information and analysis, human resource focus, process management, and business results.

Career and technical education (CTE)
Programs to help students obtain knowledge and skills leading to a first job or post-secondary technical education.

Competency-Based Curriculum (CBC) Fund
An initiative that will make funds available to train providers to develop competency-based curricula with measurable outcomes.

Economic development job training (EDJT)
Customized training to meet specific business needs; supported by Michigan Department of Economic Development grants.

Education advisory group (EAG)
A body comprising local school and college officials and business people that advises the local workforce development board on local education needs.

Michigan Technical Excellence Program (M-TEP)
An industry-led initiative to recognize high-quality technical-education programs having high levels of placement and employer satisfaction.

Sponsored by the Michigan Nonprofit Association and the Council of Michigan Foundations

cooperative education, apprenticeships, internships, school-based enterprises, and community colleges;

■ facilitating student and worker certification that is based on competency and skill standards endorsed by employers;

■ providing labor-exchange and placement services that help workers find jobs and employers find skilled workers; and

■ assessing student progress toward obtaining good jobs or further technical education.

Much of the work of the department is carried out through the network of 25 locally appointed, part-time, workforce development boards. They receive state and federal funds through the MDCD, which they use to run the 102 local "one-stop centers" (Michigan Works! agencies) and the Building Strategic Partnerships for Career Development initiative (a local and statewide strategic-planning process). The WDBs must provide certain services and programs in their service areas, but they develop their own as well—examples are computer training and permanent and temporary job placement.

Local education advisory groups (EAGs), to which members are appointed by local WDBs, partner with the boards. They primarily approve plans and recommend strategies for career-education programs—secondary, career and technical, and adult—in the WDB service region.

Together, these bodies—the MDCD, WDBs, and EAGs—oversee Michigan's career development system of worker training, learning, and placement. The system is divided into three sub-systems.

■ *Career preparation* focuses on schools and colleges, to ensure that Michigan students obtain needed academic, technical, and work-behavior skills.

■ *Workforce development* targets workers in transition; the Michigan Works! agencies offer adult education, job training (through the federal Job Training Partnership Act and the 1998 Workforce Investment Act), trade-adjustment programs, vocational rehabilitation, Work First public-assistance programs, and job-finding services.

■ *Worker enhancement* is a skills and credentialing system geared toward upgrading skills that workers need for current or future jobs. It includes employer-based training and customized training funded by state Economic Development Job Training (EDJT) grants.

In its first year of operation (FY 1999–2000), the MDCD launched a number of new initiatives.

■ *Operation Fast Break* is an eight-week, accelerated-learning program that helps students enter career-track work or college and integrates math, reading, computer technology, and employability-skills instruction.

■ *Partnership for Adult Learning* comprises private- and public-sector adult-learning programs for which funds are allocated to the WDBs by the MDCD on a formula based on the number of service-area residents (1) without a high school diploma, (2) with limited English proficiency, or (3) receiving public assistance.

■ The *Competency-Based Curriculum Fund* is a three-year, $30 million program providing financial incentives to public and private schools and education agencies to create business-education partnerships.

Michigan Works!
"One-stop" training/job-placement centers run by the workforce development boards in their service areas.

Workforce development boards (WDBs)
Part-time, private-sector entities that plan and oversee workforce development activities in the state's 25 workforce regions.

www.TalentFreeway.org
An on-line service that helps (1) Michigan residents find training and jobs and (2) employers find workers.

Sponsored by the Michigan Nonprofit Association and the Council of Michigan Foundations

■ *WorkKeys* is a workplace skills-assessment method used nationwide by employers, students, workers, and educators. A WorkKeys assessment can determine whether a person has the fundamental academic and work skills needed to qualify for career-entry work or training.

The MDCD has set five goals, with accompanying objectives, and developed a five-year strategic plan to further them.

■ *Goal 1: Develop an integrated career-development system through industry-education partnerships at the state, regional, and local levels.* The objectives are to

- provide technical assistance and resources to WDBs and educational organizations to enable them to conduct strategic planning in their region;

- direct state and federal discretionary funds to WDBs to help them and their partners to implement their goals and objectives; and

- explore ways to increase worker-training opportunities, including on-line courses, particularly those in small businesses and critical industries.

■ *Goal 2: Develop an effective, integrated, career decision-making and preparation system for youth and adults.* The objectives are to

- increase the number of pupils participating in Career Pathways schools and programs and develop program standards that ensure high quality;

- expand Operation Fast Break;

- implement the Career Education Consumer Report system, to provide information on education and training programs, including their enrollment and success rates;

- integrate separate Web-based services into a single Career Guidance System (CGS) for those seeking information about careers, education, and jobs;

- conduct a career-guidance campaign offering incentives to young people to enter fields deemed critical to the Michigan economy;

- improve the Michigan Talent Bank (the state's Internet-based employment-service system, which holds nearly a half-million resumes and lists more than 22,000 job openings, accessible through *www.TalentFreeway.org*), making it easier for people to use it to create resumes, post job orders, and conduct job and worker searches;

- help students with disabilities enter and succeed in high-demand training areas; and

- explore teacher-certification alternatives and ways to improve teacher training to make it more experience-based, competency-based, computer-assisted, and relevant to career development.

■ *Goal 3: Develop an industry-led skill-credentialing and quality-management system that will provide employers with a steady supply of well-prepared workers.* The objectives are to

- implement the Michigan Technical Excellence Program (M-TEP) to recognize technical-education programs that enjoy high placement levels and employer satisfaction;

- encourage the use of WorkKeys; and

- implement the Competency-Based Curriculum Fund.

■ *Goal 4: Inform and educate the public about Michigan's career-development system and how to access and use it effectively.* The objectives are to

- Focus public attention on the career-development system, services, and opportunities it offers to employers and job seekers;

- provide students and their parents with the information critical to successful career planning; and

- improve internal MDCD communications and staff orientation.

■ *Goal 5: Develop the MDCD into a high-performance agency by building Baldrige quality criteria into internal and external operations.*

DISCUSSION

Until recent years, the state's job-creation, -training, and -placement system was very fragmented. The myriad programs were run by many agencies at the state and local levels. The reorganization of the past decade was an effort to build a comprehensive, coherent system based on local control and employer leadership.

All state job-development programs have been pulled into one department (the MDCD), programming control has been turned over to local business people, educators, and others, and the federal and state revenue streams are directed into agencies and programs that have specific service missions.

Supporters of the new configuration say that Michigan is unique among the states in the level of local control it confers; the system works slightly differently, but similarly, in every region. They also believe that one of the system's greatest strengths is that it is "employer-driven."

Critics contend that while the new system has consolidated many programs, it also has usurped, duplicated, or made more cumbersome some programming. They point to the MDCD's involvement in education programming as an example.

Critics also believe that the department is too focused on getting people into jobs and not enough on helping them keep the jobs and advance. Even after former welfare recipients enter the program, they say, it is difficult for a new worker to put together enough education and training to advance out of the relatively small number of entry-level jobs available. Many former welfare recipients, they add, are in this predicament because they do not speak English well if at all, but the program does not allow English-as-a-second-language classes to count, as other skill-building classes do, toward participation in work-and-learn programs.

See also Higher Education Funding; Welfare Reform: TANF Reauthorization.

FOR ADDITIONAL INFORMATION

Michigan Department of Career Development
Victor Office Center, 7th Floor
201 North Washington Square
Lansing, MI 48913
(517) 241-4000
(517) 373-0314 FAX
www.michigan.gov/mdcd

Michigan League for Human Services
1115 South Pennsylvania, Suite 202
Lansing, Michigan 48912
(517) 487-5436
(517) 371-4546 FAX
www.milhs.org

Sponsored by the Michigan Nonprofit Association and the Council of Michigan Foundations

Casinos and Other Legal Gambling

BACKGROUND

Legalized gambling began in many states with a state-run lottery, but by the early 1990s many also had approved for-profit gambling enterprises such as casinos (some owned and operated by Indian tribes), riverboats, and video-lottery terminals (VLTs) at bars and restaurants. Legal gambling is big business—in 2000, Americans legally wagered more than $61 billion—and a considerable revenue source for states as well.

The forms of gambling listed below are legal but limited in Michigan. According to the Michigan Public Policy Initiative (MPPI), in 1999 legal gambling comprised a $7 billion dollar industry (most recent complete data available).

- State lottery
- Horse racing
- Charitable gaming (e.g., bingo, raffles)
- Casino gaming on Indian reservations
- Casino gaming in Detroit

Michigan does not allow dog racing, and it does not permit slot machines, video poker, or similar forms of gambling in any place other than a casino.

Casino Gambling

Indian Operations

Because Indian tribes are sovereign nations, laws prohibiting casinos do not apply to them, and, under federal law and court decrees, states do not have the right to regulate activities on Indian lands. However, states and tribes may enter into agreements that give states some regulatory oversight over a tribe's casino operations, and this has been the case in Michigan since 1993, when the governor signed the first gaming compacts with several of the state's federally recognized tribes.

Currently, Michigan has 17 Indian casinos, operated by nine tribes, and two more—one for New Buffalo and one for Battle Creek—await approval. The compacts allow the tribes to operate "class III" casinos, i.e., establishments that offer slot machines, video poker, and all other "casino style" games. The 1993 compacts with the seven tribes stated that for as long as the tribes had the exclusive right to operate casinos in the state, the revenue from slot machines and VLTs on reservations would be taxed at 10 percent of the net win: 8 percent for the state Renaissance Fund (for economic development) and 2 percent for improvements to the local communities. These compacts also stated that if any non-Indian casinos were permitted in the state, the tribes no longer would have to pay into the Renaissance Fund.

The first compacts were signed before the three Detroit casinos were on the horizon, and by mid-1999, when the first Detroit casino gaming license was granted, all seven tribes had been released from their state tax obligation. The 1993 compacts also obligate the seven tribes to paying $25,000 each annually to the state to offset the cost of

GLOSSARY

Class III casino
A gambling establishment that has slot machines, video-lottery terminals, poker, and other games commonly considered "casino style" games.

Gaming
Gambling.

Net win
A casino's receipts after winnings are paid to wagerers.

Simulcasting
In regard to horse racing, electronically transmitting a race from one track to others, where fans may bet on the race and watch it on a television monitor.

Video-lottery terminal (VLT)
A machine similar to a slot machine but offering an electronic version of blackjack, poker, or other game of chance.

casino oversight, regardless of the presence in the state of non-Indian casinos, and these payments continue.

In 1998 casino compacts were signed with four additional tribes, stating that these tribes (1) have a 10 percent state tax obligation regardless of the presence in the state of non-Indian casinos (again, 8 percent goes to economic development, via the Michigan Strategic Fund, and 2 percent goes toward local improvements); (2) annually will pay the state $50,000 (to be adjusted according to the Detroit consumer price index) to offset oversight costs; and (3) are limited to one casino each.

The total net win from VLTs and slot machines at tribal casinos in Michigan was $677 million in 1999 and even more in 2000, although the precise figure is not available. The MPPI reports that Michigan's Indian casinos provide about 4,000 jobs statewide. According to the National Indian Gaming Association, tribal gaming revenue nationwide in 2000 was $10.6 billion (less than 10 percent of the total gaming industry), and Indian casinos generated 250,000 jobs.

Detroit Casinos

Passage of a statewide ballot question in 1996 gave the go-ahead for three casinos in Detroit. Public Act 69 of 1997—the Michigan Gaming Control and Revenue Act, as amended—provides for state licensing and oversight. Among its other provisions, the act

- vests the Michigan Gaming Control Board with exclusive authority to license, regulate, and control the Detroit casinos;

- creates funds (1) to enable the control board to carry out its duties and (2) for compulsive-gambling prevention and other casino-related state programs;

- establishes a code of ethics for (1) control board members, employees, and agents, (2) casino and supplier license applicants, (3) casino and supplier licensees, and (4) others involved in gaming;

- provides for the distribution of Detroit casino tax revenue to K–12 public education in Michigan and to capital improvement, youth programs, and tax relief in the City of Detroit;

- prohibits political contributions to state/local political candidates/committees from people with a casino interest as well as from supplier license applicants and licensees;

- imposes the state wagering tax, which is 8.1 percent of each Detroit casino's net win, or adjusted gross receipts (receipts minus winnings paid to wagerers); and

- imposes an annual services fee to be paid to the state ($25 million the first year, split by the three casinos, then annually adjusted for inflation thereafter).

In 1997 Detroit officials identified the three companies with which the city would negotiate agreements to operate the casinos: Detroit Entertainment, Greektown Casino, and MGM Grand Detroit. The agreements stipulate that among other requirements, casino developers must purchase 30 percent of goods and services from Detroit-based businesses, small businesses, and minority- or women-owned businesses, and staff must be composed of at least 51 percent Detroit residents.

Several of the original investors had to be replaced because requirements pertaining to investor history caused them to be disqualified. Greektown Casino ended up becoming predominantly an enterprise of the Sault Ste. Marie Tribe of Chippewa Indians, owner of five casinos and the largest employer in northern Michigan.

All three developers quickly opened temporary facilities (two in 1999 and the third in 2000) and began operations while the permanent sites were being negotiated.

The former Detroit mayor tried to acquire enough land, using $150 million from the casinos, to cluster the three permanent casinos, each with an 800-room hotel, on the riverfront; he was unsuccessful, however, in part because of city council opposition. In March 2002 the current mayor announced a plan, agreed to by the casinos and supported by civic leaders, whereby (1) the casinos would be permitted to build smaller, 400-room hotels (Motor City and Greektown on their temporary sites and MGM at an as yet unidentified location), which would be ready for occupancy by January 2006, in time for the Super Bowl in Detroit, and (2) in exchange, the casinos would forgive the $150 million advanced to the city to buy the riverfront property. At this writing, the city council has not agreed to the plan, which it must for the plan to move forward. The cancellation of the full riverfront project may leave the city open to lawsuits by landowners who have options with the city or have closed their business in the project area.

The Detroit casinos together generated about $1 billion in revenue in 2001, up from $744 million in 2000 (see Exhibit 1). According to the American Gaming Association, the Detroit-Windsor venue was the fourth largest U.S. casino market (gross revenue) in 2000. Estimates are that when all three permanent facilities are up and running, their annual take will range from $1.2 billion to $2 billion.

EXHIBIT 1. Gross Receipts and State Wagering Tax Payments, Detroit Casinos, 1999–2001 ($ millions)

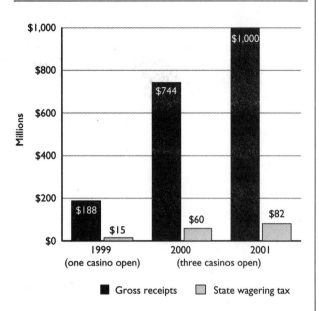

SOURCE: Michigan Gaming Control Board.

The state's share of Detroit casino revenue derives from the annual services fee ($25 million in 1999 and adjusted for inflation thereafter) paid by the three casinos and the state wagering tax (8.1 percent of net win). The latter is paid daily by each casino, through electronic transfer, and deposited into the School Aid Fund; as Exhibit 1 shows, this amounted to $60 million in 2000 and nearly $82 million in 2001.

Lottery

Established by P.A. 239 of 1972, the Michigan Lottery is governed by the Bureau of State Lottery, which makes the rules governing the games and oversees the issuance of lottery, bingo, and charitable gaming licenses. The bureau is housed in the Michigan Department of Treasury. Half of lottery revenue ($1.6 billion in FY 2001) is used for prizes and about 35 percent goes to the state School Aid Fund. About 6 percent of the fund's FY 2001 revenue came from the lottery.

Lottery sales were relatively weak from the mid-1980s through the early 1990s, and sales actually declined in some years. To boost sales, the state has increased advertising, added new instant lottery and other games, and in 1996 joined "The Big Game"—now a seven-state megalottery.

Lottery revenue climbed steadily throughout the late 1990s, but there has been a slight decrease in sales since the Detroit casinos opened, and thus the contributions to the School Aid Fund also have dropped (see Exhibit 2). The lottery has revamped its games lineup and expects sales to increase.

Charitable Gaming

The Charitable Gaming Division of the lottery was created by the Bingo Act of 1972 and licenses nonprofit organizations to sponsor bingo, Las Vegas nights, raffles, and millionaire parties as fundraisers. The division issues over 10,000 licenses annually to such qualified organizations as religious, veterans', fraternal, education, senior citizen, service groups, and political committees. In FY 2001 Michiganians spent $188 million on charitable gaming.

About 40 bingo operations raise money for candidates and political party organizations. From July 2000 to June 2001, more than $1.5 million charitable gaming dollars went to candidates. The Michigan state and local Democratic Party organizations use these events extensively, and in 1998 lottery officials investigated allegations that contribution checks were being improperly written at some of them. Although the investigation did not turn up enough evidence to put an end to political-bingo events, in 1999 the Republican Party was successful in having legislation enacted to tighten reporting rules for political-bingo fundraisers.

EXHIBIT 2. Lottery Contributions to Michigan School Aid Fund, FYs 1995–2001 ($ millions)

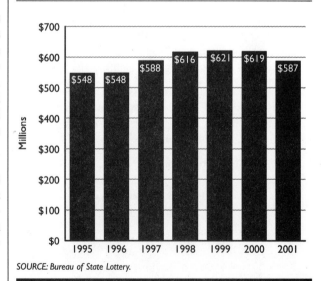

SOURCE: Bureau of State Lottery.

Charitable gaming lost market share when casinos opened in Detroit and elsewhere in the state. Beginning in 1994, the first full year that the Indian casinos were in operation, wagering at charitable gaming events declined steadily after rising an average of 6.5 percent in the previous few years. Then, in 2000, charitable gaming was given a boost by legislation (1) increasing the number of bingo events a licensee is permitted to hold weekly and (2) introducing a new bingo game that allows for progressive jackpots, i.e., is exempt from the $2,000 prize cap applied to other bingo games. The next year (2001), revenue was $188 million, an increase of $55 million over the prior year.

Horse Racing

Horse racing is Michigan's oldest form of legal gambling, established in 1933. In 2000 Michigan's seven tracks (the two largest are in the Detroit area and the other five are scattered around southern Michigan) had more than 2,300 days of live and simulcast racing, total attendance of over 1.5 million people, and almost $400 million in wagering that generated more than $13 million in state revenue. The industry suffers from competition for the gaming dollar from the lottery, casinos, and charitable gaming: In May 2001 the *Detroit News* reported that live racing took in nearly $98 million in 1998, the year before the first of the three Detroit casinos opened; when all three were open, the live-racing take went down to $44 million. All horse race wagering (both live and simulcast) dropped 6 percent, to $375 million, from 2000 to 2001.

In 1994 horse racing was roughly a $1.2 billion industry annually responsible for 42,300 jobs, $233 million in personal income, and total economic output of $439 million; these are the most recent figures available, and it may be assumed that they have dropped considerably in recent years.

DISCUSSION

Most of the current policy debate in Michigan related to gambling has to do with the Detroit casinos. The statewide ballot question on the casinos was only narrowly approved, and there was an immediate movement, which failed, to collect enough signatures to put a subsequent question on the ballot to repeal the first. Many Michiganians object to casinos for various reasons. Some feel that gambling is immoral because it encourages a "something for nothing" mentality. Many argue that gaming brings criminal activity such as drugs and prostitution to host and surrounding communities, which degrades the area; they further assert that such activity strains local resources, and local units of government do not receive sufficient compensation to enable them to deal with it.

Gambling addiction is a persistent concern for many. A United Way survey (2001) in the metropolitan Detroit area shows that 85 percent of area residents have gambled at some point: 76 percent in state-run games and 61 percent at casinos. The survey also shows that about 5 percent of gamblers, many aged 18–25 years, become addicted. Some believe that addiction is less of a problem than the survey suggests, because they do not believe that gambling is a problem until the gambler is spending more than s/he can afford, and others contend that people should be permitted to spend their money as they wish. Many, however, see gambling as leading to serious community and mental health problems that will continue to grow, even if people are informed of its dangers and offered help for their addiction.

Many Detroiters believe that the economic benefits for Detroit far outweigh the problems. Advocates for Detroit casinos used Indian-casino data to argue that casino gambling can bring minority jobs and economic stimulus to economically troubled areas. Since 1993 Indian casinos in Michigan have increased tribal employment, provided revenue for community support/improvement, stimulated other community economic development, including tourism, and helped to support tribal infrastructure. According to the Michigan Public Policy Initiative, the Indian casinos employ more than 4,000 people, often in high-paying entry-level jobs, and generate approximately $13.5 million in annual payroll, usually in low-income communities; they also result in as much as $41 million worth of local services purchased each year. Though only three years old, the Detroit casinos also appear to have become crucial to city finances; they employ 7,500 people and will provide an estimated $95 million this fiscal year in wagering taxes to the city—$22 million more than last year.

In addition to the benefit to Detroit, supporters point out that the state wagering tax—$82 million in 2001—that the Detroit casinos pay directly (and daily, via electronic deposit) to the School Aid Fund is a significant boost for schools. Others believe that while the gaming tax revenue may help to fund education, some of the people who are paying the tax, by gambling (and losing, since the taxes are based on the casinos' winnings), are those who can least afford it. Moreover, gaming opponents say, if gambling operations were to begin in a nearby city—Toledo or South Bend, for example—or if Internet gambling were to become a sizeable market, Detroit's casino profits and their beneficial effects could be diminished in the same way that Windsor's gambling profits fell when the Detroit establishments opened.

There also is criticism about the relationship of the Detroit casinos to minority communities. There is dissatis-

Sponsored by the Michigan Nonprofit Association and the Council of Michigan Foundations

faction with the fact that there is no African-American representation in the casinos' ownership. Critics point to the irony of large, elegant casinos being located in blighted neighborhoods, and they question whether the self-contained casinos will affect their surroundings positively. Auditors report that the casinos are complying with the rule that 51 percent of their employees are to be Detroit residents, and two of the three casinos are unionized, but many entry-level workers are earning less than the community had hoped, because tips in the Detroit casinos have been considerably lower than in other casino cities. In March 2002 the National Action Network called for a boycott of all MGM Mirage Inc., hotel-casinos in response to alleged racism by the gambling giant.

Finally, in October 1999 the Lac Vieux Band of Lake Superior Chippewa Indians filed a motion seeking to halt the casino process for Detroit Entertainment and Greektown Casino. The tribe challenged the preference granted to these two groups in the city's casino-developer selection process. The tribe and other parties in the lawsuit question the constitutionality of the Detroit casino-licensing process. They want the licenses of the casinos revoked and a conservator appointed to run the facilities until Detroit creates a new licensing law and reissues the operator licenses. In January 2002 a federal judge ruled that the casino licenses are "illegitimate," leaving future operations of the casinos in question.

These issues, plus some fraud cases that have arisen and the number of prospective investors and employees that have been rejected due to their background, suggest that controversy will continue to surround the Detroit casinos.

FOR ADDITIONAL INFORMATION

Bureau of State Lottery
101 East Hillsdale Street
P.O. Box 30023
Lansing, MI 48909
(517) 335-6500
(517) 335-5685 FAX
www.michigan.gov/lottery

Detroit Free Press Casino Section On Line
http://detroitfreepress.com/index/casinos.htm

Fraser, Trebilcock, Davis & Dunlap, P.C.
[Gaming practice group and publishers of *Michigan Gaming Law*]
One Woodward Avenue, Suite 1550
Detroit, MI 48226
Gaming hotline (313) 965-9038
      and
1000 Michigan National Tower
Lansing, MI 48933
(517) 482-5800
(517) 482-0887 FAX
www.michigangaming.com

Michigan 24-Hour Gambling Help Line
(800) 270-7117

Michigan Department of Community Health
Lewis Cass Building
320 South Walnut Street
Lansing, MI 48913
(517) 241-3893
(517) 335-3090 FAX
www.michigan.gov/mdch

Michigan Gaming Control Board
1500 Abbott Road, Suite 400
East Lansing, MI 48823
(517) 241-0040
(517) 241-0510 FAX
      and
3062 West Grand Boulevard, Suite L700
Detroit, MI 48202
(313) 456-4100
(313) 456-4200 FAX
www.michigan.gov/mgcb

Michigan Public Policy Initiative
1048 Pierpont, Suite 3
Lansing, MI 48911
(517) 492-2400
(517) 492-2410 FAX
www.mppi.mna.msu.edu

Office of the Racing Commissioner
Michigan Department of Agriculture
37650 Professional Center Drive, Suite 105A
Livonia, MI 48154
(734) 462-2400
(734) 462-2429 FAX
www.michigan.gov/mda

Child Care

BACKGROUND

Child care plays a critical role in child development, enables parents to work, and prepares children for success in school. Economic conditions in recent years and the new welfare system, which requires parents to work, has led to a large increase in the number of children of all ages in child care.

Child care is provided in many settings: at home; in child-care centers; in family and group daycare homes; and in residences of family and friends. Before/after-school care also may occur in any of these settings as well as in public and private schools, community-education programs, or entities such as the YMCA.

Every day in the United States, 13 million preschoolers, including six million infants and toddlers, are in child care—three of every five children in that age group. In Michigan, almost half (46 percent) of children under age five spend time in the care of someone other than a parent: about half of these are in their own or someone else's home and about half are in a child-care center, Head Start, preschool, nursery school, or school readiness or other enrichment program (1999 data).

The federal government provides substantial funding for child care and before/after-school care. Most direct payment for child care comes in the form of subsidies for low-income families. In addition, the federal government provides substantial support for middle- and upper-income families through tax credits that reimburse those families for child-care payments.

States are responsible for setting and enforcing child-care standards. In Michigan, the Division of Child Daycare Licensing in the Department of Consumer and Industry Services (MDCIS) is responsible for regulation as required in P.A. 116, the Michigan Child Care Organization Act of 1973. The Child Development and Care Division in the Michigan Family Independence Agency (FIA) is responsible for administering federal child-care funds and setting state policy for their use—e.g., eligibility criteria and amount.

Types of Child Care

Child-Care Centers

Child-care centers (sometimes called daycare centers), of which there were 4,862 in Michigan as of December 2001, must be licensed. Michigan licensing standards deal almost entirely with facilities and health and safety standards; personnel standards are minimal.

A child-care center program director must

- have completed at least 60 semester hours at an accredited college or university, including 12 hours in child development, child psychology, or early childhood education;

- have (1) been awarded the child development associates credential by the Child Development Associate Consortium (a national agency affiliated with the Association for Education of Young Children) or a similar credential approved by the

Sponsored by the Michigan Nonprofit Association and the Council of Michigan Foundations

MDCIS and (2) completed 12 hours of training in child development, child psychology, or early-childhood education; or

■ have been certified by a Montessori Teachers Institute.

Caregivers (those providing direct care, supervision, and guidance) must be

■ aged 17 and have completed at least one year of a vocational-occupational child-care training program approved by the state Department of Education, or

■ aged 18 or older (no pre-service or in-service training required).

Prior to licensing, the program director is checked for criminal convictions and substantiated abuse and neglect reports, and the premises are examined by a licensing consultant, fire inspector, and health department sanitarian. Having met all requirements, centers are issued a six-month provisional license and, if rule compliance is maintained, a two-year license thereafter; centers are re-inspected annually. Once in operation, the center must adhere to licensing rules on such matters as the caregiver-to-children ratio (see Exhibit 1), acceptable discipline techniques, number and nutritional content of meals and snacks, and type of equipment present.

Group and Family Daycare Homes

There are more than 3,300 group daycare homes and 13,000 family daycare homes in Michigan; some of the differences may be seen in Exhibit 2.

Group homes must be licensed by the state. The licensee and all adults living in the household undergo a check for criminal convictions and substantiated abuse and neglect, and the premises are inspected. The caregiver must certify that s/he meets state regulations, submit three personal references, provide health screening results, and test negative for tuberculosis. Licensees need not meet minimal education standards but must be aged 18 or older. If an aide is employed, which must be the case if more than six children are being cared for, s/he must be aged at least 14. The ratio of staff to children (including any of the staff's own who are aged under 7) shall be not less than 1:6 (i.e., there shall be no fewer than one staff member for every six children). No more than four children aged under 30 months and no more than two aged under 18 months may be cared for by a single caregiver.

Family homes need only be registered with the MDCIS. The caregiver must certify that s/he meets state regulations, submit three personal references, provide health screening results, test negative for tuberculosis, participate in orientation, and pass protective-services and crimi-

EXHIBIT 1. Required Minimum Staff-to-Children Ratio, Michigan Child-Care Centers, 2002

Age Group	Ratio of Staff to Children
Infants (up to 30 months)	1:4
2½ through 3 years	1:8
3 through 4 years	1:10
4 through 5 years	1:12
6 through 12 years	1:20
13 through 17 years	1:30
Mixed ages	Ratio required for youngest in group

SOURCE: Michigan Department of Consumer and Industry Services, Division of Child Daycare Licensing.

nal-record clearances. The home is visited by a MDCIS licensing consultant during the first 90 days of certification. Registration is valid for three years and a licensing visit is not required for renewal.

In-Home Care

Another child-care option is an in-home caregiver—e.g., nanny, babysitter, grandparent, friend, neighbor—who cares for the child in either the child's home or the caregiver's home. State regulation of these informal arrangements is not required unless care is provided for an unrelated minor for more than four weeks during a calendar year—in this case, the caregiving arrangement is supposed to be registered or licensed. In-home caregivers who are eligible for state reimbursement because they care for children of low-income families must enroll with the FIA. (According to the FIA, about 60 percent of subsidized care is in-home care.) Since these arrangements are informal, it is difficult to know precisely how

EXHIBIT 2. Differences between Group and Family Daycare Homes for Children, Michigan, 2002

Regulation	Group Home	Family Home
Maximum number of children	12	6
Number of adults required	2	1
State certification requirement	Licensure	Registration
Type of building	Private residence	Private residence

SOURCE: Michigan Department of Consumer and Industry Services, Division of Child Daycare Licensing.

Sponsored by the Michigan Nonprofit Association and the Council of Michigan Foundations

many children receive such care. The Urban Institute reported in 2000 that 40 percent of Michigan children in working families having income up to twice the federal poverty level (the 2002 poverty level is $17,650 for a family of four) are cared for by relatives; there are no figures for in-home care by others.

Before- and After-School Programs
Before/after-school care programs are subject to the same licensing rules as child-care centers, except that the director may substitute 12 credit hours in elementary or physical education or recreation for the early-childhood–related courses required of a child-center director. For children aged 6–12, the staff-to-child ratio may be not less than 1:20; for children aged 13–17, 1:30. Fire safety provisions do not apply if the program is in a public school building and the school provides documentation of compliance with safety requirements for its current, regular school-day programs.

Financing Assistance
Child care is a major family expense. The average cost for daycare and before/after-school care is $5,700 per child per year, although families may pay $10,000 or more for high-quality center-based or in-home care.

The Urban Institute finds that nationally, about half of all working families with children aged under 13 pay almost $1 of every $10 that they earn for child care. Low-income families spend a much higher proportion of their earnings: 40 percent spend an average of $1 of every $6 earned. In 1999 a Detroit family with an annual income of $15,000 and one preschool child would have spent about one-third of its total monthly income on child care.

State and federal government help by providing subsidies to low-income families (states provide them directly, while the federal government does so through block grants to the states) and by permitting tax credits or deductions to be taken by individuals and businesses.

State
In fiscal year 2000–01, the FIA paid $436 million for child care for an average of 118,700 children a month—about $570 per child. The state's share of these funds was less than half; the federal government paid the rest. The governor's FY 2002–03 budget recommendations include an increase of $23 million (includes the federal match), for child-care assistance for low-income families.

The School Readiness Program, administered by the Michigan Department of Education, had $85.5 million in FY 2000–01 for preschool programs (center- or home-based). Most programs run 2½–3½ hours, four days a week.

Twenty-seven states have tax credits or deductions for child-care expenses, and 10 have made the tax credit refundable so that the lowest-income families can benefit even when they owe no taxes. Michigan has neither a state tax credit nor deduction for child-care costs.

Federal
The Child Care and Development Block Grant, funded at $4.8 billion in FY 2001–02, provides matching funds to states to subsidize child care for families with income below 85 percent of the state median income.

The Title XX/Social Services Block Grant, funded at $1.7 billion for FY 2001–02, may be used to support child care, and Michigan's estimated allocation was $60 million.

The Child and Adult Care Food Program ($45 million for Michigan in FY 2001–02) subsidizes nutritious meals and snacks for children up to age 12 who are enrolled in child-care centers, family and group daycare homes, and before/after-school care programs. There is no minimum income requirement for this subsidy. The program, which may fund only state-regulated programs, also is an incentive for providers to become licensed/regulated.

The federal child tax credit (CTC), combined with the earned income tax credit (EITC), is a major source of income support for working families with children. Starting in tax year 2002, the $500 per child CTC will increase incrementally to $1,000 in tax year 2010. For the first time, the CTC is partially refundable for families with income over $10,000, making the credit helpful to lower-income families who otherwise would not qualify. The Congressional Joint Committee on Taxation estimates that tax law reforms of CTC and EITC will provide an additional $12 billion annually in assistance to low-income families.

Federal law permits employers to offer a Dependent Care Assistance Plan through which the employer may deduct up to $5,000 from an employee's gross salary and put it into a nontaxable spending account for child care. Social Security, federal, state, and local taxes thus are reduced for both employee and employer, and the employee can pay for child care with tax-fee dollars. The employer also may contribute to the account. (A family may not use both this plan and the child tax credit in the same year.)

Employers may receive certain other federal tax breaks if they provide or subsidize employees' child care; such programs are becoming more common but still are offered in only a few workplaces.

Sponsored by the Michigan Nonprofit Association and the Council of Michigan Foundations

Despite large increases in federal child-care assistance, there are insufficient state and federal funds to help all children from low-income families: Nine of every 10 low-income children who are eligible do not benefit from child-care financial assistance.

Availability and Quality of Care

Not only do many families have difficulty paying for child care, but they also may have trouble finding good care.

Availability

The Michigan Community Coordinated Child Care (4C) Association reports that currently, there are enough licensed daycare slots to accommodate only 80 percent of Michigan children who need it. The shortage of licensed care is especially acute for infants and toddlers, school-aged children, those with special needs, and those requiring odd-hour care because their parents work at more than one job or have an odd-hour shift. Those who work non-regular hours have limited access to centers and regulated family daycare. Welfare work requirements have created significant demand for odd-hour child care, leading many programs to add extended hours and other on-site services such as immunizations.

Before/after-school programs are among the least available to families. The National Institute on Out-of-School Time says there are about 8 million children aged 5–14 that spend part of the day without adult supervision (1999). Unsupervised time is linked to increased juvenile crime, drug use, and poor academic performance. A national survey of police chiefs finds that 86 percent believe that expanding after-school and educational child-care programs would greatly reduce juvenile crime. Michigan is considering the use of Temporary Assistance to Needy Families funding for after-school programs.

Quality

Child-care quality is higher when the following conditions exist: Adult-to-child ratios are high, teachers/caregivers have specialized training in child development, and staff is competitively compensated (Outcomes Study, University of North Carolina).

National studies measuring quality of child care consistently find that only 10 percent of child-care settings offer high-quality programs. Of the remainder, 10–20 percent fall below "adequate," and 70 percent provide only mediocre care. Even basic safety is a problem: In 1998 the national Consumer Product Safety Commission found that two-thirds of settings they visited had at least one safety hazard—for example, stairs without safety gates or soft bedding in cribs.

New research shows that high-quality child care positively affects later school achievement. The North Carolina study following children who now are in second grade finds that those who had high-quality child-care experiences are performing better in measures of both cognitive (math and language) and social (interaction with peers and teachers) skills. Similarly, a Wellesley College study finds that older children who attend good before/after-school programs have better attendance and higher grades than their peers who are not in the programs.

DISCUSSION

For years, the debate about child care was mostly about the government's role in funding and regulating programs and services. Now child care is seen as a critical factor in many families' well-being, an important support for families trying to become self-sufficient, a strong influence on school readiness for children, and a factor in academic achievement and also in preventing juvenile delinquency. Today's debate is about affordability of care, quality of care, and compensation for care providers, and the three issues are interrelated.

In 1994 the Frey, Skillman, and W.K. Kellogg foundations launched the Joining Forces Child Care Initiative in nine Michigan communities. The five-year project found that while communities are developing strategies to improve child care for low-income families, state and federal action also is needed to address the affordability, quality, and compensation issues. From the initiative's findings came recommendations to

- expand subsidy eligibility to include families with income up to 200 percent of the federal poverty level;

- raise the subsidy to reflect current market rates;

- encourage more providers to accept child-care subsidies by reducing paperwork and making timely payments;

- improve public awareness and subsidy programs and the ease with which they may be used;

- support training and better wages for child-care providers;

- base subsidies on staff training and experience; and

- increase the number of state child-care licensing consultants.

Affordability

Some advocates want government to play a substantial role in subsidizing daycare for *all* families, contending that "universal" subsidization—whether through direct assistance or employee/employer tax breaks—is necessary to ensure that all families who need it can afford good care for their children. Opponents argue that subsidized child care encourages both parents to work even when additional income is not necessary for the family's financial well-being, thus many children end up in daycare instead of at home. Others say that government should not have the primary responsibility for assuring that child care is affordable—rather, religious, charitable, and community-based organizations can do a better job of helping families get the child-care services they need.

The perspective on government's role has shifted dramatically since 1996 as welfare reform has unfolded, particularly the work requirements, which have led to more demand for child care. Policymakers have become more willing to invest in child care as a way to help people move from welfare to work. For example, Michigan, since establishing its Family Independence Program—which implemented the Temporary Assistance for Needy Families (TANF), the federal welfare-reform block-grant program—has more than doubled the amount spent for child care for low-income families: the figure went from $185 million in FY 1996–97 to $436 million in FY 2000–01. From 1997 to 1999, a study of 16 states found a median increase in state child-care spending of 78 percent. The public supports this: A large majority of Americans (86 percent) say that child-care support should be available to all low-income families so that parents may work (W.K. Kellogg Foundation poll, 1999).

Quality

On the one hand, some polls show that many families of all income levels worry about the quality of child care: For example, more than half of respondents in a *Parents Magazine* survey say they worry every week about whether their children are getting what they need in child care. On the other hand, in several surveys, parents say they are satisfied with their current child-care arrangement. (Some experts believe that many "satisfied" responses reflect parents' *need* to be satisfied because they have few or no alternatives, thus they define "satisfactory" in a way that they otherwise might not.)

While some believe that regulation is sufficient to assure quality, others say that state licensing/registration standards offer only basic health and safety protections and set the minimum number of caregivers per child but do little to address early learning. Many child-care advocates believe that federal and state government should more actively regulate child-care settings and use criteria that assess the program offered. Currently, the federal government has very little to do with setting health, safety, and quality standards, and the states require only that child-

care providers meet minimal standards. Although Michigan requires pre-service/in-service training for some who are involved in child care, it is one of only four states where none is required for center-based, non-administrative caregivers 18 and older. Those opposed to stricter or expanded regulation argue that more bureaucracy will further increase costs, draining resources that could be used to improve quality and making it ever more difficult for families to afford high-quality care.

Provider Compensation

Provider compensation affects both child-care affordability and quality. Nationally, the average annual salary of child-care professionals was $15,430 in 2000, and preschool teachers who work with children aged 3–5 make about half the salary of an elementary school teacher. Some say that raising wages will make child care less affordable and reduce access. Others say that the low wages provide little incentive for well-qualified people to enter the field and lead to high turnover—about 30 percent annually, among the highest in any profession—and these factors negatively affect the quality of child care. Programs such as TEACH (Teacher Education and Compensation Helps), implemented in Michigan in 2001, help to improve wages and reduce turnover. Many call on government to do more.

While many think there is adequate government support for child care, others see the need for more public investment to benefit both children and society as a whole, with child care as an essential part of a system of early-childhood education and care to which all families have access.

See also Children's Early Education and Care; K–12 Quality and Testing; Welfare Reform: TANF Reauthorization; Youth at Risk.

Research on this policy topic was made possible by a grant from The Skillman Foundation.

FOR ADDITIONAL INFORMATION

Children's Defense Fund
122 C Street, N.W.
Washington, DC 20001
(202) 628-8787
(202) 662-3150 FAX
www.childrensdefense.org

Division of Child Daycare Licensing
Bureau of Regulatory Services
Michigan Department of Consumer and Industry Services
7109 West Saginaw
P.O. Box 30650
Lansing, MI 48909
(517) 335-8300
(517) 335-6121 FAX
www.michigan.gov/cis

Families and Work Institute
330 7th Avenue
New York, New York 10001
(212) 465-2044
www.familiesandwork.org

Michigan 4C Association
2875 Northwind Drive, Suite 200
East Lansing, MI 48823
(517) 351-4171
(517) 351-0157 FAX
www.mi4c.org

Michigan Association for Education of Young Children
4572 South Hagadorn, Suite 1D
East Lansing, MI 48823
(800) 336-6424
(517) 336-9700
(517) 336-9790 FAX
www.miaeyc.org

Michigan Ready to Succeed Partnership
600 West St. Joseph, Suite 10
Lansing, Michigan 48933
(517) 484-4954
(517) 484-6549
www.readytosucceed.org

"Child Care Arrangements for Children Under Five: Variation Across States"
Assessing the New Federalism, The Urban Institute, Washington (March 2000)

"Child Care Expenses of America's Families"
Assessing the New Federalism, The Urban Institute, Washington (2000)

"Child Care in Michigan: A Short Report on Subsidies, Affordability, and Supply"
Assessing the New Federalism, Washington (1999)

The Child Tax Credit
Making Wages Work (2001)

Child Care Teachers Wages
National Women's Law Center, Washington (2001)

The Children of the Cost, Quality and Outcomes Study Go to School
University of North Carolina (1999)

Fact Sheet on School-Age Children's Out-of-School Time
National Institute on Out-of-School Time, Center for Research on Women, Wellesley College (2001)

From Neurons to Neighborhoods: The Science of Early Childhood Development
National Research Council and Institute of Medicine, Washington (2000)

Making Care Less Taxing: Improving State Child and Dependent Care Tax Provisions
National Women's Law Center, Washington (1998)

Preschool for All: Investing in a Productive and Just Society
Committee for Economic Development, New York and Washington (2002)

"Quality Counts 2002: Starting Early"
Education Week, Washington (January 10, 2002)

Yearbook 2001: The State of America's Children
Children's Defense Fund, Washington (2001)

Child Support

BACKGROUND

Child-support issues have become increasingly important in recent years, driven by dramatic changes in American family life, particularly with regard to children who are born out wedlock or whose parents divorce.

■ In 1960 about 4 percent of all U.S. children were born out of wedlock; the figure is closer to 33 percent today.

■ In Michigan the annual number of divorces has more than doubled since 1960; in 2000 the parents of approximately 37,000 Michigan children under age 18 were divorced.

Children born out of wedlock or whose parents divorce can face numerous economic and psychological hardships. Those who live only with their father are three times more likely to live in poverty than are children living with two parents; those living only with their mother are seven times more likely. Because children living in single-parent households frequently receive public assistance, policymakers have become increasingly concerned about the link between welfare and child-support enforcement.

A court determines whether custody of children of a divorce is granted to the mother, father, both (joint custody), or a third party. Granting sole custody to the mother is by far the most common arrangement. Michigan Department of Community Health statistics show that of nearly 19,900 court cases in which custody was awarded in 2000, mothers became the sole custodial parent in about 13,000 cases (almost 66 percent). Joint custody was awarded in about 22 percent of cases, and the father received sole custody in 11 percent. In a few instances, custody was awarded to a third party. The noncustodial parent typically incurs a legal obligation to help support the child(ren) financially.

In 1986, to increase uniformity and predictability of child support statewide, Michigan adopted a formula identifying the factors to be considered in setting awards: the child's needs, both parents' resources, and child-care and health-care costs. The state formula permits use of "imputed" income to set the support level—that is, the court may find that the noncustodial parent has the ability to earn a certain amount, even if s/he currently is not earning at that level. The formula also recognizes cases of "shared economic responsibility" (SER)—that is, the noncustodial parent has custody of a child for 128 or more overnight visits annually—and allows support payments to be reduced because the noncustodial parent is directly contributing to care.

Efforts to force noncustodial parents to pay their child support have become much more aggressive and successful in recent years. Nevertheless, the total arrearage in Michigan—the amount owed but not paid—exceeds $7 billion.

Michigan's Child-Support System

Michigan, like other states, has two child-support enforcement systems—one private and one public. The private system most often is used by parents who are financially stable and prefer to manage child support without government involvement. The public system, the subject of this piece, involves a partnership between the judicial and the executive branches of government that acts on behalf of the child.

GLOSSARY

Custodial parent
The parent awarded physical custody of a minor child and therefore responsible for day-to-day decisions affecting the child.

Child Support Enforcement System (CSES)
The computerized case-management system required of each state by the federal Family Support Act of 1988 to streamline the administration of state child-support programs.

Fragile family
Unmarried parents raising a child together; called "family" because children are being raised jointly and "fragile" because of the high risk of poverty and instability.

Imputed income
The amount a person is able to earn, even if s/he currently is not earning at that level.

Noncustodial parent
The parent who does not have custody of the child and is not responsible for day-to-day decisions affecting the child's well-being. A noncustodial parent may have rights to visit the child or have the child with him/her for periods of time ("visitation" rights and "parenting time") as well as a legal obligation to pay child support.

Shared economic responsibility (SER)
The circumstance in which a noncustodial parent has a child with him/her frequently enough (at least 128 overnights annually) to be considered directly contributing to the child's care.

Sponsored by the Michigan Nonprofit Association and the Council of Michigan Foundations

The foundation for the public system was laid in 1917 with the establishment of Friend of the Court (FOC) offices within the circuit courts of all 83 counties. Currently, the FOCs have a number of responsibilities, but two predominate: (1) They collect individual child-support payments (that is, payments made directly by the parent as opposed to payments withheld from wages) and distribute court-ordered child-support payments, and (2) they enforce court-ordered custody, parenting time, and financial support. By 2003 the payments will be collected and distributed by the Michigan State Disbursement Unit (MiSDU), as discussed below.

In the early 1970s, Congress recognized that the child-support system across the country was failing many low-income parents and added Title IV-D to the Social Security Act. At that point, child support became a federal as well as a state responsibility. Title IV-D required every state to establish a child-support agency that provides services to low-income families as well as others for a very small or no fee. Michigan's designated Title IV-D agency is the Office of Child Support (OCS), in the Michigan Family Independence Agency. The OCS retains fiscal and policy control of the Michigan child-support system and its field staff provides intake and case preparation in 128 offices statewide. The FOCs and local prosecutors perform legal and enforcement work under contract to the OCS.

Federal and State Reforms

In the 30 years since Title IV-D was created, the federal government steadily has increased its role in child-support enforcement, and many of Michigan's recent reforms respond to federal changes. Two federal laws, the Family Support Act of 1988 and the Personal Responsibility and Work Opportunity Reconciliation Act (PRWORA) of 1996, are particularly significant.

The Family Support Act required each state to establish a computerized case-management system—the Child Support Enforcement System (CSES)—by 1997. Only 17 states met the original deadline, and Michigan was not among them. As of the end of FY 1999–2000, Michigan was among only three states that still did not have a federally certified CSES, and the accrued penalties—in the form of escalating reductions in federal grants to the state child-support program—were mounting: The Michigan Senate Fiscal Agency (SFA) calculates that Michigan originally incurred nearly $69 million in penalties. The OCS notes that $35 million was recaptured as the state moved toward compliance.

The state offset the federal penalties with supplemental appropriations and General Fund transfers to child-support programming, thus, at first, child-support program-

ming was not greatly affected. But the SFA believes a failure in FY 2000–01 to complete CSES implementation would have led to an additional $50 million in penalties and severe program impacts. As of the end of FY 2000–01, Michigan does have a version of the CSES operational and ready for federal inspection. While state officials expect certification to be forthcoming, it is not certain, and the child-support budget will be precarious as long as additional penalties are possible.

PRWORA is the main vehicle of national welfare reform. While public attention focused mainly on its welfare-to-work requirements, most of the language in the new law deals with child-support enforcement. The legislation reflects the belief that children are less likely to need welfare when their parents meet legal obligations to support them. Under PRWORA, welfare recipients must turn over their child-support payments to the state and cooperate with efforts to establish a child's paternity. The law also created new child-support enforcement tools, including a (1) national "new hire" reporting system that makes it easier to locate absent parents and enforce support orders and (2) license-revocation capability that allows states to revoke professional, driver, and recreation (e.g., hunting and fishing) licenses when support is not paid.

A number of Michigan's recent policy initiatives anticipate or respond to PRWORA mandates and include the following:

■ An in-hospital paternity program that establishes responsibility for child support and gives the child inheritance rights, access to the father's medical history and insurance (if he has it), and other benefits

■ The "Fatherhood Initiative," begun in partnership with the Detroit Lions to encourage men to take a more active role in their children's lives

■ The Uniform Interstate Family Support Act, which simplifies managing interstate child-support cases

PRWORA also mandated major changes in the way states collect money. Under its provisions, states are allowed to establish Financial Institutions Data Match programs that provide access to bank and other financial data for the purpose of locating parents and enforcing child-support orders. The act also required creation of a centralized collections unit—in Michigan, the Michigan State Disbursement Unit.

Collection and Disbursement

The FOCs still are the enforcement agency of record and, therefore, the legal collector of support. Their role is greatly changed, however, by creation of MiSDU, which, by 2003,

Sponsored by the Michigan Nonprofit Association and the Council of Michigan Foundations

will collect and disburse all payments. Currently, individual payments—that is, those made by unemployed or self-employed parents—still are collected by the FOCs. But child-support payments withheld from employee wages (more than 70 percent of the total collected) now go directly from employers to the MiSDU. The MiSDU eventually will disburse as well as collect payments, but for now it sends payment authorization to the local FOC offices, which print and mail checks to the recipients.

In FY 2000–01 the state system collected $1.5 billion in child support, approximately 4 percent more than in the prior year and roughly 52 percent more than in FY 1994–95 (see the exhibit).

Much of the increase is in response to the more aggressive collection mandates required by PRWORA—especially through the Financial Institutions Data Match program. Two additional facts about state child-support collections are important because of their public policy implications:

- There often is a large gap between the amount in child-support payments that the state takes in during any given time period and the amount it pays out. At the conclusion of the 4th quarter of FY 2001, the state had on hand approximately $44 million more than it had paid out.

- The current arrearage—the amount owed by parents but not collected—is enormous: according to OCS

officials, more than $7 billion when the accumulating 8 percent interest is included.

Current Michigan Initiatives

At this writing, the Michigan House of Representatives is considering legislation that would greatly affect state child-support policy. The proposed bills would

- commit the state to a more aggressive effort to locate children and families for whom support payments have been made but not distributed (HB 4918);

- amend the Child Custody Act to create a presumption—rebuttable only by clear and convincing evidence that one parent is unfit—that a child's best interest is served by joint custody arrangements (HB 4664); and

- establish a broadly empowered Marriage and Fatherhood Commission in the state Legislative Council (HB 5545).

DISCUSSION

Many observers are dismayed at the loss of millions in federal dollars due to problems with the Child Support Enforcement System. Although money from other sources prevented wholesale erosion of child-support programs, the funds had to come from other programs. State officials contend that Michigan's decentralized system was largely to blame: local counties were able, in effect, to veto the establishment of the CSES system statewide. Critics, however, believe state officials bear responsibility too and claim that it cost far more money to implement the CSES in Michigan than in any other state (the latter is vigorously disputed by the OCS).

Debate on HB 4918, which would affect how the state uses the child-support money it collects but does not distribute, promises to be contentious. State officials argue that although technically accurate, it is misleading to claim that the gap between collected and distributed funds runs to tens of millions of dollars. The key distinction, they say, is between *undistributed* and *undistributable* funds. Money may not be distributed immediately for a variety of technical and legal reasons, but they argue that only about $700,000 actually is undistributable (because the custodial parent, to whom the money is to be directed, cannot be found). Supporters of the bill are skeptical of this claim and insist that the state must do a better job of finding custodial parents. At the very least, they say, undistributable funds should be returned to the noncustodial parents who paid them—not kept by the state.

Michigan Child-Support Collections, FYs 1995–2001 ($ billions)

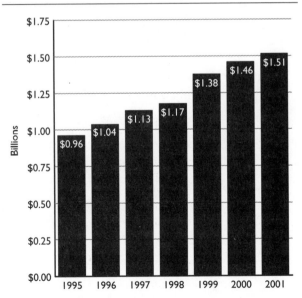

SOURCE: Michigan Family Independence Agency, Office of Child Support.

Sponsored by the Michigan Nonprofit Association and the Council of Michigan Foundations

House Bill 4664, to make joint custody the "default" arrangement, also is controversial. Organizations such as Dads of Michigan, which is dedicated to rectifying what it perceives as a systemic bias against fathers in divorce and child-support cases, support the bill. The organization argues that children are better off in joint-custody situations and also that the law would make the shared economic responsibility formula available to many more parents than use it now. The Association for Children for Enforcement of Support (ACES) takes a different view. While it generally supports joint custody, ACES opposes the presumption of joint custody unless one parent is demonstrated to be unfit. In its view, custody hearings ought to hinge on what is best for children, not on parental fitness or unfitness. Although the State Bar of Michigan has not commented directly on this legislation, members of its Family Law Section are sufficiently concerned about inequities in the use of the SER formula to appoint an *ad hoc* subcommittee to study the issue.

As so often has been the case, federal developments may affect state policy. Key federal welfare statutes are up for reauthorization in 2002, and lawmakers on both sides of the aisle express concern for the so-called fragile families—that is, arrangements in which children's unmarried natural parents, very often poor, are working together to raise them. Studies suggest that current welfare policy may create economic incentives for such couples to remain unmarried. The *New York Times* reports emerging bipartisan agreement that more should be done to create economic incentives that encourage marriage whenever possible or, at a minimum, the active involvement of both natural parents in childrearing.

The problem of the accumulating arrearage—in Michigan and elsewhere—is immense and apparently without solution for the moment. Simply "forgiving" delinquent payers would send the wrong message to parents who have conscientiously met their child-support obligations all along, but the fact is that the debt burden for some parents is now so high that they literally can never repay.

See also Welfare Reform: TANF Reauthorization; Youth at Risk.

Research on this policy topic was made possible by a grant from The Skillman Foundation.

FOR ADDITIONAL INFORMATION

Association for Children for Enforcement of Support
2260 Upton Road
Toledo, Ohio 43606
(800) 524-3206 (Ann Arbor Office)
www.childsupport-aces.org

Dads of Michigan
2677 West 12 Mile Road
Southfield, MI 48034
(888) 892-3237
(248) 559-3237
(248) 355-2511 FAX
www.dadsofmichigan.org

Family Law Section
State Bar of Michigan
306 Townsend Street
Lansing, MI 48933
(800) 968-1442
(517) 372-9030
(517) 482-6248 FAX
www.michbar.org

Office of Child Support
Michigan Family Independence Agency
Grand Tower, Suite 1215
235 South Grand Avenue
P.O. Box 30037
Lansing, MI 48909
(517) 373-7570
www.michigan.gov/fia

The Urban Institute
2100 M Street N.W.
Washington, DC 20037
(202) 833-7200
(202) 331-9747 FAX
www.urban.org

Children's Early Education and Care

BACKGROUND

Research in the last two decades confirms that early childhood, the period from birth to age five, is critically important in brain development. Later experiences also can influence one's brain capacity but in the early years, particular types of activities are necessary for certain essential aspects of brain growth. In early childhood there are several remarkably brief periods of opportunity that lay the foundation for emotional control, mathematical and language abilities, and the capacity to form social attachments. When these periods end, developing the capacity for learning in these areas becomes more difficult.

The brain grows not by adding new cells but rather by generating new connections among the cells that are present at birth. These new connections are shaped by what a child experiences: physical touch and comfort, nutrition, language, and play, among others. The good news is that most parents intuitively talk and play with young children in ways that foster their child's development.

The bad news is that neglect, stress, and trauma also affect brain development. Such experiences compromise development by affecting how the brain releases and modulates stress hormones, lowering the threshold at which one's brain activates fear and anxiety. Repeated exposure to stress usually programs a child's brain to expect and seek similar situations. Chronic stress and neglect can create a constant state of anxiety and anger that becomes a permanent trait in a child, which leads to many learning and behavior problems. Thus, early-childhood education and care has implications not only for parenting and the education field but also for the fields of health, mental health, law enforcement, and others.

Early-Intervention Research

Research is generating information about the experiences and types of care and early intervention (efforts to promote healthy development) that help children and benefit society.

- A University of North Carolina study (1999) that followed a group of children from preschool to second grade finds that the better the care center that a child attended, the better were his/her language and math skills, classroom behavior, and social skills, both in preschool and elementary school.

- The longest and most extensive evaluation of an early-childhood program is the High/Scope Perry Preschool Program (Ypsilanti). High/Scope has been following a group of individuals who had attended the preschool program when they were aged three and four. At age 27, they have higher income, fewer arrests, and less welfare participation than do members of a control group that did not participate in the program. Beyond the direct benefits to the children, every dollar invested in the program returned $7.16 to the public in reduced costs of crime, welfare, and remedial education (1993 data).

- The Chicago Longitudinal Study follows the education and social development of more than 1,500 low-income children born in 1980 who were served by the Chicago Child-Parent Center. At age 21 the participants, when compared to a peer

Sponsored by the Michigan Nonprofit Association and the Council of Michigan Foundations

group who did not receive the center's services, have a 29 percent higher rate of high-school completion, a 42 percent lower rate of juvenile arrest for violent offenses, 41 percent fewer special-education placements, and 51 percent fewer allegations of child abuse and neglect. Every dollar invested in the program returned $7.10 to the public in reduced costs of crime, welfare, and remedial education (2001 data).

■ The Michigan Department of Education (MDE) reports that children at risk of school failure who participate in the Michigan School Readiness Program are better prepared when they enter school and after five years are continuing to do better than at-risk children who do not. They score higher on the reading and math tests of the Michigan Educational Assessment Program than their classmates of similar background who were not in the readiness program, and 35 percent fewer need to repeat a grade, saving the state an estimated $11 million a year (2002 data).

Brain research shows that the young children warranting the greatest concern are those who (1) fail to get adequate nutrition; (2) do not receive physical, emotional, and intellectual stimulation; and (3) are emotionally or physically neglected or abused. Fortunately, research also demonstrates that children have a remarkable capacity to recover from the devastating effects of early deprivation and maltreatment if a nurturing environment is provided as early as possible.

Public Attention
Newsweek's 1997 special edition on early-childhood development became the most widely distributed issue in the magazine's history, translated into Japanese, Korean, and Russian and becoming the first foreign-language edition of an American magazine to appear in China. The magazine described the once-unknown link between experience and brain development, explaining that experiences stimulate electrical activity in a child's brain, which in turn "wires" the brain's circuitry to establish the structures of thought and emotion. Even vision, long thought to be genetically "hard-wired," we now know depends on visual experiences between birth and 10 months.

In 2000 *Newsweek* published another special edition on young children, presenting the continuing breakthroughs in neuroscience and genetic research, particularly the strong influence that parenting has on a child's personality. This edition also notes the explosion of parenting information available on the World Wide Web.

Michigan Initiatives and Programs
In 1999 a number of Michigan leaders from fields outside of early-childhood education and care (ECEC) attended a summit funded primarily by the state and a number of Michigan-based foundations. Out of this grew the Michigan Ready to Succeed Partnership. The goal of the partnership is to have young children enter kindergarten "ready to succeed" in school and in life.

Outcomes of the partnership's efforts since 1999 include a parent survey to learn how young children currently receive early education and care, community forums across the state to engage the public and private sectors in the effort and generate strategies to shape public policy regarding early childhood, and a Web site presenting information to the public. In 2001 participants formed an umbrella organization, the Michigan Ready to Succeed Partnership, which created the state's first public-awareness campaign on early childhood, *Be their Hero from age Zero.*®

Michigan's FY 2000–01 budget contained significant new public investment in early childhood. The MDE, Family Independence Agency, and Michigan Department of Community Health budgets had new and expanded programs for families with young children.

■ The new All Students Achieve Program—Parent Involvement and Education (ASAP–PIE) received $45 million annually for three years to provide services that help families to get their children ready to succeed in school.

■ Full-day school-readiness programs for at-risk four-years-old received $25 million, up from $5 million.

■ Reading and literacy program funding received $50 million.

■ Secondary-prevention programs, which serve families with children aged 0–3 who are at risk of abuse or neglect, received $2 million.

■ Licensed daycare providers serving children aged 0–2 received a rate increase totaling $17 million.

■ T.E.A.C.H. (Teacher Education and Compensation Helps®) was established to (1) help child-care providers working in regulated early-childhood programs obtain additional education and (2) help the programs increase the compensation of providers who have engaged in continuing education.

At this writing, economic circumstances may put some of this funding at risk of being reduced or eliminated in the current state budget, but many observers expect early-childhood programs to receive increased public support in coming years.

DISCUSSION

We know more than ever about the benefits of high-quality early education and care, both for young children and for society. But knowing the benefits and making them accessible for all families are different sides of the coin.

Most people agree that experiences play a large part in how children develop in their earliest years, and the adults in a child's life determine greatly what those experiences will be. Yet there is disagreement about what, if anything, should be done to shape these experiences. These disagreements play out in how Michigan and the nation devise and fund early-childhood education and care programs.

Nationally, families provide half the financing for early-childhood education and care. Government, mostly state and local, provides 45 percent from a tangle of federal, state, and local sources. The private sector provides 5 percent (one percent from business and the balance from philanthropy).

In Michigan, payments by families to caregivers, teachers, and programs (which vary widely in quality, content, and relationship to public schools) account for the largest expenditure for early-childhood services: $741 million annually. The combined public and private investment in children aged five and under is less than one-third of what just the public investment is for school-aged children: the annual, per child averages are $2,200 and $7,200, respectively.

Bringing brain-development research into play in public policy is challenging. Some say that it must begin with recognizing the realities of life for today's families with young children: An ever-increasing number of parents rely on other caregivers so they can go to work. Almost half (46 percent) of Michigan children under age five spend time in the care of someone other than a parent. Of those children, 47 percent are in someone else's home, and 47 percent are in a child-care center, Head Start, preschool, nursery school, or school readiness or other enrichment program.

The new knowledge about children's brain development has narrowed the distinction between "child care" and "early education." This has created debate about whether to extend formal education to children under age five. Some policy leaders say that because so many young children spend considerable time with nonparent caregivers and the quality of young children's experiences so influences their future, attention should be given to all settings where children are found: with their family, with other caregivers, and in the community. Some experts say that changing ideas about education, work, and welfare have linked two previously separate objectives—meeting labor market needs (providing child care for working parents) and fostering child development (providing education). They say that programs that *care* for young children while their parents work also must *educate*. Child care, of necessity, involves both stimulating children's thinking and supporting their social, emotional, and motor development in a safe and nurturing place.

What is the best use of public funds in the early-childhood years? Some say that children most at risk (those who will begin kindergarten at a disadvantage because of poverty and other factors) should be the first priority. Others want to move toward *universal* access—that is, making good early-childhood education and care available to *all* families. Some question whether more public investment in early-childhood services will make a difference at all, doubting that current research provides a sufficient basis for changing public policy and making a significant investment. Others suggest that rather than funding early-childhood education programs, it would be more effective to (1) reduce poverty, a major risk for positive child development, with fiscal policies such as expanding the earned income tax credit, which gives parents more income or (2) make it easier for people to work part time so they may spend more time with their children.

Among those who advocate for more public investment in early-childhood education, the balance between federal and state funding is a key consideration. For public elementary and secondary education, states and localities pay 93 percent of the costs and parents pay nothing, but for early education and care, parents and the federal government, respectively, are the biggest funders. A recent proposal from some of the nation's leading executives in business and education (the Committee for Economic Development, New York and Washington, 2002) call for (1) both federal and state government to significantly increase their investment in early education and (2) universal preschool for which each family's share of the cost would be based on income.

Regardless of the advantages of having one's children in a good program, many families cannot afford it. Unfortunately, a good many are not aware that both subsidized programs and financial assistance are available. More important, a dearth of funding limits the number of children who can be served: Despite increases in federal and state funding for early-childhood programs and child care, only three children of every five who are eligible are enrolled in Head Start, the country's most extensive investment in educating young children, and federal child-care assistance covers only about one in eight eligible children.

Sponsored by the Michigan Nonprofit Association and the Council of Michigan Foundations

A growing number of people now believe that early-childhood education clearly is linked to school success, and they want schools to take the lead in assuring universal access. Others say the schools are unable or unwilling to take on another monumental task. The debate has gone to court: Recent rulings in Arkansas, New Jersey, and North Carolina have ordered public schools to add preschool programs for at-risk children. Cases are pending in at least five additional states.

Opinion polls reveal strong public support for improving access to good child care, good after-school programs, and paid parent leave (the latter enables new parents to stay at home with the baby for a certain length of time). In a 2000 poll, respondents were asked which, to them, is more important for government to do: (1) provide access to early-childhood programs such as Head Start and after-school programs or (2) cut taxes. Nearly 70 percent come down on the side of early-childhood programs—about the same percentage who believe that shoring up Social Security and Medicare is more important than cutting taxes.

See also Child Care; Youth at Risk.

Research on this policy topic was made possible by a grant from The Skillman Foundation.

FOR ADDITIONAL INFORMATION

Children's Defense Fund
122 C Street, N.W.
Washington, D.C. 20001
(202) 628-8787
(202) 662-3150 FAX
www.childrensdefense.org

Families and Work Institute
330 7th Avenue
New York, NY 10001
(212) 465-2044
www.familiesandwork.org

High/Scope Educational Research Foundation
600 North River Street
Ypsilanti, MI 48198
(734) 485-2000
www.highscope.org

Michigan Association for Education of Young Children
Beacon Place
4572 South Hagadorn Road
East Lansing, MI 48823
(800) 336-6424
(517) 336-9700 FAX
www.miaeyc.com

Michigan's Children
428 West Lenawee Street
Lansing, MI 48933
(800) 330-8674
(517) 485-3500
(517) 485-3650 FAX
www.michiganschildren.org

Michigan Ready to Succeed Partnership
600 West St. Joseph
Lansing, MI 47833
(517) 484-4954
(517) 484-6549
www.readytosucceed.org

"Age 21 Cost-Benefit Analysis of the Title I Chicago Child-Parent Center Program"
Arthur J. Reynolds, Chicago Longitudinal Study (2001)

"Building Children's Brains"
Joan Lessen-Firestone, *First Generation of the New Century: Ready to Learn, Ready for Life*, Michigan Ready to Succeed Partnership, Lansing (1999)

The Children of the Cost, Quality and Outcomes Study Go to School
University of North Carolina (1999)

"Effects Five Years Later: The Michigan School Readiness Program Evaluation through Age 10"
High/Scope Educational Research Foundation, Ypsilanti, Mich. (2002)

From Neurons to Neighborhoods: The Science of Early Childhood Development
National Research Council and Institute of Medicine, Washington (2000)

Investing in Our Children: What We Know and Don't Know about the Costs and Benefits of Early Childhood Interventions
RAND, Santa Monica (1998)

Preschool for All: Investing in a Productive and Just Society
Committee for Economic Development, New York and Washington (2002)

Civil Rights and Liberties

BACKGROUND

The basic function of civil rights legislation in the United States has been to protect minorities from the tyranny of discriminatory treatment by the majority. In general, the federal laws set minimum standards; states are free to set higher but not lower standards of inclusion.

The civil rights movement—the most publicized and political civil rights struggle of longest standing in the United States—concerned the status of the nation's black minority and resulted in federal legislation that improved the status of ethnic and religious minorities, women, and immigrants. The first federal civil rights law since Reconstruction was enacted in 1957 and established the Commission on Civil Rights in the U.S. Department of Justice. A 1964 federal statute—the Civil Rights Act—specifically outlaws race-based discrimination in public accommodations and by employers, unions, and voting registrars. It also applies to gender-based discrimination against women (women had won the right to vote in this country only 44 years earlier). The federal Indian Civil Rights Act of 1968 gives Native Americans access to the courts for restoration of rights to their ancestral lands and reparation for lost land and natural resources.

The Michigan Civil Rights Commission was formed in 1963, when guarantees against discrimination were added to the Michigan Constitution. Article V, section 29, mandates that the commission investigate discrimination against any person because of religion, race, color, or national origin, and "secure the equal protection of such civil rights without such discrimination." This is unique in the nation: Only in Michigan does a state agency have a *constitutional* (as opposed to legislative or regulatory) mandate to eliminate unlawful discrimination in nearly all aspects of public life.

The Michigan Department of Civil Rights (MDCR) was established by legislation in 1965 to provide the staff needed to implement the policies of the Civil Rights Commission. The department is authorized under the Elliott-Larsen Civil Rights Act (Public Act 453 of 1976, as amended) and the Persons with Disabilities Civil Rights Act (P.A. 220 of 1976, as amended) to receive and investigate complaints based on unlawful consideration of religion, race, color, national origin, sex, age, marital status, physical or mental disability, arrest record, or retaliation in the areas of employment, education, housing, public accommodation, or public service (government). In addition, complaints may be based on unlawful consideration of height, weight, and arrest record in employment matters as well as unlawful consideration of family status in housing matters.

Affirmative Action

The phrase "affirmative action" first was used in President Johnson's 1965 Executive Order 11246, requiring federal contractors to "take affirmative action to ensure that applicants are employed, and that employees are treated during employment, without regard to their race, creed, color, or national origin." An important Constitutional issue causing fairly continuous public controversy has been whether and to what degree public and private institutions may use affirmative action to help members of minority groups obtain jobs or schooling.

GLOSSARY

Affirmative action
A policy or program that seeks to ensure that all people have equal opportunity, as in education and employment.

Civil rights
The nonpolitical rights of a citizen, especially the rights of personal liberty guaranteed to U.S. citizens by the 13th and 14th amendments to the Constitution and by acts of Congress.

Civil union
Legal agreement granting recognition and relationship rights that mirror many of those granted through marriage.

Domestic partnership
A documented living arrangement in which same-sex and unmarried opposite-sex partners register as a couple in order to obtain such municipal or employer benefits as health insurance, library privileges, or housing eligibility.

Hate crime
A criminal act provoked by the actual or perceived race, color, national origin, ethnicity, gender, disability, or sexual orientation of the victim.

Racial profiling
Generally, the practice of using race or ethnicity as an indicator of criminality.

Sponsored by the Michigan Nonprofit Association and the Council of Michigan Foundations

Marriage/Union/Registration

Marriage

In the United States, marriage is a restricted institution in which only one man and one woman may be joined. There are 1,049 federal statutes governing benefits, rights, and privileges for such legally married couples, and every state has up to 350 similar laws. Currently, none of these laws provides protection for same-sex couples in domestic partnerships.

Same-sex marriage is not legal anywhere in the country, and about 35 states, including Michigan, have enacted defense-of-marriage acts (DOMAs) that ban it; six have similar legislation pending. The federal DOMA (1996) holds that marriage benefits are exclusively reserved for opposite-sex couples and permits states to ignore same-sex marriages sanctioned elsewhere.

The only place where gay and lesbian couples may marry and adopt with the full privileges enjoyed by heterosexual married couples is The Netherlands. Same-sex marriages were legal briefly, during 1996, in Hawaii, but Hawaiians passed a constitutional amendment prohibiting them.

Civil Union

DOMAs do not preclude a state from enacting laws covering a different type of relationship—typically called a civil union—for same-sex couples. A civil union formalizes a same-sex relationship and may grant to same-sex couples some or all of the state benefits previously granted only to married couples, but the more than 1,000 federal rights and privileges are withheld from civil-union couples. No current civil-union plan offers the broad responsibilities, benefits, and legal and social protections that marriage does. In Vermont, legislation established a civil-union system in 2000 that offers to the partners the rights, obligations, and benefits that the state gives to heterosexual married couples. California is considering such legislation.

Domestic Partnership

Another means by which gay, lesbian, or unmarried heterosexual couples may obtain some of the legal benefits offered by marriage is through domestic-partnership registration and affidavits. More than 100 municipalities nationwide, including Ann Arbor and East Lansing, offer such registration, allowing opposite- and same-sex couples to go on public record as a non-married couple. The primary benefit of registering is to document the relationship so as to establish eligibility for partner benefits from an employer or municipality. Some employers (e.g., Ford Motor Company, DaimlerChrysler, General Motors, IBM, Walt Disney, Northwest Airlines) offer domestic-partner benefits to their workers if they sign an affidavit that defines an economic relationship. Michigan State University, the University of Michigan, and Wayne State University also offer benefits to employees' domestic partners.

Hate Crimes

Congress defines a hate crime as one in which the defendant intentionally selects a victim because of his/her actual or perceived race, color, national origin, ethnicity, gender, disability, or sexual orientation. The federal Hate Crime Statistics Act of 1990 asks states and municipalities to voluntarily report all such crimes to the FBI. The federal Hate Crimes Sentencing Act of 1994 provides for tougher sentencing in federal courts when it is proved that the offense was a hate crime. In Michigan, the Ethnic Intimidation Act of 1988 added to the state penal code the crimes of physical contact, destruction of personal property, or the threat of either with malicious intent based on the victim's race, color, religion, gender, or national origin.

Racial Profiling

Although "racial profiling" is a relatively new term and does not yet have a single, universally accepted definition, it generally refers to the practice of using race or ethnicity as an indicator of criminality. The most familiar instance is what some have dubbed "driving while black," or DWB. Such profiling occurs when law-enforcement officers stop minority motorists for minor traffic violations, but the stop really is a pretext to search for drugs or other contraband in the vehicle or to harass the occupant(s). The most common context in which racial profiling occurs is traffic stops, but there are others, including

- airport checks and searches of people/luggage by airport security or drug enforcement officials;

- questioning and searching pedestrians in public places (usually in urban areas);

- immigration-status checks of people crossing national borders; and

- ID checks of bar or club patrons.

Sexual Harassment

Sexual harassment is a form of discrimination prohibited under federal law: Title VII of the federal Civil Rights Act of 1964 and the Violence Against Women Act of 1994. Court cases have sorted sexual harassment into two basic categories.

- *Quid pro quo* harassment occurs when the perpetrator makes an aspect of employment (hiring, promotion, retention, and so on) contingent on the victim's providing sexual favors.

- A *hostile work environment* is deemed to be the case when, as defined in a unanimous 1993 U.S. Supreme

Court opinion, there is a certain frequency and severity of discriminatory conduct, it is physically threatening (not a "mere offensive utterance"), and it unreasonably interferes with an employee's work performance.

Sexual-Orientation Discrimination

Starting in the 1960s, Congress passed a number of laws designed to eradicate discrimination and prohibit employers from basing employment decisions on stereotypes or assumptions about the ability, traits, or performance of individuals with a disability or of a certain sex, race, age, religion, or ethnic group, but no federal law prohibits discrimination on the basis of sexual orientation. Although Michigan is not among them, 21 states and the District of Columbia prohibit public-employment discrimination based on sexual orientation; 12 states and the District extend this protection to the private sector. In Michigan, employers are not prohibited from firing or refusing to hire or promote an employee based on a perception of the employee's sexual orientation.

DISCUSSION

Affirmative Action

Affirmative action was meant to redress a long history of racial and gender discrimination in the United States. In the past decade, however, the concept seems to incite, rather than ease, the nation's internal divisions. An increasingly assertive opposition movement argues that the battle to guarantee equal rights for all citizens has been fought and won—and that favoring members of one group over another goes against the American grain. Defenders of affirmative action say that the playing field is not yet level—that granting modest advantages to minorities and women is more than fair given the historic discrimination that benefited whites and men.

Currently, a particularly contentious issue is whether considering race in higher-education admission decisions may be used as a means to achieve student-body diversity. Race-based admissions policies, supported by the U.S. Supreme Court's landmark 1978 decision in *University of California v. Bakke*, have been under legal attack for a decade. Most recently, two lawsuits have been brought against the University of Michigan (UM) for using race as a factor in undergraduate and law school admission. In December 2000, the UM's undergraduate admissions policy was upheld, but four months later its law school admissions policy—which is only slightly different—was struck down. The two cases, consolidated for appeal, were heard in December 2001 by the 6th U.S. Circuit Court of Appeals, which had not ruled at this writing. Regardless of the outcome, the case is expected to go to the Supreme Court.

Anti-Terrorism Efforts

Immediately following the September 11, 2001, terrorist attacks, anti-terrorism legislation was introduced at the federal and state levels. The federal USA PATRIOT Act of 2001 was signed into law on October 26, 2001, and

- allows investigators to use roving wiretaps (following a suspect rather than tapping just a particular phone);

- gives the government the power to detain immigrants for up to seven days (increased from two days) if they are suspected of being involved with terrorists;

- triples the number of immigration and border-patrol agents along the 3,000-mile border with Canada;

- provides new tools to fight money laundering by terrorists;

- allows government agencies to more easily share information about suspects and track their communications; and

- increases penalties for terrorism-related crimes.

On the three-month anniversary of the terrorist attacks, the Michigan Legislature introduced the Michigan Anti-Terrorism Act, a package of legislation to fight terrorism, improve public safety, and strengthen the state's response to emergencies. The more controversial measures would increase law enforcement's authority to investigate—including use of wiretaps—terrorist threats. Most of the bills have been enacted (among the exceptions are the wiretap measures).

Civil rights organizations such as the American Civil Liberties Union (ACLU) of Michigan and the NAACP strongly opposed the USA PATRIOT Act because they believe it infringes on civil liberties. These organizations believe that the act undermines due process and point out that it gives law enforcement extraordinary new powers, including telephone and Internet surveillance, unchecked by meaningful judicial review. The organizations also have expressed serious reservations about the Michigan anti-terrorism measures, arguing that they raise questions about the Constitutional guarantees of the Sixth Amendment right to counsel for criminal suspects and the Fourth Amendment right to be free from unreasonable search and seizure. Editorials in the *Detroit Free Press* and *Detroit News* have commented that some of the state's efforts to address terrorism may be unnecessary due to the federal action that has been taken.

Sexual-Orientation Discrimination

The Employment Non-Discrimination Act (ENDA), which had been introduced in Congress in various forms in the four previous sessions, again was introduced in 2001.

Sponsored by the Michigan Nonprofit Association and the Council of Michigan Foundations

It would extend current discrimination protections to sexual orientation. Similar legislation in Michigan (HB 4661) would amend the Elliott-Larsen Civil Rights Act to define and include sexual orientation (perceived or actual orientation toward heterosexuality, homosexuality, or bisexuality) as a protected category.

Opponents, such as the Family Research Council, believe that such legislation would give homosexual and bisexuals "special rights," equate their orientation with heterosexuality as being "normal," criminalize free speech, threaten religious freedom, and encourage lawsuits that could bankrupt small businesses. Supporters, such as the Human Rights Campaign and the ACLU, contend that affording to all citizens basic employment protection from discrimination based on irrational prejudice is not a special right. They point to a 1999 Gallup study that reports that 83 percent of Americans believe that gay people should have equal job opportunities and that more than half of the Fortune 500 companies have passed nondiscrimination policies that include sexual orientation.

Hate Crimes

When the Michigan Ethnic Intimidation Act (EIA) of 1988 was introduced, it included a prohibition on hate crimes motivated by sexual orientation, but the language was removed before passage. In 1994 the governor directed the Civil Rights Commission and the Department of Civil Rights to establish the Bias Crime Response Task Force to study the issue. One of the group's recommendations was to amend the EIA to protect against crimes committed because of the victim's actual or perceived sexual orientation and change the act's name to the Bias Crime Act. HB 4662 would implement the task force's recommendation and also classify a hate crime as a felony, thereby adding up to two years of prison time or up to a $5,000 fine to a sentence. The bill is pending; if passed, Michigan would become the 26th state to adopt anti-gay hate-crime legislation.

Gay and lesbian rights entities, such as the Triangle Foundation and the Human Rights Campaign, believe HB 4662 is necessary because hate violence against gays and lesbians is increasing in Michigan, up 36 percent in 2000. They cite numerous studies conducted by the U.S. Department of Justice and others that show that gays and lesbians are the most frequent victims of bias-motivated criminal activity. Opponents say a crime is a crime and should be prosecuted without regard to—or special consideration for—the type of motivation or victim.

Racial Profiling

There is serious concern about racial profiling. In 1999 the Michigan Civil Rights Commission adopted a policy position encouraging the collection of racial data for the purpose of determining problem areas with respect to racial profiling.

Sensitivity to the issue has prompted many law-enforcement agencies and jurisdictions to take steps to address it. Since 2000, the Michigan State Police and some local police departments (including Washtenaw County, Ann Arbor, and Grand Rapids) have been voluntarily recording gender and race at primary traffic stops. Michigan State University began collecting racial data on all campus police stops in January 2001 as part of a 12-point plan to combat the racial profiling issue before it became a problem for the university; other steps include installing video cameras in squad cars, police-student partnerships that give students a glimpse of police life and vice versa, sensitivity training for officers, pamphlets informing students of their rights when stopped by officers, and public forums on the subject.

Anti–racial profiling legislation at the state and federal level is supported by many individual-rights supporters and by such organizations as the ACLU and NAACP. In Michigan, civil rights advocates believe that the practice is widespread, citing a statewide poll conducted in 2000 by EPIC/MRA for the Michigan State Police, which found that African-Americans are more likely than Caucasian drivers to be stopped and ticketed.

Several bills addressing racial profiling have been introduced in Congress in the last several years, but none has been enacted. In terms of pending state action, HB 4927 would create the Michigan Racial Profiling and Report Statistics Act, to define and prohibit racial profiling and provide for monitoring and investigating police agencies' stop-and-search patterns. The bill also would require police to report the race of drivers in every traffic stop for at least three years and require local police departments to provide racial-sensitivity training as well as retraining for officers guilty of racial profiling. Several law-enforcement organizations denounce racial profiling, but they do not support mandated data collection on motorist stops; they express concern about how the data are interpreted and by whom, pointing out that there is no proven, empirical way to analyze the data and, therefore, misinterpretation may result.

Many organizations representing law-enforcement officers (e.g., the National Association of Police Organizations, International Association of Chiefs of Police, Michigan Association of Chiefs of Police) oppose such actions as pulling over an automobile, searching personal property, or detaining an individual solely on the basis of his/her race, ethnicity, gender, or age. Nevertheless, many in and outside the law-enforcement community believe that certain racial profiling can be lawfully used as a statistical device in preventing crimes and apprehending criminals. They cite court opinions finding, for example, that it is legitimate to consider race or ethnic background as part of a profile in airport-security measures. Criminal justice experts say that law-enforcement officers always have and always will rely in part on profiles to identify criminals, so rather than deny that racial (and other) profiling exists, it would be more constructive to accept its usefulness and inevitability and codify when and how it may be used.

See also Crime and Corrections; Emergency Preparedness and Response; Privacy.

FOR ADDITIONAL INFORMATION

American Civil Liberties Union of Michigan
60 West Hancock Street
Detroit, MI 48201
(313) 578-6800
(313) 578-6811 FAX
www.aclumich.org

Detroit Branch of the NAACP
2990 East Grand Boulevard
Detroit, MI 48202
(313) 871-2087
(313) 871-7745 FAX
www.detroitnaacp.org

Family Research Council
801 G Street, N.W.
Washington, DC 20001
(202) 393-2100
(202) 393-2134 FAX
www.frc.org

Human Rights Campaign
919 18th Street, N.W., Suite 800
Washington, DC 20006
(202) 628-4160
(202) 347-5323 FAX
www.hrc.org

Michigan Association of Chiefs of Police
2133 University Park Drive, Suite 200
Okemos, MI 48864
(517) 349-9420
(517) 349-5823 FAX
www.michiganpolicechiefs.org

Michigan Department of Civil Rights
[Offices are located statewide]
(800) 482-3604
www.michigan.gov/mdcr

Triangle Foundation
19641 West Seven Mile Road
Detroit, Mich. 48219
(313) 537-3323
(313) 537-3379 FAX
www.tri.org

Sponsored by the Michigan Nonprofit Association and the Council of Michigan Foundations

Communicable Diseases and Public Health

BACKGROUND

The term "public health" may refer to (1) the well-being of the population as it pertains to health and disease or (2) the broad system of policies, resources, practices, and programs intended to protect, maintain, and improve the health of the population. Both focus on the health of the population as a whole with an emphasis on preventing illness and attention to the range of factors (physical, behavioral, social, economic) that contribute to poor health in the population.

Evolution of the Public Health System

The public health system in the United States began in the early to mid-1800s in response to epidemics of such infectious diseases as cholera, diphtheria, smallpox, and typhoid. Local health agencies were created to carry out activities (including quarantine, isolation, and vaccination) to control communicable disease. In the late 1800s, state governments created state health boards and agencies, recognizing that environmental and communicable disease threats are not confined by local boundaries.

Communicable Disease Reporting

Infectious diseases still are one of the most common causes of suffering and death, and they impose a significant financial burden on society. Some diseases have been controlled—or eliminated—through prevention, antibiotics, and vaccines. But new diseases constantly appear, and some known diseases are reappearing in forms that resist existing drugs.

In Michigan, physicians, clinical laboratories, primary and secondary schools, child-care centers, and camps are required to report to the local health department the occurrence or suspected occurrence of any disease, condition, or infection identified in the Michigan Communicable Disease Rules. Reportable conditions include AIDS and HIV infection, chlamydia, diphtheria, gonorrhea, hepatitis, measles, meningococcal disease, meningitis, syphilis, and tuberculosis. Michigan health care professionals and laboratories also may report any condition, disease, or infection they believe may threaten public health. The following data on selected communicable diseases in Michigan are from the Michigan Department of Community Health (MDCH) unless otherwise specified.

Vaccine-Preventable Diseases

Many diseases that once were common now are controlled by vaccine. Smallpox was eliminated worldwide in 1977 and vaccination against it no longer is recommended. Poliomyelitis has been eliminated in the western hemisphere, and measles in the United States is at a record low; the organisms that cause these diseases have not disappeared, however, and they will reemerge if vaccination rates drop.

The federal Centers for Disease Control and Prevention (CDC) Advisory Committee on Immunization Practices (ACIP) recommends that all children born in the United

States be vaccinated against diphtheria, tetanus, pertussis, measles, mumps, poliomyelitis, rubella, *Haemophilus influenzae* type b, hepatitis B, varicella (hereafter, chickenpox), and pneumococcal disease. The 2001 National Immunization Survey indicates that 70 percent of Michigan's two-year-olds were fully immunized—this is down from 77 percent in 2000. Recommended immunizations for adults aged 65 years and older include a one-time immunization against pneumococcal disease (including pneumonia), a yearly "flu shot," and a tetanus-diptheria vaccine every 10 years.

In Michigan in 2001, there were only about 6,600 reported cases of chickenpox and, for the first time, none of measles.

Meningitis

For reporting purposes, meningitis is grouped into three categories.

- Meningococcal disease includes meningococcal meningitis (inflammation of the membranes surrounding the brain and spinal cord) and meningococcemia (infection in the bloodstream).

- Bacterial meningitis pertains to types of bacterial meningitis *other* than meningococcal disease.

- Viral meningitis is the most common form of meningitis, but it is the least severe and usually resolves itself.

In Michigan from 1996 through 2001, the average number of reported cases of meningococcal disease and other types of bacterial meningitis were 67 and 203 cases, respectively. Reported cases in the third category, viral meningitis, appear to increase in three-year cycles: There were 1,561 cases in 1998 and 2,542 cases in 2001.

The bacteria and viruses that cause meningitis are spread by direct contact with nose and throat secretions, usually through kissing, coughing, sneezing, and sharing drinks, cigarettes, and food. Children aged under four years and adolescents and young adults aged 15–24 are at higher risk than others for meningococcal disease. A vaccine is available that can prevent some but not all cases. In 1999 the ACIP recommended that (1) college freshman and their parents be given information about meningococcal disease and the benefits of vaccination, and (2) vaccinations be provided or made easily available to freshmen who wish to reduce their risk of disease.

Early diagnosis and treatment of meningococcal disease and other forms of bacterial meningitis are very important. Antibiotics have decreased mortality rates from 60 percent in the 1930s to 10–13 percent today, but people who recover may suffer permanent hearing loss, kidney failure, or brain injury.

Tuberculosis

Tuberculosis (TB) is a communicable disease spread through airborne respiratory secretions (droplets), usually from a cough or sneeze. The bacteria may stay in the human body for many years before causing active disease, and people who are infected but not yet sick may take medicine so that they never develop it. People who have the disease may be treated and cured, but if TB patients do not take the medicine as prescribed, the bacteria may become resistant to the medication. Sometimes the bacteria become resistant to more than one drug (multi-drug resistant TB).

At higher risk than others are people aged over 65, those with weakened immune systems (e.g., the homeless, alcoholics, substance abusers, people with HIV/AIDS) and those born in countries that have high TB prevalence.

Infectious disease
A disease caused by an infectious agent; many are communicable.

Meningitis
Inflammation of the brain and spinal cord that can result in permanent brain damage and death.

Opportunistic infection
A serious and unusual disease (e.g., rare type of cancer or pneumonia) that is virtually absent among people with a healthy immune system.

Outbreak
Sudden appearance of a disease in a specific geographic area or population.

Pandemic
An epidemic occurring over a very large area.

Sexually transmitted disease
A disease caused by any one of more than 25 infectious organisms transmitted primarily through sexual activity.

Tuberculosis (TB) disease
An illness in which TB bacteria multiply and attack any part of the body but usually the lungs; TB is spread through the air.

Vaccine
A product that produces immunity to a specific disease.

Virus
A tiny organism that multiples within cells and causes disease; viruses are not affected by antibiotics, the drugs used to kill bacteria.

Sponsored by the Michigan Nonprofit Association and the Council of Michigan Foundations

Measures to prevent the spread of TB include limited use of a vaccine in certain high-risk populations and testing/treating people in regular contact with an infected person. Early detection and treatment of infection reduces TB transmission to others.

National TB rates declined steadily from 1953 until 1985, when cases began to increase following a sharp cut in TB control resources in the 1970s and the spread of HIV/AIDS in the 1980s. Rates began to decline again after control activities were strengthened in 1992. TB continues to grow globally, with 8 million new cases a year; it causes 2 million deaths annually.

In Michigan the number of active TB cases has been almost level since 1990; 331 cases were reported in 2001—a case rate of 3.3 per 100,000 population. Michigan's case rate for TB consistently is lower than the national rate.

Sexually Transmitted Diseases

Sexually transmitted diseases (STDs) are common in the United States. Women generally suffer more serious STD complications than men, including pelvic inflammatory disease, ectopic pregnancy, infertility, chronic pelvic pain, and cervical cancer from the human papilloma virus. Blacks and Hispanics have higher rates of STD than do whites. STD disproportionately affects adolescents and young adults. In Michigan (2001 data),

■ reported cases of chlamydia (30,499) are the highest since reporting began, in 1993;

■ reported cases of gonorrhea (17,121) have been declining gradually; and

■ reported cases of infectious syphilis (428) are up, reflecting an outbreak in the Detroit area.

Several biological, social, and behavioral factors contribute to the rapid spread of STDs, including

■ the presence of only mild or no symptoms, resulting in failure to seek treatment and unknowing transmission to others;

■ the stigma associated with STDs and the general reluctance of Americans to discuss sexual behavior;

■ the poverty and marginalization of people in high-risk behavior groups (e.g., sex workers, adolescents, prisoners, migrant workers), which reduce their access to health care services; and

■ alcohol and drug abuse, which may involve the exchange of sex for drugs, anonymous sex partners, de-

creased motivation and ability to use protection, and lack of interest in medical treatment.

Early STD detection and treatment is essential, and behavior-change counseling is important to prevent recurrence and spreading it to others.

Hepatitis

Hepatitis A, B, and C are the most common types of hepatitis, a viral liver disease. Vaccines are available to prevent hepatitis A and B but not C.

■ Disease caused by the hepatitis A virus (HAV) can make people very sick but usually resolves within six months.

■ Disease caused by the hepatitis B virus (HBV) is more serious and can cause lifelong infection, cirrhosis of the liver, liver cancer, liver failure, and death. It is spread from person to person through blood or other body fluids and also may be spread from an infected pregnant woman to her fetus. (It is very important that pregnant women be tested for HBV so that if necessary, a baby may be immunized at birth.)

■ Disease caused by the hepatitis C virus (HCV) is as serious as that caused by HBV. Hepatitis C usually is transmitted through large or repeated exposures to blood—for example, through needle sharing among drug users. Consistent data are lacking regarding the extent to which sexual activity contributes to HCV transmission. Hepatitis C was discovered in 1989 and is called the "silent epidemic" because it has received little public attention. The number of documented cases is but a fraction of the total number of individuals believed to be infected. As many as 4 million Americans and 200,000 Michiganians may be infected, and the majority of them are unaware of it and the risks it poses to their health. Not only is it important to identify HCV-infected persons so that they may be treated, but, from a public health standpoint, it is critical to counsel them on ways to prevent further transmission.

The 2001 hepatitis data for Michigan are as follows: HAV, 327 cases; HBV, 618 (up from the average of 457/year in the previous five years), and HCV, 4,451 (up dramatically from 339 in 1996).

HIV/AIDS

Since reporting on Acquired Immune Deficiency Syndrome (AIDS) began, in 1981, almost half a million Americans and nearly 22 million people worldwide have died of the disease. In the United States, the number of new infections continues at about 40,000 a year, and the estimated number of people living with HIV/AIDS has increased to between 800,000 and 900,000. Racial and ethnic minority groups are disproportionately affected by HIV/AIDS and now comprise the majority of new human immunodeficiency virus (HIV) infections, people living with AIDS, and AIDS deaths nationally and in Michigan. An estimated half of all new infections nationally are among people aged under 25.

HIV is *communicable* (capable of being transmitted) and *chronic* (of long duration or slow progression). It is spread through exchange of body fluids (blood, semen, vaginal secretions, and breast milk), most commonly by sexual contact (vaginal, anal, or oral) and sharing dirty needles during intravenous drug use. Babies born to untreated HIV-positive women may be infected (perinatal transmission), but the incidence is greatly reduced when pregnant women adhere to specific therapies. Transmission from HIV-positive blood transfusions is virtually nonexistent in the United States today due to blood screening.

As of January 1, 2002, just under 10,500 people were *reported* to be living with HIV/AIDS in Michigan, but the *estimated* number is 15,500. The number of new HIV-infection diagnoses is about 825 a year, down from about 1,100 cases annually in 1995–97. Perinatal HIV transmission in Michigan dropped from 19 percent in 1993 to 3 percent in 2000, and this is credited to the state's quick adoption of U.S. Public Health Service guidelines for maternal and neonatal Zidovudine use.

HIV deteriorates the body's immune system. Most people with HIV look and feel healthy for years but can transmit the virus to others. Previously, most developed AIDS, the most serious form and final stage of HIV infection, but treatment advances that slow the progression of the disease mean that more people are remaining free of AIDS longer (but the effect's duration is unknown, and as yet there is no cure for HIV or AIDS). The most widely used treatment for HIV/AIDS is highly active antiretroviral therapy (HAART)—combinations of antiretroviral drugs. These therapies cost $1,000 to $1,500 a month and require a rigorous regimen and high patient adherence (15–20 tablets daily with periods of fasting). Low-income patients without adequate health insurance have access to drug therapy through AIDS drug-assistance programs that are funded federally and administered by the state.

Currently, avoiding certain behavior (or, put another way, engaging in safe behavior) is the only way to prevent new HIV infection. HIV-prevention programs attempt to elicit safe behavior or reduction of risk; examples of programs include education and information, abstinence programs, counseling for risk reduction, needle-exchange programs, peer training, HIV testing (because counseling accompanies it), support groups, and media campaigns. No vaccines to prevent HIV infection currently are approved for use; progress is being made, but an effective vaccine is still years away.

DISCUSSION

Generally, there is widespread public support for community-oriented activities to prevent disease and promote health. But opinion differs on how much funding should be allocated, which problems should receive highest priority, and what strategies and activities should be implemented. Conflict between individual rights and the public interest, humanitarian and economic considerations, religious and secular views, and global and local concerns complicate policy decisions related to controlling and preventing many communicable diseases.

Investing in Public Health
In 1988 the Institute of Medicine Committee for the Study of the Future of Public Health warned that "public health in the United States has been taken for granted, many public health issues have become inappropriately politicized, and public health responsibilities have become so fragmented that deliberate action is often difficult if not impossible." Today, public health professionals and advocates reiterate these concerns and assert that investment in the public health system results in lower health care costs in the long run.

Currently, economic decline has prompted state and federal budget reductions, affecting monies available to support public health efforts. But even in good economic times, state expenditures for public health have dropped: In roughly 10 years, public health spending has fallen from 2.29 percent of the Michigan budget to 2.02 percent in FY 2001–02. State and local government officials, health care providers, consumers, insurers, and employers worry about the state's commitment to the health of Michigan residents.

Funding for HIV/AIDS
In Michigan, FY 2001–02 budget cuts resulted in a 3 percent reduction in funding for HIV/AIDS services and a $600,000 cut from the $3 million originally set aside for HIV/AIDS testing and counseling.

AIDS activists say that flat or decreased funding is inadequate for prevention; the continuing number of new infections indicates that current prevention efforts are not able to reach everyone in need. They also point out that level funding for care and support programs does not meet

Sponsored by the Michigan Nonprofit Association and the Council of Michigan Foundations

the growing need for services as more people live longer with HIV/AIDS.

Conversely, the watchdog group, Citizens Against Government Waste, maintains that federally funded HIV/AIDS programs are an "epidemic of waste, fraud, abuse and mismanagement" and duplication of funding. They propose that funding be redistributed to areas where it would be more effective, such as vaccine research, international efforts, and drug subsidies. AIDS activists and human rights supporters caution that there continues to be a need for a comprehensive response to HIV and AIDS that includes prevention, care, treatment, and research.

Cost Control

Recent Michigan legislative action and policy shifts intended to contain health care expenditures have fueled debate over the allocation of resources and effectiveness of efforts. Two examples are P.A. 209 of 2000 and the Michigan Pharmaceutical Initiative.

Public Act 209 eliminated the requirement for premarital counseling of couples applying for a marriage license and requires instead that they be given written educational materials on prenatal care and on the transmission/prevention of venereal disease and HIV infection. Opponents of this change argue that required counseling was an opportunity to encourage risk-reduction behavior and provide information on HIV and STD for many who otherwise would not get the information, and they suggest that most individuals will not read written materials. Supporters of the law contend that requiring counseling was an ineffective use of prevention resources and placed an unnecessary burden on the marriage-licensing system.

The legislature directed the MDCH to develop the Michigan Pharmaceutical Initiative, a state-approved formulary (drug list) from which prescriptions paid for by state-sponsored medical programs must be selected. Opponents fear that only the least expensive drugs will be on the list, and, depending on the patient, may not be as effective as others or may have more serious side effects. AIDS advocacy groups point out that treatment with combinations of antiretroviral medications is very complex, and a drug formulary may restrict the flexibility to make the adjustments patients need. The plan's supporters contend that it will help the state to control rising drug costs, and patients will be able to obtain prior authorization if an unlisted drug is medically necessary.

Meningitis: The Power of Public Attention

The level of public concern about a particular health problem often drives health policy and legislation. While deaths from meningococcal disease are many fewer than from some other communicable diseases (AIDS, hepatitis C), the sudden death of an apparently healthy, young adult due to meningitis captures public attention, raises fears, and stimulates a call for a response.

Public Act 163 of 2001 requires the MDCH to promote dissemination of certain information about meningococcal disease (and other vaccine-preventable diseases) to Michigan high schools and colleges. Supporters point out that the legislation implements some of the ACIP's recommendations. Some argue that the new law does not go far enough, contending that all entering freshmen who live in dormitories or residential halls should be vaccinated. Yet the infection rate—even though it is higher than that of the general population—still is less than half the threshold that the CDC recommends for initiating a meningococcal vaccination campaign.

Meanwhile, complacency regarding the HIV/AIDS epidemic and lack of awareness about the spread of hepatitis C frustrate public health officials and advocates who see a need for stronger action on these issues.

Immunizations: Maintaining Public Health Gains

Many of the advances against public health problems are taken for granted, such as safe water and protection against former epidemic diseases, but public health officials warn that continuing vigilance is needed to preserve the gains that have been won. The national increase in TB during the mid-1980s is attributed in part to reduced TB control activities. Measles outbreaks—for which effective vaccination is available—continue to occur in populations where the immunization level is low.

Michigan law requires children to be inoculated before or upon school entry against polio, measles, mumps, rubella, hepatitis B, diphtheria, tetanus, pertussis, and, beginning with the 2002–03 school year, chickenpox, In addition, children entering sixth grade or enrolling in a school for the first time must present documentation that they have received, are receiving, or object to certain immunizations. Schools must report student immunization status to public health officials.

As a result of a supply shortage in the United States for some childhood vaccines, the 2002 ACIP guidelines recommend deferring some doses of tetanus, diphtheria, pertussis, and pneumonia vaccines until the supplies have been restored. The CDC indicates that the shortages may lead to increased illness and are a cause for concern but not panic. Health providers are frustrated because they see their attempts to increase immunization levels being undermined, and they fear that parents will not return to get their children immunized when the vaccines are available. Some providers call for developing backup systems to guarantee adequate supplies in the future, particularly when there is only one manufacturer of a vaccine. They point out that money spent on vaccinations saves much more in health care costs.

Sometimes concerns are raised about adverse effects from vaccines. Some health professionals fear that these concerns may threaten the gains made in immunization levels. They point out that while no vaccine is entirely free from side effects, vaccines are held to a higher standard of safety than other medicines, and numerous studies demonstrate their safety and effectiveness.

Preventing STD, HIV, and Hepatitis C
Because STDs, HIV, and hepatitis C are transmitted through sexual contact and/or injecting drug use, prevention strategies are controversial.

Sexual Abstinence versus Safer Sex
Some people advocate abstinence-only education while others promote both abstinence-based education and safer-sex education (e.g., effective condom use). As evidence of the success of abstinence-only education, Michigan Abstinence Partnership (MAP) supporters point to Michigan's significant drop in its teen pregnancy rate since the MAP began, in 1993.

Supporters of safer-sex education argue that Michigan's declining teen pregnancy rate could be due to factors other than MAP; they contend that it is a fact that many teens engage in sex and, to prevent pregnancy as well as STDs and HIV, they should be educated about how to protect themselves. Supporters of abstinence-only education fear that teaching students how to engage in safer sex promotes sexual activity; opponents point to evidence that after being educated about condom use, youths do increase condom use but not their sexual activity.

Supporters of abstinence-only education point out condoms are not 100 percent effective (due to improper use, breakage, and slippage) in preventing HIV and STDs and claim that promoting condom use is misleading if not dangerous. Supporters of safer-sex education respond that condoms do prevent transmission when used correctly, and people who are sexually active should be taught to use all the means available to protect themselves. They point to the gonorrhea decline as evidence that safer-sex education programs are effective.

Syringe and Needle Exchange
Since intravenous drug users make up a sizable proportion of HIV/AIDS and hepatitis C populations, prevention among this group is vitally important in slowing transmission of HIV and HCV. Syringe/needle-exchange programs are proven successful in reducing the risky behavior (sharing dirty needles and syringes) among intravenous drug users, but such programs rarely are supported with public funding because the risky behavior involves illegal drug use. The two programs operating in Michigan are supported by private funding. In support of public funding, advocates point to the programs' success. Opponents argue that the programs, by providing drug paraphernalia, are at the very least evincing a benign view of illegal and destructive behavior if not actually promoting it.

Individual Privacy and Disease Surveillance
All states require that AIDS cases be reported to public health authorities, but only some—including Michigan—require HIV cases to be reported as well. Some health authorities and others call for national HIV reporting (using names or codes), but others, and many people living with HIV/AIDS, fear that this could erode confidentiality rights. Proponents of wider reporting argue that not having a full HIV-surveillance system deprives health authorities of reliable information about the incidence, prevalence, and trends in HIV infection, types of behavior that increase transmission risk, or trends in specific subpopulations (e.g., minorities, women). Because of the stigma associated with HIV/AIDS, opponents fear that stricter monitoring and reporting could increase the risk of discrimination in housing, insurance, and employment as well as invade personal privacy. Opponents also worry that increased monitoring and reporting will deter people from being tested, which could result in more transmission, delayed treatment, and higher costs. The same arguments apply to reporting of other communicable diseases such as STDs and hepatitis C.

Global Health
State and local policymakers addressing communicable disease issues must deal with increasing complexity because of the permeable nature of local, state, and international borders. In an age of rapid transit and increasing mobility worldwide, a communicable disease outbreak in one country can quickly become a local threat in another.

See also Emergency Preparedness and Response; Substance Abuse.

FOR ADDITIONAL INFORMATION

AIDS Education Global Information System (AEGIS)
www.aegis.com
[one of the largest Web HIV/AIDS information sources]

Sponsored by the Michigan Nonprofit Association and the Council of Michigan Foundations

AIDS Partnership Michigan
2751 East Jefferson Avenue, Suite 301
Detroit, MI 48207
(313) 446-9800
(313) 446-9839 FAX
www.aidspartnership.org

Centers for Disease Control and Prevention
U.S. Department of Health and Human Services
1600 Clifton Road
Atlanta, GA 30333
(404) 639-3534
www.cdc.gov

Division of Communicable Disease and Immunization
Bureau of Epidemiology
Michigan Department of Community Health
3423 North Martin Luther King, Jr. Boulevard
P.O. Box 30195
Lansing, MI 48909
(517) 335-8165 or 335-8195
www.michigan.gov/mdch

HIV/AIDS Prevention and Intervention Section
Division of HIV/AIDS–STD
Michigan Department of Community Health
2479 Woodlake Circle, Suite 300
Okemos, MI 48864
(517) 241-5900
(517) 241-5911 FAX
www.michigan.gov/mdch

Michigan Association of Public Health and Preventive
    Medicine Physicians
Reportable Disease Data
www.mappp.org

Midwest AIDS Prevention Project
429 Livernois
Ferndale, MI 48220
(248) 545-1435
(248) 545-3313 FAX
www.aidsprevention.org

Sponsored by the Michigan Nonprofit Association and the Council of Michigan Foundations

Consumer Protection

BACKGROUND

Federal, state, and local governments regulate businesses to protect consumers from unfair practices and unsafe conditions and products. At the state level in Michigan, the Department of Attorney General (AG) is responsible for enforcing most consumer-protection laws. The Department of Consumer and Industry Services (MDCIS) regulates professions, corporations, and nursing homes.

Michigan created the nation's first state-level consumer-protection agency: the Consumer Protection Division, established in the AG's office in 1962. Early legislation to protect Michigan consumers covers unlawful trade practices and prohibits false representation and misleading use of words in selling, governs eviction procedures and rental agreements, regulates unsolicited merchandise, and delineates buyers' rights in home solicitation sales.

Later legislation includes the landmark Consumer Protection Act of 1976, which prohibits a variety of specific misrepresentations in commerce and advertising, regulates the return of down payments and conditions of signing agreements and service contracts, and requires sellers of business opportunities to file notice with the AG. It allows the AG to bring a class action on behalf of Michigan residents and for a person to seek a judgment, injunction, or damages against a violator of the act. Also enacted in 1976 was the item-pricing law, which requires prices to be clearly marked on individual items for sale (with certain exceptions), the volume and availability of advertised items to be posted, and a rain check offered if an advertised item is not available. Under this law, if an automatic checkout system (*scanner*) charges a price higher than that on the item, the buyer is entitled to the lower price plus 10 times the amount of the difference.

Consumer-protection legislation regarding automobiles includes a law that prohibits unfair and deceptive practices in motor-vehicle service and repair (1974) and the "lemon law" (1986); the latter provides legal remedies for buyers of new cars that do not conform to their warranty and cannot be fixed.

Product liability is a consumer-protection area pertaining to (1) damages or injuries that manufactured products may cause to users and (2) penalties and remedies imposed for such damage or injury. In the mid-1990s, business interests successfully championed a number of changes in product-liability law, among them statutes that

- eliminate *joint and several liability*, thereby making defendants responsible for only their percentage of fault unless there is criminal intent;

- establish a "state-of-the-art" defense permitting manufacturers and sellers to defend themselves from liability on the grounds that (1) their product meets current standards or is without defect, or (2) the damage/injury resulted from a risk that such a product is commonly known to possess; and

- cap rewards for noneconomic losses (that is, for the pain and suffering caused by the injury) except in instances of gross negligence or criminal fraud.

Sponsored by the Michigan Nonprofit Association and the Council of Michigan Foundations

In the late 1990s, consumer groups and trial lawyers tried but failed to achieve legislative repeal of the above changes.

In other consumer-protection areas, recent legislation

- requires home solicitors using an automated message to terminate the call when the consumer hangs up;

- prohibits sellers from sending someone to collect payment for a home-solicitation sale before the three-day right-of-rescission period has expired;

- prohibits the state from selling the driver and motor-vehicle records maintained by the secretary of state to a party that plans to use them for surveying, marketing, or soliciting;

- prohibits insurers from disclosing nonpublic, personal, financial-aid information to a third party unless the customer has been notified and given the opportunity to say no (that is, to *opt out*), and prohibits insurers from unfairly disclosing customer information for telemarketing, direct mail, or marketing through e-mail; and

- eliminates the court filing fee in cases contesting an insurer's cancellation of automobile insurance.

At the federal level, the Federal Communications Commission's (FCC) recent "truth-in-billing" guidelines require new telephone charges to be highlighted and clearly organized to prevent *cramming*—placing unauthorized or misleading charges on phone bills, a practice that has been the subject of growing consumer complaint. *Slamming*—switching consumers to another long-distance phone company without their direction—also is prohibited.

DISCUSSION

Historically, Michigan has been a leader in consumer protection, but consumer advocates assert that a pronounced business-oriented climate in state government during the 1990s blunted the protections, favoring industry over customers. Business interests respond that the earlier environment was too consumer oriented and discouraged businesses from coming to or expanding in Michigan; they believe that the changes of the last few years, particularly in product liability, put Michigan on equal footing with other states.

The AG's office, where consumers direct their complaints about unfair business practices and charities, reports that the vast majority of businesses deal fairly with consumers. Roughly 126,000 complaints were filed on a variety of businesses in 2001, and most were resolved without court

action. In the past, grievances most frequently concerned motor-vehicle repair and item pricing. More recently, complaints about telemarketing top the list, followed by grievances about natural and propane gas service and the Internet. Other complaints concern the actions of retail companies, gasoline merchants, mail-order companies, banks, automobile manufacturers, credit-reporting agencies, and contractors.

Pending Legislation

Considerable consumer-protection legislation is pending in the Michigan Legislature. Among the most significant are bills that would

- require telephone solicitors to identify themselves at the beginning of a call, prohibit them from blocking their telephone number so that it won't appear on the consumer's caller-ID, and deem it unfair or deceptive for a telephone solicitor to make certain misrepresentations (HBs 4042, 4126, 4153–54, 4250, 4506, 4631–32, 4702, 4861–63 and SBs 153–54);

- eliminate the item-pricing requirement except on food and nonprescription medicines and require that hand-held scanners with printers be available to consumers throughout an establishment (HBs 5544, 5562 and SB 1211);

- prohibit predatory lending practices, such as misrepresentation and fraud, by financial institutions, credit unions, savings and loans, secondary mortgage providers, and banks (HBs 5424–30 and SBs 776–80, 708–14, 768–774);

- include leased vehicles, motor homes, and manufactured homes in the provisions of the lemon law (HBs 4831, 5363 and SB 323);

- prohibit businesses from engaging in certain credit-transaction practices—e.g., printing the customers' credit card number on a receipt (HB 5435);

- include identity theft in the provisions of the state racketeering law (HB 5222);

- prohibit such unfair trade practices as implying that a consumer is in danger unless s/he buys a particular product or service, require disclosure to consumers of the conditions under which goods or services are offered "free" or "without charge", prohibit deceptive and unsolicited e-mail (*spam*), and prohibit disclosing to a credit-reporting agency the Social Security number of a consumer without the consumer's permission (HBs 5135, 5293, 5777);

Sponsored by the Michigan Nonprofit Association and the Council of Michigan Foundations

- regulate the travel-promotion business by requiring bonds, insurance, and consumer advice on avoiding deceptive practices (HBs 4471–72);

- require plain language in consumer contracts (except insurance policies, contracts in which language is prescribed by state or federal statute, and words or phrases that are part of a legal description of real estate) (HB 5052);

- allow consumers to recover damages beyond the limit of their property/liability policy—including damages—when an insurer unfairly denies a claim and require insurers to notify authorities when a claim is denied because arson is suspected (HBs 4740–44, 4176); and

- require health insurers to make timely payment of providers' claims—within 45 days of receipt—unless they notify the provider within 30 days of the reasons the claim is denied (SBs 451–52).

Telemarketing

Currently, federal law requires telemarketers to maintain a "do-not-call" list of consumers who have given notice to the individual calling company that they do not wish to be contacted. The Federal Trade Commission (FTC) currently is holding hearings on a plan to establish a nationwide do-not-call registry. Opponents in marketing and advertising argue that such a list would use taxpayer money to restrict First Amendment rights and, further, cause extensive job and sales losses.

In Michigan, a provision for a do-not-call registry was passed by the House, but removed from telemarketing legislation by the Senate. Critics argue that a Michigan registry would not prevent out-of-state or foreign telephone solicitation. Many consumers support such a list, and the AG, in cooperation with the Michigan AARP (American Association of Retired Persons) office, has produced new complaint forms in the absence of state legislation.

According to the AG, about one-third of the telemarketing-fraud victims are senior citizens. A recent FBI report estimates that about 14,000 illegal telemarketing operations bilk consumers nationwide of about $40 billion annually, and half the victims are aged 50 and older. Telemarketing fraud has increasingly become an international problem as American telemarketers respond to U.S. law enforcement and move operations elsewhere, often to Canada.

Internet Sales and Identity Theft

The Better Business Bureau, a private, business-sponsored organization, reports that

- fraud complaints in Michigan numbered more than 2,800 in 2001, with grievances about Internet sales and auctions topping the list, and

- identity theft claimed 3,000 Michigan victims—the most (more than a third) resulted in unauthorized use of the victim's credit card, followed by a telephone or other utility account being opened in the victim's name.

The FTC reports that nationally, identity theft was the leading consumer-fraud complaint in 2000, exceeding grievances about Internet sales/auctions and services. Thefts of someone's identity information, such as credit card or Social Security numbers, to steal money or commit fraud are rapidly increasing. Privacy advocates say that as many as 750,000 people may be victimized annually. The FTC has developed an ID theft affidavit that a victim may use when an account has been opened fraudulently in his/her name, eliminating the need for the consumer to file separate paperwork with each company with which s/he does business.

Item Pricing

The current item-pricing law is favored by consumers, the AG, and the AARP but opposed by retailers who must mark items individually even when, for example, they are in a bin under a sign stating the price. Pending legislation would remove item pricing from all goods except food and nonprescription drugs and increase penalties for scanner error from 10 times the error amount to 20 times. Supporters of the change say the 26-year-old item pricing law negates the benefit of advancing technology. The AG's annual accuracy survey of scanners at major retailers shows an error rate of 3.2 percent in 2001, a marked improvement over 16.9 percent in 2000.

Insurance

Recent hearings on the "good faith" insurance claim-payment legislation produced horror stories from consumers who said their claims had been delayed or denied without cause. Anecdotal evidence, insurers say, obscures the fact that hundreds of thousands of claims are resolved every year, and that settling claims amicably is what keeps insurers in business.

The insurance commissioner is investigating automobile insurers' practice of considering the customer's credit history in setting rates. Companies say that credit standing is an accurate predictor of loss, but consumer and agent groups say driving records should determine rates.

Lending Practices

Testimony in hearings on predatory-lending legislation suggests that the number of unscrupulous financial pro-

Sponsored by the Michigan Nonprofit Association and the Council of Michigan Foundations

fessionals is small, but the impact is sizable. Elderly consumers, first-time home buyers, and low-income people often are the victims of lending scams, fraud, and misrepresentation. Opponents say that the bills mistakenly focus on banks, credit unions, and savings and loans, whereas most predatory lending is engaged in by unscrupulous used-car dealers, home contractors, payday lenders, and others. They also contend that people who have poor credit are a high risk and lenders should be entitled to charge them a higher interest rate than other borrowers.

Plain Language

The proposal to require plain language in contracts has wide consumer support. Business groups support the concept of plain language and note that common marketplace sense dictates the need for informed consumers. They oppose the legislation, however, arguing that there is no consensus on what constitutes "plain" language, and a government agency or some other third party should not be dictating the language that will be used in a particular field of business.

See also Privacy; Telecommunications.

ADDITIONAL INFORMATION

American Association of Retired Persons
309 North Washington Square, Suite 110
Lansing, MI 48933
(517) 482-2772
(517) 482-2794 FAX
www.aarp.org/statepages/mi.html

Better Business Bureau
30555 Southfield Road, Suite 200
Southfield, MI 48076
(248) 644-9100
(248) 644-5026 FAX
www.detroit.bbb.org

Consumer Information Bureau
Federal Communications Commission
445 Twelfth Street, S.W.
Washington, DC 20554
(888) CALL FCC
(202) 418-0232 FAX
www.fcc.gov/cgb

Federal Trade Commission
600 Pennsylvania Avenue, N.W.
Washington, DC 20580
(202) 326-2222
www.ftc.gov

Michigan Bankers Association
222 North Washington Square, Suite 320
Lansing, MI 48933
(517) 485-3600
(517) 485-3672 FAX
www.mibankers.com

Michigan Chamber of Commerce
600 South Walnut Street
Lansing, MI 48933
(517) 371-2100
(517) 371-7224 FAX
www.michamber.com

Michigan Department of Attorney General
525 West Ottawa Street, 7th Floor
Lansing, MI 48913
(517) 373-1140
(517) 335-1935 FAX
www.ag.state.mi.us

Michigan Insurance Federation
334 Townsend Street
Lansing, MI 48933
(517) 371-2880
(517) 371-2882
www.mifassoc.org

Michigan Manufacturers Association
P.O. Box 14247
Lansing, MI 48901
(517) 372-5900
(517) 372-3322 FAX
www.mma-net.org

Michigan Retailers Association
603 South Washington Avenue
Lansing, MI 48933
(517) 372-5656
(517) 372-1303 FAX
www.retailers.com

Sponsored by the Michigan Nonprofit Association and the Council of Michigan Foundations

Crime and Corrections

BACKGROUND

The Michigan State Police and the Federal Bureau of Investigation (FBI) classify crimes as *index* or *non-index*. The eight index crimes are murder, rape, robbery, aggravated assault, burglary, larceny, arson, and motor-vehicle theft. Because of their serious nature, these offenses are considered a better indicator of the crime situation than is total crime, which includes many minor infractions.

As the exhibit shows, the *number* of index crime offenses in Michigan generally has been dropping for the last decade: down 29 percent from 1991 to 2000 (most recent data available). The concurrent decline in the Michigan crime *rate* (the number of crimes per 100,000 residents—6,138 in 1991 and 4,144 in 2000) closely parallels that of the nation as a whole, for which the rate of serious crime declined every year from 1991 to 2000.

Juvenile Crime

The dip in adult crime has been accompanied by a decline in crimes committed by juveniles (youth aged 16 and younger). The Michigan State Police reports that juvenile arrests for violent crime declined by more than 30 percent over the past five years. According to the Uniform Crime Report, the FBI's standardized measure of reported

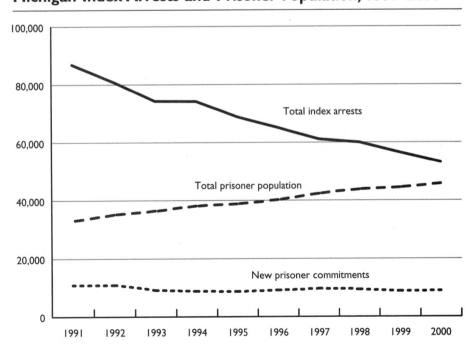

Michigan Index Arrests and Prisoner Population, 1991–2000

SOURCES: Michigan State Police, 2000 Uniform Crime Report ; Michigan Department of Corrections, 1999 Statistical Report and 2000 Annual Report.
NOTE: "Index" crimes are eight serious crimes—murder, rape, robbery, aggravated assault, burglary, larceny, arson, and motor vehicle theft—for which the rate of occurrence is believed to be a reliable indicator (index) of overall crime.

Sponsored by the Michigan Nonprofit Association and the Council of Michigan Foundations

crimes, Michigan juvenile arrests as a percentage of total arrests (about 13 percent on average) remain below the national norm. Juvenile offenders generally are the responsibility of the Family Independence Agency (FIA) Bureau of Juvenile Justice, which operates public-delinquency residential-care programs at 14 sites around the state.

Incarceration

The U.S. Justice Department reports that as of June 2000, more than 1.9 million people were confined to the nation's jails and prisons—a national incarceration rate of 702 per 100,000 people. Nationwide, from 1990 to midyear 2000, the incarcerated population grew 5.6 percent annually on average. The exhibit shows that Michigan too has seen a rise in its incarcerated population.

Although the size of the prison population is influenced by the crime rate, there is not a one-to-one correlation. The rise in incarceration rates despite falling crime rates reflects society's sterner attitude toward crime and criminals. There is a resolve to "get tough" on both. In recent years, Michigan legislators have enacted numerous statutes affecting law enforcement and corrections policy. Among them are measures that

■ make Michigan's drunk driving laws substantially more stringent;

■ create a $10 million grant program to encourage community policing (e.g., to establish foot patrols, to bring officers into closer touch with residents and businesses); and

■ set out new sentencing guidelines that establish minimum sentences.

Controlling and managing the state prison population is the responsibility of the Michigan Department of Corrections (MDOC), which has nearly 19,000 employees and oversees operation of 44 correctional institutions and 11 camps. Jails are the responsibility of counties.

In recent years Michigan has seen extraordinary growth in its state prison system. Since 1998 space for nearly 5,000 new prisoners has been created by expanding eight prisons, converting two camps to prisons, and constructing two new prisons. The expansion enabled the state, in 2000, to stop leasing beds in a medium-security Virginia state prison, where for two years it had been housing some 2,000 Michigan inmates. At $1.60 billion, the FY 2001–02 MDOC appropriation was the third largest in the budget; the governor has recommended $1.63 billion for FY 2002–03. The 1.8 percent increase restores some of the funds lost in the budget cuts of late 2001 but does not allow for any expansion.

Although the number of *new* prison commitments as a portion of total arrests has remained relatively constant over the past decade (2.7 percent in 1991, 2.2 percent in 1999), society's tougher stance on crime has manifested itself in ways that keep people in prison longer.

■ The legislature has mandated, and the courts are imposing, longer sentences for violent offenses (nearly 14,000 inmates in the state system are serving 10 years or more).

■ "Good time" credit has been eliminated for offenders whose crimes occurred after January 1, 1999, and all offenders whose crimes occurred after December 15, 2000, must serve their entire minimum sentence prior to being considered for parole.

■ There has been a decline in the number of paroles granted to people convicted of violent and assault crimes. This is particularly true with regard to sex offenders (the number serving time has more than tripled since 1988).

■ MDOC has cracked down on probation and parole violators, sending or returning them, respectively, to prison more often; this has brought about the biggest rise in prison admissions.

To stem the increasing necessity for beds in the state prison system, MDOC has established two major funding programs for counties. These programs offer them financial incentives to handle certain offenders locally who otherwise would be bound for a state prison.

■ Under the jail reimbursement program, which began in 1988, counties have been paid more than $122 million to house certain offenders in local jails instead of sending them to a state prison. In FY 1999–2000, MDOC paid counties nearly $18 million to house 3,900 offenders.

■ Grants totaling over $219 million have been awarded to counties to help them better manage their offenders through a variety of programs, including residential placement for probationers and jail expansion.

Capital Punishment

Michigan is one of only 12 states (and the District of Columbia) that does not impose the death penalty. In 1846 Michigan became the first government in the English-speaking world to abolish capital punishment for murder and lesser crimes. At this writing, no resolutions to permit the death penalty for a crime prosecuted under Michigan law have been proposed since 1999. Readers interested in a full discussion of the death penalty are referred to *Michigan in Brief, 6th Edition,* which may be found on line at *www.michiganinbrief.org.*

DISCUSSION

Crime and Imprisonment Rates

Crime statistics should be viewed with caution. First, law-enforcement practices can affect the number of crimes reported. Second, reporting is not necessarily uniform nationwide or even statewide. Third, the number of incidents reported may reflect the current public attitude about certain kinds of crimes; for example, some observers speculate that an increase in the number of rapes may result from an increased willingness of victims to report the crime. Last, there always is a gap between reported and unreported crime.

The public's perception of the crime rate often is swayed by factors other than the number of crimes committed. Many people believe that the tremendous growth in prison population is due to a continuing escalation of crime, but this is inaccurate. The prison population both nationally and in Michigan has increased over the past decade, even as crime rates have dropped. Similarly, media coverage of crime stories can fuel the perception that a crime problem is more severe than it is.

While it is reasonable to suppose that the many "law and order" measures enacted in recent years have had some effect on crime rates, it also is true that a number of important factors associated with the incidence of crime are beyond the reach of public policy. For example, states—and areas within states—that have a higher rate of index crimes than others also have more people aged 16–39 (the most crime-prone group), a larger concentration of urban population, and more pockets of poverty.

The rate of new prisoner intake has slowed since 1998, but changes in sentencing laws will keep many offenders behind bars longer, continuing the need for prison beds. Budget cuts in FY 2001–02 necessitated by the economic downturn brought the MDOC appropriation down 1.2 percent, which the department is absorbing by reducing expenditures for new-employee training and eliminating the prisoner rehabilitation education program. In addition, one camp and two corrections centers will be closed.

Some observers fear that the current economic problems and the accompanying rise in unemployment will cause the crime rate, and the attendant burdens on law enforcement and the jail/prison system, to rise again.

Other

In the wake of the terrorist attacks in September 2001, anti-terrorist activity has moved up on the crime-fighting agenda. The events have increased discourse among citizens and policymakers alike about "terrorists among us" and to what extent law-enforcement agencies must take action. In early 2002 a bipartisan anti-terrorism package of bills was enacted that characterizes certain activities as criminal, sets penalties for engaging in such activities, and gives law enforcement expanded powers in enforcing anti-terrorism and other measures.

Before September 11, racial profiling was already a civil rights issue related to the criminal stereotyping of non-whites, and certain law-enforcement practices were being called into question. Now there is a dual concern that some Arab-Americans may be a threat but also that Arab-Americans in general may be unjustly singled out as threatening. (Michigan has the largest concentration of Arab-Americans in the nation). House Bills 4927 and 5307, pertaining to racial profiling, are pending.

Privacy is another concern. Advocates of a proactive approach to combating terrorism and other crimes believe that laws must be changed to accommodate new technology and allow law-enforcement officials to keep closer tabs on people with a suspected terrorist or criminal connection; SBs 803 and 806, pertaining to electronic surveillance, are pending. Civil liberties advocates warn about the possibility of privacy invasion and due-process violations when wiretapping and other search-and-seizure powers are expanded.

The Michigan criminal-justice landscape has been further altered in recent years by new sex-offense and concealed-weapons legislation and the establishment of a criminal DNA database.

■ In 1999 a number of Michigan laws related to sex offenses took effect. Convicted sex offenders in Michigan receive harsher prison sentences than before, and when their time has been served, their photograph and personal information are added to a registry of sex offenders by the local criminal-justice agency that dealt with them originally. The registry may be searched on line by the public, and the offender must update his/her information for at least 25 years by contacting the local law-enforcement agency on specified dates annually. The purpose of the registry is to prevent future sexual victimization, and all states and the District of Columbia have some such law. There is much concern, however, that these laws violate the *ex post facto* clause of the U.S. Constitution that protects individuals from legislation that "further increases the penalty

Sponsored by the Michigan Nonprofit Association and the Council of Michigan Foundations

by which a crime is punishable." At this writing, the Alaska law is scheduled for consideration before the U.S. Supreme Court, and the outcome may affect the registry laws in some or all states.

■ In 2000, new state concealed-weapons laws took effect, changing the procedures by which Michigan residents apply for and receive a license to carry a concealed weapon. The intent of the laws was to standardize and streamline the licensing process and to keep the license information in a centralized database. Legislation has been introduced (HB 5683) to exempt retired police officers from the safety-training requirement and to waive some restrictions on where peace officers may carry firearms. There also is legislation proposed (SB 329) to allow 18–20 year olds to carry a concealed pistol in certain circumstances.

■ In 2000 the criminal DNA database mandates took effect, requiring adults convicted of a felony and certain misdemeanors to submit a DNA sample that is retained in a database. In addition, juveniles who are "waived" to a criminal court in family or circuit court and *convicted* of a felony or specified sex-related misdemeanor are subject to the expanded profiling. DNA profiling has been hailed for enabling law-enforcement officials to identify the perpetrator of a crime and ruling out innocent suspects. Those who oppose the laws cite the excessive nature of profiling *all* felons, even those associated with nonassault crimes; there also is concern about privacy, since DNA can provide information that far exceeds what is necessary for a criminal investigation. No legislation has been introduced to amend these laws.

See also Civil Rights and Liberties; Emergency Preparedness and Response; Firearms Regulation; Privacy; Substance Abuse; Youth at Risk.

FOR ADDITIONAL INFORMATION

Civil Law and the Judiciary Committee
Michigan House of Representatives
P.O. Box 30014
Lansing, MI 48909
(517) 373-0106
(517) 373-5791 FAX

Criminal Justice Committee
Michigan House of Representatives
P.O. Box 30014
Lansing, MI 48909
(517) 373-6576

Judiciary Committee
Michigan Senate
P.O. Box 30036
Lansing, MI 48909
(517) 373-6920
(517) 373-2751 FAX

Michigan Council on Crime and Delinquency
1115 South Pennsylvania Avenue, Suite 201
Lansing, MI 48912
(517) 482-4161
(517) 482-0020 FAX

Michigan Department of Corrections
P.O. Box 30003
Lansing, MI 48909
(517) 373-0720
(517) 373-2628 FAX
www.michigan.gov/corrections

Michigan State Police
714 South Harrison Road
East Lansing, MI 48823
(517) 332-2521
(517) 336-6551 FAX
www.michigan.gov/msp

National Criminal Justice Reference Service
P.O. Box 6000
Rockville, MD 20849
(800) 851-3420
(301) 519-5500
www.ncjrs.org

Senate Fiscal Agency
Victor Center, Suite 800
201 North Washington Square
P.O. Box 30036
Lansing, MI 48909
(517) 373-2768
(517) 373-1986 FAX
www.senate.state.mi.us/sfa

Domestic Violence

BACKGROUND

Domestic violence is abusive behavior that threatens the health, safety, physical or mental well-being or financial security of a household member; the state's response to incidents of domestic violence depends on whether the victim is a child, spouse, or elderly person.

GLOSSARY

Child Abuse
An action by an adult responsible for a child's health and welfare that (1) harms or threatens harm to the child's health and welfare and (2) occurs through nonaccidental physical or mental injury, sexual abuse, sexual exploitation, or maltreatment.

Neglect
Harm or threatened harm that occurs through negligent treatment, such as failing to provide adequate food, clothing, shelter, or medical care; includes placing someone at an unreasonable risk by failing to intervene when one can and knows, or should know, of the risk.

Stalking
Willful and repeated harassment that terrorizes, frightens, intimidates, threatens, or molests someone.

Child Abuse

A recent study by Prevent Child Abuse America estimates that nationally, $258 million is spent every day as a direct or indirect result of child abuse and neglect. Every dollar spent on prevention is estimated to save $19 in future spending. In Michigan, state government focuses on detecting and protecting abused children as well as on prevention and the continuum of services needed to support families and thus prevent child abuse and neglect.

The Michigan Family Independence Agency (FIA) is required by law to respond to every report of suspected child abuse or neglect within 24 hours; an FIA children's protective services (CPS) caseworker must (1) dismiss the complaint, (2) begin an investigation to be completed within 30 days, or (3) refer the complaint to law-enforcement officials.

In FY 2001 the FIA received nearly 140,000 allegations of child abuse and/or neglect, investigating more than 67,000 allegations and substantiating nearly 16,500. The largest number of allegations involved physical neglect or physical injury; additional cases related to improper supervision, failure to protect, mental injury, and other types of abuse/neglect. Parents in the home perpetrated the vast majority of abuse or neglect.

In FY 2001, 49 Michigan children died from abuse/neglect and 8,654 were removed from their home.

Although anyone may report child abuse, the following, if they suspect it, are required by law to report their suspicions to the FIA: a physician, physician's assistant, coroner, dentist, hygienist, medical examiner, nurse, licensed emergency medical care provider, psychologist, audiologist, social worker, law-enforcement officer, regulated child care provider, school administrator, marriage and family therapist, professional counselor, and teacher.

The last two decades have brought significant change in matters of child abuse. A number of state laws and policies have been enacted to deal with the problem. Recent legislation

■ requires attorneys to be made available for children in child protection and guardianship proceedings;

■ revises judicial-assignment processes for the Family Division of circuit court;

■ expands the list of offenses allowing for accommodation of child witnesses;

■ eliminates competency determinations for child witnesses aged under 10;

Sponsored by the Michigan Nonprofit Association and the Council of Michigan Foundations

- gives protective services caseworkers access to children's medical and mental health records;

- establishes a central registry of abusers, with access allowed to CPS workers;

- includes nonparent adults as "persons responsible for a child's health and welfare";

- applies child abuse penalties to live-together partners;

- protects health care workers and corporations from criminal liability when they report an injury caused by violence;

- increases the penalty for failing to report child abuse;

- protects individuals from abandonment charges for leaving a newborn (birth to 72 hours) at a hospital, police station, or fire department; and

- requires emergency service providers to take possession and provide care for abandoned children.

Pending legislation would

- increase the penalty for abuse resulting in a child's death (HBs 5384–85);

- require criminal background checks for those employed in child-care organizations (SB 275, HB 4058);

- create a rebuttable presumption that custody will be refused to perpetrators of domestic violence (SB 428, HB 4546); and

- establish, in placement cases, a court-appointed special-advocate program for children through which volunteers will conduct independent investigations regarding the child's best interest (SB 370).

Specific changes in administrative procedures and laws are proposed annually in the report of the Office of the Children's Ombudsman, which investigates complaints about FIA protective services. Frequently, these proposals result in further action to better protect children. The 2000 report recommends three policy changes regarding protective services: (1) require a home visit at a child's residence during the course of every investigation, (2) hold a case open for a minimum of 90 days when a "preponderance of evidence" indicates the risk of future harm is "high" or "intensive," and (3) refrain from placing a child with a relative who has a substantiated history of child abuse or neglect. The FIA agrees at least in part with each of the recommended changes.

In addition to state laws and policies, there are numerous entities actively addressing child abuse, abuse prevention, and policy. Three are listed here.

- The Children's Trust Fund, established in 1982, provides a permanent funding source for county-level prevention programs statewide. These programs target populations that are not part of the active FIA children's protective services caseload. The fund is financed by interest, donations, federal grants, and a new source of revenue: license plate sales promoting the trust fund. Since its creation, the fund has provided services to more than 2.5 million children and 500,000 families.

- The Michigan League for Human Services and Michigan's Children jointly sponsor annual KIDS COUNT reports that develop data on child welfare in local communities; the objective is to influence public policy related to children and families. The project reports county data on children—including that on abuse; it also establishes partnerships with local communities to address child welfare concerns, especially abuse and neglect.

- Children's Charter of the Courts of Michigan is a private, nonprofit organization involved with issues that bring children in contact with the court system. The group assists communities with abuse-prevention and family-support programs and advocates for legislative and administrative change to reduce child abuse and neglect.

Each county FIA office operates a hotline for reporting child abuse. There also is a statewide hotline number for parenting help, crisis intervention, and referrals: (800) 942-4357.

Domestic Abuse

Abuse by an intimate partner is recognized as a violent criminal act and investigated by the police. In FY 1999–2000, domestic-violence programs in Michigan received more than 61,000 calls and sheltered 13,600 women and children.

Although the state is not directly engaged in programs having do with spouse abuse, the FIA Domestic Violence Prevention and Treatment Board coordinates and partially funds Michigan's 45 private, nonprofit, local domestic-violence centers. The shelters receive local, state, and federal funds as well as varying amounts—determined by a formula based on the geographic size and population of the area served—from the board.

The lieutenant governor's Domestic Violence Homicide Prevention Task Force report (April 2001) states that in 1999 more than 100 Michigan women died as a result of domestic violence. To prevent such deaths in the future and to protect survivors, the task force recommends

- increasing public awareness and education about domestic violence;

- increasing victim protection throughout judicial proceedings;

- creating uniform standards for reporting and tracking domestic-violence crimes and offenders; and

- enhancing domestic-violence prevention training for judges and law-enforcement personnel.

A considerable body of law addressing domestic violence has been enacted in the last few years, including measures that respond to the task force's findings. The more recent legislation

- prohibits insurers, health maintenance organizations, and Blue Cross Blue Shield of Michigan from charging higher premiums or refusing to cover domestic-violence victims;

- allows the Family Division of circuit court to issue personal protection orders (PPOs) and permits warrantless arrest of juveniles for violating a PPO;

- expands the scope of PPOs and domestic-violence reports;

- revises procedures for the warrantless arrest of someone who violates a PPO;

- prohibits disclosure of student information to a person against whom a PPO has been issued;

- includes violation of an out-of-state PPO in the definition of domestic violence;

- honors PPOs from other states;

- requires an explanation for denial or approval of a PPO involving nonrelationship stalking;

- requires that PPO violators be tracked through fingerprinting;

- requires increased reporting on criminal contempt convictions for violating a PPO;

- extends the statute of limitations from three to five years for domestic-violence actions;

- protects people in dating relationships;

- authorizes creation of state and local fatality-review teams;

- allows courts to consider out-of-state domestic assault convictions in imposing sentences for domestic assault in Michigan;

- requires the State Police to develop standard reporting forms for domestic-violence crimes; and

- increases criminal penalties in some domestic-violence cases.

Pending legislation would

- prohibit offenders, under some circumstances, from being released from jail on interim bond (SBs 132, 727);

- allow certain hearsay evidence in domestic-violence cases (HB 4765); and

- permit evidence of prior domestic-violence acts to be presented at trial (SB 733, HB 5283).

The Michigan Coalition Against Domestic and Sexual Violence is a statewide organization that provides training and technical assistance for domestic-violence professionals and volunteer organizations, participates in public policy initiatives, provides emergency and support services through member agencies, and promotes public awareness of domestic and sexual violence.

The State Bar of Michigan has a pro bono project for domestic-violence victims and in 2001, with support from several government agencies, trained 219 Michigan attorneys in providing legal representation to domestic-violence victims.

The hotline for reporting domestic violence is (800) 799-SAFE [7233].

Elder Abuse
Although statistics on elder abuse are uncertain at best, the *New England Journal of Medicine* estimates that nationally, incidents range from one million to two million a year. Incidence is believed to be vastly underreported; public agencies may be notified of as few as one in 14 occurrences.

Michigan's FIA is required to investigate all complaints of abuse, neglect, or exploitation of people aged 18 and over, in settings other than nursing homes and other public facilities, who are vulnerable because of mental or physical impairment or the frailty and dependency of age. The FIA adult protective services (APS) unit must investigate immediately if serious injury is suspected, otherwise within 24 hours. If APS substantiates abuse or neglect, it provides or makes arrangements for whatever services are needed—social, health, remedial, or legal—to correct or relieve the problem. Physicians and other health professionals are required to report suspected abuse.

According to the APS unit, caseloads have doubled during the past decade, reaching 3,324 in 2000. Approxi-

Sponsored by the Michigan Nonprofit Association and the Council of Michigan Foundations

mately 70 percent of elder abuse and neglect falls into the category of self-neglect—that is, people are not a victim of someone else but of their own neglect. About 15 percent are victims of physical abuse or neglect and 15 percent are victims of financial exploitation, a growing category of abuse.

Legislation strengthening Michigan's 1982 Adult Protective Services Act and additional legislation in the past decade have enhanced protections for vulnerable adults; pending measures would increase penalties for crimes against senior citizens and vulnerable adults (SBs 276, 514 and HBs 4557, 4973). A *vulnerable adult* is redefined as a person over 18 with developmental disability, mental illness, or physical disability; this applies whether or not the person has been determined by a court to be incapacitated and requiring supervision or lacking competency. A 2000 law prohibits embezzlement of the money or property of a vulnerable adult by anyone in "a position of trust," such as a court-appointed guardian, conservator, personal representative, or trustee. Penalties may include imprisonment and a fine of three times the value of the money or property obtained or attempted to be obtained.

The Michigan Office of Services to the Aging (OSA) contracts with 16 area agencies on aging (AAAs) to serve Michigan's senior citizens, and their programming includes elder-abuse prevention. The AAAs contract with private organizations for many services such as operating hotlines and training law-enforcement personnel, prosecutors, and others to recognize and deal with elder abuse.

Triad, a program designed to fight crimes that target seniors, was established by the National Sheriffs Association in partnership with the International Association of Chiefs of Police and the American Association of Retired Persons (AARP). Triad has helped to form 16 regional triads that train local law enforcement, local agencies, and senior citizens to deal with crimes that involve elderly people as victims or witnesses. Local triads also survey seniors about crimes they perceive as most prevalent in their area. Triad annually co-sponsors a conference of workshops and informational seminars relating to crimes against the elderly.

The statewide hotline number to report abuse of vulnerable adults is (800) 996-6228.

DISCUSSION

The challenge for Michigan protective services workers—especially child caseworkers—lies in complying with a state mandate to make a reasonable effort to maintain or reunite the family unit and an equally strong mandate to protect citizens from harm.

The Families First program, founded on the concept of keeping children in their home if at all possible, offers intensive, short-term, in-home counseling and correction services. Early in the program's history, some child advocates criticized the minimal training being given caseworkers even though the program's success depends on highly skilled personnel. In the late 1990s, mandatory staff training increased substantially. Families First reports that 84 percent of participating families remain intact 12 months after leaving the program. The Office of the Auditor General concludes that Families First generally has been effective in providing a safe alternative to out-of-home placement of children at imminent risk of being removed from their home.

Funding for many programs dealing with domestic violence increased significantly in the late 1990s, when state revenue reflected a thriving economy, but budget cuts in late 2001 reduced monies in several areas. While no reductions were made directly to children's protective services, secondary effects from sharp cutbacks in the funds directed to domestic-violence shelters and other community health services may affect protective services for children. For example, the Michigan Domestic Violence Prevention and Treatment Board budget was trimmed by nearly $1 million.

Although Michigan's anti-stalking law was enacted in 1992, it was challenged in court as being vague and too broad. In 2001 the U.S. Circuit Court of Appeals upheld the law, which was one of the first in the nation to address the central harm of stalking behavior (causing the victim to feel terrorized, intimidated, or harassed) rather than requiring specific intent by the perpetrator. It is hailed as a valuable tool by law enforcement, prosecutors, and domestic-violence experts.

After a five-year lapse during which programs were funded on previous formulas, the federal Older Americans Act was reauthorized by Congress in October 2000. Numerous state programs benefit from the act, including those designed to combat elder abuse and provide education on elder-abuse prevention.

Advocates for the elderly note that funding to combat domestic violence, regardless of the total level, short-changes programs targeted at senior citizens. Nationally, funding to combat child abuse receives 96 percent of all monies, domestic violence gets 3 percent, and elder abuse less than one percent. With improved outreach on elder abuse, the reported incidence is rising and some caseworkers for the elderly are overburdened. They frequently earn less than other domestic-violence workers but must deal with such complex crimes as financial exploitation.

See also Aging; Foster Care and Adoption; Substance Abuse; Youth at Risk.

FOR ADDITIONAL INFORMATION

American Association of Retired Persons
309 North Washington Square, Suite 110
Lansing, MI 48933
(517) 482-2772
(517) 482-2794 FAX
www.aarp.org/statepages/mi.html

Children's Charter of the Court of Michigan
324 North Pine Street, #1
Lansing, MI 48933
(517) 482-7533
(517) 482-2626 FAX
www.childcrt.org

Children's Trust Fund
235 South Grand River Avenue, Suite 1411
Lansing, MI 48933
(517) 373-4320
(517) 241-7038 FAX
www.michigan.gov/fia

Domestic Violence Prevention and Treatment Board
Family Independence Agency
235 South Grand Avenue, Suite 506
Lansing, MI 48909
(517) 335-6388
(517) 241-8903 FAX
www.michigan.gov/fia

Michigan's Children
428 Lenawee Street
Lansing, MI 48933
(517) 485-3500
(517) 485-3650 FAX
www.michiganschildren.org

Michigan Coalition Against Domestic and Sexual Violence
3893 Okemos Road, Suite B-2
Okemos, MI 48864
(517) 347-7000
(517) 347-1377 FAX
www.mcadsv.org

Michigan League for Human Services
115 South Pennsylvania Avenue, Suite 202
Lansing, MI 48912
(517) 487-5436
(517) 371-4546 FAX
www.milhs.org

Office of Child and Family Services
Family Independence Agency
235 South Grand Avenue, 5th Floor
Lansing, MI 48909
(517) 335-6158
(517) 335-6177 FAX
www.michigan.gov/fia

Office of Children's Ombudsman
Michigan National Tower, Suite 100
P.O. Box 30026
Lansing, MI 48909
(517) 373-3077
(517) 335-4471 FAX
www.michigan.gov/oco

Office of the Lieutenant Governor
P.O. Box 30026
Lansing, MI 48909
(517) 373-6800
(517) 241-3956 FAX
www.michigan.gov/ltgov

Office of Services to the Aging
Department of Community Health
611 West Ottawa Street, 3d Floor
P.O. Box 30676
Lansing, MI 48909
(517) 373-8230
(517) 373-4092 FAX
www.miseniors.net

Sponsored by the Michigan Nonprofit Association and the Council of Michigan Foundations

Elections: Campaign Finance and Voting

BACKGROUND

Michigan has complex laws regulating contributions to and expenditures of (1) candidates for state and local office and (2) committees that seek to influence election outcomes. (Federal law governs candidates for federal office—e.g., Congress.) All campaign funds must be disclosed.

The Michigan Department of State has responsibility for election matters in the state. The Bureau of Elections supervises campaign finance laws: From the time a person begins raising money to run for office or a group organizes a committee to raise money to influence an election, certain statements must be filed with the bureau. The bureau also supervises voter registration, and it maintains extensive Internet services for prospective and registered voters, media, the public, candidates, and committees. The Bureau of Legal Services receives and investigates campaign and election complaints.

Election Committees

There are several types of election committee. The exhibit presents their contribution limits.

- *Candidate committees* are directed and controlled by a state or local candidate for office. (Candidates for federal office are governed by federal law.) Candidates must use the money they receive for their own nomination or election or to pay expenses incidental to holding the elective office.

- *Political party committees* are statewide, congressional-district, or county-level political party organizations that receive or spend at least $500. Examples are the Michigan Republican and Democratic parties.

- *Political action committees (PACs)* typically start out as "political committees" formed to support/oppose one or more candidates, ballot questions, or recalls. If they operate for longer than six months, receive contributions from 25 or more people, and support/oppose three or more statewide candidates, they evolve into "independent committees." *Independent committees* typically are formed by businesses, labor organizations, advocacy groups, partisan legislative caucuses, and professional and trade associations. An independent committee may contribute ten times the amount that a political committee is permitted to give.

- *Ballot-question committees* support/oppose a ballot question, e.g., a local millage question, a statewide referendum or initiative, or a proposed amendment to the state constitution. They are prohibited from contributing or spending money in support/opposition to a candidate. Unlike the other types of committee, they may receive money from treasury funds of corporations, labor organizations, Indian tribes, and persons holding a casino interest.

GLOSSARY

Bundling
The practice whereby individuals or groups raise money from individuals on behalf of a candidate and combine it into a single contribution.

Election cycle
A full election cycle starts on the day following a general election for an office and ends on the day of the next general election for the same office. Shorter cycles pertain to the specific elections: special, primary, and general.

Hard money
Cash or checks given directly to a candidate for campaign expenses; similarly, the funds spent by candidates on their campaigns. All sources and expenditures must be disclosed.

Issue advertising
A commercial or ad in support of or opposition to an issue; may infer that a particular candidate is on the "right" or "wrong" side of the issue.

Political action committee (PAC)
A catchall phrase referring to committees, including "segregated funds" established by businesses, labor unions, Indian tribes, professional and trade associations, advocacy groups, or individuals with the objective of influencing elections.

Fundraising Limits

Michigan committees have no limits on how much money they may raise. Candidate committees must account for all funds received, and annual, pre-convention, post-convention, pre-election, and post-election filings are required. Other committees have different reporting schedules, depending on their type and whether registered at the state or county level. All committees must immediately report large amounts received close to an election (contribution sizes and deadlines vary by type of committee).

All state and local candidates are restricted as to how much money they may receive from donors, whether individuals or committees.

Spending Limits

Committees and candidates (except gubernatorial candidates who accept public funds) have no spending limits, but, as with collections, several filings are required and large, last-minute expenditures must be reported immediately.

Gubernatorial Campaigns

Since the mid-1970s, candidates for governor may receive public funds collected from taxpayers who check off $3 ($6 for a joint return) on their state personal income tax return. So long as sufficient taxpayer funds are on hand, a candidate in a gubernatorial primary may qualify for up to $990,000; s/he may raise additional funds and spend up to $2 million. Following the primary, each major-party nominee for governor who accepts public funds receives $1,125,000 (state funds permitting) and, again, may spend up to $2 million. (Independent and minor-party candidates may qualify for varying amounts of public funding.) Exempt from the spending limit are certain expenses, such as security costs, fees associated with state reporting requirements, and a one-time advertise-

Soft money
Money not given directly to a candidate for campaign expenses. Usually given to political parties or used to purchase "issue" advertising. Individuals, business, labor unions, and advocacy groups may give unlimited contributions, which are unregulated, in this way.

Straight-ticket (straight-party) vote
Casting one's vote for all the candidates of one party.

Contribution Limits for a Full Election Cycle, Michigan, 2002

Office	Individual and Political Committee	Independent Committee	Legislative Caucus Committee	District or County Political Party	State Political Party
Governor (with public funding)[a]	$3,400	$34,000	$34,000	$30,000	$750,000
Governor (without public funding)[a]	3,400	34,000	34,000	34,000	68,000
Secretary of state, attorney general, or statewide education post	3,400	34,000	34,000	34,000	68,000
Michigan Senate	1,000	10,000	Unlimited[a]	10,000	10,000
Michigan House of Representatives	500	5,000	Unlimited[a]	5,000	5,000
Local and judicial offices in jurisdictions of 250,000 or more	3,400	34,000	34,000	34,000	68,000
Local and judicial offices in jurisdictions of 85,001–249,999	1,000	10,000	10,000	10,000	20,000
Local and judicial offices in jurisdictions of 85,000 or fewer	500	5,000	10,000	5,000	10,000

SOURCES: Public Sector Consultants, Inc., and Michigan Department of State, Bureau of Elections.
[a]Candidates may make unlimited contributions to their own campaign. The exception is gubernatorial candidates who are accepting public funds; they are limited to a total of $50,000 from themselves and their immediate family.
[b]A legislative-caucus committee may not contribute to a legislative candidate in a contested primary.

Sponsored by the Michigan Nonprofit Association and the Council of Michigan Foundations

ment in response to the editorial endorsement (newspaper, radio, or television) of an opponent.

A gubernatorial candidate may waive public funding in either the primary or general election or both, avoiding the $2 million expenditure cap. One alternative to accepting public money is to raise all one's campaign funds through private contributions. Another is to personally finance one's campaign; in such a case (and only in this case), the self-financed candidate's opponents in the primary or general election may receive public funds but are excused from the spending limit.

DISCUSSION

Campaign Costs
Campaign costs have risen sharply, largely because media advertising costs have skyrocketed, and as campaigns become more sophisticated, more is being spent on consultants and staff. Spending sets a new record in virtually every election cycle.

In 2000 the median spending for all Michigan House campaigns was just under $43,000, but the hotter the contest, the higher the spending. In the most expensive contest, the candidate benefited from slightly more than $683,000 in direct, indirect, and independent expenditures. That year the 10 most heavily funded House races accounted for about one-third ($4.6 million) of the $14.3 million in total spending in all 110 House districts. Increasingly, the parties' legislative caucuses and the political parties are the biggest donors to legislative campaigns.

Michigan Supreme Court seats have become an important prize to political parties and special interests, and campaign spending for a seat on the high bench has increased dramatically: In 1994 average spending per candidate was $287,000; in 2000 it was more than four times that—almost $1.3 million.

Critics of the current political-fundraising system argue that big-money contributors overwhelm the voices of ordinary voters and beholden officeholders to their largest donors. They argue for full disclosure of *soft* money (see below) and, to reduce candidates' reliance on private contributions, for more public funding. Yet the U.S. Supreme Court, in *Buckley* v. *Valeo* (1976), upheld the right to unlimited candidate spending as a right of free speech protected by the First Amendment. Other federal court rulings have found that curbs on "issue" advertising by groups violate their First Amendment rights.

Supporters of the current fundraising system point out that spending for political advertising still is far outstripped by that for commercial products, such as motor vehicles, and the democratic electoral process is at least as important.

Soft Money
"Soft" money is so called because it is used to indirectly influence political outcomes (as opposed to "hard" money, which goes directly to a candidate). Groups, businesses, or individuals usually (1) use soft money to purchase issue advertising or (2) give it to political parties (instead of candidates), which may channel it to candidates or use it for their own issue advertising. Soft money contributions are unlimited and unregulated.

Soft money use ballooned in the 1990s, when special interest groups and national political parties discovered a loophole in federal campaign finance laws: Groups were limited by law in how much they could give directly to a federal *candidate* but not in how much they could give to *parties*, and they began donating huge sums to the national Republican and Democratic parties. The national parties used the money to donate heavily to congressional and presidential candidates and they transferred some of it to the state parties, enabling them to channel it to state races. In 2000 the national parties transferred more than $24 million to Michigan's state parties, and this money found its way into campaigns for local and state, as well as federal, office and also into the state parties' own issue advertising.

Soft money's other big use is for issue advertising through which political parties and interest groups, on their own and ostensibly in support/opposition to an issue, condemn or praise a candidate's votes or stand in regard to the issue. The idea is to move voters toward or away from a candidate. So long as the candidate does not participate in the content or placement of such ads, the spending is legal and avoids Michigan's candidate-contribution limits and source/expenditure disclosure requirements. Michigan soft-money opponents want state regulation requiring full disclosure of who is contributing to issue advertising and how the funds are spent but, as mentioned above, federal courts have been reluctant to uphold many restrictions on issue advertising.

At the federal level, opponents of soft money prevailed in the recent enactment of the federal McCain-Feingold law. Depending on which parts of the law survive the court challenges that immediately were filed, the use of soft money in federal elections (i.e., presidential and congressional) will be variously regulated, limited, or prohibited.

Supporters of the use of soft money argue that every individual or group should have an unfettered right to espouse political and ideological beliefs. They also believe that

Sponsored by the Michigan Nonprofit Association and the Council of Michigan Foundations

the low limits on contributions to federal, state, and local candidates have forced the parties and interest groups to use soft money and issue advertising as ways to influence voters.

Recent State Statutory Changes

Recent changes in state election law affect campaign funding and the ballot. The most controversial changes strictly regulate "bundled" contributions and ban straight-party ("straight-ticket") voting.

Bundled Contributions

Some political groups "bundle" contributions from supporters. That is, they raise funds from individuals on behalf of a candidate and then turn them over *en masse* to the candidate. EMILY's List (a national group that directs money to Democratic female candidates who support the pro-choice position) and the Pioneers (a national group that directs money to George W. Bush) are examples of such groups. Public Act 250 of 2001 (1) requires that groups that bundle contributions must disclose the individual contributions and (2) stipulates that the sum given to one candidate may not exceed the limit for a contribution from an independent committee.

Democrats argue that the new law is designed solely to limit to $34,000 the contribution of EMILY's List to its endorsed 2002 gubernatorial candidate, when otherwise, several times that sum would have been expected to flow to her campaign. Republicans counter that disclosure requirements and limits should be consistent, regardless of whether a committee bundles or does not bundle its contributions.

Ballot Changes

For decades, Michigan voters have been able, with a *single action*, to vote a straight ticket—that is, by pushing one lever, punching one hole, or marking one box, they could cast their vote for all the candidates of one political party. One- to two-thirds of Michigan voters (it varies by location) historically have chosen to so vote, but in 2001 Michigan enacted a law to do away with the practice. Republican supporters of the ban argue that it follows a nationwide trend (32 states currently prohibit single-action straight-ticket voting) and reduces the chance that voters will skip the nonpartisan contests—e.g., for judicial seats—and ballot questions, which are below the partisan contests on the ballot.

Democrats and many local clerks counter that single-action straight-party voting greatly speeds up election day balloting and enables people to easily cast a vote for candidates of the same philosophical persuasion. Underlying the parties' positions is a practical consideration: While many Republicans cast a straight-party vote, even more Democrats do.

The ban on straight-party voting likely will be subjected to referendum on the November 2002 ballot. At this writing, more than the required number of signatures have been obtained and await certification by the State Board of Canvassers.

2001 saw enactment of several other changes in voting laws, largely as a response to Florida's vote-casting and vote-tallying problems in the 2000 presidential contest. Under one new law, Michigan will convert to a uniform voting method if the federal government provides the roughly $20 million needed to do so. Currently, about 25 percent of local jurisdictions use the punch card system, 56 percent use an optical scan, and the remainder use lever machines or paper ballots. The measure also requires an expedited recount if a presidential election in the state is decided by 25,000 or fewer votes, and it raises training standards for election workers as well.

Proposed Reforms

Further suggested changes in campaign finance include

- permitting public, tax-supported dollars to be used for state legislative, judicial, or executive offices in addition to governor;

- requiring full disclosure of issue-advertising contributions and expenditures;

- prohibiting PAC contributions to candidates when the legislature is in session;

- shortening campaigns;

- requiring media to donate space/time for campaign advertising or greatly reduce their rates;

- limiting contributions to state political parties;

- limiting how much legislative-caucus campaign committees may contribute to candidates; and

- requiring electronic filing of contributions and expenditures.

Critics of one or more of these proposals point out that courts consistently have decided cases by erring on a broad interpretation of the First Amendment and the right of free speech. They also argue that any restrictive law or regulation motivates special interests, parties, and candidates to find loopholes to avoid constraints on campaign spending.

Sponsored by the Michigan Nonprofit Association and the Council of Michigan Foundations

Further suggested changes in voting include

- instituting a vote-by-mail or vote-by-Internet system;

- designating an election day holiday;

- permitting an absentee ballot for any reason;

- allowing voter registration to occur at the polls rather than requiring it in advance; and

- extending election-day hours or expanding voting to multiple days.

Supporters of such changes assert that they would increase voter ease and participation. The percentage of eligible people who vote has been declining fairly steadily: In the 1960 presidential election in Michigan, 73 percent of voting-age adults cast a ballot; in the 2000 presidential election, 58 percent voted.

NOTE: In May, just before this edition went to print, the Board of State Canvassers approved the straight-party voting question for the November 2002 ballot. A second question on the November ballot pertains to bonding for sewer construction and renovation. On the primary ballot, in August, there will be questions pertaining to compensation for certain elected state officials and funding/investment of a number of natural resources trust funds.

FOR ADDITIONAL INFORMATION

Bureau of Elections
Michigan Secretary of State
Mutual Building, 4th Floor
208 North Capitol Avenue
Lansing, MI 48918
(517) 373-2540
(517) 373-0941 FAX
www.michigan.gov/sos

Committee to Protect Voters' Rights
112 East Allegan Street
Lansing, MI 48933
(517) 374-7274
(517) 374-8605 FAX

League of Women Voters of Michigan
200 Museum Drive, Suite 104
Lansing, MI 48933
(517) 484-5383
(517) 484-3086 FAX
www.lwvmi.org

Michigan Campaign Finance Network
1310 Turner Street, Suite B
Lansing, MI 48906
(517) 482-7198
(517) 482-6132 FAX
www.mcfn.org

Michigan Chamber of Commerce
600 South Walnut Street
Lansing, Ml 48933
(517) 371-2100
(517) 371-7224 FAX
www.michamber.com

Michigan Democratic Party
606 Townsend Street
Lansing, MI 48933
(517) 371-5410
(517) 371-2056 FAX
www.mi-democrats.com

Michigan Republican Party
2121 East Grand River Avenue
Lansing, MI 48912
(517) 487-5413
(517) 487-0090 FAX
www.migop.org

Michigan Voters for Clean Elections
Common Cause in Michigan
109 East Oakland Street
Lansing, MI 48906
(517) 484-5385
(517) 484-5385 FAX (call ahead)
www.commoncause.org/states/michigan

Emergency Preparedness and Response

BACKGROUND

Most people's idea of civil emergency preparedness and response is demarcated sharply by September 11, 2001. Before that, a "disaster" usually meant a flood, tornado, or other natural event after which the affected towns and counties need additional help to tend to the needs of local residents and businesses. Since September 11 and the delivery of anthrax-tainted mail during the following two months, we have become acutely aware that a disaster may be caused by humans as well as nature. This awareness has shone a bright light on how government is and should be prepared to respond to all calamities, from a storm to a train derailment to a biological attack. Michigan is served by its Emergency Management Act, enacted in 1976, and a number of task forces, teams, and other bodies charged with protecting state residents and infrastructure.

In Michigan law, emergency and disaster are precisely defined, but in practice the former has to do with the *potential* for harm and the latter with *actual* harm having been done. Almost every year a number of situations are declared by the chief executive to be an emergency or disaster. Since January 1, 2000, situations in Michigan have been the subject of five gubernatorial and two presidential declarations.[1]

Emergency Response in Michigan

When there is an emergency or disaster in Michigan, it is likely that among the first people on the scene (first responders) will be local law-enforcement or public-safety personnel. [Hereafter, for simplicity, "emergency" should be read as meaning either emergency or disaster.] Working through the local chain of command, responders may request additional resources from other government units with which the affected local government has a mutual aid compact. A mutual aid compact is a binding agreement among local units of government that sets out payment, liability protection, and rules for police, fire, or other public personnel responding to an emergency in the jurisdiction of another compact member. Without such an agreement, law-enforcement and other public-safety personnel who respond outside of their jurisdiction may lack authority to offer assistance and may be unprotected from liability.

Local personnel also may contact their county's emergency-management coordinator. Every Michigan county and all municipalities with 25,000 or more residents are required by state law to have an emergency coordinator. (It is optional for smaller municipalities.) When a local official declares a state of emergency and asks for state assistance, the formal request is transmitted from the county's emergency coordinator to the Emergency Management Division (EMD) of the Michigan State Police (MSP). The EMD is the lead emergency agency in Michigan and is responsible for

- coordinating local, state, and federal emergency-management activities;

- preparing and maintaining the Michigan Emergency Management Plan;

- proposing and administering a statewide mutual aid compact;

[1]Gubernatorial declarations: heavy snow in Emmet County; severe winds in Kalamazoo County; flooding in Genesee County; urban flooding in Wayne County; gasoline pipeline rupture in Jackson County. Presidential declarations: urban flooding in Wayne/Oakland counties; blizzard in 39 counties.

APRIL 1, 2002 113

Sponsored by the Michigan Nonprofit Association and the Council of Michigan Foundations

---

GLOSSARY

Disaster
A situation resulting in loss of life, property damage, and/or a threat to public health and safety.

Emergency
A situation that may result in loss of life, property damage, and/or a threat to public health and safety.

Emergency management assistance compact
A formal interstate agreement defining how and under what conditions states will aid one another during a disaster or emergency.

First responders
The first people sent to a disaster or emergency site—e.g., firefighters, emergency medical personnel, local law enforcement.

Mutual aid compact
A contract between two or more units of government setting out payment, liability protection, and rules for police, fire, or other public personnel in the event of an emergency or disaster.

Weapon of mass destruction (WMD)
Usually, a weapon containing a nuclear, biological (e.g., anthrax, smallpox, salmonella) or chemical (e.g., nerve agent) payload, but some agencies use a broader definition. For example, the FBI considers the 1995 Oklahoma City bombing to be a WMD attack due to the amount of conventional explosives used and the resulting harm to life and property.

- providing and maintaining the state Emergency Operations Center;

- issuing rules and establishing standards for emergency-training programs; and

- preparing recommendations to the governor for executive orders, proclamations, and regulations in times of emergency.

The state director of emergency management (MSP director), working with the EMD commander (MSP deputy director), has the power to

- direct state disaster-relief forces;

- administer state and federal disaster-relief funds and money;

- make recommendations to the governor;

- assign general missions to the National Guard or state defense force to assist with relief operations; and

- receive and investigate requests for assistance from local governments.

Together, the EMD and State Police heads determine whether a state of emergency exists in the requesting locality. Depending on the nature, scope, and magnitude of the event, the EMD may recommend to the governor that s/he declare a state of emergency because local resources have been exhausted. A gubernatorial declaration permits the governor to assume certain extra powers with regard to the emergency area for up to 28 days, including the authority to

- issue executive orders, proclamations, and directives having the force of law;

- seek and accept federal assistance;

- suspend a regulatory statute, order, or rule;

- commandeer or use private property; and

- direct mandatory evacuations and control access to the emergency site.

The nature of the event determines which state or federal agency has the primary responsibility to respond. In the event of a forest fire, for example, the Michigan Department of Natural Resources is the primary agency, while the response to an oil spill on the Great Lakes would be led by the U.S. Coast Guard. The assignment of primary and supporting roles for a wide range of emergencies is set out in the *Michigan Hazard Analysis* framework and other state and federal planning documents.

Considerable Michigan legislative activity followed the September 11 attacks. Among the first laws enacted were Public Acts 247 and 248 of 2001, making Michigan a member of the national Emergency Management Assistance Compact. The compact establishes procedures whereby member states may request training and emergency assistance from the compact and provides for (1) command and control of responding personnel and (2) limited liability immunity for personnel rendering assistance in another state. Michigan, which had been planning to join the compact prior to the September 11 attacks, became the 43d signatory. In addition to this step, the State Police, attorney general, secretary of state, and legislative leaders reached agreement on various other anti-terrorism measures to be introduced as legislation. In total, 46 bills were introduced, 34 of which have been enacted as of this writing (see the exhibit); the remainder still are under consideration.

Michigan's Statewide and Regional Emergency Response Resources

- *Michigan National Guard Civil Support Team* This group—officially a Military Support Detachment/Rapid Assessment and Initial Detection (MSD/RAID) team—is a 22-member group of National Guard troops who have specialized training and equipment enabling them to respond to attacks involving weapons of mass destruction (WMDs). Until November 15, 2001, Michigan's team was a "light" team—that is, it comprised part-time guard members; the nearest "heavy" (full-time) team was located in Peoria, Illinois. On that date, the U.S. Department of Defense authorized a full-time team to be deployed in Michigan, bringing the total number of national teams to 32. The Michigan team expects to be certified in late 2002, after each member completes more than 650 hours of training from the Michigan State Police, U.S. departments of Defense and Energy, and U.S. Environmental Protection Agency. The team will be located at Fort Custer (near the Battle Creek Air National Guard base).

- *Michigan Hazardous Materials Training Center* Operated by the State Police, the center provides hazardous-materials training to public and private responders. The center was created in 1991 with private-sector donations and is located adjacent to the Michigan State Police Training Academy, in Lansing. Courses include such topics as confined-space rescue, monitoring and sampling hazardous materials, and terrorism-incident planning and response.

- *Michigan Urban Search and Rescue Team (MUSAR)* This is a privately funded team of skilled

Michigan Anti-Terrorism Legislation, 2001–02

Act Number (All 2002 unless otherwise indicated)	Synopsis and Effective Date
P.A. 225 of 2001	Prohibits firearms, explosives, knives, or other dangerous weapons on commercial airport property. 4/1/02
P.A.s 247–248 of 2001	Make Michigan a member of the Emergency Management Assistance Compact, a mutual-aid agreement among the states, territorial possessions, Puerto Rico, and the District of Columbia. 1/8/02
P.A. 24	Provides sentencing guidelines for possessing a dangerous weapon on commercial airport property. 3/6/02
P.A. 112	Allows a judge to suppress delivery of an affidavit to a person served a search warrant if necessary to protect an investigation or the safety of a victim or witness. 4/22/02
P.A. 113	Creates the Michigan Anti-Terrorism Act and declares an act of terrorism—and providing material support for terrorism—to be a felony. 4/22/02
P.A. 114	Clarifies procedures under which law-enforcement agencies may share grand jury information about terrorism-related investigations and crimes. 5/1/02
P.A. 115	Prohibits a person from obtaining or possessing a blueprint or other diagram of a public building for the purpose of committing an act of terrorism. 4/22/02
P.A. 116	Amends the list of "vulnerable targets," adding stadiums, transportation structures (including bridges and tunnels), public utilities (e.g., gas pipelines and electric generating plants), airports, and port facilities; additional felony penalties apply to someone convicted of committing an act of terrorism against them. 4/22/02
P.A. 117	Prohibits a person from using the Internet or other telecommunications device to impair public safety or government operations with the intent to commit an act of terrorism. 4/22/02
P.A. 118	Prohibits drivers from transporting hazardous material without a hazardous-material endorsement on their operator's license. 5/1/02
P.A. 119	Includes acts of terrorism punishable by life imprisonment among the crimes to which a statute of limitations does not apply. 4/22/02
P.A. 120	Requires someone convicted of an act of terrorism to reimburse affected government entities for incident-related expenses, including emergency response and prosecution. 4/22/02
P.A. 121	Gives National Guard members certain protections with regard to their civilian job when they are called into state service; makes Michigan's protections the same as federal protections. 4/1/02
P.A. 122	Defines as felonies terrorist threats, acts of terrorism that do not cause death, and soliciting support for an act of terrorism. 4/22/02
P.A. 123	Amends the Michigan Code of Criminal Procedure to include sentencing guidelines for poisoning (or making a false report of poisoning) food, drink, medicine, or water supplies. 4/22/02
P.A. 124	Amends the definition of racketeering to include an act of terrorism. 4/22/02
P.A. 125	Requires hospitals to develop and maintain a plan for detecting and handling biohazards. 4/1/02
P.A. 126	Amends the Michigan Vehicle Code to increase the penalty for creating, possessing, selling, or obtaining a fake driver's license. 4/22/02
P.A. 127	Amends the Michigan Code of Criminal Procedure to include sentencing guidelines for forging, selling, or possessing a fake driver's license. 4/22/02
P.A. 128	Specifies that a search warrant, affidavit, or tabulation contained in any court file or record-retention system is not public information. 4/22/02
P.A. 129	Allows a person to be prosecuted for a criminal offense—even if s/he is not located in Michigan—if the offense was conducted partly in Michigan or resulted in substantial and detrimental effects in Michigan. 4/22/02
P.A. 130	Exempts from Freedom of Information requests a public body's emergency-response plans, risk planning and threat assessments, and domestic-preparedness strategies. 5/1/02
P.A. 131	Defines a terrorist organization and excludes First Amendment activities from the definition of terrorism. 4/22/02
P.A. 132	Amends the Emergency Management Act to extend the maximum effective duration of an emergency or disaster from 14 to 28 days; authorizes the State Police Emergency Management Division to administer statewide mutual-aid compacts; and permits "heightened state of alert" declarations to warn of terrorist activities and gives the governor limited emergency powers during such a state. 5/1/02

Sponsored by the Michigan Nonprofit Association and the Council of Michigan Foundations

P.A. 133	Amends the Michigan Military Act to grant additional law-enforcement powers to the National Guard when responding to terrorism or protecting the state's vital resources, including military installations. 5/1/02
P.A. 134	Establishes possession of a fake incendiary device, explosive, or bomb as a felony. 4/22/02
P.A. 135	Increases the punishment for tampering with a food, drink, nonprescription medicine, or pharmaceutical product or poisoning a spring, well, reservoir, or public water supply. 4/22/02
P.A. 136	Expands the definition of money laundering to include proceeds from acts of terrorism. 4/22/02
P.A. 137	Amends the Code of Criminal Procedure to include sentencing guidelines for acts of terrorism. 4/22/02
P.A. 140	Amends the list of "vulnerable targets," adding petroleum refineries, storage facilities, and pipelines; vehicles, trains, aircraft, or boats used to transport the public; and federal, state, and local governmental buildings. Additional felony penalties apply to someone convicted of committing an act of terrorism against them. 4/22/02
P.A. 141	Requires that someone convicted of terrorism to make monetary restitution to victims and units of government for the terrorism act(s). 4/22/02
P.A. 142	Adds an act of terrorism to the list of situations in which real and/or personal property may be seized by and forfeited to state and local government. 5/1/02
P.A. 143	Amends the Code of Criminal Procedure to add sentencing guidelines for acts of terrorism. 4/22/02

NOTE: These are 34 of the 46 anti-terrorism bills proposed in the wake of September 11, 2001. The remaining 12 bills are in various stages of the legislative process.
SOURCE: Public Sector Consultants, using information from the legislation, House and Senate fiscal agency analyses, and House Legislative Analysis Section documents.

responders from the State Police and local law-enforcement, public-safety, and private-sector organizations. The team, comprising members from across the state, consists of four specialty groups: search, rescue, technical, and medical. The Federal Emergency Management Agency (FEMA) has a national network of 28 urban search and rescue teams nationally, and MUSAR is pursuing such certification. Currently, the nearest FEMA search and rescue teams are located in Ohio and Indiana.

■ *Michigan Regional Response Team Network* This is a network of 12 teams throughout the state that are composed of local police, fire, and medical agencies. Teams may use MUSAR resources as well as local and state bomb squads. The teams can respond within two hours to a situation involving a weapon of mass destruction anywhere in the state.

■ *Michigan Homeland Security Task Force* The task force was established as the Michigan Terrorism Task Force in 1996 in the wake of the World Trade Center and Oklahoma City bombings. Its purpose is to facilitate information sharing among agencies about Michigan's domestic anti-terrorism preparedness. The task force was renamed in 2002 and is composed of 18 officials from federal, state, and local agencies. Federal agencies represented are the Department of Defense, Environmental Protection Agency, Public Health Service, and Federal Bureau of Investigation. State agencies represented are the State Police, National Guard, and departments of Agriculture, Community Health, Environmental Quality, and Natural Resources. Local government is represented by law-enforcement officials. The task force meets quarterly and is chaired by the Michigan State Police.

DISCUSSION

The horrific events of late 2001 raised the priority of emergency management and preparedness nationwide. In Michigan, policymakers undertook a review of the state's emergency-management plans and are addressing the changes needed and the challenges in implementing them.

Preparedness Drills
First-responder training is a key component of many of the emergency-preparedness and response plans at all government levels. But even with billions of promised federal dollars, states and local governments cannot train all potential first responders for all potential situations. Large-scale drills—in which units of government respond to a disaster complete with volunteer "casualties"—are an excellent way to train responders, but they also are expensive. Less costly but effective are such smaller-scale exercises as "What if . . .?" discussions and analysis/study of other localities' responses to various situations. The "Dark Winter" exercise (in mid-2001), in which a mock smallpox outbreak was responded to, provided both direct training for the many federal officials involved and indirect training for the state and local responders nationwide who now are studying the exercise.

Preparedness is only as good as the information available to those who must respond. For example, during the anthrax attack in October 2001, medical professionals at first did not know that anthrax spores could be made finely enough to pass through the microscopic pores in envelopes, and the public health system was ill-prepared to simultaneously test a large number of samples, conduct an epidemiological investigation, meet inoculation demands, and assist the FBI with its criminal investigation.

Sponsored by the Michigan Nonprofit Association and the Council of Michigan Foundations

In Michigan, a number of preparedness drills are coordinated by the Michigan State Police each year, and the Michigan National Guard participates in the MSP drills and also conducts its own for guard forces. In recent years, drills have pertained to nuclear-power-plant accidents/disasters, terrorist attacks, use or threatened use of a weapon of mass destruction, civil unrest, airplane crashes, and biological outbreaks (e.g., foot and mouth disease). Preparedness drills may involve one or several local, state, and federal agencies; formats include discussions, classroom training, "tabletop" scenarios (wherein the command structure responds as if the event were occurring), or simulated incidents.

Budget Battles: Distribution and Disbursement

In 2002 the president requested nearly $38 billion for new homeland defense activities focusing on four key areas: preparation for bioterrorism, emergency response, airport and border security, and improved intelligence gathering and information sharing. In Michigan, the governor's 2002–03 budget proposes $9.5 million to strengthen the state's public health infrastructure and $60 million in bonding for airport security improvements. Michigan will receive millions more in federal homeland defense funds.

Federal/state policymakers face politically charged questions about how the money shall be allocated. Should enhanced protection, training, equipment, and supplies be provided equally to all states/counties? To the more populous states/counties? To states/counties that are home to high-profile targets? To statewide teams that can be deployed rapidly to any county?

How the money shall be channeled is another question. Supporters of channeling all monies to local governments through the EMD assert that it would permit the agency to coordinate training and resources and assure appropriate coverage statewide. Most FEMA dollars currently are administered in Michigan by the EMD, but this is not the case with other anti-terrorism money. The Michigan Department of Community Health recently was notified that it will receive more than $30 million from the Federal Centers for Disease Control to strengthen the department's bioterrorism preparedness. Some anti-terrorism funding goes directly to local units of government via Justice Department grants, and while this allows for flexibility in seeking funding to meet local priorities, it also can mean overlapping or duplicate services. Monies sought and received directly by local governments and agencies could result, for example, in two similar-sized cities receiving (1) vastly different grants as a result of Congressional pressure and/or grant-writing prowess or (2) grants with which they purchase equipment that is incompatible with that used elsewhere in Michigan (e.g., emergency radios using different frequencies).

Interagency Communication

The events of September 11 revealed that there was inadequate communication among and within U.S. immigration, intelligence, and law-enforcement agencies. In many cases, one federal agency had information that was not passed to others that could have acted on it. Protecting national borders, an important issue in Michigan, is an area in which interagency communications are important but complicated: Responsibility falls to the U.S. Coast Guard, Customs Service, and Immigration and Naturalization Service, and to various state agencies—in Michigan, the National Guard, local police and sheriffs, State Police, and Michigan Department of Transportation. Policymakers and law-enforcement officials must jointly define, monitor, and adjust organization structures to ensure that all partners share all relevant information at all times. In Michigan, this coordination is being managed by the EMD and the Homeland Security Task Force in conjunction with federal anti-terrorism task forces directed by the U.S. attorneys' offices.

Changes to Michigan Laws

Even before September 11, the Michigan emergency-management command structure was considering needed changes in the guiding document, the Michigan Emergency Management Act (P.A. 390 of 1976). For example, the act gave the governor emergency powers for up to 14 days unless the period were extended by the legislature, but it did not specify how the legislature shall grant an extension.

As mentioned, following September 11, Michigan legislative and executive branch leaders developed 46 bills that they believe are necessary to improve Michigan's security. The 34 that have been enacted as of this writing include an extension of the governor's emergency powers to 28 days and establishment of a process by which the legislature may further extend the duration.

One challenge for policymakers was to sort out which of the many proposals were adequate and appropriate responses and which marked an unacceptable intrusion into individual liberty. One issue that remains particularly contentious is expanded wiretap authority (this was not part of the 46-bill package but received attention during its deliberation). Expansion supporters believe that authorizing state and local law enforcement to conduct wiretaps will increase the effectiveness of investigation and prosecution of major crimes, including terrorism, abduction, computer crime, and crime involving children and computers. In addition, supporters point out that wiretaps

Sponsored by the Michigan Nonprofit Association and the Council of Michigan Foundations

must receive advance approval by multiple law-enforcement and judicial entities. Opponents argue that the expanded wiretapping authority will lead to abuses and threaten personal liberties, and they point to the extremely high cost of wiretaps (the House Legislative Analysis Section reports an average exceeding $54,000).

U.S. Office of Homeland Security

Another question for emergency management in Michigan is how the new federal Office of Homeland Security will interact with and affect Michigan's emergency-management agencies and plans. The mission of the federal office is to "develop and coordinate the implementation of a comprehensive national strategy to secure the United States from terrorist threats or attacks." How effective this office will be at integrating disparate agendas, gathering and controlling funding, and getting buy-in from local, state, and federal partners is a question that concerns the emergency-preparedness community at every level of government.

As of this writing, it is unclear both how much of the $38 billion in federal homeland defense monies will make its way to Michigan and which agency or agencies in the state will be in charge of disbursing it. Adding to the confusion is that the federal office is not expected to distribute funding directly. Rather, it will distribute it through other federal agencies (e.g., the departments of Justice, Agriculture, Energy). As is the case with existing emergency-preparedness dollars, Michigan policymakers will face distribution and disbursement questions: How shall the money be allocated, and which agency will control distribution?

See also Privacy.

FOR ADDITIONAL INFORMATION

ANSER Institute for Homeland Security
2900 South Quincy Street, Suite 800
Arlington, VA 22206
(703) 416-2000
(703) 416-3343 FAX
www.homelandsecurity.org

Emergency Management Division
Michigan State Police
4000 Collins Road
Lansing, MI 48909
(517) 336-6198
(517) 333-4987 FAX
www.michigan.gov/msp

Federal Emergency Management Agency
500 C Street, S.W.
Washington, DC 20472
(202) 646-4600
(202) 646-4086 FAX
www.fema.gov

Michigan Association of Chiefs of Police
2133 University Park Drive, Suite 200
Okemos, MI 48864
(517) 349-9420
(517) 349-5823 FAX
www.michiganpolicechiefs.org

Michigan State Police
714 South Harrison Road
East Lansing, MI 48823
(517) 332-2521
www.michigan.gov/msp

National Emergency Management Association
Council of State Governments
P.O. Box 11910
Lexington, KY 40578
(859) 244-8000
(859) 859-8001 FAX
www.nemaweb.org

Office of Homeland Security
The White House
1600 Pennsylvania Avenue
Washington, DC 20502
(202) 456-1414
(202) 456-2461 FAX
www.whitehouse.gov/homeland

Sponsored by the Michigan Nonprofit Association and the Council of Michigan Foundations

Firearms Regulation

BACKGROUND

A rticle 1, section 6, of the Michigan Constitution states that "Every person has a right to keep and bear arms for the defense of himself and the state," and there has been relatively little legal debate over the intent or purpose of Michigan's constitutional language. This is in sharp contrast to the diverse opinion about the meaning of the Second Amendment to the U.S. Constitution, (". . . the right of the people to keep and bear arms, shall not be infringed"), but nevertheless, the issue of firearms regulation in Michigan has been the focus of heated debate in recent years.

Both federal and state law regulate the purchase and use of firearms. Federal law primarily focuses on the sale of firearms by licensed gun dealers. For example, federal law

- requires gun manufacturers, distributors, and dealers to hold a federal firearms license (FFL);

- prohibits FFL holders from selling a handgun to someone aged under 21 or a rifle or shotgun to someone aged under 18;

- prohibits the private sale of a handgun to someone aged under 18;

- prohibits importation of small, poor-quality handguns (so-called Saturday night specials) and some foreign assault weapons;

- prohibits production of certain assault weapons and magazines capable of holding more than 10 rounds of ammunition (however, it is not illegal to own or sell pre-1994 weapons and magazines);

- prohibits the manufacture, import, or sale of fully automatic machine guns (however, it is not illegal to own/sell pre-1986 weapons); and

- prohibits anyone aged under 18 from possessing a handgun or ammunition suitable only for a handgun; and

- prohibits certain categories of people—convicted felons, fugitives from justice, subjects of restraining orders, or those convicted of domestic violence—from possessing guns.

Compliance with the last provision listed above occurs through the FBI's National Instant Check System (NICS). FFL holders are prohibited from selling any gun without performing the NICS background check. According to a February 2000 report by the Bureau of Alcohol, Tobacco and Firearms, the background-check system prevented purchases by prohibited persons about 180,000 times during its first year of operation (1999). The NICS system applies only to sales by FFL holders, however. A sale by any other person (e.g., unlicensed seller, individual owner) in any venue (e.g., garage sale, gun show, private residence) does not require a background check.

While federal law focuses on the sale of firearms by licensed dealers, Michigan laws regulate their sale, possession, and use by individuals. In Michigan,

- selling automatic weapons is prohibited;

GLOSSARY

Automatic weapon
A firearm that can fire continuously until the ammunition is exhausted or the trigger released.

Concealed weapon
In Michigan, a firearm, either loaded or unloaded, that (1) is 30 inches or shorter or (2) by appearance or construction, does not look like a firearm.

Firearm
Under Michigan law, rifles, shotguns, automatic weapons, pistols, pellet guns, and flare launchers are firearms; BB guns and blank-cartridge pistols are not.

Handgun
A firearm that can be used with one hand; includes pistols.

Rifle
A firearm with a grooved bore; designed to be fired from the shoulder.

Semiautomatic weapon
A firearm that ejects the shell and loads the next ammunition round automatically after each shot has been fired; unlike an automatic weapon, the trigger must be pulled for each shot.

Shotgun
A smooth-bore firearm that fires shot over short ranges.

Sponsored by the Michigan Nonprofit Association and the Council of Michigan Foundations

- rifles and shotguns may not be sold to someone aged under 18;

- selling armor-piercing ammunition is prohibited;

- selling or using hardware to convert a semiautomatic weapon to fully automatic is illegal;

- discharging a firearm from a vehicle is prohibited;

- handguns may be purchased only if a permit is granted by a local police agency and the applicant has passed a background check;

- anyone convicted of committing a crime with a firearm is subject to an additional penalty of two years in prison without opportunity of early parole;

- schools must expel students who possess a weapon, including a firearm, on school property;

- discharging a firearm within a public right-of-way, in cemeteries, or on farm property without the consent of the farm's owner is prohibited; and

- carrying a firearm while under the influence of a controlled substance or alcohol is prohibited.

Michigan's firearm laws are relatively strict: In March 2000, the Open Society Institute (New York) published "Gun Control in the United States: A Comparative Survey of State Gun Laws," ranking the 50 states on the stringency of their laws concerning ownership, possession, sale, and transfer of guns. Michigan ranks 14th among the 50 states in the strictness of its gun laws. Using a scale on which 0 equates to consistency with federal law, negative numbers indicate more leniency than federal law, and positive numbers indicate more strictness than federal law, Michigan scores 15. Massachusetts is most strict, with a score of 76, and Maine most lenient, with a score of –10. The national average is 9.

Of the 669 murders committed in Michigan in 2000, firearms were used in 474: handguns in 231, rifles in 19, and shotguns in 24 (the remainder were not classified by firearm type). By age of victim, 258 were 25–39, 174 were 17–24, and 40 were 16 and younger. By race of victim, 185 were Caucasian, 463 were African-American, and two were of Asian or Pacific descent (the remainder were not identified by race).

Michigan's New Concealed-Weapons Laws

In July 2001 Michigan law regarding the acquisition of a license to carry a concealed weapon (CCW) underwent a dramatic change. A concealed weapon, as defined by Michigan law, is a (1) loaded or unloaded firearm that is 30 inches or shorter or (2) a firearm that looks like something other than what it is (e.g., a pen or camera).

Under the former CCW laws, county licensing boards comprising a representative of the sheriff, prosecutor, and state police decided whether an applicant could obtain a CCW license, and the applicant had to prove that s/he was qualified and needed to carry a concealed weapon. Licensing boards were prohibited from issuing licenses to several types of applicants—youth aged under 18, non-U.S. citizens, convicted felons, and others. Acceptable reasons for needing to carry a concealed weapon varied from county to county. Some boards granted many CCW licenses, while others issued very few. If one was turned down for a CCW, there was little right of appeal.

The legislative intent of Michigan's new CCW laws is to

> create a standardized system for issuing concealed pistol licenses to prevent criminals and other violent individuals from obtaining licenses to carry a concealed pistol, to allow law abiding residents to obtain a license to carry a concealed pistol, and to prescribe the rights and responsibilities of individuals who have obtained a license to carry a concealed pistol. It is also the intent of the legislature to grant an applicant the right to know why his or her application for a concealed pistol license is denied and to create a process by which an applicant may appeal that denial.

The old statute, because of the local discretion permitted, was known as a "may issue" law. The new statute, which requires a county licensing board to issue a permit unless it can show that the applicant is *not* eligible, is known as a "shall issue" law.

The new laws outline the basic requirements for CCW license eligibility. Applicants must

- be aged 21 or older;

- be a U.S. citizen or legal alien and a Michigan resident for six months;

- not be prohibited under the Michigan Penal Code from having a firearm;

- never have been convicted of a felony in Michigan or elsewhere and have no felony charges pending;

- not have been dishonorably discharged from the U.S. armed forces;

- not have been convicted of a misdemeanor violation for certain offenses for eight years prior to application;

- not have been convicted of any misdemeanor for three years prior to application;

Sponsored by the Michigan Nonprofit Association and the Council of Michigan Foundations

- never have been cleared of a crime due to a plea of insanity;

- never have been involuntarily committed for mental illness; and

- be in a sound mental state when applying.

Finally, it must be clear to the county board that issuing the license will not endanger the safety of any person; a decision to deny a license for this reason must be based on

> . . . clear and convincing evidence of civil infractions, crimes, personal protection orders or injunctions, or police reports or other clear and convincing evidence of the actions of, or statements of, the applicant that bear directly on the applicant's ability to carry a concealed pistol.

Two additional provisions of the new laws (1) require that two sets of fingerprints must be submitted by the applicant, one for the State Police and the other for the FBI, and (2) designate certain areas as "pistol free." The latter include

- schools and school property (unless the carrier is a parent or legal guardian dropping off or picking up a student);

- daycare centers and child-care agencies;

- sports arenas and stadiums;

- customer areas of businesses licensed under the state liquor control code (unless the carrier is an owner or employee);

- places of worship (unless the presiding official allows concealed weapons);

- entertainment facilities with a seating capacity of 2,500 or more;

- hospitals;

- college or university classrooms and dormitories;

- casinos; and

- airports (added in 2002).

In addition, all applicants for a CCW license must complete a certified pistol safety-training course that offers at least eight hours of instruction, including three hours on a firing range.

DISCUSSION

There are two groups of opponents to Michigan's new CCW laws. One argues that the laws are too tough, that there is no evidence that restrictions on concealed weap-

ons will reduce crime, and that the new restrictions on where concealed weapons may be carried is a step backward. They also assert that the fingerprinting requirement is a step toward national registration of firearms, which they vehemently oppose.

The other group fears that Michigan's being a shall-issue state means that the number of pistols in circulation and being carried will increase dramatically. They point out that in Wayne County alone, from 1990 to 1998, 5,264 youngsters aged under 17 were charged with carrying a concealed weapon. They are afraid that with CCW permits being more easily obtained, such statistics will worsen in the years ahead. They also contend that removing local discretion in issuing permits means that local circumstances cannot be taken into account.

Supporters of the new laws believe that they provide much-needed uniformity in granting licenses, impose important restrictions on where concealed weapons may be carried, and improve security by raising the minimum age, from 18 to 21, for obtaining a permit.

There also are dramatic differences of opinion on other firearm-related issues.

- In 1990 Michigan enacted a law prohibiting cities or other jurisdictions from bringing legal action against gun manufacturers or distributors for death or injury resulting from a firearm. Such litigation has been brought by cities in some other states. The law was vigorously opposed by gun-control advocates and vigorously supported by gun-control opponents.

- Michigan is one of 40 states that prohibits or restricts municipalities from enacting local gun legislation that is more restrictive than the state's. Opponents argue that local units of government should have the authority to impose tougher standards than the state if necessitated by local circumstances or the desires of the residents. Supporters believe that law-abiding gun owners should be able to travel anywhere in the state without being in danger of violating local law.

- Four states—California, Maryland, South Carolina, Virginia—have a "one-gun-a-month" law, meaning that a person may buy no more than one handgun a month. The intent is to prevent illegal gun traffickers from buying and reselling multiple handguns. Proponents of such a law in Michigan argue that it would cut down on the trafficking of illegal handguns. Opponents argue that law-abiding gun purchasers should not be restricted in the number of purchases they are permitted.

Sponsored by the Michigan Nonprofit Association and the Council of Michigan Foundations

- Finally, four states—California, Connecticut, Hawaii, Massachusetts—require guns in the home to be kept locked or unloaded. Proponents of such a measure for Michigan (Senate Bill 538) believe that "safe storage" requirements would dramatically reduce firearm accidents, particularly involving children. Opponents argue that such regulation is unnecessary and constitutes government intrusion into the home, violating personal freedom.

See also Crime and Corrections.

FOR ADDITIONAL INFORMATION

Brady Campaign
1225 I Street, N.W., Suite 1000
Washington, DC 20005
(202) 898-0792
(202) 371-9615 FAX
www.bradycampaign.org

Coalition to Stop Gun Violence
1000 16th Street, N.W., Suite 603
Washington, DC 20036
(202) 408-0061
(202) 408-0062 FAX
www.gunfree.org

Michigan Coalition of Responsible Gun Owners
P.O. Box 14014
Lansing, MI 48901
(517) 484-2746
(517) 484-2798 FAX
www.mcrgo.org

Michigan Partnership to Prevent Gun Violence
1501 North Shore Drive, Suite B
Lansing, MI 48823
(517) 332-4299
(517) 332-4392 FAX
www.mppgv.org

Michigan Rifle and Pistol Association
P.O. Box 1802
Midland, MI 49641
(989) 631-3079
www.michrpa.com

Michigan State Police
714 South Harrison Road
East Lansing, MI 48823
(517) 336-6176
(517) 336-6551 FAX
www.michigan.gov/msp

Michigan United Conservation Clubs
2101 Wood Street
P.O. Box 30235
Lansing, MI 48909
(517) 371-1041
(517) 371-1505 FAX
www.mucc.org

National Rifle Association
11250 Waples Mill Road
Fairfax, VA 22030
(800) 672-3888
(703) 267-3918 FAX
www.mynra.com

Open Society Institute
400 West 59th Street
New York, NY 10019
(212) 548-0600
(212) 548-4609 FAX
www.soros.org

Sponsored by the Michigan Nonprofit Association and the Council of Michigan Foundations

Foster Care and Adoption

BACKGROUND

Foster Care

When children must be removed from their own home, the state may place them temporarily in family foster care. Foster care can be necessary for various reasons, such as when a child's family is unable or unwilling to provide minimum care and supervision, when there are safety concerns attributable to abuse or neglect, or when parental rights are terminated.

During the 1960s, growing awareness of child abuse/neglect led to (1) public financial support for children in foster care and (2) mandates that various professionals who have contact with children (e.g., doctors, teachers) must report suspicions of abuse/neglect to the authorities. The latter led to increased knowledge of instances of abuse/neglect and resulted in more children being placed in foster care. Nationwide, the most recent data say that on September 30, 1999,

- 568,000 children were in foster care,

- 118,000 children awaited adoption,

- 171,000 victims of child maltreatment had been placed in foster care during the previous year, and

- 1,100 children died as a result of maltreatment (22 in foster care).

In the 1980s state policy—through federal funding incentives and legislation enacted to comply with federal requirements—was to make a "reasonable effort" to keep children with their families, avoiding the necessity of foster placement when possible and shortening the length of stay when it was not. When children could not be safely returned to their family, states were encouraged (as they are now) to facilitate the children's adoption. For several years, family preservation and reunification took precedence over other child-welfare concerns, but this has changed in light of (1) too many instances of continued maltreatment and even death among children returned to their family and (2) harm done to children languishing in the foster-care system, which frequently involves a child being in a number of foster-care placements.

In Michigan, the landmark report of the Children's Commission (Binsfeld Commission, 1995) and the annual reports of the state Office of Children's Ombudsman scrutinized the workings of the Michigan child-welfare system and proposed changes that led to a considerable body of legislation making the safety and best interests of children (often preservation of the family unit) the primary goals of the system. Among the changes that affect foster care are reforms that

- allow the state to more rapidly sever parental rights in egregious cases of sexual and psychological child abuse and make these children available for adoption as quickly as possible;

- waive some foster-home licensing requirements, to enable sibling groups to be placed together;

- give parents of abused children priority for substance abuse treatment;

GLOSSARY

Direct-consent adoption
The instance in which birth parents identify, before the birth, the person(s) to whom they will release the child for adoption.

Foster care
Temporary full-time care of children by person(s) other than their parents.

Michigan Adoption Resource Exchange (M.A.R.E.)
An organization that tracks adoption-eligible permanent court and state wards with special needs, produces a monthly photo book and maintains a Web site featuring children in state care who are awaiting adoption, and recruits families for children with special needs.

Open adoption
The instance in which the biological and adoptive parents know one another and may maintain some form of contact after the adoption.

Relative care/adoption
The care or adoption of a child by an adult who, by marriage, blood, or adoption, is the child's relative (e.g., grandparent, sibling, step sibling, uncle, aunt); also called kinship care/adoption).

Special-needs children
Children who have physical, emotional, or mental impairments often resulting from abuse or neglect.

Voluntary-release adoption
The instance in which a child's birth parents release the child to a private adoption agency, and s/he is adopted from the agency.

Sponsored by the Michigan Nonprofit Association and the Council of Michigan Foundations

- revise the duties of the foster-care review boards, requiring them to examine the history of children in foster care in each county, monitor progress made toward fulfilling their *permanency* plans (a plan, prepared by the state Family Independence Agency [FIA] caseworker when a child is placed in foster care, to achieve permanent placement for the child), and hear appeals of proposed placement changes;

- require an attorney to be available to act on behalf of a child who is the subject of a child-protection or guardianship proceeding;

- require that foster parents be given prior notice of proposed placement changes (unless the child is endangered), provide for review-board investigation of proposed changes, with a court hearing if necessary, and require foster parents to be given all pertinent reports;

- provide foster parents with medical and education records on children in their care; and

- furnish each child in the welfare system with a portable "medical passport" to facilitate ongoing care.

In 1998 the FIA began intensive caseworker education that includes specific training on foster care, kinship care, and adoption. More recently, the FIA and the State Court Administrative Office have jointly sponsored similar training for judges, attorneys, court personnel, and additional FIA staff.

Since 2000 the family court must conduct a permanency planning hearing within one year after the FIA first files a petition to terminate parental rights; if the parent is found to have abused the child, parental rights may be terminated immediately and the hearing must occur within 28 days after the petition. The court must then review the progress of the child towards permanency every 90 days.

In 2000 about 19,500 Michigan children were in 8,201 licensed foster-care homes and 3,422 kinship homes. Foster parents receive a basic-care allowance of $14 a day for children aged birth–12 and $17.30 for older children; additional funds are paid for medically fragile children. To date, the recent budget cutting does not affect funds for foster care or adoption.

The 2000 FIA Supervising Agency "report card" on the FIA and private child-placing agencies finds that the average length of time from termination of parental rights to adoption is about 13 months for children aged under 14 and about 24 months for older children. About 46 percent of children in foster care have had more than one caseworker, and 5 percent have had four or more.

Among the several nonprofit organizations concerned with foster-care issues are the three large groups listed here.

- The Michigan Foster and Adoptive Family Association promotes communication, cooperation, and coordination among people involved with the child-welfare system. A major focus is on recruiting, retaining, and educating foster and adoptive families. The association works closely with the FIA to find homes for special-needs children.

- The Michigan Federation of Private Child and Family Agencies is a statewide organization of nonprofit, private, charitable agencies that serve children, youth, and families through foster care, residential care, adoption, and other services. The federation advocates for policies and legislation that protect children and strengthen families.

- The Child Welfare League of America, a national organization of 1,100 public and private nonprofit agencies, develops and promotes federal programs and policies to protect children, especially those who are abused/neglected, and strengthen families.

Adoption

The various kinds of adoption are defined in the glossary. In 1999, 36,000 children were adopted nationwide—64 percent by their foster parents, 15 percent by relatives, and 21 percent by nonrelatives—and 10,000 more were waiting.

The number of Michigan adoptions climbed appreciably after (1) passage of the federal Adoption and Safe Families Act in 1997, which provides funding incentives to states for increasing adoptions; (2) further federal legislation that prohibits delaying or denying foster or adoptive placement on the basis of the child's or foster/adoptive parent's race or ethnicity; and (3) the passage in Michigan of the "Binsfeld legislation," which, among other measures, makes it easier than before to terminate parental rights and begin the adoption process. From 1997 to 1999, Michigan adoptions rose by 18 percent, or nearly 330 children (due in part to enabling foster parents to adopt more quickly than before and also to increased publicity about available children); this qualified the FIA for nearly $1 million in federal awards, more than half of which the FIA passed on to adoption agencies for post-adoptive services.

In Michigan in fiscal year 2000–01, more than 2,900 adoptions were finalized, of which more than half were placed by private agencies. Exhibit 1 presents the statistical breakdown of these 2,900 children.

EXHIBIT 1. Characteristics of Michigan Adoptions, FY 2000–01 (2,900 total)

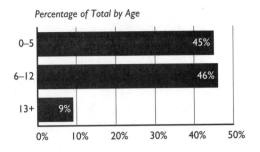

Percentage of Total by Age

Age	%
0–5	45%
6–12	46%
13+	9%

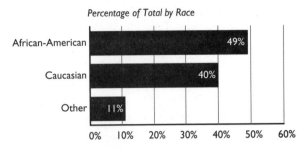

Percentage of Total by Race

Race	%
African-American	49%
Caucasian	40%
Other	11%

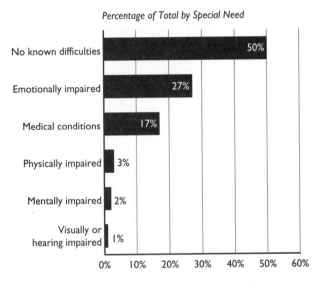

Percentage of Total by Special Need

Special Need	%
No known difficulties	50%
Emotionally impaired	27%
Medical conditions	17%
Physically impaired	3%
Mentally impaired	2%
Visually or hearing impaired	1%

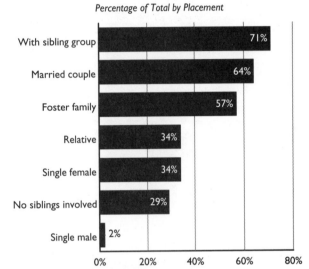

Percentage of Total by Placement

Placement	%
With sibling group	71%
Married couple	64%
Foster family	57%
Relative	34%
Single female	34%
No siblings involved	29%
Single male	2%

SOURCE: Family Independence Agency, AFCARS Adoption Reporting System.

In its March 2002 monthly issue, the Michigan Adoption Resource Exchange, which promotes the adoption of state wards with physical, mental, or emotional problems, lists 427 children available for adoption. Exhibit 2 presents the statistical breakdown of these children.

Michigan, which allows an income tax credit for adoption expenses, is among the leaders in placing special-needs children in permanent homes.

Michigan law permits certain information to be released to and about an adopted adult (that is, an adopted child who has reached adulthood).

- An adopted adult, his/her direct descendants (if s/he is deceased), an adoptive parent, a birth parent, or a birth sibling may obtain *nonidentifying* information, such as medical history, about an adoptee's birth parent(s).

- An adopted adult may receive *identifying* information on his/her birth parents and siblings through the FIA's Central Adoption Registry, if the parties have filed statements of consent.

- Birth parents and siblings may receive an adopted adult's *identifying* information if s/he provides written consent through both the agency and court that completed the adoption.

DISCUSSION

With the shift to measuring child welfare by the yardstick of safety, permanency, and well-being for the child, all decisions concerning placement in foster care or adoption are guided by the best interest of the child. This emphasis exacerbates an already severe shortage of foster families. Of particular difficulty is placing special-needs children, minorities, older children, and sibling groups of two or more.

Sponsored by the Michigan Nonprofit Association and the Council of Michigan Foundations

EXHIBIT 2. Characteristics of Michigan Special-Needs Children Available for Adoption, March 2002 (427 total)

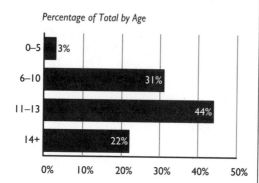

Percentage of Total by Age

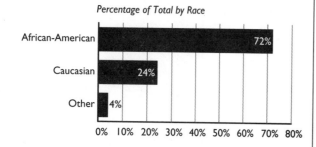

Percentage of Total by Race

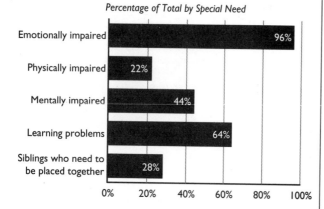

Percentage of Total by Special Need

SOURCE: Michigan Adoption Resource Exchange.

The foster-home shortage is aggravated by the proliferation of two-income families, the mounting number of single-parent homes, a rise in substance abuse, the aging of current foster parents, and the many foster parents who adopt their charges (60–70 percent) and drop out of the foster-care network.

Eighty percent of foster-home placement changes occur at the request of the foster parents, who cite the fatigue and complexity of caring for special-needs children, the lack of adequate support and training for their role, financial reimbursement that does not always cover care, and the sometimes poor relationship between families and social workers. These placement changes mean that the children involved—frequently those who most need stability—are being shuttled from one placement to another.

Meeting the needs of foster parents and children is considered crucial to retaining capable foster parents and promoting placement permanency. Pending legislation (HB 5242) would establish foster- and adoptive-care resource centers. For foster parents, the centers would coordinate much-needed respite care for them, assist them in obtaining daycare for their charges, and help agencies to retain foster parents. Other measures pending would

- prohibit removal of a child from a relative's home, unless the child is at risk of harm, while the relative is petitioning for custody (HB 4858);

- require the state to support several focus groups in which current and former foster children would provide firsthand input about the effect of foster-care policy on their lives (HB 5484); and

- require the FIA to provide the same level of financial and other support for relative care as for foster care (HB 5292).

For adoptive parents, the resource centers would address the need for more post-adoption support that was borne out by a 1999 statewide survey of 638 adoptive families involving 1,350 adopted children. Nearly one of four families report needing post-adoption services it did not receive, including counseling and support groups for parents, children, and adolescents, respite care, and such education support as tutoring. More than one-third of the families report facing a behavioral emergency (e.g., an arrest) with one or more of their adopted children and finding nowhere to go. Half of the families did use available post-adoption support and report that special education services are the most helpful, followed by support groups for parents and psychological counseling. In 2000, new federal and state funds addressed some of these needs.

Other measures pending relating to adoption would make it a misdemeanor to intentionally misidentify a man as a biological father in order to deceive in an adoption proceeding and prohibit consideration of age in prospective adoptive parents.

One area that concerns child-welfare advocates is the need for more spending for subsidies to parents of adopted special-needs children. The subsidy currently is $14–33 a day, depending on the child's age and need at adoption, and is

Sponsored by the Michigan Nonprofit Association and the Council of Michigan Foundations

locked in—regardless of whether the child's problems diminish or worsen—until the child is aged 18. Because Michigan has been successful in securing adoptive homes for these children, subsidy spending has risen steadily, to $161 million in 2001; the subsidy caseload was more than 20,400 at the end of 2001 and is expected to exceed 24,000 by 2003. Supporters of at least maintaining the subsidy, if not raising it, make two points: (1) A subsidy is necessary to achieve a permanent home for many children because of the expense of raising a special-needs child (60 percent of families who adopt a special-needs child have an annual income under $40,000); and (2) many special-needs children are adopted by their foster parents, and if the adoption subsidy falls below or becomes more uncertain than the foster care subsidy, these families will opt not to adopt. Some suggest that part of the expense of raising the subsidy could be offset by lowering or terminating it for parents of children whose medical, physical, or emotional problems have diminished or disappeared before they reach 18.

Similarly, care by relatives is a desired option for children needing out-of-home placement, but only under certain conditions are kinship homes paid the same amount as licensed foster homes. Some relatives of modest means are willing to care for a child but unwilling to go through the process of becoming a licensed foster home, which involves numerous training hours, background checks, and sometimes housing alterations.

See also Children's Early Education and Care; Domestic Violence; Youth at Risk.

Research on this policy topic was made possible by a grant from The Skillman Foundation.

FOR ADDITIONAL INFORMATION

Child and Family Services Administration
Michigan Family Independence Agency
235 South Grand Avenue, 5th Floor
P.O. Box 30037
Lansing, MI 48909
(517) 335-6158
(517) 335-6177 FAX
www.michigan.gov/fia

Child Welfare League of America
440 First Street N.W., 3d Floor
Washington, DC 20001
(202) 638-2952
(202) 638-4004 FAX
www.cwla.org

Michigan Adoption Resource Exchange
330 West Michigan Avenue
P.O. Box 6128
Jackson, MI 49204
(800) 589-6273
(517) 783-6273
(517) 783-5904 FAX
www.mare.org

Michigan Federation of Private Child and Family Agencies
309 North Washington Square, Suite 011
Lansing, MI 48933
(517) 485-8552
(517) 485-6680 FAX
www.michfed.org

Michigan Foster and Adoptive Family Association
2450 Delhi Commerce Drive, Suite 10
Holt, MI 48842
(517) 694-1056
(517) 694-3092 FAX
www.mfapa.org

Sponsored by the Michigan Nonprofit Association and the Council of Michigan Foundations

Genetic Cloning, Testing, and Research

BACKGROUND

Recent advances in the field of genetics have expanded with dazzling speed, bringing with them the challenge of wide-ranging and often unknown consequences. Over the years, genetic manipulation has been used for purposes such as improving crop yields and accelerating animal growth. Cloning an animal from embryonic cells and, more recently, from adult cells, vaulted genetics into the daily headlines, then, in 2001, there came the announcement that a very early human embryo had been produced.

Genetic Cloning

The birth of Dolly, the sheep cloned in 1997, generated both anticipation and fear that human cloning would not be far behind. At the federal level, an executive order immediately banned the use of federal funds for human cloning. Extensive discussion ensued in Congress about the ethics of cloning, and numerous bills were introduced in an effort to prohibit human cloning without restricting promising research. Cloning began to be discussed in terms of *therapeutic cloning* (to create an embryo for a supply of stem cells for research or therapy, thus destroying the embryo) and *reproductive cloning* (to produce a human being). Currently, Congress is considering legislation to ban all cloning, including therapeutic cloning, and alternatively, legislation to ban only reproductive cloning.

Michigan enacted laws in 1998 making human cloning a felony, setting penalties for cloning, and prohibiting state funds from being used for it. California, Louisiana, and Rhode Island also have such a ban, and other states have similar legislation pending.

Related controversy surrounds research using embryonic stem cells, which are believed to hold potential for leading to treatment for diseases such as Alzheimer's, Parkinson's, diabetes, and heart disease. The president announced in August 2001 that he would allow the award of government funds for research that uses embryonic stem cells being cultured in laboratories around the world but would prohibit funding to develop new lines that involve creating and destroying additional embryos.

In early 2002 two biotechnology companies announced that they had cloned pigs that do not have a specific gene that appears to cause the human body to reject pig organ transplants; the breakthrough is thought to be an important step in the field of *xenotransplantation*—animal-to-human transplants. In addition, human embryonic stem cells have been developed into tiny blood vessels, a crucial step in someday using such cells to repair blocked arteries.

Genetic Testing and Profiling

Genetic testing is the process of examining human chromosomes for genetic markers that may indicate the presence or likelihood of diseases or conditions that sometimes can be treated. Hundreds of genetic tests are available, and seven are required of newborns in Michigan. Similarly, genetic profiling records an individual's DNA makeup and can be used to identify a person with near certainty.

GLOSSARY

Biotechnology
The use of living organisms, cells, or substances from living organisms to make products, improve plants or animals, or develop microorganisms.

Chromosome
The structure in the nucleus of a cell, composed of DNA, that contains genes.

Clone
An exact genetic copy of an organism.

Deoxyribonucleic acid (DNA)
A chemical, found in the nucleus of a cell, that carries genetic information—that is, the instructions for making all the structures and materials the body needs to function.

Embryo
The prefetal product of conception from implantation through the eighth week of development. An embryo conceived through sexual reproduction receives half its genes from each sexual parent; that is, half from the sperm and half from the egg. A cloned embryo receives all its genes from one parent—the DNA donor.

Gene
A component passed from one generation to the next that occupies a specific location on a chromosome and helps determine a particular characteristic in an organism.

Sponsored by the Michigan Nonprofit Association and the Council of Michigan Foundations

Legislation

In 1999 the report of the Michigan Commission on Genetic Privacy and Progress recommended ways to protect genetic data, prevent discrimination, and maximize the beneficial uses of new genetic medical knowledge. Legislation followed in 2000 that

- prohibits health insurance companies from requiring genetic information before issuing coverage,

- requires a person's informed consent before undergoing genetic testing, and

- prohibits the use of genetic tests as a condition for obtaining employment.

Pending Michigan legislation (HB 4936) would require separate written consent from the patient for disclosure of genetic information to another party, except as allowed by law or Medicaid policy. Another bill (SB 1214) would set conditions under which DNA test results may be considered as the basis for a new trial of someone convicted of a felony.

Effective January 2002, Michigan law expanded DNA profiling to the entire felon population, including those convicted of specific sex-related misdemeanors.

Although considerable federal legislation has been introduced regarding genetic testing, none has been enacted to date. In 2000 the president issued an executive order prohibiting federal agencies from using genetic information in making employment or promotion decisions and declaring genetic information subject to the same privacy protections as other medical information. The president has urged Congress to pass legislation extending these protections to all citizens.

Biotechnology

Biotechnology is the practice of using living organisms, cells, or substances from living organisms to make products, improve plants or animals, or develop microorganisms other than human cloning. Nearly 300 "biotech" businesses in Michigan generate $2 billion in annual revenue and employ more than 16,000 workers.

In July 1999 the state agreed to invest $1 billion over 20 years in a "life sciences corridor" designed to make Michigan a leading state in developing biotechnology applications. The lead Michigan research institutions—Michigan State University, the University of Michigan, Wayne State University, and the Van Andel Institute—have been joined in proposing biotech projects by other institutions and universities. The initial investment was $100 million, which, along with all future monies awarded under the program, is allocated in three areas: 40 percent on basic research; 50 percent on collaborative research, with emphasis on developing emerging discoveries; and 10 percent on commercializing developments through start-up companies. The proposals are awarded competitively after peer review by a third party, most recently the American Association for the Advancement of Science.

The awards, administered by the Michigan Economic Development Corporation, are intended as a catalyst for bringing health-related products to the consumer while also building companies that create high-technology jobs. The funds are augmented by substantial private money, and 21 new life-science companies were formed in or attracted to Michigan in 2001. Interest from public and private researchers generated nearly 300 project proposals for $45 million to be awarded in 2002. While some proposals are in the field of genetics/genomics, 40 focus on bio-defense.

Genetic marker
A known DNA sequence associated with a particular gene or trait; some are associated with certain diseases and conditions.

Genetic profile
The record of a person's genetic makeup.

Genome
The complete collection of an organism's chromosomes. Except for red blood cells, all human cells contain a complete genome.

Genome sequencing
Determining the order of the chemical bases that make up DNA; that is, "reading" the genetic makeup of an organism. This order spells out the exact instructions required to create a particular organism with its own unique genetic traits.

Stem cell
A cell that has the ability to divide for indefinite periods in culture and to give rise to specialized cells such as skin or heart cells; embryonic stem cells are undifferentiated and thus more capable of being nurtured into various types of tissue than are non-embryonic stem cells.

Stem cell line
The continuing division of a particular stem cell; as cell lines age, they lose their capacity to differentiate into various kinds of tissue.

Sponsored by the Michigan Nonprofit Association and the Council of Michigan Foundations

At the international level, the massive, ongoing Human Genome Project is designed to identify and sequence the genes in human DNA and develop tools for analyzing the resulting data. A feature of the U.S. government's part in the project is transferring technology to the private sector through licensing and awards for innovative research. In 2000 the government and a private company announced that a first draft of the entire human genome had been sequenced, and, more recently, three chromosomes of the total 24 in the human genome have been decoded to a high scientific standard.

DISCUSSION

Stem cell research and cloning pit doubts about the morality of embryo experiments against the promise of treating disease. Some people believe that harvesting stem cells from human embryos is tantamount to homicide and any benefits derived from such research are morally tainted. Others counter that stem cells offer staggering potential to treat disease, and research should not be limited, as the president has decreed, to existing stem cell lines.

The National Academy of Sciences and the Institute of Medicine assert that public funding of research on human stem cells derived from both adults and embryos will provide the most efficient and responsible means to fulfill the promise of stem cells for achieving medical breakthroughs. The academy notes that new stem cell lines will be needed in the future to replace existing lines compromised by age and to address concerns about cultures using animal cells and serum that could result in health risks for humans. The academy report continues,

> Although stem cell research is on the cutting edge of science today, it is still in its infancy, and an enormous amount of basic research remains to be done before it can result in medical treatments . . . Public sponsorship of basic research would help ensure that many more scientists could pursue a variety of research questions and that their results are made widely accessible . . . In addition, public funding offers greater opportunities for regulatory oversight and scrutiny of research . . . [However] Human reproductive cloning should not now be practiced. It is dangerous and likely to fail.

Opposition to cloning a human being is nearly universal. Advanced Cell Technology, the private company that produced a very early, six-cell human embryo, denies interest in cloning a human; its stated goal is to produce stem cells for research. While a very few scientists have expressed interest in cloning a human, most believe that apart from moral or ethical issues, it is simply too dangerous at the current level of knowledge.

In 2001 the U.S. House of Representatives passed a measure to prohibit human cloning. A few months later, during consideration of an unrelated bill, the Senate defeated an amendment that would have placed a six-month moratorium on all cloning, but it has not acted on the cloning-prohibition bill itself. The Council of Catholic Bishops condemns this inaction as "morally irresponsible," and asserts that the successful early-stage cloning of human embryos has dangerous implications of playing God and devaluing human life. Right to Life of Michigan also deplores the Senate's inaction. At this writing, debate continues on the prohibition bill and on a second Senate bill that would ban reproductive cloning but allow continued cloning for medical research. The president has affirmed his intention to sign a bill banning human cloning if it comes to his desk.

Current policy of the American Medical Association directs its member physicians not to participate in human cloning "at this time because further investigation and discussion regarding the harms and benefits of human cloning are required."

The final report of the National Bioethics Advisory Commission (its charter expired in October 2001) concludes that the federal oversight system should protect the rights and welfare of human research participants, regardless of whether the research is publicly or privately sponsored. Since no current entity has the authority to develop federal policy for all research involving human participants, the commission called for legislation creating a single federal office.

Three to five percent of the U.S. Human Genome Project budget is devoted to studying the ethical, legal, and social issues surrounding the availability of genetic information; this is the largest bioethics program in the world. Among the issues under study are the following:

- Fairness in the use of genetic information by insurers, courts, schools, adoption agencies, and the military: Who should have access and how will it be used?

- Privacy and confidentiality of genetic information: Who owns and controls it?

- Stigmatization due to an individual's genetic differences: How does personal genetic information affect society's perceptions of that person?

- Reproductive issues such as adequate informed consent for complex procedures and reproductive rights: How reliable is fetal genetic testing? What larger issues are raised by new reproductive techniques?

- Clinical issues, including the education of professionals and the public, and the implementation of standards in testing procedures: How will genetic tests be evaluated and regulated for accuracy? How do we balance limitations and social risk with long-term benefits?

- Uncertainties associated with gene tests for susceptibilities and complex conditions: Should testing be performed when no treatment is available?

- Philosophical implications regarding human responsibility, free will versus genetic determinism, and concepts of health and disease: Do people's genes make them behave in a particular way? Where is the line between medical treatment and enhancement?

- Health and environmental issues concerning genetically modified foods and microbes: Are such foods safe to humans and the environment?

- Commercialization of products, including property rights such as patents and copyrights and accessibility of products: Who owns genes and other pieces of DNA? Will patenting DNA sequences limit their accessibility and development into useful products?

The questions surrounding genetic cloning, testing, and research are controversial and growing more complicated with every announcement from genetic science and biotechnology, and they can be expected to be present on the political agenda, in scientific research, and in public debate for some time.

See also Abortion; Crime and Corrections; Privacy.

FOR ADDITIONAL INFORMATION

American Medical Association
515 North State Street
Chicago, IL 60610
(312) 464-5000
(312) 464-4184 FAX
www.ama-assn.org

Human Genome Project Information
Oak Ridge National Laboratory
1060 Commerce Park, MS 6480
Oak Ridge, TN 37830
(865) 576-6669
(865) 574-9888 FAX
www.ornl.gov/hgmis

Michigan Economic Development Corporation
300 North Washington Square
Lansing, MI 48913
(517) 373-9808
(517) 335-0198 FAX
http://medc.michigan.org/lifescience

National Academy of Sciences
2001 Wisconsin Avenue, N.W.
Washington, DC 20007
(202) 334-2000
www.nationalacademies.org

Sponsored by the Michigan Nonprofit Association and the Council of Michigan Foundations

Great Lakes Concerns

BACKGROUND

The Great Lakes—Erie, Huron, Michigan, Ontario, and Superior—and their connecting channels form the largest fresh surface-water system on Earth. Covering more than 94,000 square miles, the Great Lakes and connecting waterways comprise about 90 percent of the nation's supply of fresh water and 18 percent of the world's. If the volume of Great Lakes water were spread over a surface area the size of the lower 48 states, it would create a lake nearly 10 feet deep. With 3,288 miles of Great Lakes shoreline, Michigan has a longer coastline than any state except Alaska. More than 200 Michigan rivers flow into the Great Lakes.

This system greatly affects the quality of life in Michigan and throughout the Great Lakes basin, the region drained by the lakes. It is a major source of domestic and industrial water; it provides an economical way to transport raw materials, agricultural products, and manufactured goods; it is the cornerstone of the tourist industry of the region; and it provides a wealth of recreation opportunities. The Great Lakes affect the region's weather and provide unique water and coastal habitats that support a wide range of plants and animals.

Problems

In the 1960s, reports of serious Great Lakes problems began to alarm the region's residents. Domestic water supplies were threatened, swimming beach closures were common, and toxic chemicals, including mercury, DDT, and polychlorinated biphenyls (PCBs), were found to be accumulating at alarming levels in fish and wildlife. Moreover, alewife—which had been limited to the Atlantic Ocean and Lake Ontario until the 1932 Welland Canal expansion around Niagara Falls—had become the dominant species in lakes Huron and Michigan, and the annual die-off was fouling beaches and clogging water-intake systems.

In the last three decades significant progress has been made in controlling pollution and improving the quality of Great Lakes water. There is heightened public awareness about how land use and waste-disposal practices affect the lakes. Federal law requires the governors of the eight Great Lakes states to agree to any significant diversion of Great Lakes water outside of the basin. However, the following issues are still of major concern:

- Toxic contamination
- Nonpoint-source pollution and excessive nutrients
- Exotic species
- Water diversions
- Lake levels
- Habitat loss

Lakes Management

While the legal ownership of Great Lakes bottomland rests with the eight states and two Canadian provinces that border the lakes, the interests of the two countries in commercial navigation and pollution control in this shared water resource prompts strong

GLOSSARY

Bioaccumulation
The increase in concentration of a substance by a biological organism above the level found in its food supply or environment; often the concentration increases through successive levels of the food chain (biomagnification).

Consumptive use
Human consumption of basin waters through agricultural and industrial processes (e.g., evaporation from irrigation and steam emitted from power plants) plus that incorporated into products (e.g., milk).

Ecosystem
The interdependent relationship among members of a biological community and their natural environment.

Great Lakes basin
The hydrological unit (region) drained by the Great Lakes; also referred to as the Great Lakes watershed.

Great Lakes states
The eight U.S. jurisdictions bordering the Great Lakes: Illinois, Indiana, Michigan, Minnesota, New York, Ohio, Pennsylvania, and Wisconsin. Two Canadian provinces also border the lakes: Ontario and Quebec.

Non-native species (exotics)
Species not native to a locale.

Nonpoint-source discharge
A diffuse discharge (one that does not have a single point of origin)— e.g., rain or runoff from adjacent lands that enters a water body; may carry pollutants.

Point-source discharge
A single, identifiable source of a discharge, (e.g., pipe or smoke-stack); may carry pollutants.

Sponsored by the Michigan Nonprofit Association and the Council of Michigan Foundations

federal interest. Under the Boundary Waters Treaty of 1909, Canada and the United States established the International Joint Commission (IJC) to prevent and resolve disputes over water use and provide independent advice on such other transboundary environmental issues as air pollution.

Under the auspices of the IJC, in 1972 the two governments entered into the Great Lakes Water Quality Agreement (GLWQA) to "restore and maintain the chemical, physical, and biological integrity of the waters of the Great Lakes basin ecosystem." The focus of the IJC and the cooperating federal, state, and provincial agencies for nearly 30 years has been to develop and implement pollution-abatement measures that will restore and maintain beneficial uses of the lakes.

DISCUSSION

Toxic Chemical Contamination

The Great Lakes basin is vulnerable to the accumulation of pollutants released as by-products of agriculture, manufacturing, power generation, and waste incineration. The IJC has identified at least 360 pollutants in the water, sediments, and wildlife of the Great Lakes, including many persistent toxic chemicals that are of significant concern: dioxin, PCBs, mercury and lead, poly-aromatic hydrocarbons, and several pesticides. These pollutants are toxic at low concentrations, accumulate in fish and wildlife (bioaccumulation), and increase in concentration at successive levels of the food chain (biomagnification).

Toxic chemicals enter the Great Lakes by direct discharge from such "point sources" as manufacturing sites and waste-water treatment facilities, from atmospheric deposition (precipitation containing toxic particles), and through runoff from the land. Studies show that atmospheric deposition accounts for as much as 90 percent of the PCBs, lead, and mercury that annually reach the lakes, coming from as far away as Mexico and South America. State and regional initiatives to protect the lakes from toxic deposition include the Regional Great Lakes Air Toxics Emissions Inventory, a collaborative monitoring effort among the Great Lakes states.

In cooperation with state food-inspection agencies, the federal Food and Drug Administration regulates the chemical levels allowed in commercial food products, including commercially caught fish. The Great Lakes states and provinces, however, are responsible for protecting their residents from the health risks of consuming contaminated, non-commercially caught fish and wildlife. This is accomplished by issuing consumption advisories for the general population (and sensitive subpopulations, such as pregnant women, nursing mothers, and children) when a lake's fish/wildlife are found to contain concentrations above a certain level of such chemicals as mercury and dioxins. In Michigan, the advisories are issued annually by the Michigan Department of Community Health and recommend limiting or avoiding consumption of certain fish/wildlife from specific water bodies.

Nonpoint-Source Pollution and Excessive Nutrients

Nutrients—including phosphorus, various forms of nitrogen, and other elements—provide the basic building blocks for biological productivity of aquatic organisms, and they support the production of small plant organisms (i.e., phytoplankton) that are the primary link in the Great Lakes food chain. Too many nutrients, however, can cause significant problems. Excessive phosphorus in Lake Erie led to widespread algae blooms, odors, poor aesthetics, and lowered dissolved oxygen to the point that in the 1960s Lake Erie was declared "dead."

One major source of phosphorus is household laundry detergent. Since 1972 the United States and Canada have spent approximately $10 billion on building and upgrading sewage treatment facilities, and this has reduced all nutrients, but primarily phosphorus, that eventually find their way to the lakes. In addition, in the 1970s, Michigan imposed a phosphorus content restriction on laundry detergents sold in the state.

Another source of lake nutrients is runoff, or non-point source pollution: When rainfall or melting snow flows across the landscape, it washes soil particles, bacteria, pesticides, fertilizer, animal waste, oil, and numerous other toxics into the lakes and the tributaries that feed them. This is one of the leading causes of water-quality problems in Michigan and the Great Lakes. Through both voluntary and regulatory programs, the Michigan Department of Environmental Quality's (MDEQ) Nonpoint Source program targets activities to reduce the effect of polluted runoff in Michigan.

Non-Native Aquatic Nuisance Species (Exotics)

So-called exotic species of plants and animals are those that have been transported from their natural range into new territory. Many are highly beneficial: Most U.S. crops and domestic animals, many sport fish and aquaculture species, numerous plants, and most biological-control organisms originated elsewhere. Many exotic species, however, cause significant environmental, socio-economic, and public health damage because they have no natural predators in their new locale. They can negatively affect commercial and recreational fishing, power generation, manufacturing, navigation, tourism and beach use, natu-

Sponsored by the Michigan Nonprofit Association and the Council of Michigan Foundations

ral area/native species appreciation, public water supplies, and whole populations of native plants and animals. A Cornell University study (1999) tags the annual cost of harmful exotics in the United States at $138 billion.

Since the 1800s, more than 160 exotic aquatic organisms, including plants, fish, algae, and mollusks have become established in the Great Lakes. About 10 percent have created severe problems. These species out-compete more desirable species for food and habitat and carry diseases that are transmitted to other fish and wildlife. One, the zebra mussel, was discovered in Lake St. Clair in 1988 and now has been found in all five Great Lakes and 165 inland Michigan lakes and is spreading across the country. The zebra mussel is particularly troublesome to industries and municipalities that rely on large-scale water withdrawals from the Great Lakes because they attach themselves in barnacle-like colonies to water-intake screens and restrict water flow, costing millions annually to keep intakes free of them.

More than one-third of the current exotics have been introduced in the past 30 years, a surge that coincides with the St. Lawrence Seaway expansion. Once successfully established, a non-native organism is virtually impossible to eradicate. The most effective defense is to prevent unintentional introductions in the first place. Shipping practices, most notably the discharge of ballast water from ocean-going vessels, primarily are responsible for introduction of exotics, but they also can enter the Great Lakes through aquaculture, bait harvesting operations, aquarium trade, and other ways.

In 1993 the U.S. Coast Guard issued regulations requiring that ships destined for the Great Lakes from abroad and not fully loaded with cargo must discharge and exchange their ballast water in the ocean; the intent is to flush out potential invaders. Although this is an important step in reducing future exotic invasions, it is not completely effective. Critics point out that the regulations exempt approximately 80 percent of the 500 or so vessels transiting here each year from conducting any type of ballast-water management or treatment. These are the infamous "NOBOB" (no ballast on board) vessels. "No ballast" is a misnomer, because they actually may be carrying up to 100 metric tons of unpumpable water and residual sludge, which mixes with the Great Lakes ballast water that they take on and discharge as they off load cargo at one port (e.g., steel at Gary) and take on cargo at another (e.g., grain at Duluth).

Michigan Public Act 114 of 2001 addresses the ongoing invasion of exotic species. The law requires the MDEQ to

- determine whether vessels operating on the Great Lakes and the St. Lawrence Seaway are complying with ballast-management techniques adopted by the Shipping Federation of Canada (for oceangoing vessels) and by the Lakes Carriers' Association and the Canadian Ship Owners' Association (for non-ocean-going vessels);

- determine whether ballast-water management practices have been made a condition of passage on the St. Lawrence Seaway;

- determine whether oceangoing vessels operating on the Great Lakes are using a ballast-treatment method to prevent introduction of exotics; and

- compile and maintain lists of vessels that comply with the management practices or treatment methods, maintain the lists on the MDEQ Web site, and provide them to the governor, certain legislative committees, and shippers.

The act has focused public attention on the severity of problems related to the ongoing invasion of exotics, but some suggest that it relies largely on voluntary compliance and is only a beginning step in reducing the risk of future invasions. Given interstate commerce protections under the U.S. Constitution, international trade agreements, and the geographic scope of the Great Lakes, many believe that more stringent federal action is required to address this issue.

Water Diversion

The present means of managing diversions from the lakes are the Great Lakes Charter, a voluntary agreement signed in 1985 by the Great Lakes governors and Ontario and Quebec premiers, and the U.S. Water Resources Development Act (WRDA), enacted in 1986.

Great Lakes Charter

The charter and a recently adopted amendment (Annex 2001) set out a diversion notice-and-consultation process by which no Great Lakes state or province will proceed with any new or increased diversion or consumptive (human) use of Great Lakes water exceeding five million gallons/day average over 30 days without notifying, consulting, and seeking the consent of all affected states and provinces. The amendment provides a framework through which new agreements may be reached among the states/provinces to take such actions as changing the water-withdrawal limit, collecting water-use data by jurisdiction, implementing environmentally sound and economically feasible water-conservation measures, and resolving disputes regarding proposed diversions and consumptive uses of Great Lakes water.

Sponsored by the Michigan Nonprofit Association and the Council of Michigan Foundations

Water Resources Development Act

The WRDA requires that the eight Great Lakes governors unanimously approve any diversion from the lakes or their tributaries for use outside the basin. In reviewing proposals subject to the act, the governors consider whether the proposed diversion (1) is necessary to protect the requesting locality's public health, safety, and welfare, (2) is consistent with water resource planning and existing uses of basin waters, (3) has incorporated environmentally sound and economically feasible water-conservation practices, and (4) is necessary because there is no reasonable alternative.

Lake Levels

Great Lakes water levels have fluctuated for thousands of years. Unlike oceans, where the ebb and flow of tides are constant and predictable, Great Lakes fluctuations rarely are regular, and they cannot be predicted accurately for the long term. The major influences on the hydrology of the lakes and their connecting channels are weather and climate. Water enters the system via precipitation, runoff, and groundwater inflow. It leaves the system via surface evaporation, groundwater outflow, consumptive use and diversion, and the St. Lawrence River. Because most of these factors cannot be controlled or accurately predicted for more than a few weeks, humans' ability to regulate the lake levels is very limited. Nature has the last word.

Recent years have seen a drop, to lows not experienced since the mid-1960s, in lake levels, particularly in lakes Michigan and Huron. This is due partly to low precipitation in the Lake Superior region during the winter of 1998–99, which reduced runoff into the lake, and partly to higher air temperatures throughout the region in 1999–2000, which warmed the water and increased evaporation. Any dramatic change in lake levels or temperatures causes problems. For example, high water causes erosion, and low water affects boaters and the marine industry; in addition, the recent warmer weather (and, thus, warmer water) has resulted in more algal blooms than usual.

The rapid increase in atmospheric carbon dioxide (CO_2) concentrations and greenhouse gasses in the last century is believed to have resulted in a significant rise in the global average temperature, and a warmer climate with either more or less precipitation could result. The potential effects on Great Lakes water levels could be significant. Large fluctuations have important impacts on wetlands, fisheries, habitats, and human use of the shoreline.

Habitat Loss

Adequate high-quality physical and chemical habitat is necessary to ensure the successful growth, survival, and reproduction of plants and animals that make up a healthy ecosystem. A decline in ecosystem health often may be attributed directly to the loss of critical habitat.

The Great Lakes system is home to hundreds of thousands of plant, fish, and wildlife populations, a good many of which depend on near-shore habitat—that is, they breed, grow, and/or live some or all of their life on the land or in the water along the shoreline of the big lakes and the connecting rivers, streams, and channels. These areas are greatly affected by both water level changes and human use.

Human activity contributes to habitat degradation and loss through agriculture, urban and industrial development, exotic species introduction, mining, nonpoint-source pollution and sedimentation, solid waste disposal, recreation, air emissions, water discharges, and water-level management.

The full picture of the state of Great Lakes habitat is insufficiently documented and largely anecdotal, but many researchers and experts contend that loss and degradation are severe—indeed, existing data collection and research, which are largely local and piecemeal, support this view. The biennial State of the Lakes Ecosystem Conference (SOLEC, hosted by Environment Canada and the EPA to deliver a bi-national, science-based review of the state of the basin ecosystem without assessing agency programs), reviews research and papers on habitat health but there currently is no funding or plan in either country to tackle the big picture.

Directional Drilling

Directional drilling—that is, drilling that begins in one location (e.g., on land) and angles to reach an oil or gas deposit in another location (e.g., under a lake)—is used when it is undesirable or impossible to position a well-head directly above the mineral deposit. Until recently, Michigan was the only state that permitted such drilling in the Great Lakes, and it was a matter of considerable controversy. The practice was banned in Michigan with enactment of Public Act 148 of 2002. The act prohibits the Michigan Department of Natural Resources from entering into a contract that allows drilling operations for the exploration or production of oil or gas beneath Great Lakes bottomlands, connected bays or harbors, or connecting waterways.

Great Lakes Conservation Task Force

In January 2002, the state Senate's bipartisan Great Lakes Conservation Task Force released *The Citizens' Agenda: An Action Plan to Protect the Great Lakes*, presenting 17 issue briefs as well as findings and recommendations. The plan is expected to provide the basis for legislative

Sponsored by the Michigan Nonprofit Association and the Council of Michigan Foundations

proposals to address the matters raised in public meetings and through other input that the panel received.

See also Air Quality; Water Quality.

Research on this policy topic was made possible by a grant from the Frey Foundation.

FOR ADDITIONAL INFORMATION

Citizens' Agenda: An Action Plan to Protect the Great Lakes
Michigan Senate Great Lakes Conservation Task Force
(2002), *www.senate.state.mi.us/gop/greatlakesreport/
index.html*

Great Lakes Commission
400 Fourth Street
Ann Arbor MI 48103
(734) 665-9135
(734) 665-4370 FAX
www.glc.org

Great Lakes Environmental Research Laboratory
National Oceanic and Atmospheric Administration
2205 Commonwealth Boulevard
Ann Arbor, MI 48105
(734) 741-2235
www.glerl.noaa.gov

Great Lakes Information Network
400 Fourth Street
Ann Arbor, MI 48103
(734) 665-9135
(734) 665-4370 FAX
www.great-lakes. net

Great Lakes National Program Office
U.S. Environmental Protection Agency
77 West Jackson Boulevard
Chicago, IL 60604
(312) 886-4040
(312) 353-2018 FAX
www.epa.gov/glnpo

Great Lakes United
P.O. Box 3040
Ann Arbor, MI 48106
(734) 998-0760
(734) 998-0821 FAX
www.glu.org

International Joint Commission
Great Lakes Regional Office
100 Ouellette Avenue
Windsor, Ontario N9A 6T3
Canada
(519) 256-7821
(519) 256-7791 FAX
www.ijc.org

Michigan Environmental Science Board
Michigan Department of Environmental Quality
Constitution Hall
P.O. Box 30680
Lansing, MI 48909
www.michigan.gov/mesb

Michigan Sea Grant College Program
Natural Resources Building, Room 334
Michigan State University
East Lansing, MI 48824
(517) 353-9568
(517) 353-6496 (FAX)
www.miseagrant.org

Office of the Great Lakes
Michigan Department of Environmental Quality
Lansing, MI
(517) 335-4056
(517) 335-4053 (FAX)
www.michigan.gov/deq

Health Care Access, Medicaid, and Medicare

BACKGROUND

In regard to health care, "access" refers to the ease with which people can obtain the care they need in a timely fashion. People sometimes do not get care because

- their insurance does not cover certain services, or they do not have insurance at all;

- if they have insurance, high copayments or deductibles may discourage them from seeking necessary care;

- there are few or no providers (e.g., doctors, hospitals, clinics) within convenient distance;

- language or cultural barriers between them and their provider(s) make it hard for them to receive the care they need;

- insurance companies deny their claims; or

- they do not have transportation, cannot get time off from work, or cannot find a babysitter.

Health Care Insurance

Insurance is most often the key factor that determines whether people have access to health care services; without it, many cannot afford care. Those with no or minimum coverage often forgo preventive services or put off getting care until their problems advance and become harder (and more costly) to treat than they would have been otherwise. Many people or their dependents are without coverage because

- their employer does not provide it (employers are the greatest single source of U.S. health insurance, but some find it too expensive to carry for their workers);

- their employer covers them but not their dependents (one way that employers control costs);

- they have declined their employer's coverage because they cannot afford their share of the premium; or

- they are not working but are ineligible for the public programs that cover some low-income adults and many low-income children (Medicaid and MIChild) or people aged 65 and over, blind, or disabled (Medicare).

In 2000 (at this writing, the latest year for which comparable data are available), one million Michiganians (10 percent of the state population) were without health insurance for the entire calendar year. Nationwide, the figure was 39 million (14 percent). Such factors as age, income, and employment status play a role in determining whether a person has coverage.

GLOSSARY

Categorically needy
People who qualify for Medicaid because their family is eligible to participate in certain public-assistance programs (e.g., Temporary Assistance for Needy Families).

Federal poverty level (FPL)
The minimum annual income required by a family to meet food, shelter, clothing, and other basic needs: in 2002, $15,020 for a family of three; the figure varies by family size and is calculated by a formula established by the federal government.

Medicaid
The federal/state program that pays for health care services delivered mainly to low-income people, including many elderly, children, and pregnant women who qualify; states also may choose to cover medically needy people.

Medically needy
People who are Medicaid eligible because they have substantial medical costs and their income is too high to qualify them as categorically needy.

Sponsored by the Michigan Nonprofit Association and the Council of Michigan Foundations

- In Michigan and nationwide, the nonelderly (those aged 0–64) are less frequently covered by health insurance than are the elderly, mainly because Medicare covers virtually everyone aged 65 and older. A plurality of the uninsured population is aged 18–29.

- In general, nonelderly minority populations have a substantially higher uninsured rate than do whites. In Michigan, 10 percent of nonelderly whites, 14 percent of nonelderly blacks, and 32 percent of nonelderly Hispanics are uninsured. Nationally, the figures are 11 percent, 20 percent, and 34 percent, respectively.

- Despite Medicaid, 36 percent of the nation's nonelderly poor—those with income below the federal poverty level (FPL) (in 2000, the year in which these figures were compiled, the FPL was $13,853 for a family of three)—are uninsured. In Michigan, the number is 29 percent. Sixty percent of Michigan's uninsured (and 64 percent of the nation's) live in households with income below 200 percent of the FPL.

- People living in working households comprise more than 70 percent of the country's uninsured population.

- In Michigan, health insurance is offered by 98 percent of businesses with 50 or more employees and 57 percent of businesses with fewer.

In 2000, 68 percent of Michiganians (64 percent of Americans) were covered by private insurance either offered by their employer or union or individually purchased. Twenty-one percent (22 percent nationwide) were covered by government-sponsored health insurance, such as Medicare, Medicaid, or a military health plan.

Provider Availability

Another critical factor in accessing health care is provider availability. A person living in a rural area may have excellent insurance, but if the nearest provider is an hour's drive away, his/her access to care suffers limits.

In 2000, according to the *Primary Health Care Profile of Michigan* (Michigan Primary Care Association), one-third of the Michigan population lived in a county with an extreme shortage of primary care physicians. In general, the population-to-physician ratio in these counties is at least 3,500:1. A ratio of 1,500:1 is the national standard.

Government Health Care Coverage

The nation's Medicare and Medicaid programs (titles XVIII and XIX, respectively, of the Social Security Act) were implemented in 1966. Medicare (a federal program) and Medicaid (a federal/state program) are intended to ensure that certain vulnerable populations have health care coverage. Today, Medicare targets mainly the elderly, and Medicaid targets mainly the poor. Over time, the two programs have become much more expensive than originally envisioned.

- From 1970 to 2000, total federal Medicare expenditures grew from $8 billion to $224 billion.

- From 1970 to 2000, total state and federal Medicaid expenditures grew from $5 billion to $203 billion.

- By 2000 Medicare accounted for 17 percent of the nation's total health care costs, which had reached $1.3 trillion (more than 13 percent of the gross domestic product); Medicaid (including state and federal spending) accounted for 16 percent of total health care costs.

Medicare
The federal program that pays for many health care and related services for people aged 65 and older or those who are blind and/or have long-term disability. Part A (hospital insurance) is funded entirely by the government; Part B (medical insurance) must be paid for in part by the recipient.

Temporary Assistance for Needy Families (TANF)
A federal block grant; in Michigan it funds the Family Independence Program (FIP) as well as child care, transportation, and other services for people receiving public assistance.

The two programs also have become much more expensive: Since first initiated, both have undergone substantial change in regard to the people they help and the health care services they cover.

Medicare

In Medicare's first year, there were just over 19 million enrolled; by 2001—despite no major Medicare eligibility expansion since the 1970s—the number had more than doubled, to 39 million. About 87 percent of the program's enrollees are elderly (aged 65 and older); the remainder are blind or disabled. In Michigan, approximately 1.4 million people are eligible for Medicare benefits.

Today Medicare provides beneficiaries with two types of coverage: hospital insurance (Part A) and medical insurance (Part B).

■ Medicare Part A reimburses participating providers for care rendered; coverage includes inpatient hospital services, care for a limited time in a skilled nursing facility, home health services, and hospice care. Part A is financed by the Medicare Trust Fund, which is funded by a 2.9 percent payroll tax that is split between employer and employee.

■ Medicare Part B coverage is optional, and, to obtain it, recipients must pay a monthly premium ($54 in 2002), which accounts for one-quarter of Part B funding; the rest is paid for by general tax revenue. Almost all people entitled to Part A choose also to enroll in Part B, which covers the following:

- Physician services (in both hospital and nonhospital settings)

- Clinical laboratory tests

- Durable medical equipment

- Flu vaccinations

- Drugs that cannot be self-administered (except certain anti-cancer drugs)

- Most medical supplies

- Diagnostic tests

- Ambulance services

- Hospital outpatient and ambulatory surgical-center services

- Some cancer screening and bone-mass measurement

- Some physical therapy

- Blood products not covered by Part A

Medicare does not cover routine physical examinations, most dental care and dentures, outpatient prescription drugs (except certain self-administered anti-cancer drugs), routine eye care and eyeglasses, hearing aids, and certain other services. (Some of these services may be covered under Medicare+Choice, through which qualified health maintenance organizations cover Medicare beneficiaries.) Medicare covers only 100 days of skilled nursing home care.

Medicaid and MIChild

Medicaid is a state/federal cost-shared program that provides medical assistance for certain individuals and families with low income and limited assets. The federal government has established certain parameters within which each state may establish its own eligibility standards, determine the type/amount/duration/scope of services, set payment levels for services, and administer the program.

Medicaid does not provide medical assistance for all poor people—only for designated groups (categories). Although there are only two eligible populations—the categorically and medically needy—the categories have been expanded numerous times.

Categorically Needy

Originally, this category included only families receiving cash assistance through Aid for Families with Dependent Children (AFDC) and aged, blind, and disabled people receiving Supplemental Security Income benefits. In 1997 AFDC was incorporated on the national level into Temporary Assistance for Needy Families (TANF), a federal block grant that funds Michigan's Family Independence Program (FIP), child care, transportation, and other services for people receiving public assistance. Over the years, "categorically needy" has been expanded to include

■ infants, children, and pregnant women in lower-income families;

■ low-income elderly and disabled persons; and

■ individuals eligible for transitional Medicaid (provided for 12 months to beneficiaries who get a job or a better job and, because of the income increase, become ineligible for Medicaid).

Within the categorically needy population, there are many for whom states *must* provide Medicaid services and others for whom the state may *choose* to provide services; most states choose to extend Medicaid services to their

Sponsored by the Michigan Nonprofit Association and the Council of Michigan Foundations

most vulnerable populations who meet certain asset and income levels.

Medically Needy

States may choose, as Michigan has done, to establish programs for this category of people—those who have substantial medical costs but their income is too high for them to be eligible for Medicaid. Such people are eligible for assistance if their medical costs consume enough of their income/assets to bring the latter down to a level at which they meet Medicaid eligibility requirements.

Scope of Services

Medicaid services have expanded over time. When the Michigan Medicaid program was implemented, in 1966, it was to cover services "of a curative, not a preventive, nature," and routine medical examinations and immunizations were excluded. Today, the program's focus is different: For example, the Early and Periodic Screening Diagnosis and Treatment program (EPSDT) places a strong emphasis on immunization and preventing diseases among children.

Originally, the federal government required states to cover only five Medicaid services. Since 1966 the list has expanded substantially and now includes the following:

- Inpatient and outpatient hospital services
- Services provided at rural health clinics and federally qualified health centers
- Laboratory and x-ray services
- Nursing home services
- Physicians' services, including medical and surgical services provided by a dentist
- Services provided by a nurse midwife, certified pediatric nurse, and certified family nurse practitioner
- Home health services
- EPSDT for youth under age 21
- Family-planning services and supplies
- Necessary medical transportation

Michigan's Medicaid program also covers numerous optional services (for some, the state may require recipients to make a copayment), including the following:

- Prescribed drugs
- Clinic services
- Dental services and dentures

- Physical, occupational, and speech therapy
- Podiatry, optometry, and chiropractic services
- Hospice care
- Inpatient psychiatric services for people aged 21–65 and intermediate-care-facility services for persons with mental retardation
- Eyeglasses, hearing aids, and prosthetic devices

Eligible Populations

Currently, Michigan's Medicaid program serves numerous eligible populations that fall roughly into the following categories:

- Family Independence Program participants
- Supplemental Security Income recipients
- Infants and pregnant women in families who have annual income under 185 percent of the poverty level
- Children older than one year but younger than 18 in families with income below 150 percent of the FPL
- Elderly and disabled persons with income below the poverty level
- Former FIP recipients whose cases were closed due to employment but who do not have health insurance (this is referred to as the transitional Medicaid population)
- Medically needy

In Michigan approximately 1.2 million people are enrolled in Medicaid. In 2001 the state's total spending (including state and federal funds) on Medicaid totaled $7.9 billion, including about $3.5 billion in state funds. Of the people who receive Medicaid services in Michigan,

- 42 percent are children,
- 31 percent are low-income adults,
- 20 percent are blind or disabled, and
- 7 percent are elderly.

Although more than 40 percent of Michigan's Medicaid population are children, nearly three-quarters of the program's spending goes to the elderly, disabled, and blind.

- 13 percent of Medicaid spending is for children (averaging $907/child/year),
- 13 percent is for low-income adults ($1,242),
- 50 percent is for persons who are blind or disabled ($7,113), and

Sponsored by the Michigan Nonprofit Association and the Council of Michigan Foundations

■ 24 percent is for the elderly ($9,615).

Nationwide, only 10 million people were enrolled in the program in 1960; now more than 41 million are served. Nationally, in 2000, Medicaid financed health care for approximately

■ 21 million children,

■ 9 million adults in low-income families,

■ 7 million people who are blind and disabled, and

■ 4 million elderly.

Almost 14 percent of the American population is eligible to receive Medicaid benefits—up more than 35 percent from 1990.

MIChild

In 1997 Congress enacted the State Children's Health Insurance Program (SCHIP) to supplement existing Medicaid coverage of low-income children. Michigan's SCHIP program is called MIChild, and coverage is almost identical to Medicaid. As is the case in other states, Michigan receives a greater percentage of its funding for MIChild from the federal government than it does for Medicaid.

MIChild covers children (1) aged under one living in a household with income of 185–200 percent of the FPL and (2) aged 1–18 in a household with income of 150–200 percent of the FPL. MIChild enrollment was 26,331 as of February 2002.

DISCUSSION

For the large majority of people, health insurance—provided through an employer or government plan—covers a large portion of their health care costs. If the plan does not pay the entire bill, the individual must pay the balance out-of-pocket. For many, the out-of-pocket portion imposes a manageable burden, but for others it can be considerable. Those without health insurance must pay for all treatment out-of-pocket, and this can mean financial ruin. If a person simply is unable to pay his/her health care bill, s/he either must forgo treatment, or the provider(s) must absorb much—and sometimes all—of the expense (this means higher health care bills and restricted access for others).

Federal law requires providers to render emergency care to everyone who needs it, regardless of ability to pay, but it does not require providers to give preventive care (e.g., regular checkups) to those who cannot pay.

Proponents of the current U.S. health care delivery system contend that it ensures that virtually everyone has access to medical services: Most families have private coverage; millions of elderly, disabled, and low-income Americans are covered by Medicare, Medicaid, and other government programs; and the uninsured are able to receive critically needed care on a charity basis.

Critics argue that the system, as good as it is, has serious flaws. They point out, for example, that people can amass ruinous health care bills even if they are insured, because a plan may not cover or may cover only part of needed services. Critics also believe that the system reduces health care to a commodity that is provided as charity to the poor but enjoyed at will by the more affluent. They contend that access to basic health care is a privilege that should be equally available to all.

Some policymakers favor a universal (covers everyone) delivery system that would ensure at least certain health care benefits for everyone, regardless of employment status or income. A universal plan receives most support from those who believe that access to basic health care is a right; they argue that it is government's responsibility to guarantee people's rights, and, therefore, it should make sure that health care coverage is provided for all citizens. Opponents argue that the law already ensures people's access to care by requiring providers to render emergency service. They maintain that it should not be government's responsibility to guarantee health care. If it were, the government would have to tax heavily and limit its provision of numerous other non-health (e.g., education, defense, foreign aid) services.

Although most Americans are satisfied with the current care delivery system, many also believe that it needs substantial repair. Rather than revamp the entire system, policymakers are focusing on reforms that will extend health care access, either in the form of coverage or in coverage of more benefits (e.g., prescription drugs). The following summarizes the major national and state policy initiatives to improve access to care.

Tax Incentives to Purchase Health Insurance

State and federal legislation has been proposed to give employers and individuals tax incentives to purchase health insurance. The most prominent of these initiatives currently is the president's FY 2002–03 budget proposal to offer $89 billion in tax credits to individuals not covered by employer-sponsored insurance: Families with two or more children and annual household income under $25,000 could obtain up to $3,000 in tax credits for health insurance costs.

Sponsored by the Michigan Nonprofit Association and the Council of Michigan Foundations

Proponents of such tax breaks for *individuals* point out that businesses are allowed to deduct all costs in providing health insurance to their employees, and they argue that workers also should be permitted deductions. They contend that tax breaks will encourage more people to buy into health insurance plans and also provide relief to insureds who incur substantial medical expenses despite their coverage.

Those who support additional *employer* tax breaks (that is, tax credits and not just tax deductions) argue that many firms do not offer health insurance to their workers, and they should be encouraged as much as possible to offer at least basic coverage.

Others contend that tax breaks alone are insufficient to encourage people to buy health coverage themselves or employers to purchase it for them: Even with the proposed deductions and credits, individuals and employers still must assume a great majority of the cost themselves.

"One-Third Share" and Other County Programs

Several Michigan counties have stopgap programs that offer some health benefits to the uninsured. These programs usually offer a low-cost alternative, covering fewer benefits, to private and public health insurance. A few offer or are considering "one-third share" plans for uninsured workers and their dependents, under which employers, county and/or state government, and the workers each contribute one-third of the premium for a low-cost policy.

Several other counties have community programs that cover some residents who are ineligible for Medicaid and do not have private insurance. These programs rely on funding from county, state, federal, and sometimes private sources, and they offer limited benefits—inpatient hospital care usually is excluded—to qualified individuals. Unlike the one-third share plans, these programs are not employer based.

In two locations—the City of Detroit and Ingham County—the W.K. Kellogg Foundation has funded Community Voices (CV) projects, expansive efforts to improve residents' access to health coverage and care. The project brings together residents, neighborhood groups, community-based nonprofit organizations, care providers, public health departments, and others in a coordinated effort that addresses not only coverage but also barriers to access such as provider-availability problems, cultural and ethnic issues, and transportation needs.

Medicaid and Medicare

In America and the states, Medicaid and Medicare have been the primary means by which access to health care has been extended to a larger share of the population. The most recent significant expansion, SCHIP, for children, is basically a Medicaid expansion even though some states (like Michigan) have chosen to create new programs under the SCHIP banner. As health care costs continue to rise, Medicaid and Medicare struggle to balance cost control and expansion of access. The recent economic downturn and the attendant shortfalls in federal and state budgets have exacerbated this struggle. Policymakers face a difficult question: How do we expand access (or even protect the access that we have now) in the face of budget problems?

The Medicaid and Medicare programs have grown substantially, and federal and state spending for them soon will be unable to keep pace with the demand for services. The Medicare program is in particular jeopardy: In 2000 there were only 34 million American elderly, but by 2025 there will be almost 61 million. Additional utilization and spending because of this population's growth is expected to push the program's cost beyond $500 billion by 2008. Costs will accelerate even more when the babyboomers begin retiring, around 2010.

Current demographic trends portend a considerable problem for Medicaid as well. Although the elderly (aged 65 and over) account for the smallest segment of this program's population, their care is the most expensive. In Michigan, annual Medicaid services cost $907 per child but $9,615 per elderly adult. As the number of elderly who qualify for the program grows, so will the cost.

To address access and cost, state and local policymakers are considering several proposals, the most prominent of which are MIFamily (a Michigan initiative) and an outpatient prescription-drug benefit for Medicare (a federal initiative).

MIFamily Initiative

In his FY 2002–03 budget, the governor proposed MIFamily, a program to cover more low-income people not currently eligible for Medicaid. A federal waiver will be required and, if approved, will allow the state to cover these adults under Medicaid although with fewer benefits than current Medicaid eligibles receive.

Proponents of this Medicaid expansion argue that it will help uninsured adults. Others are wary, contending that the viability of Michigan's Medicaid program has been in question for years because the state does not pay health plans and providers enough to cover their costs to deliver care. Another Medicaid expansion, they say, will make this situation worse, especially if funded in part by payment cuts to plans and providers. Health plans and providers further argue that inadequate payments threaten access to care for those who are already on Medicaid, because more doctors and others may decide that they cannot accept Medicaid patients. Defenders of the current Medicaid program counter that the state has controlled Medicaid spending without jeopardizing access. They cite independent quality-review studies in support of their position. In addition, they point out that Michigan has used special financing mechanisms to obtain over $1 billion in additional federal funds for Medicaid, while other states have to operate without the additional monies.

Medicare Proposals

Balancing access and cost is no less difficult with Medicare. In recent years, there have been proposals to lower the Medicare-eligibility age and allow others—the uninsured and those aged 55–64—to buy into the program with a $300–400 monthly premium. Others have proposed raising the eligibility age, from 65 to 67, but many believe that the idea failed because it is unpopular with the elderly, who are a powerful lobbying force and tend to vote regularly and in great number.

Rather than raise the eligibility age, Congress has considered requiring the affluent to pay a higher Medicare premium. Opponents argue that people aged 65 and over already paid for their Medicare services through the payroll taxes that fund the program. Supporters argue that those who can afford to pay more out-of-pocket for their health care ought to do so and that the elderly receive much more in benefits than they contributed in payroll taxes.

The Medicare initiative currently receiving the most attention pertains not to extending Medicare to more beneficiaries but to improving current beneficiaries' access to a benefit (outpatient prescription drugs). Before the events of September 11, 2001, and the economic downturn, which reordered federal budget priorities and left less money to fund this expansion, the addition of an outpatient prescription-drug benefit to Medicare seemed likely. Policymakers and advocates agreed that prescriptions are essential to managing many illnesses and conditions; the obstacles were cost and benefit design: Which drugs would Medicare cover and how much in deductibles and copayments would beneficiaries have to pay?

In his FY 2002–03 budget, the president proposed $190 billion over 10 years to fund a drug benefit, but as yet there are no specifics on how the benefit would be structured. Some critics say this is far too little to be much help. Other critics, including many provider and health plan groups, contend that any expansion of Medicare benefits is likely to come at a cost in access. They fear that funding for a drug benefit will come from payments to providers for other Medicare services, and this will compromise access.

Access to Providers

Although discussion about public and private health insurance seems to monopolize the access debate, also important to patients is doctor/hospital availability. In some places there is an oversupply, while in many others there is a shortage. The latter is a pressing matter in many communities, but it is difficult to address directly—lawmakers cannot require a hospital to locate in a particular area or force doctors or nurses to practice in one place rather than another.

To address this problem, Michigan and many other states allow doctors and nurses to reduce or eliminate their student-loan burden by agreeing to practice for a given number of years in a rural community or underserved inner city, and many patient advocates are encouraging funding for clinics that serve as hospital outposts in such locations. With the nursing shortage worsening in Michigan and across the nation, policymakers are considering numerous initiatives to attract people to nursing, provide financial assistance for schooling, and help keep nurses in the profession.

Conclusion

Today's policymakers have the unenviable task of maintaining, if not improving, vulnerable populations' access to health care and, at the same time, managing the cost of doing so. This tension pinpoints the tradeoffs involved with access to health care: Given finite funding for government programs, policymakers must balance (1) the number and kind of people covered (recognizing that some need more services than others), (2) the services/benefits covered, and (3) the payments to health plans and providers for delivering the covered benefits. Any increase or decrease in any of these factors affects spending on behalf of and access for some people. Any significant decrease in any of these will severely compromise access for many people. As a state or a country, we could choose to provide everyone with public or private health insurance, but to do so would mean that we would have to offer fewer benefits or pay providers less for the services we use.

The only way to avoid trading off among these three factors is for policymakers to expand significantly the funding for health care, which, given other priorities—e.g., education, defense, corrections—is no simple task. The biggest question for state and federal officials is whether (1) the responsibility for access to health care should continue to be government's, or (2) a greater share should be assumed by the private sector—employers and individuals.

Sponsored by the Michigan Nonprofit Association and the Council of Michigan Foundations

See also Aging; Health Care Costs and Managed Care; Immigrants: Human Services Benefits; Long-Term and Related Care; Mental Health Funding and Services; Substance Abuse; Tobacco Settlement; Youth at Risk.

FOR ADDITIONAL INFORMATION

American Association of Retired Persons
309 North Washington Square, Suite 110
Lansing, MI 48933
(517) 482-2772
(517) 482-2794 FAX
www.aarp.org

Center for Medicare and Medicaid Services
U.S. Department of Health and Human Services
7500 Security Boulevard
Baltimore, MD 21244
(410) 786-3000
(410) 786-3252 FAX
www.cms.gov

Families USA
1334 G Street, N.W.
Washington, DC 20005
(202) 628-3030
(202) 347-2417 FAX
www.familiesusa.org

Medical Services Administration
Michigan Department of Community Health
400 South Pine Street
P.O. Box 30479
Lansing, MI 48909
(517) 335-5501
(517) 335-5007 FAX
www.michigan.gov.mdch

Medicare/Medicaid Assistance Program
6105 West St. Joseph Highway, Suite 209
Lansing, MI 48917
(800) 803-7174
(517) 886-1305 FAX
www.mymmmap.org

Michigan Council for Maternal and Child Health
318 West Ottawa Street
Lansing, MI 48933
(517) 482-5807
(517) 482-9242 FAX

Michigan League for Human Services
1115 South Pennsylvania Avenue, Suite 202
Lansing, MI 48912
(517) 487-5436
(517) 371-4546 FAX
www.milhs.org

Michigan Health and Hospital Association
6215 West St. Joseph Highway
Lansing, MI 48917
(517) 323-3443
(517) 323-0946 FAX
www.mha.org

Michigan Primary Care Association
2525 Jolly Road, Suite 280
Okemos, MI 48864
(517) 381-8000
www.mpca.net

Michigan State Medical Society
120 West Saginaw
East Lansing, MI 48823
(517) 337-1351
(517) 337-2490 FAX
www.msms.org

Office of Financial and Insurance Services
Michigan Department of Consumer and Industry Services
Ottawa Building, 2d Floor
P.O. Box 30220
Lansing, Michigan 48909
(517) 335-3167
(517) 335-4978 FAX
www.michigan.gov/cis/ofis

Health Care Costs and Managed Care

BACKGROUND

Unless otherwise noted, all national data presented are from 2000, and all Michigan data are from 1998; these are the latest years for which adequate comparable data are available.

- National health expenditures reached $1.3 trillion in 2000, up 6.9 percent over 1999. Preliminary estimates place 2001 growth at more than 8 percent. The rise in 1999 and 2000 health spending outpaced growth in the gross domestic product (GDP), signaling the end of the nine-year stability of health spending's share of the GDP. Health spending now comprises 13.2 percent of the nation's economy.

- In 1998 Michigan personal health expenditures—total health expenditures less medical research and facility-construction costs—were estimated at $35.6 billion.

Programs and Payers

Exhibit 1 shows that public programs account for almost half (45 percent) of the nation's health care bill. The major public programs are

- *Medicare*, the federal program that provides a wide range of health services to the elderly, blind, and disabled; and

- *Medicaid*, the joint federal-state program that offers comprehensive health services to some adults living in poverty and to children—depending on their age—living in households at or below 185 percent of the federal poverty level.

GLOSSARY

Capitation
A payment method in which a managed-care plan, group of health care providers, or individual provider receives a fixed monthly fee in return for delivering certain or all health services to a single patient or family. The capitation fee is paid regardless of how many instances of care occur.

Federal poverty level
The minimum annual income required by a family to meet food, shelter, clothing, and other basic needs: in 2002, $15,020 for a family of three (the amount varies by family size); set according to formula by the federal government.

Health maintenance organization (HMO)
A type of managed-care plan; offers enrollees comprehensive coverage for specific health services for a fixed, prepaid premium.

Managed care
A broad term for a comprehensive approach to health care delivery that (1) provides care to enrollees, usually on a capitated basis; (2) coordinates care, to ensure appropriate use of services; and (3) monitors and measures provider performance, to control costs and maintain or improve care.

Medicaid
The federal-state program that pays for health care services to many low-income people, including elderly who qualify.

EXHIBIT 1. National Health Expenditures, by Program, 2000

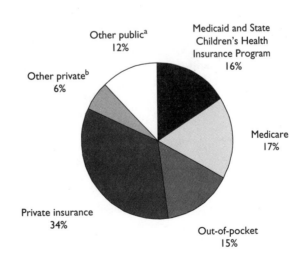

SOURCE: *Centers for Medicare and Medicaid Services, Office of the Actuary, National Health Statistics Group.*
[a]*Includes such programs as workers' compensation, public health activity, Department of Defense, Department of Veterans Affairs, Indian Health Service, and state and local government hospital subsidy and school health.*
[b]*Includes industrial in-plant, privately funded construction and nonpatient revenues, including philanthropy.*

Sponsored by the Michigan Nonprofit Association and the Council of Michigan Foundations

Together, these two programs make up 37 percent of Michigan's health spending and 33 percent of the nation's.

- Medicare spending amounted to 22 percent of the state's health bill and 17 percent of the nation's (national spending was $224 billion in 2000).

- Medicaid spending amounted to 15 percent of the state's health bill and 16 percent of the nation's (national spending was $202 billion in 2000).

- Other government programs (public health, health care for military personnel, and others) accounted for 12 percent of the nation's bill in 2000.

The exhibit also shows that private health insurance, much of it offered by employers to their employees, paid a third—$442 billion—of the nation's health bill in 2000. Most of the remainder ($195 billion)—for copayments, deductibles, and other health services and products not covered by health insurance—was paid out-of-pocket by patients.

The private-spending share of health expenditures grew between 1997 and 1999, offsetting public-share declines caused primarily by slower Medicare spending growth. In 2000 public and private spending grew at about the same rate. In the near future, private-expenditure growth is expected to outpace public-sector health spending because outpatient prescription drug costs, which Medicare does not cover, are rising rapidly.

More recent data on employer-based health insurance show that after five years of record low inflation (1994–98), health insurance premiums rose dramatically in 1999, 2000, and 2001. In fact, premiums increased 11 percent between the spring of 2000 and 2001. Smaller businesses—those with fewer than 100 employees—saw higher increases (12.5 percent on average) than did large firms (10.2 percent). When employer and employee shares of health insurance premiums are combined, the average cost of individual coverage was $221 a month ($2,652 a year) in 2001. Family coverage averaged $588 a month ($7,056 a year).

As premiums rose, employers increased the employee share of the family premium from $122 to $150 a month, on average, between 1996 and 2001, but the proportion of the premium paid by employees stayed about the same (27–28 percent). Employers have been requiring employees to pay higher deductibles and copayments, however, which means that workers are bearing a growing proportion of their health insurance costs.

Providers

Health care expenditures also may be broken down by provider, as shown in Exhibit 2. Nationally, more than half of health dollars go for hospital services and physician care (32 percent and 22 percent, respectively); these portions of the nation's health spending have not changed much since 1960. Declining in the last four decades have been the shares taken up by dental care and drugs, the latter dramatically despite rising drug costs in recent years. Nursing-home and home-health care and other professional services have grown significantly in the same period.

In Michigan, hospitals received 41 percent of health dollars in 1998. Physician and other professional services received 26 percent, drug and other medical supplies 14 percent, nursing homes 7 percent, dental services 6 percent, home health care 2 percent, eyeglasses and other durable medical equipment 2 percent, and other personal health care 2 percent.

Although drugs' share of the national and state health dollar has declined in recent decades, it is likely to start growing—perhaps significantly—in the years ahead. The

Medicare
The federal program that pays for many health care services for people who are blind, disabled, or aged 65 and older.

Panel
The group of providers—physicians, hospitals, pharmacists, others—authorized by a managed-care plan to care for the plan's enrollees.

Point-of-service plan (POS)
An HMO variation that allows enrollees to seek care outside the plan's panel of providers without having to pay the entire cost.

Preferred provider organization (PPO)
A group of providers that agrees to furnish services, at negotiated fees, to a payer's enrollees in exchange for the likelihood of increased patient volume; functions similarly to POS plans, but PPOs contract with HMOs and insurers rather than acting as insurers themselves.

Primary care provider
The physician in charge of all aspects of a patient's care, including referral to specialists.

Qualified health plan (QHP)
An HMO that meets certain state requirements; QHPs are used by the state to serve most of the Medicaid population.

Sponsored by the Michigan Nonprofit Association and the Council of Michigan Foundations

EXHIBIT 2. National Health Expenditures, by Provider, 2000

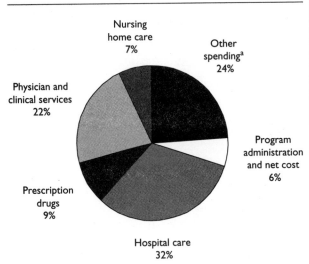

SOURCE: Centers for Medicare and Medicaid Services, Office of the Actuary, National Health Statistics Group.

[a]Includes dentist services, other professional services, home health, durable medical products, over-the-counter medicines and sundries, public health, research and construction.

average yearly cost of prescription drugs per person nationally in 1993 was $195; by 2000 it was $417. Drug costs are rising primarily for three reasons.

- More people are taking prescription drugs and those who already were taking them are taking more of them.

- Newer, more expensive drugs are entering the market, replacing older, less expensive counterparts.

- Prices are rising on existing drugs.

Managed Care

Managed care is a broad term for any comprehensive approach to health care delivery that (1) provides care to enrollees usually on a capitation (fixed monthly fee) basis (2) coordinates patient care so as to ensure the appropriate use of services, and (3) routinely monitors and measures the performance of health providers so as to control costs and maintain or improve care.

Managed-care plans almost always practice selective contracting—that is, they ask only some physicians, hospitals, pharmacists, and other providers in a geographic area to join their panel (the group that the plan authorizes to care for its enrollees). Many plans also require enrollees to choose a primary care physician, who is in charge of all aspects of their care, including referrals to a specialist (the plan will not pay for specialist treatment unless the patient was referred by his/her primary care physician). There are three common types of managed-care plan.

- *Health maintenance organizations* HMOs are the best-known type of managed-care plan. They offer enrollees comprehensive coverage for specific health services for a fixed, prepaid premium. If enrollees obtain health care from a provider not on their plan's panel, they must pay the full cost for the care out of their own pocket.

- *Point-of-service plan (POS)* This is an HMO variation that allows enrollees to seek care outside the panel without having to pay the entire cost. POS plans are becoming more popular because many view them as a way to preserve a wider choice of providers than with a conventional HMO.

- *Preferred provider organization (PPO)* PPOs are groups of providers that agree to furnish services to a payer's enrollees at negotiated fees in exchange for the likelihood of increased patient volume. PPOs generally function like POS plans—with enrollees required to pay more for a service if they use a non-PPO provider—but they usually do not monitor provider costs and performance as closely as HMOs do.

Managed care is a driving force in the evolution of the U.S. health care system, but it no longer is viewed by most employers and federal and state governments as the primary means by which health care costs can be brought under control. The past two years have shown that health care costs can rise significantly even as managed-care enrollment rises. As the numbers below illustrate, many more employees are in less restrictive health plans (PPOs and POS plans, sometimes called "managed care lite") than are in HMOs, which makes it more difficult for employers to control health care costs.

In 2001, 93 percent of the nation's workers were in an HMO, POS plan, or PPO, up from 40 percent in 1992. Only 7 percent of workers with employer-sponsored health insurance were in traditional indemnity plans.

- HMO enrollment peaked in 1996 at 31 percent of the working population; in 2001 the figure was 23 percent.

- PPO enrollment has risen from 28 percent in 1996 to 48 percent in 2001.

- POS plans covered 14 percent of workers in 1996 and 22 percent in 2001.

Sponsored by the Michigan Nonprofit Association and the Council of Michigan Foundations

- In Michigan, as of September 30, 2001, 29 HMOs served almost 2.7 million members (more than one-quarter of the state's population). Medicare beneficiaries enrolling in HMOs have declined in recent years, as many health plans withdrew from the federal program because of inadequate payment for services. In Michigan in 2001, about 79,000 beneficiaries were enrolled in Medicare HMOs; the number is projected to be lower in 2002. Michigan has moved most Medicaid beneficiaries into qualified health plans (QHPs), HMOs that meet certain state requirements; as of December 2001, 742,000 are enrolled in a QHP—90 percent of those eligible for a QHP and almost two-thirds of the total Medicaid population.

DISCUSSION

Why Health Costs Rise

Health care costs rise for several reasons.

- *Inflation and population growth* These factors are persistent and, for the most part, outside the health care sector's control. As the huge baby boom generation (those born between 1946 and 1964) ages, its use of health care services will drive up costs dramatically.

- *Health price inflation* This exceeds general inflation and annually contributed an average of 3 percent to 1999–2001 health cost increases.

- *Frequency and intensity of use of services* The higher the use, the higher the expenditures. Use of services is increasing within certain age groups (e.g., the elderly), which may be compounded by the increase in the size of the age group (again, the elderly are an example). New technologies and drugs also contribute to rising costs, especially when they do not fully replace other diagnosis and treatment methods.

In the mid-to-late 1990s, managed care was successful in limiting the growth in two of the factors above—inflation and utilization—largely by negotiating fee discounts with providers, limiting unnecessary care, and requiring cost-conscious decision-making by providers. There are limits to such actions, however, and in recent years there has been a resurgence in health cost increases. Most experts agree on several reasons for accelerated health spending in 1999–2001.

- To gain market share, managed-care plans had accepted lower revenue/profits, but they could not continue this practice and stay in business.

- Managed-care plans had forced providers (mainly hospitals and physicians) to accept reduced reimbursement for several years, but providers no longer are willing to accept this and are strengthening their negotiating leverage through consolidation.

- Health care is labor intensive, and significant shortages of professionals, particularly nurses, mean that to attract and keep sufficient numbers of these professionals, health care employers have had to increase compensation.

- Public and provider backlash against certain cost-control practices is leading (1) managed-care plans to alter their practices "voluntarily" and (2) state and federal lawmakers to press for legislation limiting ways that plans may cut costs.

- Advances in pharmaceutical and medical technology—such as new biotechnology drugs and improvements in artificial limbs, valves, and organs—prolong life, but they are expensive and few people want any limit placed on the development and appropriate use of such advances.

- The population continues to age, and an older population uses more health care services.

Managed Care

Some experts contend that managed care can control costs without jeopardizing the quality of care. They point out that when working properly, managed-care plans and providers are rewarded financially for keeping people healthy, which limits cost increases and improves quality. They add that managed care's greater use of preventive services and patient education helps to cut costs, as has the development of clinical guidelines that allow physicians to forgo costly procedures that have little likelihood of improving a patient's health. As medical science is able to define more precisely what works and what does not, they assert that unnecessary care can be identified and reduced and quality enhanced.

Supporters of health plans also note that through the National Committee for Quality Assurance (NCQA), HMOs voluntarily may seek accreditation—an indicator of a certain level of quality and financial stability. NCQA reviews are rigorous on- and off-site evaluations, conducted by physician teams and managed-care experts. The reviews assess such clinical quality indicators as frequency of regular breast-cancer screening and childhood immunization, advice to smokers to quit, first-trimester prenatal care, and use of appropriate medication following a heart attack. To receive accreditation, an HMO must meet specific standards in clinical care, prevention of illness and injury, patient satisfaction, and financial stability. An increasing number of employers are requiring HMOs to have NCQA accreditation before they will contract with them.

Health plans are enmeshed in a complex battle among health care interest groups. Critics of managed-care plans, including some consumers/employees and providers, argue that their practices threaten quality. They contend that most health plans focus primarily on the bottom line and that to do so means that they must deny care that physicians and other caregivers deem necessary. Other critics, including some employers, believe that managed-care plans have not succeeded at controlling costs.

The call in recent years for federal and state "patient bill of rights" legislation confirms that there is conflict among health plans, employers, consumers, and providers. Many consumers want a wide choice of providers, particularly physicians, whom they may see without financial penalty. Many managed-care plans, however, view restricting their provider panel as essential to controlling costs—it is the only way that they can steer patients to cost-effective hospitals and physicians. The rapid growth of POS plans suggests that managed care is attentive to consumers' demand for greater choice, but it remains to be seen whether this demand will continue as health insurance premiums rise and employers ask consumers to pay a greater share of the premium.

Current legislative debate about health care centers on many practices of managed-care plans and government's role in regulating them. Congress and almost every state have proposals or new laws to toughen HMO regulation. The most common initiatives would

- expand patients' legal recourse if they believe an HMO has denied or delayed necessary care;

- give certain patients direct access to specialists;

- prohibit "gag rules"—that is, proscribe managed-care plans from limiting what physicians may tell patients about treatment alternatives;

- prevent HMOs from denying payment for emergency services because the HMO determines after the fact that the patient's symptoms did not warrant an ER visit;

- prohibit routinely discharging new mothers and/or their newborns from the hospital in less than two days (normal delivery) or four days (caesarean section);

- prevent outpatient surgery for mastectomies;

- require that certain information about the plan be disclosed to plan members (e.g., certain indicators of quality, how the HMO selects panel providers, and any financial incentives the HMO offers to providers to keep costs down);

- require a consumer ombudsman within or outside the plan to act as a patient advocate; and

- require that members be afforded access to a sufficient number and mix of specialty physicians and other providers.

Proponents of many of these provisions contend that they protect quality of care. Opponents of some measures contend that HMOs rarely engage in the practices that the bills address and therefore legislation is unnecessary. As to limiting access to specialists, experimental treatment, and emergency care, however, they argue that managed care's ability to control costs and maintain quality depends on being permitted to take these very actions.

Controlling Costs

There have been many efforts to control health care costs. Employers are starting to shift more costs onto their employees, and this probably will accelerate during the economic downturn because workers are more likely to accept the increases than to try to move to another job.

Employers, government, and health plans also are working to address rapidly escalating prescription drug costs. Employers have increased prescription copayments, often by dividing brand-name drugs into preferred and nonpreferred categories, which creates a three-tiered drug benefit: Generic drugs have the lowest copay, preferred brand-name drugs have a higher copay, and nonpreferred brand-name drugs have the highest. Campaigns to get prescribers and patients to use generic drugs more frequently when appropriate also are underway. Large employers and government long have sought to limit drug costs by bulk purchasing and, very recently, with price controls. Michigan and a few other states recently notified drug companies that their products will be excluded from Medicaid's preferred list of drugs if they do not lower their prices. The drug companies and others contend that Medicaid beneficiaries will be denied the medication they need under such an action.

Improving Quality

Most health care experts believe that the efforts discussed above will fail to control health care costs. Others add that such efforts could even threaten the quality of care. To make matters worse, the cost of new technology and drugs and, especially, the aging of the population will drive up health care costs for the foreseeable future.

To try to confront this seemingly intractable problem, health policy experts and practitioners increasingly are focusing on the issue of quality. They believe that the only way to gain control of unsustainable increases in health costs is to improve the quality of care because, they con-

Sponsored by the Michigan Nonprofit Association and the Council of Michigan Foundations

tend, too much care is unnecessary or unproven. Doing this means better identification and elimination of unnecessary care and delivering only care that will benefit the patient as efficiently as possible. They argue that more must be done to

- translate into medical practice the procedures known from research to be effective in restoring patients to health and managing chronic disease (called "evidence-based medicine");

- limit the use of procedures for which there is no solid basis in research;

- reduce errors in the health care *system* that are not the fault of individual professionals but are a factor in thousands of preventable deaths every year;

- endeavor to better coordinate patient care among physicians and other professionals, especially for the millions of Americans with chronic illnesses such as diabetes, high blood pressure, and arthritis; and

- emphasize prevention of illness and injury by promoting healthy behavior (e.g., regular exercise, good nutrition, seat belt use, modest alcohol consumption, no tobacco consumption).

Perhaps the most prominent nationwide initiative to put these ideas into practice is the Leapfrog Group. Comprising many large employers—including the big three automakers, General Electric, and Verizon—the Leapfrog Group focuses on developing tangible leaps in patient safety and quality, rewarding high-quality care providers, and informing employers and consumers about these efforts. Currently, three tangible leaps are sought.

- *Computerized physician-order entry* Physicians' handwriting can be misread, leading to serious prescription errors. Hospitals would require physicians to enter medication orders into a computer linked to prescribing-error-prevention software.

- *Intensive-care-unit physician staffing* Research shows that patients do best in an intensive care unit that is staffed with intensive-care specialists.

- *Evidence-based hospital referral* Employers should direct patients and health plans to hospitals that have demonstrated high quality of care for certain common procedures.

In our state, the Michigan Health and Safety Coalition (MH&SC)—with active participation from automakers, labor, providers, insurers, state government, and others—is helping to carry out the Leapfrog initiatives and other programs to improve the quality of care.

Everyone agrees that Americans use too much health care and that the value of much of it is unproven, but there is no consensus on how to eliminate rationally and humanely the services we do not need. Leapfrog and similar efforts offer promise. What is certain is that the battles today are only a dress rehearsal for those that we will see in a decade, when the huge baby boom generation begins to reach age 65, and its health care needs intensify.

See also Aging; Communicable Diseases and Public Health; Health Care Access, Medicaid, and Medicare; Long-Term and Related Care; Mental Health Funding and Services; Substance Abuse; Tobacco Settlement; Youth at Risk.

FOR ADDITIONAL INFORMATION

American Association of Health Plans
1129 20th Street, N.W., Suite 600
Washington, DC 20036
(202) 778-3200
(202) 331-7487 FAX
www.aahp.org

American Association of Retired Persons
309 North Washington Square, Suite 110
Lansing, MI 48933
(517) 482-2772
(517) 482-2794 FAX
www.aarp.org

Blue Cross Blue Shield of Michigan
600 East Lafayette Boulevard
Detroit, MI 48226
(313) 225-8113
(313) 225-6764 FAX
www.bcbsm.com

Center for Medicare and Medicaid Services
U.S. Department of Health and Human Services
7500 Security Boulevard
Baltimore, MD 21244
(410) 786-3000
(410) 786-3252 FAX
www.cms.gov

Families USA
1334 G Street, N.W.
Washington, DC 20005
(202) 628-3030
(202) 347-2417 FAX
www.familiesusa.org

Sponsored by the Michigan Nonprofit Association and the Council of Michigan Foundations

Medical Services Administration
Michigan Department of Community Health
400 South Pine Street
P.O. Box 30479
Lansing, MI 48909
(517) 335-5001
(517) 335-5007 FAX
www.michigan.gov/mdch

Michigan Association of Health Plans
327 Seymour Avenue
Lansing, MI 48901
(517) 371-3181
(517) 482-8866 FAX

Michigan Consumer Health Care Coalition
600 West St. Joseph Highway
Lansing, MI 48933
(517) 484-4954
(517) 484-6549 FAX

Michigan Health and Hospital Association
6215 West St. Joseph Highway
Lansing, MI 48917
(517) 323-3443
(517) 323-0946 FAX
www.mha.org

Michigan Health and Safety Coalition
27000 West 11 Mile Road
Mail Code B713
Southfield, MI 48034
(248) 448-6266
(248) 448-0058 FAX
www.bcbsm.com/blues/mhsc.shtml

Michigan State Medical Society
120 West Saginaw Street
Lansing, MI 48823
(517) 337-1351
www.msms.org

National Committee on Quality Assurance
2000 L Street, N.W., Suite 500
Washington, DC 20036
(888) 275-7585
www.ncqa.org

Sponsored by the Michigan Nonprofit Association and the Council of Michigan Foundations

Higher Education Funding

BACKGROUND

Michigan's 15 public universities and 28 community colleges fulfill a vital function: They play a central role in preparing the work force, giving graduates the means to earn a higher income than otherwise, and they contribute to the personal and intellectual development of the citizenry. Universities generally offer programs resulting in a four-year or post-graduate degree. Community colleges provide programs resulting in a two-year degree or non-degree certification. In total, Michigan's institutions of higher education schooled more than 330,000 fiscal year equated students (FYES) in FY 2000–01.

Universities

Michigan has 15 public four-year institutions of higher education, including the University of Michigan branch campuses in Dearborn and Flint. (Michigan also has 45 independent colleges and universities, but they do not receive state funds.) The Michigan Constitution grants public universities autonomy in all decisions regarding their operations and policies, but state government may exert indirect control via the appropriations process. State appropriations for universities come almost entirely from the General Fund. Unlike K–12 schools, universities have no "earmarked" funding from sales or other tax revenue, and, unlike community colleges, they cannot raise funds by levying a millage. This means that for their entire state appropriation, universities must compete against other parts of the state budget—and sometimes take a back seat to other state priorities.

State funding for public universities grew steadily throughout the 1970s and 1980s, nearly doubling. In the 1990s, growth continued but more slowly: In the last 12 years, from FY 1991–92 through FY 2001–02, General Fund appropriations for universities have increased by 46 percent, from $1.3 billion to $1.9 billion. Exhibit 1 presents the appropriation per FYES for this period.

GLOSSARY

Fiscal year equated student (FYES)
The number of students attending an institution, adjusted for part-time enrollment—i.e., a student attending half time is counted as one-half FYES. Full-time enrollment is considered to be 30 semester-credit hours a year.

Headcount enrollment
The total number of students attending an institution either full or part time.

EXHIBIT 1. State Appropriations per Fiscal Year Equated Student, Michigan Public Universities, FYs 1991–2002

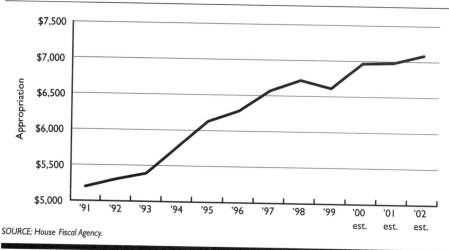

SOURCE: House Fiscal Agency.

Annual increases in state support for universities varied during the 1990s. In the first few years of the decade, when the economy was in recession or pulling out of one, universities received minimal annual increases of about one percent. The situation had improved by FY 1999–2000, a year in which the U.S. and Michigan economies were enjoying the largest peace-time expansion in history. That year, universities received a 5 percent increase, well above the Detroit–Ann Arbor inflation rate of 3.4 percent. However, the economic weakness in 2001 led again to stagnant university appropriations—in FY 2001–02 they are slated to receive only a one percent increase over the previous year.

The appropriation for FY 2002–03 is $1.94 billion for state universities—again, only a marginal increase. Of this, $1.6 billion is recommended for the schools' general operations, $250 million for financial aid to students, and $73.6 million for various other purposes. In total, university funding will use approximately 21 percent of the state General Fund, the same as in FY 2001–02.

Community Colleges

Michigan has 28 community colleges, two-year institutions that confer an associate's degree. Their primary role is to provide general education, job training, and career and technical instruction at a reasonable cost. Community colleges also offer remedial programs for students lacking college entrance skills, opportunities for adults to continue their education, and a gateway for students not yet academically prepared or financially able to enroll at a university.

Approximately 417,400 attended a Michigan community college full- or part-time in FY 2000–01; fiscal year equated enrollment was 110,000. In the 1990s the FYES peaked at 130,500 (FY 1992–93) and bottomed out at 107,500 (FY 1997–98); in the last few years it has remained relatively stable.

Community colleges are governed by locally elected boards and have three major funding sources: property taxes, state aid, and tuition and fees. In FY 2000–01, property taxes and state allocations each contributed roughly one-third (with the edge going to the former), tuition and fees about one-quarter, and the balance came from such other sources as endowments and investment income (see Exhibit 2).

State funding for community colleges fluctuated throughout the 1990s. For example, in FY 1994–95 they received a 1.1 percent decrease, but they received increases above the inflation rate in four of the next five years. Like universities, community colleges have no earmarked source of state funding, and they tend to suffer when state revenues drop—for FY 2002–03, in an economic decline, a "continuation" budget for community colleges has been enacted, giving them just a 0.04 percent increase.

Unlike universities, community colleges are permitted, if voters approve, to levy a local property tax on residents in their tax district. In return, tax-district residents get a break on tuition: in-district tuition tends to be about 50 percent lower than out-of-district tuition. Growth in property tax revenue is restricted because a property's assessed value is prohibited from rising more than 5 percent or the inflation rate, whichever is less. Community colleges are able to increase their property tax revenue above the inflation rate only by raising the millage *rate*, which requires voter approval.

Tuition and Fees
Universities
The governing boards of Michigan universities annually set tuition and fees, and they are among the highest in the nation for public institutions. Tuition has risen rapidly over the last decade. From FY 1990–91 to FY 2000–01, average annual in-state tuition rose an average of about 8 percent, more than double that of inflation as measured by the Detroit–Ann Arbor cost-of-living index. The figures presented below are for undergraduate in-state students enrolled for 30 semester credits in FY 2000–01.

- The average tuition was $4,329.

EXHIBIT 2. Funding Sources, Michigan Community Colleges, FY 2000–01

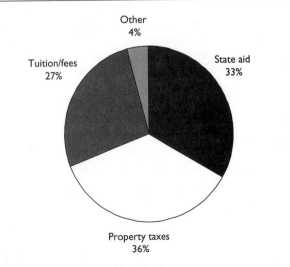

SOURCE: *Michigan Department of Career Development.*

Sponsored by the Michigan Nonprofit Association and the Council of Michigan Foundations

- The University of Michigan had the highest tuition: $6,513 for undergraduates.

- Michigan State University, the largest state school (40,000 FYES), had the second-highest tuition: $5,170.

- Saginaw Valley State University had the lowest: $3,607 (about 80 percent lower than UM's).

Community Colleges

As with universities, community college tuition has increased rapidly over the last decade. From FY 1990–91 to FY 2000–01, the in-district average rose an average of 4.1 percent a year. The figures presented below are per credit hour for FY 2001–02.

- For in-district students, tuition averages $53.87 per credit hour.

- For out-of-district students, tuition averages $79.70.

- Mott Community College, in Flint, has the highest in-district tuition: $61.15.

- Kalamazoo Valley Community College has the lowest in-district tuition: $43.25.

DISCUSSION

Universities

High tuition rates are a barrier to a university education for many low- and middle-income families. Also, the expense of a university education can force students to work part time (often delaying graduation until the fifth or sixth year), borrow money, and/or attend a less expensive school regardless of its reputation or curriculum offering in the student's chosen field.

As mentioned, state government is limited in how much it can directly control tuition increases, but for the last several years, legislators and governors have used the power of the purse to provide incentives to universities to keep tuition increases low. For example, the FY 2000–01 budget reduced, by 1.5 percent, state aid for any university that increased tuition by more than 4 percent from the previous fiscal year. In the FY 2002–03 budget, the legislature has addressed the issue by making an agreement with university leaders that total appropriations would not be reduced from the FY 2001–02 level if universities agree not to raise tuition by more than 8.5 percent or $425, whichever is greater. Even so, an 8.5 percent increase is a sizable hike and will exceed the inflation rate by more than 200 percent.

Supporters of increased state funding for universities point out that studies find a direct link between state appropriation levels and tuition/fee levels—when state funding goes down, tuition goes up and vice versa; they believe that the solution to high tuition is greater state support.

Those opposed to increasing university funding contend that higher education is big business, and, as in all businesses in this day and age, management must become leaner and production more efficient. Specifically, they call for privatizing such services as bookstores, food service, and health service and for redesigning course schedules to facilitate student graduation in four years. Some also call for ending faculty tenure, which they contend allows some low-performing but high-paid faculty members to undeservedly remain on staff. Some observers also are concerned by duplication of course offerings among colleges, and they call for better coordination statewide.

Supporters of higher university funding believe that to prepare students for the workplace of the 21st century, universities are under pressure to add technology and make other expensive improvements, thus the consumer price index no longer is the appropriate standard against which to measure tuition increases. They acknowledge that universities are not as efficient as businesses but argue that they should not be expected to be so, since efficiency sometimes comes at the expense of academic integrity and quality of education.

Community Colleges

While community colleges play a significant role in workforce training, some believe that they take a back seat to universities when it comes to state funding. They argue that while universities receive an average state appropriation per FYES of approximately $7,000, community colleges receive only about $3,300.

Community college supporters point out that in addition to being more affordable than universities, the colleges offer many advantages to their community that four-year institutions do not.

- Community colleges provide opportunities to those who do not participate in university education because of economic or social barriers, such as many minorities, single parents, people with disabilities, people with low income, and the educationally disadvantaged.

- They are geographically accessible. Ninety-five percent of Michigan residents live within commuting distance of a community college.

Sponsored by the Michigan Nonprofit Association and the Council of Michigan Foundations

- Because they stress applied skills that lead directly to employment, community colleges are able to respond to the needs both of adults who need re-training as well as first-time learners.

- Community colleges offer customized or contract training—for example, firms contract with a community college to train employees in the specific skills that the companies need.

Rising costs, sometimes-stagnant state appropriations, and voter reluctance to increase millage rates leave community colleges with only the option of raising tuition if they wish to maintain or expand programs, and this can have the unfortunate effect of making a community college education less affordable to thousands of people. Community college advocates maintain that since such colleges were founded, their hallmark has been their ability to provide a good education at a reasonable cost. As the costs of attending four-year institutions skyrocket and as jobs require increasingly higher education/skill levels, supporters believe that it is imperative that community colleges remain affordable.

Currently, only 76 percent of the state's taxable value (the value on which property taxes are levied) is in a community college district, and some observers suggest that redistricting should be explored as a way to increase community college revenue. Redrawing existing borders so that every area of the state is in a community college tax district, proponents claim, would have several advantages: More local property tax revenue would be available to the two-year institutions; post-secondary education would become more accessible to all because there would be no need to charge out-of-district tuition; and eliminating the two-tiered tuition system (whereby in- and out-of-district students are charged different rates) would reduce administrative costs.

Redistricting is viewed with skepticism by those who fear that implementing it statewide might be an administrative and political nightmare because of the so-called Headlee amendment, which requires that any new taxes levied on a locality be approved by the affected voters.

Moreover, because community colleges can levy taxes, every annexation of a locale not already in a service district would require the locale's voters to approve the annexation.

See also Career Development.

FOR ADDITIONAL INFORMATION

American Association of Community Colleges
One Dupont Circle, N.W., Suite 410
Washington, DC 20036
(202) 728-0200
(202) 883-2467 FAX
www.aacc.nche.edu

House Fiscal Agency
Michigan House of Representatives
124 North Capitol Avenue
Lansing, MI 48933
(517) 373-8080
(517) 373-5874 FAX
www.house.state.mi.us/hfa

Michigan Community College Association
222 North Chestnut Street
Lansing, MI 48933
(517) 372-4350
(517) 372-0905 FAX
www.mmca.org

Michigan Department of Career Development
Victor Office Center, 7th Floor
201 North Washington Square
Lansing, MI 48913
(517) 241-4000
(517) 373-0314 FAX
www.michigan.gov/mdcd

Presidents Council, State Universities of Michigan
Michigan Dental Building
230 North Washington Square, Suite 302
Lansing, MI 48933
(517) 482-1563
(517) 482-1241 FAX
www.pcsum.org

Sponsored by the Michigan Nonprofit Association and the Council of Michigan Foundations

Highway Funding and Safety

BACKGROUND

In 1913 the Michigan Legislature passed the State Trunk Line Act, authorizing a state highway network. Then, it totaled about 3,000 miles of roadway; today it comprises nearly 122,000. Responsibility for today's roads is split among the state (9,711 miles), counties (89,499 miles), cities and villages (20,667 miles), and the federal government (2,102 miles).

The Michigan Department of Transportation (MDOT) has jurisdiction over the state highway system, identified by *I*, *U.S.*, and *M* designations. County roads are under the jurisdiction of the 83 county road commissions, and municipal streets are owned by 535 incorporated cities and villages. The federal government is responsible for roads in national forests, parks, and federal installations.

Funding

Monies for the state's transportation system comes from state, local, and federal sources. State-generated revenue supplies the majority of the income and is collected primarily through Michigan's fuel taxes (19 cents per gallon on gasoline and 15 cents per gallon on diesel fuel), motor-vehicle registration fees, and sales tax collected on vehicles. This revenue is *earmarked* (dedicated) to transportation, and it may be spent only for purposes established by law. Local units of government help to fund the construction or reconstruction of state trunk lines in their jurisdiction.

The federal government provides funding for transit and state highways through the Transportation Equity Act for the 21st Century (TEA-21). Signed into law in 1998, TEA-21 allocates to the states a share of the 18.4-cents-per-gallon federal gasoline tax for state use on highway, highway safety, transit, and other surface-transportation programs. Michigan's allocation during the program's six-year life (1998–2003) is expected to exceed $800 million a year.

Michigan's transportation programs and the appropriation of revenue collected for them are governed by Public Act 51 of 1951, as amended. The Michigan Transportation Fund (MTF) is the primary collection and distribution fund for transportation monies; from it dollars are allocated, using the statutory funding formula, to state, county, and city and village road agencies as well as to the special funds: Critical Bridge Fund, Comprehensive Transportation Fund (in support of public transit programs), and Economic Development Fund (for roads in support of economic development projects). This description greatly simplifies the complicated Act 51 MTF distribution formula, and for more information, readers are directed to "Road Funding," in *Michigan in Brief, 6th Edition*, which may be found at *www.michiganinbrief.org*.

In addition to creating the MTF and setting out the spending formula, Act 51 specifies how the state and locals shall spend the money from the various funds, how federal funds shall be allocated (roughly 75 percent for repairing and rebuilding state roads and 25 percent for building, repairing, and rebuilding local federal-aid eligible roads), and how compliance and reporting shall be accomplished.

GLOSSARY

Transportation Equity Act for the 21st Century (TEA-21)
Federal law that authorizes federal surface-transportation programs for highways, highway safety, and transit for the six-year period from 1998 to 2003.

Trunk line
Any road for which the Michigan Department of Transportation has responsibility.

Sponsored by the Michigan Nonprofit Association and the Council of Michigan Foundations

The FY 2001–02 state transportation budget of $3.1 billion is approximately $1.3 billion more than the FY 1995–96 budget—an increase of 70 percent in six years. This is due partially to the enactment of TEA-21 in 1998, which is bringing an additional $300 million a year in federal funding for Michigan roads and transit systems. Also, Build Michigan, Governor Engler's three-phase transportation funding program of $5 billion over 10 years has increased revenue: A 4-cents-per-gallon gasoline tax hike and increases in commercial truck registration fees are bringing $300 million more annually to the state transportation budget.

Safety

According to the National Highway Transportation Safety Administration (NHTSA), traffic crashes are a leading cause of death in the United States (*the* leading cause for 5–27-year-olds) and cost Michigan taxpayers nearly $10 billion a year.

The good news is that while the number of vehicles on Michigan roads and the number of miles traveled are increasing, traffic crashes and fatalities are not, and this probably is due to a number of actions taken in recent years.

- *Seat-belt use enforcement* As of March 2000, Michigan law enforcement personnel may issue a citation whenever they observe an unbelted driver or passenger. The NHTSA estimates that annually this will save about 150 Michigan lives, prevent almost 3,600 crash-related injuries, and save $2.6 million. Indeed, there were 8 percent fewer fatalities in the state in 2001 than in 2000 (the figure dropped from 1,382 to 1,267).

- *Graduated driver licensing* Michigan's graduated driver licensing (GDL) program has lowered crash rates among teenaged drivers. It is a three-stage licensing process for new drivers: In the first stage they have a learner's permit (allowing them to drive only with supervision); in the second they have an intermediate license (requiring supervision at certain times of the day); and in the third they receive full licensure (imposing no restrictions). A recently released study by the University of Michigan Transportation Research Institute reports that crash rates among 16-year-old drivers are down 25 percent since 1996, when the GDL program began.

- *Repeat-offender limitations* In 1999 several laws were enacted to crack down on people who repeatedly commit traffic offenses. Repeat offenders may not only have their driver's license revoked, but their vehicle license plate may be confiscated, their vehicle immobilized, they may be prohibited from being issued license plates and titles, and anyone who co-owns a vehicle with a repeat offender may be denied registration for and title to the vehicle. For drivers convicted of alcohol-related offenses, an ignition interlock may be required (this is a device that renders a vehicle inoperable when a driver fails to pass a breath test for alcohol), and they may be required to obtain substance-abuse treatment. The laws also classify several actions as a crime, including causing serious injury while driving on a suspended license, causing death while driving on a suspended license, allowing another person to drive on a suspended license and causing serious injury, allowing another person to drive while suspended and causing death, and driving while drunk with a person under age 16 in the vehicle.

DISCUSSION

Build Michigan

The Build Michigan program has been the topic of debate since its debut in 1992. The 4-cent gasoline tax hike was particularly onerous to some and, more recently, Build Michigan III has been criticized because it requires a one-time $100 million General Fund/General Purpose (GF/GP) appropriation and an additional $800 million from bonding. Critics disapprove of using GF/GP monies for roads; they point out that many important programs have no source of funds other than GF/GP, whereas roads get upwards of $2 billion a year from revenue dedicated solely to that purpose. They further disapprove of engaging in long-term borrowing to fund road improvements, which they equate to the state's getting a credit card and making future generations pay off the debt. Supporters contend that long-term debt is appropriate in this instance because future generations will benefit greatly from the projects, which were carefully selected to address safety, congestion, and economic development, because they will serve the state for 100 years. Local road agencies worry that some of the money needed to repay the bonds could be diverted from road maintenance and construction.

Although Build Michigan III has $900 million in funding in addition to the $12.5 billion set aside for Michigan roads in the next five years, organizations such as the Southeast Michigan Council of Governments (SEMCOG) and the Michigan Road Builders Association (MRBA) say it is insufficient to meet growing needs. SEMCOG predicts that by 2025, the metropolitan Detroit area alone will have a $17 billion shortfall in meeting its transportation needs, which include public transit and rail as well as roads.

Many are concerned about Build Michigan III's emphasis on expanding the highway system to the detriment of repairing roads. Although traffic volume has increased 30

Sponsored by the Michigan Nonprofit Association and the Council of Michigan Foundations

percent since 1991 and capacity only 3 percent, critics question the wisdom of failing to fix deteriorating roads before taking on expansion projects. Environmental organizations fear that Build Michigan III's focus on expansion will widen urban sprawl by leading to more development in rural areas. Organizations such as the Michigan Land Institute claim that the Build Michigan program has ignored public transit, and they recommend increasing and stabilizing transit funding.

Supporters point out that Build Michigan I repaired more roads than any other program in a similar period of time in Michigan history, and, furthermore, Build Michigan III is not focused solely on expansion. Moreover, according to MDOT, the Build Michigan II and III programs have focused on "fixing the worst roads first," with a goal of bringing 90 percent of state roads to good condition by 2007. The department points out that annually, less than 25 percent (and sometimes much less) of the state's transportation budget is invested in new roads. They also dispute environmentalists' claims that new road construction leads to urban sprawl, saying that this phenomenon generally is caused by local land-use planning.

TEA-21 Reauthorization

Organizations such as MDOT and the MRBA have begun working on the reauthorization package that is expected to replace TEA-21 in 2003. Although TEA-21 brought record investment and improvements in all forms of Michigan transportation, current allocation formulas return only 90.5 cents for every federal gas tax dollar sent to Washington. To bring more transportation funding to Michigan and address certain safety and security concerns, they are lobbying for several changes that will benefit the state.

- *Full funding of federal-aid highway and transit programs* This could be accomplished through continuing the Revenue Aligned Budget Authority from TEA-21 or allowing states to spend down unobligated balances in the federal Highway Trust Fund.

- *Higher return on the money that states send to the Highway Trust Fund* MDOT believes that each state should get at least a 95 percent return on its contributions to both the highway and transit accounts of the Highway Trust Fund.

- *Significant reinvestment in the high-level road system (interstates, freeways, and national highways)* This becomes more vital every year as Michigan falls further behind in modernizing the interstate system and addressing capacity issues, especially in urban areas.

- *Protocols and funding to address security issues* Michigan has an international border and the security issues that go with it. Michigan also must review security/safety risk in all areas of transportation—highways, pipelines, rail transit, facilities, bridges, and so on. In addition, the state must address its need to monitor traffic on these systems, especially "HAZMAT" (hazardous materials) shipments by truck and rail.

- *More flexibility for states in determining how programs are structured and money is spent* MDOT supports consolidating federal categorical funding (that is, funding dedicated to specific programs) into block grants to the states. The current multitude of categorical grants, set-asides, and discretionary grant programs complicate the funding process and make it difficult to direct funding to the most-needed transportation improvements.

- *Streamline federal planning and program-delivery requirements* MDOT believes that state transportation agencies should lead statewide planning and have as much authority as possible in administering federal transportation programs in their states.

Diesel Fuel Tax

Legislation (House Bills 5733–36) has been introduced to extend the 4-cents-per-gallon gasoline-tax hike to diesel fuel and simplify its collection. Opponents (including the Michigan Trucking Association) argue that truckers already pay their fair share through other fees and taxes, and they contend that it would negatively affect the industry, which already is suffering in the declining economy.

Proponents (including MDOT, county road commissions, the Michigan Association of Counties, and the MRBA) cite a recent Federal Highway Administration study that estimates that commercial trucks are responsible for up to 40 percent of the cost to design, build, maintain, and repair roads and bridges; in 2000 the trucking industry contributed only 16 percent of Michigan funding for such work. MDOT reports that equalizing the tax by extending it to truck fuel will yield an additional $38 million annually in revenue and, if at the same time, reporting and collection are simplified, an additional $10 million will be realized.

Safety

In late 2000 federal legislation was enacted requiring all states either to adopt .08 percent blood-alcohol concentration (BAC) as the presumptive level of intoxication for driving or lose a portion of their federal highway monies. Michigan's BAC level currently is .10 percent, and legislation to lower it to .08 (HBs 4084 and 4134) was introduced in 2001. The Michigan Licensed Beverage Association and Michigan Beer and Wine Wholesalers oppose lowering tolerances on the ground that when driving is a factor in a serious accident, the driver's blood-alcohol level more often is near or above .15 percent. They favor targeting these drivers and repeat offenders. Road safety advocates, such as Mothers Against Drunk Driving, strongly support lowering the limit to .08 percent.

Since 1966 Michigan has required motorcyclists to wear helmets while operating their machines, but many motorcyclists vociferously oppose the requirement. Many consider the law an abridgement of freedom—an example of the state dictating behavior to persons who should be free to choose how to live their lives. Safety organizations urge continued resistance to allowing exceptions to this law, claiming that all society pays a price when a cyclist or passenger is injured or killed. House Bill 4823, which would limit the helmet requirement to operators under 21 years old, awaits action.

See also Emergency Preparedness and Response; Land Use and Sustainability; Substance Abuse.

FOR ADDITIONAL INFORMATION

Michigan Department of Transportation
P.O. Box 30050
Lansing, MI 48909
(517) 373-2090
(517) 373-8518 FAX
www.michigan.gov/mdot

Michigan Field Office
Federal Highway Administration
Federal Building, Room 207
315 West Allegan Street
Lansing, MI 48933
(517) 377-1844
(517) 377-1804 FAX
[See "Highway Statistics 2000," available at *www.fhwa.dot.gov/ohim/hs00*]

Michigan Road Builders Association
924 Centennial Way, Suite 460
Lansing, MI 48917
(517) 886-9000
(517) 886-8960 FAX
www.mrba.com

Michigan Secretary of State
Treasury Building
430 West Allegan Street
Lansing, MI 48918
(517) 373-7296
(517) 373-2510 FAX
www.michigan.gov/sos

Michigan State Police
Office of Highway Safety Planning
4000 Collins Road
P.O. Box 30633
Lansing, MI 48909
(517) 336-6477
(517) 333-5756 FAX
www.michigan.gov/msp

Sponsored by the Michigan Nonprofit Association and the Council of Michigan Foundations

Housing Affordability

BACKGROUND

In 2000, after a decade of unprecedented economic growth, the Michigan State Housing Development Authority (MSHDA) estimated that more than 670,000 Michigan households may be classified as "housing needy"—meaning that their dwelling is overcrowded (has more than one person per room), is substandard (i.e., lacks complete plumbing, does not have a private kitchen, lacks adequate heating, or is physically deteriorated), or eats up more than 30 percent of household income in rent or mortgage payments. Recent U.S. Census figures suggest that the national number could be as high as one million households.

Home Ownership

Home ownership is out of reach for a sizeable portion of the population: In Michigan the average sale price for new and pre-owned houses is $134,058 (Michigan Board of Realtors, 2001). Manufactured housing is more reasonable than traditional housing, averaging $31,800 for a new, basic unit and $50,200 for a larger unit with more amenities (National Housing Conference); used units cost less, of course.

Rental Housing

The demand for affordable rental housing is immense because many would-be homeowners have to settle for renting. At the same time, the amount of rental housing is decreasing and some of what exists is deteriorating badly.

One problem with privately owned rental housing is the difficulty in enforcing housing codes (for such reasons as agency understaffing, absentee landlords, and legal hurdles), which contributes to the deterioration and eventual loss of existing rental housing. Moreover, enforcement is inconsistent—too lax in some locales and too strict in others.

Much of the public rental housing was built in the 1930s and 1940s and badly needs replacement or major renovation, but government-funded new construction has nearly ended, and the U.S. Department of Housing and Urban Development (HUD) reports that federal funding for rehabilitation has been cut more than 60 percent over the past decade. The largest federal effort—the section 8 Housing Program—has been reduced significantly since 1980. Federal funding for rental-housing construction and for rent-subsidy assistance has been halved in the past 20 years, dropping from $32 billion (1980) to $16 billion (2000).

Moreover, as HUD acknowledges, conditions in many public housing developments are unacceptable: poor management, poor maintenance, deterioration, and high crime rates. As a result, vacancy rates are high—not because there is a lack of demand for such housing, but because people who ordinarily would live there are forced to choose between such conditions and looking elsewhere. HUD has been severely criticized for mismanaging public housing, and major steps have been taken to improve the agency's efficiency and effectiveness.

Much privately owned rental housing that was subsidized by the federal government has been converted to market-rate units—which is permitted after a number of years following construction (the length of time depends on how the mortgage was structured) if the owner forgoes further federal subsidies.

Either as a result of deterioration or through conversion, more than half of the nation's affordable rental units (one million of 1.9 million units) were lost in the late 1990s. In Michigan in 2002 alone, MSHDA reports that the state is at risk of losing some 6,700 affordable apartment units as a result of owners opting out of their contract with MSHDA and putting the units in the more lucrative open market. The agency reports that it is pursuing several strategies to prevent the loss.

There is little or no new construction in the private sector to replace the lost affordable rental units—although in 2001 MSHDA funded 1,228 new units and, through its Low-Income Housing Tax Credit program, helped to finance another 8,322.

Addressing Michigan's Needs

Of the 3.8 million Michigan households, more than one-third (1.5 million) are low-income, and many live in housing that is overcrowded or substandard. HUD reports that 30 percent of all low-income housing in Michigan is considered substandard. Needy renters outnumber needy owners two to one.

Newly built or existing housing is not affordable for some middle-income and most low-income families. Michigan's efforts to address this need are coordinated through MSHDA. The agency was established in 1966 and is widely recognized for its innovative programs. It receives no state appropriations but instead sells tax-exempt bonds and notes and lends the proceeds at below-market interest rates to developers of rental housing, buyers of single-family homes, and others. In the past 20 years, the agency has

- financed more than $1.8 billion for nearly 52,000 units of affordable rental housing in Michigan;

- helped to finance approximately $3.5 billion in single-family mortgages, making it possible for Michiganians to purchase almost 80,000 homes; and

- allocated more than $150 million in housing tax credits, primarily to developers, which has helped to create more than 40,000 additional rental units.

The housing authority also

- administers certain federal housing programs;

- provides grants to and works with neighborhood groups to finance construction and renovation of low-income housing;

- makes funds available to homeless shelters; and

- provides low-interest loans to help landlords make property repairs.

Michigan has roughly 149,000 low-cost, rent-subsidized housing units plus 18,000 covered under the section 8 low-income certificates and vouchers program—half in municipal housing developments; most are supported by federal programs and some have state subsidies.

Since passage of the National Affordable Housing Act in 1990, Michigan has received approximately $200 million in Home Funds and is using it for housing rehabilitation and ownership programs and rental assistance. MSHDA administers most of the funds statewide, although some are allocated directly to communities for use in local programs. In addition, such federal programs as Community Development Block Grants, Emergency Shelter Grants, and Housing Opportunities for Persons with AIDS funneled nearly $76 million into the state last year, with portions or all of each program being used to meet housing needs.

According to MSHDA, 62 percent of those with housing problems who live in central cities are renters. The Detroit Housing Commission reports that nearly half of its renters are inadequately housed and about a third of low-income homeowners live in substandard housing or are paying more than 30 percent of their income for housing. The Detroit Housing Commission provides about 5,800 public housing units, with a vacancy rate of 47 percent; some 1,100 of the total are scheduled to be demolished and 550 are undergoing renovation. Another 4,900 units are covered under the section 8 low-income rent certificates and vouchers program.

DISCUSSION

Government at all levels is being criticized for failing to address the shrinking supply of affordable housing. In recent years, the federal emphasis has shifted from constructing and rehabilitating low-income housing to giving subsidies to low-income renters for the portion of their housing costs that exceeds 30 percent of income. Various tax reform measures since the mid-1980s have established incentives for developers and owners of low-income housing, but the absence of enough affordable housing stock in Michigan and the nation suggests to many that not enough is being done.

Sponsored by the Michigan Nonprofit Association and the Council of Michigan Foundations

With diminishing federal responsibility, many believe that state government should expand its role in improving access to adequate low-income housing. Some argue that in limiting its role to that of a financing agency without state appropriations, MSHDA is restricted in its ability to address Michigan's low-income housing problems.

Various measures have been enacted in recent years to improve Michigan's stock of affordable housing. Public Act 147 of 1992, for example, created "enterprise zones"—an economic redevelopment tool under which rehabilitated housing is taxed at a lower rate than it would be elsewhere in the community. By designating up to 10 percent of their geographic area as enterprise zones for up to 12 years, about 30 of Michigan's larger municipalities have considerably increased rehabilitation in those areas.

Public Act 376 of 1996 made 22 "renaissance zones" possible. These provide virtually tax-free housing and business operations in depressed areas. Affordable housing opportunities are believed to have been created in these zones, but the number of units is unknown.

In 2000 the state directed $25 million of federal Temporary Assistance to Needy Families (TANF) funds to provide housing help for families on public assistance. These funds are administered by MSHDA via an interagency agreement with the Michigan Family Independence Agency (FIA) and allocated as follows:

- $9 million to Habitat for Humanity, to help 300 families reduce the principal owed on their home

- $11 million to help with down payments, relocation, credit repair, and home inspections

- $2.8 million to help people who (1) had never owned a home, (2) had not owned a home in the three years prior, or (3) were purchasing a home in a federally targeted area

- $1 million to provide MSHDA's section 8 voucher program families with lead-safe rental units

- $1.2 million to MSHDA for administrative costs

Nearly all of the funds have been expended, and the response to this program suggests to many that a significant number of Michiganians need help in getting affordable housing. Housing advocates feel that the key problem is finding homes for families below 25 percent of the state median income ($43,448, according to the 2000 Census).

The *State and Local Sourcebook* (*Governing* magazine, 2001) ranks Michigan 48th among the states in state and local government per capita spending on housing. Al-though the state does administer affordable rental and home ownership programs, much of the funding for it comes from federal resources.

Because some believe that the state needs to make more funding available for comprehensive affordable housing solutions, legislation (HBs 4682–84) has been introduced to create a state housing trust fund focused on the needs of low-income, very-low income, and extremely low-income households.

The bills would create the Affordable Housing Program in MSHDA and the Michigan Affordable Housing Fund in the Department of Treasury. The bills do not establish a revenue source for the fund, although they allow for potential appropriations and contributions and would create a single business tax credit as one way to encourage contributions (one analysis says the SBT credit could yield as much as $28 million annually until the tax is phased out). The bills provide for grants or loans to eligible applicants (not-for-profit corporations, for-profit corporations, and MSHDA-approved for-profit/nonprofit partnerships) for

- land and building acquisition;

- new construction or rehabilitation;

- predevelopment and development costs;

- preservation of existing housing units;

- infrastructure and community facilities directly supporting housing development;

- insurance premiums;

- operating and replacement reserves;

- down-payment and security-deposit assistance; and

- support services.

Projects would have to fit into their surroundings, and a portion of the program's annual allocation would have to be directed at "special populations," including people who are homeless, have physical and mental disabilities, or live in a distressed or rural area.

Supporters of the bills say that Michigan has a severe housing problem and needs a comprehensive, long-term solution. They assert that a state program and trust fund comprise the best way to develop a responsible program and target those most in need. They point out that for every $1 spent from a housing trust fund, another $5–10 is leveraged in other public and private resources (National Low Income Housing Coalition). Proponents further assert that there are economic as well as humanitarian reasons in support of affordable housing: Areas that lack affordable housing are unattractive to business because absence of such housing makes it difficult to maintain a suitable, stable work force.

The bills' skeptics fear that for-profits would use fund money to build and sell affordable housing and then use the profits, however modest, for more-lucrative, nonpublic ventures. The bills' proponents counter that even if some money were to "escape" in this way, including private-sector builders in the program would result in construction of many more affordable housing units than nonprofits could efficiently build on their own.

FOR ADDITIONAL INFORMATION

Detroit Housing Commission
1301 East Jefferson Avenue
Detroit, MI 48207
(313) 877-8639
(313) 877-8769 FAX
www.ci.detroit.mi.us/housecomm

Investing in Affordable Housing in Michigan
Public Sector Consultants, Inc. (May 2001),
www.publicsectorconsultants.com/publications.html

Michigan Association of Realtors
720 North Washington Avenue
P.O. Box 40725
Lansing, MI 48901
(517)372-8890
(517)334-5568 FAX
www.mirealtors.com

Michigan State Housing Development Authority
755 East Michigan Avenue
P.O. Box 30044
Lansing, MI 48912
(517) 373-8370
(517) 335-4797 FAX
www.michigan.gov/mshda

U.S. Department of Housing and Urban Development
451 7th Street, S.W.
Washington, DC 20410
(202) 708-1112
(202) 619-8365 FAX
www.hud.gov

Sponsored by the Michigan Nonprofit Association and the Council of Michigan Foundations

Immigrants: Human Services Benefits

BACKGROUND

Prior to 1996, immigration policy and welfare policy had little to do with one another. The federal Immigration and Naturalization Service (INS) administered the Immigration and Naturalization Act (INA) and made basic decisions about who would be allowed into the country and under what conditions. While "undocumented" or "illegal" immigrants never were presumed to have access to welfare benefits, immigrants legally residing in the country did.

This changed in 1996, with passage of the federal Personal Responsibility and Work Opportunity Reconciliation Act (PRWORA), commonly known as welfare reform. With regard to immigrants, PRWORA had two main effects.

- For the foreseeable future, the act altered immigrants' eligibility for benefits under such programs as Supplemental Security Income (SSI), Food Stamps, Medicaid, and Temporary Assistance for Needy Families (TANF) as well as various state-funded programs.

- It created an important role for the states, empowering—but not requiring—them to create programs for immigrants.

The law remains formidably complex, even for people with long-time familiarity with welfare programs and benefits. Essentially, PRWORA grafted very complex laws dealing with immigration onto very complex laws dealing with welfare eligibility. The act divides the American immigrant population into two groups.

- *"Qualified" immigrants* have some welfare rights. This group includes lawful permanent residents and certain refugees and those given asylum for humanitarian or political reasons.

- *"Unqualified" immigrants* have no welfare rights. This group includes undocumented immigrants as well as those with temporary status, such as students and tourists.

Moreover, PRWORA distinguishes among qualified immigrants, depending on their status as of August 22, 1996, the date the law was enacted. Immigrants who arrived on or before that date are called pre-enactment immigrants; those arriving after are called post-enactment immigrants. As the exhibit makes clear, pre-enactment qualified immigrants have many more rights than those arriving after August 22, 1996, who either are ineligible for benefits altogether or barred from receiving them for five years.

The exhibit accurately depicts the general thrust of the PRWORA provisions and the effect on the immigrant population, but it does not deal with the law's myriad exceptions based on an immigrant's military or work experience or status as a refugee or asylum seeker.

Role of the States

Perhaps most important, PRWORA left many key decisions about immigrant welfare policy in the hands of the states, including two of particular consequence: (1) whether to provide TANF and Medicaid benefits to pre-enactment immigrants and (2) whether

GLOSSARY

PRWORA
Personal Responsibility and Work Opportunity Reconciliation Act of 1996, the main vehicle of national welfare reform that shifted many decisions regarding welfare—including those affecting immigrants—to the states.

Qualified immigrants
Immigrants with permanent resident status and others who may be entitled to welfare benefits. PRWORA further divides this group into "pre-enactment" immigrants (those who arrived in the United States on or prior to August 22, 1996) and "post-enactment" immigrants (those arriving after). The pre-enactment group has considerably more welfare rights.

Temporary Assistance to Needy Families (TANF), Supplemental Security Income (SSI), Medicaid, Food Stamps
The main state/federal funding and programs through which cash assistance, medical care, and nutrition assistance are provided to the needy.

Unqualified Immigrants
Generally, immigrants who are in the United States temporarily—for example, students and visitors—or illegally. In general, unqualified immigrants are not entitled to benefits.

Sponsored by the Michigan Nonprofit Association and the Council of Michigan Foundations

Noncitizen Benefit Eligibility, United States, 2002

Group	Program and Eligibility				
	SSI	Food Stamps	Medicaid	TANF[a]	State/Local Benefits
Qualified pre-enactment immigrants	Eligible[b]	Eligible[b]	State option	State option	State option
Qualified post-enactment immigrants	Ineligible	Ineligible	Ineligible for first five years; state option thereafter	Ineligible for first five years; state option thereafter	State option
Unqualified immigrants	Ineligible	Ineligible	Eligible for emergency services only	Ineligible	Ineligible without passage of state legislation

SOURCE: The Urban Institute, Washington, D.C., 1999.
[a] In Michigan, the TANF block-grant monies are used for the Family Independence Program (FIP) and other services for people receiving public assistance.
[b] Eligibility is only partial. SSI is available only to the disabled or to those receiving benefits as of August 22, 1996. Food stamp eligibility is limited to those aged under 18, aged 65 or older, blind, or disabled.

to provide state-funded substitute benefits for post-enactment immigrants who either lost or had not yet attained eligibility for food stamps, SSI, TANF, and Medicaid.

In short, whether a state's immigrant population receives benefits is no longer just a federal decision—individual states have a great deal to say in the matter. The states were nearly unanimous in their decision to continue to grant TANF and Medicaid benefits to pre-enactment qualified immigrants. With regard to state-funded substitute benefits for the post-enactment group, however, there is considerable variation among the states. The differences among four particular states that have large a immigrant population suggest that factors such as welfare philosophy and effective advocacy probably play a bigger role than does straightforward consideration of immigrant need: California and Massachusetts are very generous in the degree to which they offer benefits to this population; Texas and Florida are considerably less so.

Michigan Benefits

Michigan has a relatively large immigrant population. According to information developed by the Center for Civil Justice (Saginaw), there were approximately 519,000 foreign-born residents of Michigan in 2000, comprising 5.4 percent of the state population. Traditionally, many of these residents have come from India, Mexico, Canada, China, and a number of Middle Eastern countries. Many of the most recent arrivals came from Bosnia, Iraq, and portions of the former Soviet Union.

Michigan's immigrant population is certainly not disproportional in terms of the national immigrant population, nor has the increase in the population exceeded the national average over the last decade. The percentage and number of foreign-born residents here does not begin to approach that of California, New York, Florida, Texas, or New Jersey.

Michigan gives TANF and Medicaid eligibility to pre-enactment qualified immigrants, but for the post-enactment group Michigan does not go much beyond what is required under federal law. Post-enactment immigrants are ineligible for SSI (in Michigan, state disability assistance) or food stamps and must wait five years for eligibility for Medicaid or TANF (in Michigan, the Family Independence Program).

DISCUSSION

The aims of the immigrant provisions of PRWORA are similar to the general aims of the act itself and reflect a desire to give states flexibility in providing services and welfare assistance in a way that encourages and supports work. With specific reference to immigrants, part of the federal policy goal was to encourage naturalization among immigrants who had lived here a long time without seeking full U.S. citizenship.

Welfare reform, including the immigrant provisions, has many supporters. For example, the American Public Human Services Agency (APHSA)—a group that includes many state agency professionals—argues that shifting welfare authority to the states was "indisputably the right course of action." Proponents often cite declining welfare rolls, a greater commitment to work, and many innovative state programs as evidence that PRWORA is a policy success.

Sponsored by the Michigan Nonprofit Association and the Council of Michigan Foundations

But the act has many critics. While some concede that PRWORA worked well for the first five years, they wonder how it will fare during tough economic times, when jobs are scarce. Critics also emphasize the fact that similarly situated immigrants are treated differently depending upon the state in which they reside. They ask if the federal government, which has exclusive control over immigration, should not do more to ensure the well-being of immigrants.

Critics also note that the provisions of PRWORA, particularly those that apply to post-enactment immigrants, have a perverse effect in that services are provided in inverse proportion to an immigrant's need for them. For example, the Center for Civil Justice cites evidence suggesting that the immigrant population often is upwardly mobile and thus unlikely to need welfare benefits five years after entry. Yet they do need benefits when they are newly arrived and without work and when language frequently is a barrier, but this is precisely when they may not be eligible for some programs.

Finally, of course, critics point to the complexity of the act itself. When many English-speaking professionals have trouble determining who is eligible and who is not, how can new arrivals who are unfamiliar with the law, customs, and language be expected to understand their obligations and rights?

Regardless of one's opinion of PRWORA, it is clear that the law has changed immigrant participation in welfare programs.

- Children born in the United States are citizens whether their parents are or not, and thus they may be eligible for such benefits as food stamps. Yet studies suggest that among citizen children living in immigrant households, the number receiving food stamps has dropped substantially nationwide. While it is not possible to directly confirm this trend in Michigan, the U.S. Department of Agriculture estimates that food stamp participation in Michigan fell from nearly 839,000 in FY 1997 to just over 641,000 in FY 2001, a decline of about 24 percent. It is reasonable to assume that at least some of the decline was among immigrants or among children of immigrants who are eligible for benefits because they were born in this country. Although the latter are eligible, their parents may not understand eligibility requirements and do not enroll them.

- The Michigan Department of Community Health reports that in October 1997 there were about 3,900 emergency services only (ESO) beneficiaries in the Michigan Medicaid program. In October 2001 that number had risen to more than 14,500, an increase of over 270 percent. One may receive ESO assistance if s/he is poor enough to qualify for Medicaid but does not meet one or more of the other eligibility criteria that would qualify him/her for full Medicaid benefits. It is reasonable to assume that at least some of the ESO increase is attributable to immigrants, who, prior to PRWORA, would have qualified for full Medicaid benefits but now may get only ESO care.

Although Michigan is not particularly generous in regard to immigrants, demographic statistics show that this is at least in part a response to economic reality. Immigrant poverty is a problem in Michigan, but the evidence also suggests that it is not as severe a problem here as in the country generally. In 1996 the percentage of Michigan immigrants living in poverty (24 percent) was below the national average (28 percent). Also in 1996, noncitizens made up some 6.4 percent of the national poverty population, whereas in Michigan the figure was 12.5 percent.

Advocacy groups such as the Center for Civil Justice point out that the suffering that immigrants endure here still is real, and the center would like, at a minimum, to see food stamp privileges restored for post-enactment qualified immigrants. While acknowledging that any new state programs are unlikely in light of Michigan's fiscal picture, advocacy groups stress that there are practical ways to reduce barriers to access that would be effective and save money. These include

- reducing disparities in the way in which immigrant benefits are offered from county to county, and

- providing a more aggressive outreach program to ensure that immigrants who are entitled to benefits are aware of their rights.

Such recommendations are met with some sympathy from state officials, but they point out that the state of the budget is such that it is unrealistic to expect any new state-funded program for immigrants or, for that matter, anyone else. Some policymakers argue that federal changes are necessary to make the food stamp program more understandable and accessible to others as well as immigrants. The Michigan Family Independence Agency director noted in testimony to the U.S. House of Representatives that the sheer complexity of the food stamp program has led to a situation wherein "many immigrants just assume they are ineligible and do not apply for benefits that would help their families."

Early in 2002 the federal administration announced that it would support aligning food stamps eligibility with

TANF eligibility. The proposal is being debated as part of the new federal farm bill. If passed, post-enactment qualified immigrants will become eligible for food stamps after residing in the United States for five years.

See also Welfare Reform: TANF Reauthorization.

FOR ADDITIONAL INFORMATION

American Public Human Services Association
810 First Street, N.E., Suite 500
Washington, DC 20002
(202) 682-0100
(202) 289-6555 FAX
www.aphsa.org

Center for Civil Justice
320 South Washington, 2d Floor
Saginaw, MI 48607
(800) 724-7441
(517) 755-3558 FAX
www.mlan.net/ccj

Michigan League for Human Services
1115 South Pennsylvania Avenue, Suite 202
Lansing, MI 48912
(517) 487-5436
(517) 371-4546 FAX
www.milhs.org

Office of Communications
Michigan Family Independence Agency
Grand Tower, Suite 1510
235 South Washington Square
P.O. Box 30037
Lansing, MI 48909
(517) 373-7394
www.michigan.gov/fia

The Urban Institute
2100 M Street, N.W.
Washington, DC 20037
(202) 833-7200
(202) 331-9747 FAX
www.urban.org
[See especially, Wendy Zimmerman and Karen C. Tumlin, "Patchwork Policies: State Assistance for Immigrants under Welfare Reform" (1999).]

Sponsored by the Michigan Nonprofit Association and the Council of Michigan Foundations

K–12 Funding

BACKGROUND

After 25 years of futility and 12 ballot proposals, in 1994 Michigan voters approved Proposal A, which revamped the way the state funds K–12 education. Voters reduced the state's relatively high property taxes, which had been about 35 percent above the national average before the reforms and now are about the same as the national average. Proposal A not only gave property tax relief but reduced funding disparities among school districts—spending had ranged from $3,400 to $10,300 per pupil.

Local property taxes for schools were largely replaced with new state education taxes. The reforms

- increased the state's 4 percent sales tax to 6 percent and earmarked the increase for the School Aid Fund;

- created several new revenue sources for schools, including a 6-mill state education property tax and a 75-cent per pack cigarette tax;

- limited annual property tax increases on each parcel of property to the lower of (1) the inflation rate or (2) 5 percent;

- stipulated that school districts on the low end of the funding spectrum would receive bigger annual funding increases than would the "richer" schools; and

- eliminated a number of categorical (special) grants and rolled the funds into the foundation allowance.

Funding Distribution

To reduce funding disparities among school districts, a "foundation allowance"—a per pupil amount of operating funding—was established for each district in the state. This allowance was influenced by the amount of funding a district had received before Proposal A was passed, meaning that districts that had higher property values before Proposal A were assigned a higher foundation allowance. (In the first year of Proposal A, foundation allowances for K–12 districts ranged from $4,200 to $10,294.) A "minimum" foundation allowance—the least amount a district would receive—was established at $4,200 in FY 1994–95 and has increased each year to the current level of $6,500.

A basic foundation allowance (the "basic")—a target amount to which lower-funded districts one day would be raised—also was established. In FY 1994–95, the first full fiscal year of the new school finance system, the basic was $5,000 per pupil. Districts with a foundation allowance *below* the basic received an increase in their per pupil funding of up to twice the dollar amount of the increase in the basic. For example, if the basic increased from $5,000 to $5,153, as it did from the first to second year of the reforms, all districts with a minimum foundation allowance of $4,200 in FY 1994–95 received a per pupil increase of twice this $153 rise, or $306. However, every district that was *above* the basic received only $153 per pupil—the amount of increase in the basic. (See the exhibit.)

GLOSSARY

Charter school
A public school, sometimes with a particular educational approach, that is exempt from certain state regulations; also known as a public school academy.

Foundation allowance
A per pupil amount of state funding that pays for school operations.

Intermediate school district (ISD)
An education service agency that provides support to school districts within a geographic area (frequently approximates the county).

Millage
A monetary unit equal to 1/1000 of a dollar. Millage is the tax rate on property—the number of mills assessed against the property's taxable value.

Public school academy
A charter school.

School Aid Fund
A fund into which certain state revenues are deposited and from which funds may be spent only on K–12 education.

Taxable value
The amount of property value upon which property taxes are levied.

History of the School Foundation Allowance, FY 1994–95 to FY 2001–02

Fiscal Year	Minimum Foundation Allowance	Basic Foundation Allowance	Maximum Foundation Allowance	Dollar Increase in the Basic
1994–95	$4,200	$5,000	$6,500	NA
1995–96	4,506	5,153	6,653	$153
1996–97	4,816	5,308	6,808	155
1997–98	5,124	5,462	6,962	154
1998–99	5,170	5,462	6,962	0
1999–2000	5,700	5,700	7,200	238
2000–01	6,000	6,000	7,500	300
2001–02	6,500	6,500	7,800	300
% Change, FYs 1995–2002	54.8%	30.0%	20.0%	NA

SOURCE: Public Sector Consultants, Inc., using data from the House Fiscal Agency.
NOTE: The FY 2001–02 allowance includes a $200 per pupil "equity payment" designed to raise the lowest foundation allowance from $6,300 to $6,500.

Emerging Issues

The 2003–04 legislative session will see Proposal A's 10-year anniversary. This occasion, along with budget cuts caused by the current recession, no doubt will bring the "new" system's strengths and weaknesses under scrutiny, and the following issues are likely to be part of the debate.

Reducing the Funding Gap

As stated above, Proposal A has achieved the goal of bringing all districts up to the basic foundation allowance. The exhibit shows that the minimum foundation allowance has increased nearly 55 percent from the first year of Proposal A, more than twice the 20 percent increase of the maximum foundation allowance. The per pupil funding gap between the highest- and lowest-funded district has narrowed from $6,900 to $5,255. While it is good news that all districts have reached the basic foundation allowance, it also means that all districts now will receive the same dollar increase each year, and the gap will not be further narrowed without additional legislation.

Infrastructure and Capital Improvements

Proposal A was targeted toward school operating funds, which are used to pay for wages and salaries, textbooks, and other day-to-day operational expenses. It was not intended to address capital needs such as building, expanding, or improving school buildings; these still are funded primarily from voter-approved debt millage. However, the aging of the state's stock of school buildings and the necessity to equip buildings for computer technology are escalating the need for capital improvements, for which money must be raised locally. The value of the property in the district affects the amount of money per mill that a district can raise for capital expenses—for example, in Northport one mill raises about $816 per pupil, but in Highland Park it raises only about $32 per pupil.

Declining Enrollment

Proposal A tied a district's funding much more to enrollment than was the case under the old system, so for every pupil a district gains or loses, it now also gains or loses money. In FY 2001–02, more than 300 of the 554 local districts lost pupils and therefore funding. Although total school enrollment is increasing statewide, much of the growth is found in the state's 190 charter schools rather than in traditional school districts. In future years, total school enrollment is expected to decline statewide, meaning that even more districts, as well as charter schools, will see fewer pupils enter their doors.

Local Revenue-Raising Ability

As part of the effort to provide tax relief and reduce funding disparities, Proposal A severely limits a district's ability to levy additional mills in order to increase operating funds. Under the old system, districts were relatively free to ask voters to approve new millage for operations. Since Proposal A, however, districts may ask at any given time for only up to three "enhancement" mills for operation. In 1997 additional restrictions were imposed, and districts now must request enhancement mills on an intermediate school district (ISD)-wide basis. In other words, they must ask all voters in the ISD in which they are located to approve the additional mill(s) and, if approved, share the resulting revenue on an equal, per pupil basis with all districts in that ISD. Since 1997 only one such millage request has been approved, and it is unlikely that many others will follow.

Sponsored by the Michigan Nonprofit Association and the Council of Michigan Foundations

School Revenue Growth and Stability

When Proposal A passed, there were questions about whether, over time—in a good and bad economy—the new system would provide sufficient revenue to support schools. It appears that during a good economy, school revenue has been sufficient and has exceeded the inflation rate. From FY 1994–95 to FY 2001–02, a period during which the national and state economies were expanding, the foundation allowance grew from $5,000 to $6,500, an average annual increase of 3.8 percent, which exceeds the 2.7 percent Michigan inflation rate. At this writing, the School Aid Fund is larger than the entire state General Fund, the fund that pays for the operation of nearly all of the rest of state government.

In March 2001 the National Bureau of Economic Research declared that a recession was underway in the United States for the first time in ten years. The resulting decline in state revenue for schools forced lawmakers to reduce the FY 2001–02 budget from its enacted level, marking the first school budget cut since the Proposal A reforms came into being. It is too soon to determine whether in a recession schools will suffer more under Proposal A than they would have under the old system, but early evidence suggests that this may be the case, and this question deserves analysis when sufficient data become available.

DISCUSSION

Reducing the Funding Gap

As stated above, legislation is required to further close the school funding gap. Indeed, in FY 2001–02, a one-time "equity payment" was allocated to reduce the gap between the minimum and maximum foundation allowances from $1,500 to $1,300. This payment gave up to $200 per pupil to districts having a foundation allowance below $6,300, effectively raising the foundation allowance to $6,500. The cost to the state was $129 million. While many people support the concept of greater equity among school districts, the price tag of such an effort is an obstacle. The recent economic downturn makes it unlikely that the state will be able to afford another equity-enhancing program in the near future.

Infrastructure and Capital Improvements

Not since the 1970s, when the state provided funds for "millage equalization," has Michigan provided direct state assistance for infrastructure. Many school representatives and others are pressing for state help with infrastructure needs, but such assistance could cost billions if fully funded. Proponents argue that a state role is necessary because of the vast inequities in local districts' ability to raise such money. They also argue that Proposal A makes it harder for districts to get a debt millage passed, since there is a

misperception among many that the reform meant there would be no more millage elections. Opponents counter that the current School Aid Fund was created to pay only for school operations and it is up to the locals to get their debt millages approved by voters and provide their own bricks and mortar. Others may not oppose state assistance on principle but argue that the state simply does not have sufficient funding to provide such support or has higher funding priorities.

Declining Enrollment

Supporters of financial help for districts with declining enrollment argue that such a decline can be caused by demographic or economic factors beyond a district's control. They point out that shrinking enrollment could one day affect almost all districts, as the total Michigan school-aged population is expected to decline 1.9 percent from FY 2001–02 to FY 2005–06. Opponents argue that many districts lose pupils to charter schools or other districts, and the state should not reward a district with extra funding when it simply could not compete with other schools. Others say that schools should adapt by cutting spending when enrollment declines.

Local Revenue-Raising Ability

Support seems to be growing to allow local districts to levy additional local operating millage. In 2001–02, legislation was introduced (House Bill 4917), for the first time since Proposal A passed, to permit districts to go to voters for additional operating millage. Supporters say that if voters are willing to pay more to support their local schools, they should be allowed to so. They also point to the fact that many of the higher-funded districts have received less-than-inflationary increases in their per pupil funding since Proposal A went into effect, and they argue that a millage would help them to keep up with rising costs. Opponents say that allowing additional local mills would erode the property tax relief granted under Proposal A; they also could argue that new operating mills in some districts would once again allow the funding gap between rich and poor districts to widen. As the state constitution requires that the enabling legislation for any type of new school millage must be passed by a three-fourths affirmative vote by both legislature chambers, enacting an operating-millage bill would be difficult.

See also K–12 Quality and Testing; K–12 Schooling Alternatives; Special Education.

FOR ADDITIONAL INFORMATION

Michigan Association of School Administrators
1001 Centennial Way, Suite 300
Lansing, MI 48917
(517) 327-5910
(517) 327-0771 FAX
www.gomasa.org

Michigan Association of School Boards
1001 Centennial Way, Suite 400
Lansing, MI 48917
(517) 327-5900
(517) 327-0775 FAX
www.masb.com

Michigan Department of Education
Hannah Building
608 West Allegan Street
P.O. Box 30008
Lansing, MI 48909
(517) 373-3324
(517) 373-4022 FAX
www.michigan.gov/mde

Michigan Department of Management and Budget
P.O. Box 30026
Lansing, MI 48909
(517) 373-1004
(517) 373-7268 FAX
www.michigan.gov/dmb

Michigan Education Association
1216 Kendale Boulevard
East Lansing, MI 48826
(800) 292-1934
(517) 337-5598 FAX
www.mea.org

Sponsored by the Michigan Nonprofit Association and the Council of Michigan Foundations

K–12 Quality and Testing

BACKGROUND

Article VIII, section 2, of the Michigan Constitution requires the legislature "to maintain and support a system of free public elementary and secondary schools as defined by law," and many people see this as one of state government's most important functions.

The state has become increasingly involved in overseeing the performance of K–12 students, particularly since the 1994 school finance reforms, which made the state the largest K–12 funding source. The state's interest in education quality stems from the obvious need for a well-educated citizenry, a deep-held belief that a good education is essential to a person's well-being, and a need to document the return on investment for state education dollars.

The state and the nation have struggled in recent years to find a fair, realistic, and accurate way to measure academic performance. This has proven to be no easy task. Some commonly used indicators of a school's quality include its graduation rate, dropout rate, and funding level. However, these indicators, while easily calculated, provide little information on classroom learning.

Standardized testing is becoming commonly used nationwide to quantify and compare academic outcomes across districts and time. Michigan uses such testing and has been administering its own standardized evaluation tool, the Michigan Education Assessment Program (MEAP) test, to students since the 1970s.

Measuring Quality

Michigan Education Assessment Program

Arguably, the most controversial test given in Michigan classrooms is the MEAP test, which is used by state educators to assess student performance. The tests are administered in five grades on various subjects.

Each year the state publishes the MEAP scores—the percentage of students in each school building and district in the state that scored at, above, or below state standards. The exhibit presents the grades and subjects tested and the statewide results for FY 2000–01.

Schools have a strong incentive to perform well on their MEAP tests because the scores are used in school accreditation, in giving school achievement awards (e.g., the "Golden Apple"), and in awarding college scholarships (the Merit awards) to individual students. MEAP scores are used by some parents in choosing the school district in which their child will be educated; this decision brings additional revenue to the district receiving the new pupil and costs revenue for the district losing him/her.

Federal Legislation: No Child Left Behind

Standardized testing is expected to increase nationwide in coming years due to enactment of the federal No Child Left Behind Act of 2001. Beginning in the 2005–06 school year, this act requires states, as a condition of receiving federal funding, to test all 3d–8th graders annually on reading and math. In Michigan this will increase standardized

MEAP Testing and Statewide Results, FY 2000–01

Grade Level	Subjects Tested	Percentage of Students Meeting or Exceeding State Standards
4	Reading	60%
	Math	72
5	Science	42
	Writing	61
	Social studies	19
7	Reading	58
	Math	68
8	Science	20
	Writing	67
	Social studies	30
11	Math	68
	Reading	74
	Science	60
	Writing	69
	Social studies	27

SOURCE: Michigan Department of Treasury, "Michigan Merit Award and MEAP Information."

testing substantially: Currently, in this age group, 3d and 6th graders are not MEAP tested at all and only 4th and 7th graders are tested in both reading and math.

Simply described, the new federal guidelines penalize subperforming districts that do not produce sufficient increases in test scores over time. After two years of no improvement, schools must permit parents to send their child to a different school and provide transportation to the new school. Also, for students attending persistently failing schools (that is, a school that has failed to improve sufficiently for three of four consecutive years), the local district must use part of its federal funding to pay for supplemental instruction, such as tutors, for its students. These stringent federal testing requirements are evidence that policymakers increasingly are relying on test scores to both evaluate and improve the nations' schools.

Accreditation

Accreditation, an evaluation system commonly used in higher education, recognizes whether a school has met certain standards set by the State Board of Education and the legislature. Public Act 25 of 1990 initiated the state accreditation program. Until very recently, MEAP test scores were the primary determining factor in whether a school achieved accreditation, but in response to objections by many to using this test as nearly the sole evaluation tool, the State Board of Education developed a new accreditation system that uses additional measures as well.

Quality-Improvement Strategies

Potential strategies for improving education quality are nearly limitless. Some of the most common are briefly described here.

Early-Childhood Education

Support for early-childhood education (preschool) as a school-improvement strategy is growing. Currently, the Michigan School Readiness Program provides preschooling for approximately 26,000 four-year-olds thought to be at risk of future academic failure. This is a highly rated program, and studies (e.g., by the High/Scope Educational Research Foundation) show that children who have good early education perform better in school than do children with similar backgrounds who have not.

Parent Involvement

Parent involvement—e.g., requiring homework to be finished on time, attending parent-teacher conferences—is found to be a positive influence on student achievement. Michigan recently attempted to increase parent involvement in education: P.A. 29 of 2001 requires the Michigan Department of Education (MDE) to develop a model voluntary contract that schools may use to encourage parents to be more involved in their children's education.

Professional Development

Professional development involves improving education through improving the knowledge, skills, and abilities of teachers and other school professional staff. All Michigan school districts are required to provide at least five days annually of professional development.

Schools of Choice and/or Charter Schools

In Michigan, parents may choose to send their child to a public school other than the one assigned by the child's school district. Michigan has relatively progressive alternative-schooling laws, allowing charter schools, home schooling, and school choice across district lines.

State Takeover

If the legislature and governor believe it necessary, legislation may be enacted permitting the state to take control of a school district in order to improve its performance. In Michigan, the state has taken over the Detroit school district—the state's largest—and appointed a so-called reform board to replace the local school board.

Statewide Core Curriculum

Some states mandate that schools statewide teach a "core" curriculum—a standardized course of study. Michigan has

Sponsored by the Michigan Nonprofit Association and the Council of Michigan Foundations

a *model* core curriculum that schools may use or not, as they choose.

Technical Assistance

Technical assistance involves experts assisting struggling districts in identifying and implementing specific actions to improve education quality. Michigan offers some limited technical assistance to schools exhibiting difficulty in obtaining accreditation.

DISCUSSION

Standardized Testing

There is strong disagreement about whether standardized tests measure academic achievement or simply test-taking skills. Opponents say that using standardized test scores to compare one school or district to another excludes such critical factors as parent involvement, student mobility, cultural differences, and socioeconomic status. Some go so far as to argue that the test is a better measure of family income than it is of a school's ability to teach, because academic performance and income are highly correlated. Test scores are not adjusted to reflect differences in family income or other factors, and critics contend that this results in schools being unfairly judged or stigmatized for matters beyond their control.

Others object to the increasing amount of time that students spend preparing for and taking standardized tests. They argue that teachers are forced to "teach to the test" or to prepare students by teaching lessons for the sole purpose of helping them to test well. They point out that standardized tests, unlike tests normally given in the classroom to assess performance, are not used to provide feedback to students to improve their performance—in fact, students typically never find out how they did on specific test questions.

Standardized-test supporters argue that taxpayers pay billions of dollars annually for public schools and have a right to hold schools accountable—something they feel is not possible absent standardized tests. Members of the business community and others argue that classroom grade-point averages cannot be used to compare schools, since an "A" in one district (or building or classroom) does not necessarily have the same meaning as an "A" in another. Giving the same test to all students, they assert, is the only way to get an accurate comparison of student performance. They argue that in the absence of such tests, parents, employers, and colleges would have no objective data to tell them whether students in one district are better or more poorly prepared for the future than are students elsewhere. Not only are these tests necessary to compare schools, but they also are needed to track the performance of schools over time.

Most supporters of standardized tests have no objection to "teaching to the test." On the contrary, they assert that this is one of the objectives of giving such a test. The MEAP test, for example, is designed to test knowledge of subject matter covered in the state's model core curriculum, one that supporters believe is based on high standards. If, in giving the MEAP test, schools are forced to teach to these high standards, students stand only to gain. Thus, MEAP supporters say, standardized tests not only measure student success but also contribute to it.

Accreditation

The state superintendent of education recently announced a new accreditation system for Michigan schools (Education YES!) that relies less on MEAP scores than did the earlier system. Under Education YES!, each school building will receive an overall letter grade plus additional letter grades for six specific indicators, three that pertain to the MEAP test and three that do not. The overall grade will be based primarily on MEAP test scores, which will comprise about two-thirds (67 percent) of the score. The remaining third will be based on other indicators, such as teacher quality and professional development. The superintendent has created an Accreditation Advisory Committee to develop the details of the accreditation plan and says that schools may expect to receive their first accreditation report in December 2002. The House and Senate must approve the new system, although some policymakers believe that the superintendent has the legal authority to implement the plan regardless of legislative action (this issue is unresolved at this writing).

Education YES! is receiving some positive reaction because it relies on factors in addition to MEAP scores. Some object to the use of letter grades at all, stating that disadvantaged schools are at risk of being unfairly branded with low grades. Many school-reform proponents object to any reduced reliance on test scores, arguing that assessment could become too "soft" to be a useful evaluative tool or school-improvement incentive. Others point to the strict new federal assessment requirements and contend that the state accreditation system should be aligned with the federal requirements.

Other Quality Issues
State Takeover of Poorly Performing Districts

In 1999 a law was enacted directing the state to take over the Detroit school district, which prompted intense opposition from many Detroit lawmakers, residents, and others. The elected school board was disbanded and a new, state-appointed board (the reform board) took the helm.

The board hired a new superintendent, who is making administrative and other changes throughout the district. In 2004 Detroit residents will be allowed to vote on whether to keep the reform board or again elect a local board. While Detroit currently is the only takeover district in Michigan, others, including Benton Harbor, had been under takeover consideration, and the issue is likely to resurface.

Takeover proponents argue that in poorly performing school districts, state trustees can break through the "usual way of doing business" and force change. They assert that it is a district's students who really suffer when a district is not performing well, and the state has a responsibility to step in when school districts fail their students. Opponents decry the loss of local control and suggest that more state support, such as financial and technical assistance, would be as or more effective in bringing about change than a state takeover.

Core Curriculum

Supporters of state-mandated basic curriculum contend that it is the only way to ensure that students across the state graduate with the same essential skills. Opponents argue that such a mandate would interfere with one of the most dearly held aspects of the Michigan public school system: local control. Supporters of statewide adherence to a core curriculum point out that local districts still would be free to decide how to teach the core courses and also to offer supplemental studies.

See also Children's Early Education and Care; K–12 Funding; K–12 Schooling Alternatives.

FOR ADDITIONAL INFORMATION

Mackinac Center for Public Policy
140 West Main Street
P.O. Box 568
Midland, MI 48640
(989) 631-0900
(989) 832-0666 FAX
www.mackinac.org

Michigan Association of School Administrators
1001 Centennial Way, Suite 300
Lansing, MI 48917
(517) 327-5910
(517) 327-0771 FAX
www.gomasa.org

Michigan Association of School Boards
1001 Centennial Way, Suite 400
Lansing, MI 48917
(517) 327-5900
(517) 327-0775 FAX
www.masb.org

Michigan Business Leaders for Education Excellence
Michigan Chamber of Commerce
600 South Walnut Street
Lansing, MI 48933
(517) 371-2100
(517) 371-7224 FAX
www.michamber.com

Michigan Congress of Parents, Teachers and Students
1011 North Washington Avenue
Lansing, MI 48906
(517) 485-4345
(517) 485-0012 FAX
www.michiganpta.org

Michigan Education Association
1216 Kendale Boulevard
East Lansing, MI 48826
(800) 292-1934
(517) 337-5598 FAX
www.mea.org

Office of the Superintendent
Michigan Department of Education
608 West Allegan Street
P.O. Box 30008
Lansing, MI 48909
(517) 373-3324
(517) 373-4022 FAX
www.michigan.gov/mde

U.S. Department of Education
400 Maryland Avenue, S.W.
Washington, DC 20202
(800) 872-5327
(202) 401-0689 FAX
www.ed.gov

Sponsored by the Michigan Nonprofit Association and the Council of Michigan Foundations

K–12 Schooling Alternatives

BACKGROUND

One of the most hotly debated topics in K–12 education is schools of choice (or "school choice" or, simply, "choice"), whereby parents are permitted to choose the venue in which their children will be educated. In Michigan, school choice generally refers to the following:

- Interdistrict (cross-district) choice
- Charter schools
- Vouchers
- Home schooling

Interdistrict Choice

Since 1994, when Proposal A (the school-finance reform initiative) passed, the amount of state funding a school district receives depends more on the number of students it enrolls than previously was the case. Schools now receive from the state a certain amount (the foundation allowance) per pupil; thus, if a student leaves his/her current school district for any reason, the district's state funding is reduced. Losing students can have very serious financial consequences for a district: for example, a district receiving the minimum foundation allowance ($6,500) in FY 2001–02 will forgo $162,500 if it loses just 25 students.

School choice in Michigan has been permitted since passage of Public Act 300 of 1996, but it is not unlimited. Students may transfer only to another district that is located within (1) the boundaries of the intermediate school district (ISD) in which they live or (2) a contiguous ISD. In addition, there are certain restrictions.

- School districts may choose whether to participate in the schools of choice program—that is, whether they will accept transferring students.
- Districts that choose to participate must publish a list of grades in which they will accept nonresident students and the number of students they will allow in each.
- Schools must accept students on a first-come-first-served basis; they may not discriminate on the basis of race, academic ability, or any other factor.
- Parents must provide their own transportation.

In the 1996–97 school year, the first that the law was in effect, almost 8,000 Michigan students attended a school outside their home district. In 2001–02 the number more than quadrupled, to about 33,500.

Of the state's 554 local school districts, two-thirds (64 percent) are accepting students from outside their district. Since more districts are expected to experience declining enrollment in coming years, it is likely that in the future more will participate with the aim of increasing their revenue.

Sponsored by the Michigan Nonprofit Association and the Council of Michigan Foundations

Charter Schools

In 1994, as part of school-finance reform, lawmakers passed P.A. 362 of 1993, the so-called charter-school law. The law permits "public school academies" to be established. Michigan was among the first states to take such a step, and, according to one education-reform organization, the Michigan law is one of the most far-reaching in the nation—second only to Arizona's and Delaware's in the amount of autonomy given charters, the kind allowed, and other factors.

Michigan charter schools operate under the auspices of an *authorizer*, one of four types of public entity: a state university, school district, ISD, or community college. The authorizer is responsible for monitoring the charter school's progress and its adherence to state regulations as well as providing other oversight; the authorizer may revoke a school's charter if it believes the school is not performing satisfactorily. The number of charter schools that state universities collectively may authorize is 150, and this ceiling was reached in FY 2000–01, meaning that universities may not charter additional schools unless an existing one closes. Although there is no cap on the other types of authorizers, they are confined to authorizing charters in their service area, whereas a university may authorize schools statewide.

Charter schools are subject to most of the same laws as traditional schools; for example, they must employ only certified teachers, are prohibited from charging tuition or teaching a religion-based curriculum, and must accept students on a first-come-first-served basis. Unlike traditional public schools, however, they need not (1) accept all applicants if they do not have available space, which means they can control school and class size, (2) hire unionized teachers, or (3) participate in collective bargaining.

Currently, Michigan has approximately 190 charter schools. Only a minority of Michigan youngsters attends a charter school (see Exhibit 1). The amount of state funding lost to traditional schools is about $420 million (out of $11 billion).

Vouchers

Under a voucher system, the state would provide funding for parents to send their children to a school of their choice, be it public or private. A voucher system would be a substantial departure from the current system, where state aid flows only to public school districts and parents of private-school students foot the bill themselves.

Five states—Florida, Maine, Ohio, Vermont, and Wisconsin—currently offer voucher programs that pay tuition at private schools. Most are confined either to a specific city

---

EXHIBIT 1. Enrollment in Michigan Public Charter and Traditional Schools, FY 2001–02

Charter schools
64,500 students[a]
3.8% of all students

Traditional schools
1.6 million students[a]
96.2% of all students

SOURCE: House Fiscal Agency, using data from the Michigan Department of Education.
[a]Full-time equivalent, blended pupil numbers; these are the figures used to calculate schools' state aid.

(e.g., Milwaukee) or are targeted to students who have an identifiable risk of academic failure. Six other states offer tax credits for private-school expenses or scholarships, and some observers consider this to be a form of voucher.

Article VIII, section 2, of the Michigan Constitution specifically prohibits using public monies to fund private- or religious-school education. This means that to have a voucher system in Michigan, a majority of voters must approve a constitutional amendment. In 2000 Michigan voters turned down, by more than a two-to-one margin, a ballot proposal to institute a sweeping voucher program in the state. The measure would have allowed vouchers in any district having a graduation rate of less than two-thirds or in which a majority of voters approved a voucher system. Potentially, all of the state's districts could have been voucher districts. Had it passed, the amendment would have created the first statewide voucher system in the nation in which any district and any student living there could participate.

The U.S. Supreme Court currently is considering a pivotal voucher case, *Zelman* v. *Simmons-Harris*, regarding whether a six-year-old voucher program in Cleveland violates the Constitution because 96 percent of the students in this state-sponsored program attend schools that have a religious affiliation. If the decision, expected in July 2002, upholds the program, it could lead to an increase of such

Sponsored by the Michigan Nonprofit Association and the Council of Michigan Foundations

programs nationwide; if it rules against the program, the question of whether vouchers may be used at religious-affiliated schools may be laid to rest permanently.

Home Schooling

The Revised School Code of 1976 states that a child is not required to attend a public school if s/he is

> being educated by his or her parent or legal guardian at the child's home in an organized educational program that is appropriate given the age, intelligence, ability, and any psychological limitations of the child, in the subject areas of reading, mathematics, science, history, civics, literature, writing, and English grammar.

This provision makes home schooling legal in Michigan. The state's home-school laws are among the least restrictive in the nation—only a handful of other states have laws that are as or more permissive than Michigan's. See Exhibit 2 for a comparison of states' home-schooling requirements.

The Michigan law requires home-schooling parents to teach certain subjects, but this is one of the few requirements it imposes. Home-school parents may choose their own curriculum as long as it addresses the subjects required by the state. They may select their own textbooks, issue their own diplomas, and, if they wish, teach a religion- or philosophy-based curriculum. Home-schooled students are not required to take Michigan Educational Assessment Program (MEAP) tests, and there are very little data collected on the education performance of home-schooled students.

Although there are various reasons why people choose to educate their children at home, among the most commonly expressed are dissatisfaction with the quality of public education, concern about violence in the public schools, a desire for the child to have individualized instruction, and preference for a curriculum that reflects parents' values, religious or otherwise.

The number of home-school students is growing. In the decade from school years 1990–91 to 2000–01, the num-

EXHIBIT 2. Home-Schooling Requirements, States and the District of Columbia

States with High Regulation[a]	States with Moderate Regulation[b]	States with Low Regulation[c]	States Requiring No Contact with State[d]
Maine	Arkansas	Alabama	Alaska
Massachusetts	Colorado	Arizona	Idaho
Minnesota	Connecticut	California	Illinois
New York	Florida	Delaware	Indiana
North Dakota	Georgia	District of Columbia	Michigan
Pennsylvania	Hawaii	Kansas	Missouri
Rhode Island	Iowa	Kentucky	New Jersey
Utah	Louisiana	Mississippi	Oklahoma
Vermont	Maryland	Montana	Texas
Washington	North Carolina	Nebraska	
West Virginia	Nevada	New Mexico	
	New Hampshire	Wyoming	
	Ohio		
	Oregon		
	South Carolina		
	South Dakota		
	Tennessee		
	Virginia		
	Wisconsin		

SOURCE: Home School Legal Defense Association, Purcellville, VA.
NOTE: The year for which this information is presented was not indicated.
[a]State requires parents to notify the state that they are home schooling, submit achievement test scores and/or professional evaluation of student progress, and perhaps meet other requirements (e.g., use state-approved curriculum, meet teaching qualifications, submit to home visits by state officials).
[b]State requires parents to notify the state that they are home schooling, submit achievement test scores and/or professional evaluation of student progress.
[c]State requires parents only to notify the state that they are home schooling.
[d]State imposes no requirement on parents to initiate contact with the state.

Sponsored by the Michigan Nonprofit Association and the Council of Michigan Foundations

ber is believed to have more than doubled—from around 825 students to 1,915. Because parents are not required to report that they are home schooling their children, these numbers are estimates and likely to be low.

DISCUSSION

The 1998–99 education poll, conducted by Public Sector Consultants, Inc., found that 58 percent of respondents statewide believe that students should be allowed to attend any public school they choose, even one outside their home district. The same poll found that 53 percent agree in concept with giving public money to private schools. Alternatives to public schooling are seen by some as the solution to the ills of public schooling and by others as a destructive force in education, and the debate may be expected to continue for years to come.

Choice and Competition

Supporters of school choice claim that choice and its resulting competition among schools is necessary to improve education quality in Michigan. They argue that if public schools lose their "education monopoly," they will have to respond more quickly and appropriately to changing student and parent demands. This market-driven approach, choice supporters say, will help the education system identify good and bad schools and find ways either to improve or eliminate the ones not serving students well.

Supporters of school choice also believe that there is no one best way to learn or teach, therefore students and educators should be entitled to choose among diverse programs, teaching styles, and school schedules. They contend that students will be better and more enthusiastic learners if they may choose a school or program compatible with their learning style, and teachers and administrators will be more enthusiastic and effective in schools that support their personal philosophy of education. The result, they posit, is better education.

Opponents of the choice concept counter that the market analogy is not appropriate for K–12 education. They argue that unlike businesses, schools do not have control over the "raw material"—the students—who enter their halls. They assert that by draining resources from traditional public education, school choice actually is detrimental, rather than beneficial, to the quality of local public schools. They argue that a healthy system of public schools is necessary in a democratic society and weakening the public school system to accommodate the needs of a few is not in the best interest of the state or nation.

Opponents also argue that public education can be best improved by working within the current system through such improvements as adopting a statewide core curriculum (that is, ensuring that all schools teach the same basic subject matter) and giving schools the technical assistance they need to deal with low levels of academic performance. They also assert that there now are many more choices than in the past within traditional public schools themselves, and the needs of individual students usually are accommodated.

Charter Schools

Charter-school supporters say that these schools give parents more options, foster competition among public schools, and are laboratories where education innovation can be explored and the findings used to help improve all schools. They point out that there is a strong parent demand for charter schools, as evidenced by the waiting lists for admission. They also say that charters serve many of the state's economically disadvantaged students and point out that the majority of charter schools are in urban areas, where traditional public schools frequently face the most difficulty.

Opponents contend that charter schools are damaging local public schools by taking funding from them. Moreover, they assert that charters "skim" students from traditional schools—that is, for the most part they take the better students and also the least expensive to educate (lower-grade students and those without special needs). Also, since charters typically do not hire unionized teachers (who generally draw higher salaries and benefits than non-union teachers) and are permitted to limit the number of students they enroll, they may have smaller class sizes, which gives them an unfair advantage in competing for students. All of this, opponents say, further hurts traditional schools. They further contend that studies, such as that conducted by Public Sector Consultants in 2000, find a lack of education innovation in charter schools, rendering invalid the argument that charter schools serve as education laboratories to develop and test new teaching methods. They also point to a recent state audit report that finds that charter schools are not sufficiently monitored by their authorizers, and they argue that these schools should come under much closer scrutiny.

Proponents are fighting to get the cap on the number of university-chartered schools increased from the current limit of 150. They argue that as about three-quarters of the charters are authorized by universities, the cap unfairly limits growth in the number of charter schools. Charter-school opponents disagree, contending that until there is greater oversight over existing schools, new ones should not be started. At this writing, the issue is under study by a task force appointed by the legislature, and lawmakers have agreed to delay their vote on raising

Sponsored by the Michigan Nonprofit Association and the Council of Michigan Foundations

the cap until the task force's report, which is expected soon, has been submitted.

Vouchers

Voucher supporters argue that parents of private-school students pay taxes just as parents of public school students do, but they do not receive the same benefit from their tax dollars. They also point out that wealthy families can afford to "escape" the public schools if they are dissatisfied with them, but low-income parents, who cannot afford private-school tuition, are forced to place their children in a local public school whether they feel the school is adequate or not. Vouchers, they contend, would provide equity for these parents and their children.

Voucher opponents counter that private-school parents voluntarily have opted not to send their children to public schools, thus they voluntarily have chosen to forgo the tax benefit derived from public education. They further assert that using public funds to help pay for private schooling would be expensive and drain substantial resources from public schools. Finally, they object to vouchers because they believe their use would violate separation of church and state in that the vouchers, which could be used to attend private, religious schools, would be paid for with public dollars.

Home Schooling

In regard to home schooling, many supporters feel that whatever an individual's reasons for home schooling, it is a parent's civil right. They argue that in public schools, children may encounter ideas, philosophies, and even physical danger to which their parents do not want them exposed. Opponents fear that home-schooled students will suffer from lack of socialization with other pupils and argue that the state should monitor the academic progress of home-schooled students. They believe that home-schooled children easily could "fall through the cracks" educationally unless there is more state monitoring and assessment.

See also K–12 Funding; K–12 Quality and Assessment.

FOR ADDITIONAL INFORMATION

Charter Schools Office
Central Michigan University
2520 South University Park Drive
Mt. Pleasant, MI 48859
(989) 774-2100
(989) 774-7893 FAX
www.cmucso.org

Home School Legal Defense Association
P.O. Box 1152
Purcellville, VA 20134
(540) 338-8899
(540) 338-2733 FAX
www.hslda.org

Michigan Association of Public School Academies
215 South Washington Square, Suite 210
Lansing, MI 48933
(517) 374-9167
(517) 374-9197 FAX
www.charterschools.org

Michigan Association of School Administrators
1001 Centennial Way, Suite 300
Lansing, MI 48917
(517) 327-5910
(517) 327-0771 FAX
www.gomasa.org

Michigan Department of Education
Hannah Building
608 West Allegan Street
P.O. Box 30008
Lansing, MI 48909
(517) 373-3324
(517) 373-4022 FAX
www.michigan.gov/mde

Michigan Education Association
1216 Kendale Boulevard
East Lansing, MI 48826
(800) 292-1934
(517) 337-5598 FAX
www.mea.org

Local Government Organization and Issues

BACKGROUND

Collectively, if authorities are included, there are more than 2,700 government units in Michigan (see Exhibit 1), and they fall into two categories.

- *General-purpose* units are counties, cities, villages, and townships; all have an elected board as their legislative body.

- *Special-purpose* units are K–12 school districts, intermediate school districts (ISDs), regional educational service agencies (RESAs), community colleges, and authorities; all have a governing body that may be elected or appointed.

General-Purpose Government

General-purpose units of government operate with restricted power, that is, the unit's authority is granted by the state, either through the constitution or statute. Whether a unit is empowered to engage in an activity depends on whether the state has expressly granted it authority to do so. (By contrast, local governments in most western states operate with *permissive* power, that is, they may exercise any authority that the legislature has not expressly prohibited or restricted.) In Michigan, counties, townships, and villages begin as general-law units, but if they meet certain statutory requirements, they may change to charter (home-rule) units. By law, all cities are charter units.

EXHIBIT 1. Michigan Local Governments, by Type and Number, 2002

Type	Number
General Purpose Government Units	
Counties	83
Townships	1,242
Cities	272
Villages	261
TOTAL	1,858
Special Purpose Government Units	
K–12 districts	555
Intermediate school districts	57
Community colleges	28
Authorities	200+
TOTAL	840+

SOURCES: Michigan Municipal League; Michigan Townships Association.

Sponsored by the Michigan Nonprofit Association and the Council of Michigan Foundations

- *General-law* units may organize themselves and exercise authority only in the way that the state constitution and statutes have specifically set forth for this type of government.

- A *charter* (home-rule) unit has more control over its organization and broader authority than does a general-law unit. The unit's charter sets forth the taxing and borrowing limits (subject to state law), number of departments, and types of services to be delivered to residents.

Counties

All Michigan counties but one are general-law units. (Wayne County is the exception; the electorate adopted a charter in 1980.) The difference between a general-law county and a charter county is found in administrative and legislative functions.

Under state law, general-law counties may adopt, with voter approval, a "unified" form of government—that is, they may centralize their administration by having either an elected county executive or a county manager appointed by the elected board. Only Bay and Oakland counties have adopted the unified form, both with an elected executive.

The state Charter County Act permits voters in a charter county with population exceeding 1.5 million (only Wayne) to choose to have either an elected county executive (as Wayne does) or an appointed county manager, who handles the county's day-to-day operations. Whether an elected executive has veto power, how staff functions are handled, and over which line department s/he has control depend on the provisions of the charter adopted by the electorate.

Townships

State law gives the home-rule (charter) option to townships of 2,000 or more residents. One advantage of home rule for townships is some protection against being annexed by adjacent cities. Townships may achieve charter status via (1) a resolution adopted by the township board or (2) a vote of township residents. The latter course gives a township greater taxing authority than the former: five mills upon voter approval of charter status plus authority to go to the voters for additional mills. If charter status is achieved by resolution, the authority to tax property is restricted to the amount levied on the date the resolution is adopted. A charter township board also may appoint a superintendent or manager to serve as the township's chief administrative officer (general-law townships are administered by the elected township board). Of Michigan's 1,242 townships, 130 have opted for charter status.

Villages

A Michigan village may establish itself, with voter approval, as either a general-law or (if its population is 750 or more) a home-rule (charter) unit. Although both types may levy up to 20 mills for operation, general-law villages are limited as to how they may use the millage: streets (5.0 mills), cemeteries (2.5 mills), and general government operation (12.5 mills). Of the 261 villages in Michigan, 213 are general law and 48 are home rule.

Cities

All of Michigan's 272 cities are home-rule units. A city's residents, in adopting a charter, determine the form their government shall take; three options are available.

- *Council, manager*   Under this structure, which has been adopted by 180 cities, the city council appoints a city manager who administers the day-to-day operations of city government; the council is responsible for policy decisions and adopting the annual budget.

- *Strong mayor, council*   This structure is used most often in larger cities where the mayor is elected directly by voters and is not a member of the legislative body (council). The mayor is the chief administrative officer and appoints/removes administrative officials designated by the charter as reporting directly to him/her.

- *Weak mayor, council*   This structure is found mostly in smaller cities where the mayor is a council member and elected to the mayoralty by fellow council members. The mayor chairs council meetings and serves as the city's chief administrative officer.

Special-Purpose Government

K–12 districts, ISDs, RESAs, community college districts, and authorities are special-purpose governments—that is, they have been created to produce and provide a specific government service. They have limited property-taxation authority and are governed by an elected or appointed board. Among the purposes for which authorities may be created are to operate an airport, harbor, or port; finance and oversee building or transportation projects; promote downtown development; construct and operate sewer and water systems; or operate emergency (police, fire, ambulance) services.

Authorities are of two general types, depending on how they are created.

- *By vote*   If the authority is created by a vote of the residents in the general-purpose government jurisdiction(s) that wish the authority to exist, the

Sponsored by the Michigan Nonprofit Association and the Council of Michigan Foundations

voters also decide whether the unit shall have power to levy a property tax as a source of revenue.

■ *By resolution* If the authority is created by resolution by the general-purpose government(s), it does not have the power to levy a millage for operations and must rely on other funding (e.g., an appropriation from the board[s] that created it).

Intergovernmental Cooperation and Consolidation

Cooperation

The Michigan Legislature has enacted several statutes permitting intergovernmental cooperation. Basically, any local governments authorized to engage in a given activity or provide a given service may do so collaboratively. Numerous examples of intergovernmental contracting and cooperation may be found, ranging from joint fire departments to sewer/water authorities. Intergovernmental collaboration usually arises from locals' wish to reduce costs through specialization or take advantage of economies of scale in producing and providing services.

Consolidation

There are three types of consolidation, although only two occur regularly: functional and geographical (the third is political and last occurred in 1837).

■ *Functional* consolidation is service specific—for example, consolidating fire, police, or emergency-service departments. Across the state there are numerous instances of functional consolidation.

■ *Geographical* consolidation is embodied in the wave of school consolidations that occurred from the 1930s to the 1960s, when Michigan reduced the number of public school districts from 6,200 to the present 554. Geographical consolidation ignores political or jurisdictional boundaries and focuses on a service area, in this case the reasonable geographic boundary of a school district.

Property Taxes

The property tax is an important revenue source for local governments, and its distribution as a percentage of total collections has shifted since the 1994 passage of Proposal A. As Exhibit 2 shows, prior to Proposal A, about 72 percent of the property taxes collected annually were directed to education, primarily K–12, and the balance went to other local units. Local government now receives about 42 percent of total property tax collections—an increase of about 14 percent from before Proposal A (2000 data). Thus, while Proposal A reduced property taxes, it increased the share of revenue available for non-education local government.

EXHIBIT 2. Property Tax Revenue Distribution, by Type of Unit, 1993, 1994, and 2000

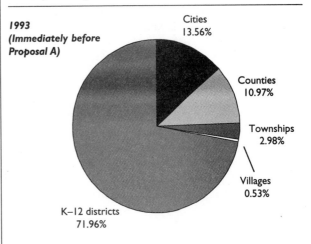

1993 (Immediately before Proposal A)

Cities 13.56%
Counties 10.97%
Townships 2.98%
Villages 0.53%
K–12 districts 71.96%

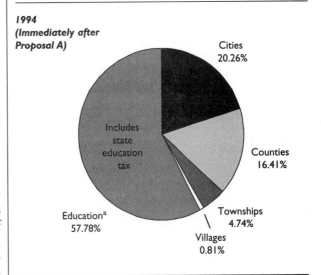

1994 (Immediately after Proposal A)

Cities 20.26%
Counties 16.41%
Townships 4.74%
Villages 0.81%
Education[a] 57.78%
Includes state education tax

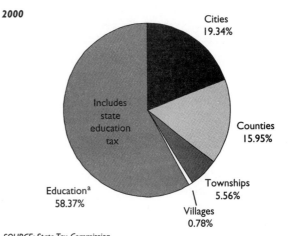

2000

Cities 19.34%
Counties 15.95%
Townships 5.56%
Villages 0.78%
Education[a] 58.37%
Includes state education tax

SOURCE: State Tax Commission.
[a]Education = Local K–12 schools, community colleges, ISDs, RESAs.

Sponsored by the Michigan Nonprofit Association and the Council of Michigan Foundations

State Revenue Sharing

The State of Michigan shares some of its tax revenue—more than $10 billion in the 1990s—with local units of government. Funding for the revenue-sharing program is based both in the constitution and in law.

In Michigan, revenue sharing is *unrestricted*—that is, there are no strings attached: local governments may use it as they see fit. Until 1996, when the state revenue-sharing program was changed, local governments had received a portion of revenue from four taxes levied by the state: sales, income, intangibles, and single business. These funds were distributed to cities, villages, and townships in two ways: *per capita* and by *relative tax effort* (RTE). Per capita distribution is straightforward: High-population units (e.g., Oakland County) receive more than low-population units (e.g., Montmorency County). Relative tax effort rewards units according to how their taxation level stacks up against the state average: high-tax units receive more than low-tax units.

The 1996 changes (1) removed income, intangibles, and SBT revenue from the revenue-sharing pool (these were offset by the new sales tax revenue) and (2) began to phase out the use of RTE as a basis for revenue sharing. Constitutional revenue sharing now is distributed solely on a per capita basis, and the statutory sales-tax share is distributed according to

- a percentage share of the unit's FY 1997–98 share of revenue—the percentage is decreasing every year as the RTE is phased out;

- the per capita value of the unit's total taxable property;

- yield equalization—a formula that offsets variances in taxable-property wealth among local units and helps units that have low such wealth; and

- a formula whereby a unit's population is multiplied by a weight factor assigned to that type of unit.

The movement from RTE to full per capita distribution is creating winners and losers. Winners are units of government with large and rapidly expanding population (e.g., townships that are being suburbanized); losers are units with slow-growing or declining population (e.g., older, land-locked cities).

State revenue sharing is particularly important to townships, which currently derive about 40 percent of their general fund revenue from the program.

DISCUSSION

All local governments share three problems, and all have to do with money: declining authorized millage rates, the difference between the state-equalized and taxable value of property, and fluctuating state revenue sharing. The so-called Headlee amendment (1978) amended the state constitution to clarify the responsibility of state government with respect to revenue sharing with local units, and it has provided some legal recourse for local units in their attempts to secure funding from the state. (Readers are directed to *Michigan in Brief, 6th Edition,* which may be found at *www.michiganinbrief.org,* for specific information about the Headlee amendment.)

Such issues as transportation funding, fire protection, land use, solid waste management, and consolidation and intergovernmental contracting also are persistent concerns for many local officials. Problems in these areas frequently have to do with local control—either among local jurisdictions or between the locals and the state. The line between state and local authority sometimes is vague, and spheres of influence often are overlapping, ambiguous, and contested.

Municipal Residency

More than 100 large cities nationwide require their employees to live within city boundaries. Detroit did so in 1999, hoping to create a safer and more vibrant city by bringing its employees (especially police and firefighters) into the community and encouraging economic growth as these new residents lived, raised their families, and spent money in the city. Residency opponents argued that such requirements violate individual freedom of choice. In 1999 the Michigan Legislature enacted a law prohibiting Michigan jurisdictions from imposing residency requirements, although they are permitted to require that employees live within 20 miles.

Land Use

How local land shall be used—for agriculture, recreation, housing, industry, small business, and so on—and the extent to which larger areas or the state should be involved in land-use decision-making is a contentious matter and is discussed elsewhere in this book.

Living Wage

ACORN, a community-advocacy organization, reports that nationwide about 60 local government units require businesses with which the unit has contracts to pay employees working under the contract a wage that is higher than the federal minimum ($5.15 an hour) plus certain benefits, enabling the workers to earn a so-called living wage. Michigan jurisdictions that have such a law are

- the cities of Ann Arbor, Detroit, Eastpointe, Ferndale, Kalamazoo, Warren, and Ypsilanti;

- Ypsilanti and Pittsfield townships; and

- Washtenaw County.

Debate about the wisdom of a living wage is heated, and state legislation to prohibit locals from imposing one has been introduced. Among the arguments opponents make against such laws are that

- wage minimums should be set at the federal level, for consistency;

- when laws vary from jurisdiction to jurisdiction, doing business with the jurisdictions becomes complicated and expensive, particularly for new businesses;

- they discourage firms from locating in living-wage jurisdictions;

- enforcement requires additional local-government resources;

- they discourage competition in bidding for jurisdiction jobs;

- they cost local units more when purchasing goods and services;

- studies (e.g., Michigan State University, 1999) show that they result in there being fewer low-level jobs available, because firms cut back on the number of workers to compensate for the higher payroll; and

- they pose a particular hardship for nonprofits (e.g., the Salvation Army has moved its headquarters out of Detroit, contending that it could not financially comply).

Proponents for living-wage laws argue that

- studies (e.g., Wayne State University, Urban Studies Center and Labor Studies Center, 1999) show that the maximum possible cost to both living-wage jurisdictions and employers is minor; and

- most important—and they assert that this position trumps all others—ensuring that workers earn a livable wage and receive benefits (e.g., medical coverage) not only helps workers and their families but also the jurisdiction, the state, and society.

"Let Local Votes Count"

Local units had been anxious about encroachment on their rights for many years, and in 1999 the Michigan Legislature passed the municipal-residency ban, right-to-farm act, and imposed a state construction code. This lead Michigan cities, in 2000, to craft a ballot initiative—Let Local

Votes Count—to amend the state constitution to require a two-thirds vote of the legislature (rather than a simple majority) to pass any state law dealing with an issue that could be addressed by city, county, village, or township government. The Michigan Municipal League, which represents about 500 cities and villages, headed the effort. Opponents argued that requiring a two-thirds vote would permit a minority to disrupt crucial legislation that in any way affected local matters. Proponents argued that something was necessary to protect the state from running roughshod over the wishes of local citizens and the authority of the local officials who speak for them. The initiative did not pass, and local governments' scope of authority is likely to remain the same, at least for now.

See also Highway Funding and Safety; Land Use and Sustainability; Solid Waste and Recycling; Taxes on Businesses; Taxes on Consumers.

FOR ADDITIONAL INFORMATION

Bureau of Local Government
Michigan Department of Treasury
430 West Allegan Street
Lansing, MI 48922
(517) 373-3305
(517) 373-2621 FAX
www.michigan.gov/treasury

Michigan Association of Counties
935 North Washington Avenue
Lansing, MI 48906
(800) 258-1152
(517) 372-5374
(517) 482-4599 FAX
www.miaco.org

Michigan Association of Intermediate School Administrators
1001 Centennial Way, Suite 300
Lansing, MI 48917
(517) 327-5910
(517) 327-0771 FAX
www.melg.org/maisa

Michigan Association of School Administrators
1001 Centennial Way, Suite 300
Lansing, MI 48917
(517) 327-5910
(517) 327-0771 FAX
www.gomasa.org

Michigan Association of School Boards
1001 Centennial Way, Suite 400
Lansing, Michigan 48917
(517) 327-5900
(517) 327-0775 FAX
www.masb.org

Sponsored by the Michigan Nonprofit Association and the Council of Michigan Foundations

LOCAL GOVERNMENT ORGANIZATION AND ISSUES

Michigan Municipal League
1675 Green Road
Ann Arbor MI 48105
(800) 653-2483
(734) 669-6300
(734) 662-8083 FAX
www.mml.org

Michigan Townships Association
512 Westshire Drive
P.O. Box 80078
Lansing, MI 48908
(517) 321-6467
(517) 321-8908 FAX
www.michigantownships.org

Office of Revenue and Tax Analysis
Michigan Department of Treasury
430 West Allegan Street
Lansing, MI 48922
(517) 373-2864
(517) 373-8414 FAX
www.michigan.gov/treasury

Readers are directed to *Michigan in Brief, 6th Edition*, which may be found at *www.michiganinbrief.org*, for a list of publications pertaining to local government organization and issues.

Sponsored by the Michigan Nonprofit Association and the Council of Michigan Foundations

Long-Term and Related Care

BACKGROUND

Long-term care (LTC) covers a range of medical and/or social services for people who have disabilities or chronic care needs. It may refer to nursing-home care or to other types of care listed in the glossary, and its importance is growing because

■ Americans are living longer;

■ people aged 85 and over comprise the fastest-growing segment of the population; and

■ the oldest of the "babyboomers" are aged 55 and will begin to use LTC services in this decade.

In 2000 there were more than one million Michiganians aged 65 and older, and more than 90 percent of those who require LTC in a given year are in this group. The U.S. Bureau of the Census projects that by 2020 this group will number nearly 1.7 million, and half will spend time in a nursing home. The financial implications of the future demand for LTC are staggering.

■ In 2001 the average annual cost per resident for nursing home care in Michigan was $54,000; assuming 3.3 percent annual inflation, the cost in 2020 will be $97,000.

■ Home-health care is considerably less expensive than nursing home care but still averages $12,500 annually; annual inflation of 3.3 percent brings the cost in 2020 to $22,500.

■ Michigan Medicaid spending for LTC in 2001 totaled about $1 billion; 3.3 percent annual inflation brings the bill in 2020 to $1.9 billion (this projection does not take into account the burgeoning growth of the LTC age group).

■ Nationwide, in 2000, LTC nursing home spending from all sources (state, federal, public, private) was $92 billion; the Congressional Budget Office estimates that LTC will grow nationally by 2.6 percent annually and in 2020 the figure will reach $207 billion (again, the growth in the LTC age group is not calculated into the projection).

From 1995 to 2000, nationwide Medicaid LTC spending for the 65-and-older age group increased an average of 4 percent annually, more than the general rate of inflation. Although the growth rate has slowed recently, it still presents a major problem for policymakers and consumers who must find a way to continue paying for LTC. Assuming a 3.3 percent annual inflation rate, a nursing home that costs $150/day now will cost $268/day in 20 years.

Today Medicaid and out-of-pocket spending are the primary financing sources for LTC for the elderly in the United States (see the exhibit). Although Medicare picks up almost 10 percent of total LTC costs, its coverage is limited: Medicare pays for care provided by skilled medical personnel for certain medical conditions (referred to as *skilled* care) but only for 100 days (the full amount for the first 20 days and all but $101.50 for days 21–100); it does not cover helping a person to perform activities of daily living (*custodial* care). After Medicare coverage is exhausted, nursing-facility care may be

GLOSSARY

Adult day care
Mainly nonmedical, daytime supervision and arranged social interaction for seniors; typically paid for with personal funds. May enable some seniors to reside at home by allowing the caregiver—e.g., spouse or child—to work while the senior is in a supervised environment. Facilities must be approved by the state, but state licensure is not required.

Adult foster care
Care provided in facilities that offer transitional or long-term living for people aged 18 and older who need supervision, personal, and other basic care. Residents may be aged, mentally ill, developmentally disabled, and/or physically challenged, but they do not require continuous nursing care. Supplemental Security Income often offsets/covers residents' costs. State licensure is required.

Assisted/independent living
A residential arrangement for seniors who can live independently; may be government subsidized or unsubsidized; out-of-pocket rent is based on the person's income. Housekeeping and limited medical services are available. State licensure is not required.

Basic care
Supervision and assistance with the needs of daily living that can be provided by nonlicensed personnel.

Cost shifting
In the LTC context, shifting payment for care from the public to the private sector.

Sponsored by the Michigan Nonprofit Association and the Council of Michigan Foundations

Home health care

Medical and personal care, homemaker and chore services (e.g., heavy cleaning, yard work), meals, and transportation provided to homebound by nurses, other health professionals, or home-health aides; may be covered in part or in total by Medicaid, Medicare, or private insurance.

Homes for the aged

Facilities that provide custodial/personal care for individuals aged 60 and older and not capable of living independently; for residents, it is similar to living in their own home except that they reside in a group setting. Supplemental Security Income often offsets/covers the cost of such care. State licensure is not required.

Hospice

Offers palliative care, including pain management, to terminally ill patients. Some hospice care is covered by Medicare and Medicaid. Hospice providers are state licensed.

Managed care

A broad term for any comprehensive approach to health care delivery that (1) coordinates patient care so as to ensure the appropriate use of services and (2) routinely monitors and measures health providers' performance so as to control cost and maintain or improve the quality of care. Under capitated managed care, a fixed amount per beneficiary is paid to the health insurance carrier.

Medicaid

The federal/state program that pays for many health care services for low-income people who qualify, including children, pregnant women, and the elderly.

Medicare

The federal program that pays for many health care services for people who are (1) blind and/or have a long-term disability or (2) aged 65 and older.

MIChoice

The state program (with some federal funding) that provides participants with resources (e.g., homemaker services, home-delivered meals, transportation) that make it possible for them to stay in their own residence.

Payment Sources for Long-Term Care, 2001

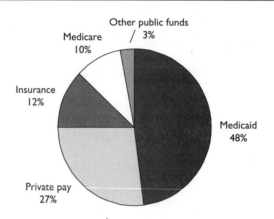

SOURCE: Centers for Medicare and Medicaid Services (formerly Health Care Financing Administration), 2001.

covered by Medicaid—if the patient's income is sufficiently low—which picks up 48 percent of the nation's LTC costs. Patients and their families pay for 27 percent, usually from savings, pensions, and annuities; private health insurance pays for 12 percent; and other public funds cover the remainder.

If LTC costs continue to climb at the current rate, it is unlikely that Medicaid and Medicare will be able to pick up the portion of costs that they traditionally have. Policymakers at the state and federal levels are exploring strategies to reduce LTC expenditures for the elderly while improving the quality of care provided.

DISCUSSION

Long-term care costs are increasing principally because

- the nation's elderly population is burgeoning;

- far more women—traditionally, the elderly's primary caretakers—are employed now than in the past and, therefore, are unavailable to provide informal long-term care for their loved ones; and

- neither public policy nor LTC industry practices have been able to keep pace with changing demand.

There are no practical ways to affect the consequences of the first two causes, so debate on reducing the system's expense focuses mainly on public policy changes and industry reform. There are two generally accepted strategies that policymakers may use to control spending: (1) shifting the cost, i.e., offsetting government expenditures by increasing private contributions and (2) reforming the delivery system so as to provide care less expensively.

Cost Shifting

The debate about generating additional private resources to offset LTC costs traditionally absorbed by Medicaid and Medicare—and thus by state and federal government—revolves primarily around

- encouraging people to carry private long-term care insurance;

Sponsored by the Michigan Nonprofit Association and the Council of Michigan Foundations

Nursing home (basic)
A facility providing regular medical, nursing, social, and rehabilitation services, in addition to room and board, for people who cannot live independently; provides basic medical services short of 24-hour skilled nursing care and must meet state licensure requirements. Most residents qualify for Medicaid.

Nursing home (skilled)
A facility providing intensive, around-the-clock nursing care and supervision; registered nurses, licensed practical nurses, and nurse aides provide services under the guidance of the patient's physician. Medical nursing care is provided as well as restorative, physical, occupational, and other therapy. About one-third of patients pay from private funds; the remainder receive Medicaid and/or Medicare benefits. Facilities must be licensed by the state.

Respite care
In-home service, provided through a community-based program, that gives intermittent care to people in their residence; its purpose is to relieve the primary caregiver of responsibility for periods ranging from a few hours to a few weeks. Services may range from simply being present to providing the complex care needed by someone on life-support equipment.

Skilled care
Care that requires licensed nursing personnel.

Subacute care
Features services more intensive than those provided in skilled nursing facilities but less intensive than acute care (hospitalization); provides treatment for specific, complex medical conditions immediately after or instead of hospitalization. Facility must be licensed by the state.

Supplemental Security Income (SSI)
Federal assistance program for people aged 65 and older and meeting certain asset and income requirements; SSI also assists the blind or extremely visually impaired and those who suffer from a physical or mental disability.

■ more strictly enforcing the asset-related provisions of the laws governing Medicaid; and

■ reducing Medicaid eligibility, reimbursement, and services.

Long-Term Care Insurance

Currently, only 6–7 percent of the elderly have private LTC insurance. States are trying to encourage people to purchase such policies so as to enable them to pay for their own LTC rather than relying on government programs. Pending federal legislation would allow LTC-insurance purchasers to deduct from their income tax the total cost of the premiums. Analysts say, however, that this is unlikely to provide enough tax relief to encourage people to buy the insurance.

Many people do not purchase LTC insurance because of the cost: $400 to $5,000 a year, depending on the insured's age, health, and the policy's benefits. Studies find that only 10–20 percent of the elderly can afford it. Moreover, even with LTC coverage, individuals may have out-of-pocket costs not covered by their insurance; for example, a policy may cover $120/day in a nursing home, but if the cost is $160, the resident is liable for the remaining $40. Michigan P.A. 4 of 2001 requires LTC insurance carriers to define and provide policyholders with a detailed coverage explanation.

Asset Enforcement

A second way to increase nongovernment payment for LTC is to enforce Medicaid-related asset transfer/recovery provisions. There is evidence that many people, to become eligible for Medicaid benefits, purposefully divest their assets. The purpose of such transfers—so-called Medicaid estate planning—is to appear poor on paper while preserving private wealth for one's heirs. Although Congress repeatedly has legislated against such practices, many point out that the prohibitions are easy to circumvent and the practice of Medicaid estate planning has surged in recent years.

Another asset-related concern for government-funded LTC is estate recovery. According to the U.S. Department of Health and Human Services, only about one-half of one percent of Medicaid nursing home expenditures are recovered each year, despite a federal law requiring states to recover them from the estate of deceased program beneficiaries. Michigan has not yet instituted such a program. The Michigan Department of Community Health contends that it cannot implement a recovery program without legislation, and the legislature has not acted for a number of reasons. First, it has not been determined how much such a program will cost or recover, although an earlier (FY 1994–95) recovery estimate was about $4 million. Second, the success of recovery attempts elsewhere has been limited. For example, Colorado's program has yet, after four years, even to recover the cost of running the program. To date, the federal government has not imposed penalties for noncompliance.

Reducing Program Scope

If government does not succeed in substantially increasing private LTC contributions by encouraging the purchase of private insurance and/or discouraging private asset transfer, it will have to consider more traditional cost-shifting options (which also will result in individuals having to pay more out-of-pocket). These include

■ cutting the rates at which LTC facilities are reimbursed for their services (since 1997 states have almost complete freedom in setting nursing-home payment rates);

■ raising eligibility standards for government-funded LTC services (e.g., setting more stringent income standards for people who wish to have Medicaid pay for nursing home care); and

Sponsored by the Michigan Nonprofit Association and the Council of Michigan Foundations

- limiting the extent to which long-term care services are covered.

Effect of Cost Shifting

Although many applaud personal accountability and responsibility when it comes to long-term care, others argue that cost shifting harms those who most need the government's support—the frail elderly and their families. This view is leading policymakers at all government levels to find ways not just to shift LTC costs but to reduce them without sacrificing quality.

System Reform

The second general strategy for controlling LTC costs is to reorganize the delivery system to make it more efficient. Many states, including Michigan, are seeking to accomplish such reform by

- integrating acute (hospital) and long-term care systems under the managed-care umbrella;

- creating a managed-care system that encompasses LTC only; and/or

- offering more home- and community-based services.

Managed Care

People who need LTC services often encounter a fragmented financing and delivery system: Private insurance and Medicare mainly finance acute care; Medicaid mainly finances LTC. This separation of financial responsibility creates an incentive for the federal and state governments to shift costs to one another. It also results in a breakdown of coordination in service delivery.

Policymakers increasingly are looking at *capitated* managed-care—an arrangement whereby a single, state-administered payment is made, on a per-patient basis, to a managed-care organization (e.g., health maintenance organization) to pay for an enrollee's care. For such a system to incorporate LTC and function smoothly, many policymakers argue that monies from Medicaid (the principal payer for LTC) and Medicare (the principal payer for most other health costs for seniors) must be combined.

Various states have applied for a federal waiver to create a capitated managed-care system that incorporates LTC and combines Medicaid and Medicare funds to pay for it; Minnesota and Wisconsin have received approval. Michigan has not applied for a waiver, instead choosing to focus on integrating health-care financing and delivery only for Medicaid services.

Home- and Community-Based Services

Managed LTC is evolving slowly, but there are alternatives that may result in LTC savings. One is to expand home- and community-based services for older adults, and Michigan has received federal approval to do so.

In 1992 the Health Care Financing Administration (now the Centers for Medicare and Medicaid Services) approved Michigan's Home and Community Based Services for the Elderly and Disabled, and in 1998 it became available statewide. The program gives recipients access to personal care, homemaker services, home-delivered meals, transportation, help with chores, respite care, counseling, personal emergency response, home modifications, equipment aids, adult daycare, training, durable medical equipment, medical supplies, and private-duty nursing. The expansion is part of Michigan's MIChoice initiative, which is meant to provide participants with resources (e.g., homemaker services, home-delivered meals, transportation) that make it possible for them to stay in their own residence.

Many policy experts believe that home health care actually will increase LTC expenses. The reason is the so-called woodwork effect: Many people will forgo LTC if the only choice is a nursing home but will use it if home-care services are an option. Thus, providing broad-based home care could increase demand for LTC services, resulting in expenses that exceed any cost savings stemming from reducing the demand for nursing home care.

Quality Control

Although expense is the major issue surrounding LTC, policymakers and industry officials also struggle with improving LTC quality. According to a 2000 survey conducted by the Health Care Association of Michigan (HCAM, an association of for-profit nursing homes), 89 percent of respondents reported being satisfied with the services they or their loved ones receive in a Michigan nursing home. The association reports that nationally, on average, there were 8.3 citations per facility in 2000 for violations of the quality regulations that were implemented in 1995. Michigan averaged 2.4 citations per facility, well below the national average.

In 2001 Michigan officials investigated 1,704 complaints and reports of poor care. Many LTC providers argue that many deficiencies found in Michigan facilities may not necessarily be due to inadequate staff and administrative practices but rather to the regulation system, which they say is extreme: It encompasses a zero-tolerance policy toward mistakes or errors—even those that have little to do with patient care. LTC providers also complain that the system is based on subjective opinion and is vulnerable to surveyor bias.

Critics of the LTC system argue that enforcement is not strict enough, and they say that serious violators go undetected and unpunished. They contend that the few facilities that do provide poor care (most of the violations involve only 45–50 of the state's 437 nursing homes) do not receive nearly enough regulatory attention.

In recent years two programs to improve LTC care in Michigan have been implemented.

- *Resident Protection Initiative*   This program identifies homes that need accelerated review and, in some cases, such intervention as directed in-services or a clinical or administrative advisor to assist in complying with regulations. The Michigan Department of Consumer and Industry Services (MDCIS) has received national attention for this effort.

- *Governor's Quality Care Awards*   This program recognizes outstanding Michigan care providers who go the extra mile in creating a safe, healthy, and nurturing environment for the elderly.

The MDCIS also provides facility licensure status and inspection reports on its Web site, and this helps consumers and their families to choose an LTC option that will give good care—in terms of cost *and* quality—to the patient. In addition, measures are pending to (1) require administrators to give residents a monthly itemized bill for services rendered (SB 574), (2) create a consumer rating index for nursing homes and require that residents be surveyed annually as to their satisfaction with the facility (SB 572), and (3) allow electronic monitoring of nursing home residents (SB 1120 and HB 5603).

Conclusion

Given the growing need for and expense of LTC services both in Michigan and nationwide, LTC reform is inevitable. Policymakers are exploring numerous options to make LTC affordable both for individuals and government. Most believe that success best can be achieved through both cost shifting and system reform. The challenge is to determine the optimal degree to which both should be pursued. Debate on this matter is heated, but regardless of any disagreement among policymakers, most agree that the goal is to develop a system that ensures the availability of affordable, high-quality long-term care.

See also Aging; Consumer Protection; Domestic Violence; Health Care Costs and Managed Care.

FOR ADDITIONAL INFORMATION

American Association of Retired Persons
309 North Washington Square, Suite 110
Lansing, MI 48933
(517) 482-2772
(517) 482-2794 FAX
www.aarp.org

Citizens for Better Care
4750 Woodward Avenue, Suite 410
Detroit, MI 48201
(800) 833-9548
(313) 832-7407 FAX
www.cbcmi.org

Division of Health Facilities and Services
Bureau of Health Systems
Michigan Department of Consumer and Industry Services
G. Mennen Williams Building, 5th Floor
P.O. Box 30664
Lansing, MI 48909
(517) 241-2626
(517) 241-1981 FAX
www.michigan.gov/cis

Health Care Association of Michigan
P.O. Box 80050
Lansing, MI 48908
(517) 627-1561
(517) 627-3016 FAX
www.hcam.org

Michigan Association of Homes and Services for the Aging
6512 Centurion Drive, Suite 380
Lansing, MI 48917
(517) 323-3687
(517) 323-4569 FAX

Michigan Hospice and Palliative Care Organization
6015 West St. Joseph Highway, Suite 104
Lansing, MI 48917
(800) 536-6300
(517) 886-6667
(517) 886-6737 FAX
www.mihospice.org

Office of Services to the Aging
Michigan Department of Community Health
611 West Ottawa Street, 3d Floor
P.O. Box 30676
Lansing, MI 48909
(517) 373-8230
(517) 373-4092 FAX
www.miseniors.net

Sponsored by the Michigan Nonprofit Association and the Council of Michigan Foundations

Mental Health Funding and Services

BACKGROUND

The public responsibility for caring for people with developmental disabilities and mental illness was set out in Michigan more than 150 years ago, in the 1850 state constitution. The state's first mental institution, the Kalamazoo Asylum for the Insane, began receiving patients in 1859. The most recent state constitution (1963) also stipulates that care for this population is an explicit responsibility of the state. Article VIII, section 8, says,

> Institutions, programs, and services for the care, treatment, education, or rehabilitation of those inhabitants who are physically, mentally, or otherwise seriously disabled shall always be fostered and supported.

In practice, the state system for mental health care that has evolved over the years was designed to meet the needs of two very different client populations:

- the *developmentally disabled*—people with mental retardation, autism, cerebral palsy, or epilepsy, and

- the *mentally ill*—adults and children afflicted by such conditions as schizophrenia, manic-depressive disorder, and serious depression.

Delivery System

State hospitals and centers originally were the main means of treating and caring for the mentally ill and developmentally disabled. In the first half of the 1900s, the capacity of state institutions grew dramatically. However, by the 1960s there evolved a general consensus among mental health professionals and the public that the needs of most mental health patients best can be met in community programs located as close to a patient's family as possible. In 1974 the Michigan Mental Health Code (Public Act 258) transferred the authority and funding for the care and treatment of adults and children with mental illness and developmental disabilities from the state to community mental health services programs (CMHSPs), agencies sponsored by Michigan's 83 counties and overseen by the Michigan Department of Community Health (MDCH).

Today there are 48 CMHSPs; some are single-county, some are multi-county, and one is city-county. Each CMHSP offers a variety of services that may include

- psychosocial rehabilitation,

- assertive community treatment,

- supported employment,

- inpatient and outpatient services,

- day programs,

- special services for children and adolescents, and

- emergency and telephone crisis services.

GLOSSARY

Assertive community treatment
Team treatment that provides comprehensive, community-based psychiatric treatment, rehabilitation, and support to people who have serious and persistent mental illness.

Case management
Coordination of a person's health care needs through a plan overseen by a case manager.

Developmental disability
A mental or physical incapacity, such as mental retardation, autism, cerebral palsy, or epilepsy, that arises before adulthood and usually lasts through life.

Managed care
The effort to "manage," or control, utilization and costs through alternative care-delivery systems and specific management techniques. Health maintenance organizations (HMOs) are a well-known managed-care delivery system; individual case management and utilization review are typical managed-care techniques.

Medicaid
The federal/state program that pays for many health care services for low-income people who qualify.

Mental illness
Any mental or emotional disorder that substantially impairs normal life activity. Examples are schizophrenia, manic-depressive disorder, and serious depression.

For the past three years, the MDCH has operated a managed-care specialty-services program for the mentally ill and developmentally disabled Medicaid population. The department sees managed care as a way to

- facilitate freedom for people with mental health needs,

- retain state-county-community partnerships,

- ensure accountability and integrity, and

- promote efficiency.

Under the program, the MDCH has contracted with each CMHSP to operate as a specialty prepaid health plan (SPHP) responsible for providing Medicaid-covered mental health and developmental disability services in its area.

In 2002 the MDCH will begin to select SPHPs differently, no longer automatically contracting with the 48 CMHSPs. To continue to serve as a SPHP, a CMHSP must meet certain requirements and have specified capabilities, among them having

- at least 20,000 Medicaid beneficiaries living in its service area,

- the ability to serve the mental health population in its geographic area,

- adequate administrative capability,

- established cost limits on mental health services,

- the capacity to ensure client access to services,

- established practices that ensure consumers equal treatment and inclusion in their care decisions, and

- a focus on consumer-directed services and consumer participation in planning and governing.

A CMHSP that does not have the required number of Medicaid recipients in its service area is permitted to join another for SPHP purposes. Initially, only CMHSPs may apply, but if a CMHSP application is found wanting, a competitive process will be used to find an organization qualified to act as the SPHP in that geographic area. Although it may be possible for private, mental-health management companies to act as SPHPs, all existing CMHSPs probably will be successful in receiving a SPHP designation—either individually or as part of a group—because they have the first opportunity to bid and have acted as SPHPs for the past three years. If a CMHSP were not to receive the SPHP designation, it would lose state Medicaid dollars and thus the vast majority of its business. It could continue to function, albeit at a greatly reduced level, relying on the non-Medicaid dollars it receives from the state and clients' private-insurance and out-of-pocket payments.

State Facilities

The state has closed 24 state mental health institutions since 1981, 16 of them since 1990. Currently, six state-operated hospitals and centers serve mentally ill adults and children and people with developmental disabilities. They are

- the Caro Center, Kalamazoo Psychiatric Hospital, Northville Psychiatric Hospital, and Walter Reuther Psychiatric Hospital, which serve mentally ill adults;

- the Hawthorn Center, which serves mentally ill children; and

- the Mt. Pleasant Center, which serves developmentally disabled clients.

Parity
The proposition that limitations or restrictions on mental health insurance benefits should be no greater than those on other medical services.

Psychosocial rehabilitation
Combined psychological and social services to help people develop and improve the skills needed to live and participate in the community.

Psychotropic drug
Medication that modifies mood, cognition (e.g., awareness, perception, reasoning, judgment), or behavior.

Specialty prepaid health plan (SPHP)
A plan whereby for a fixed amount of funding per person, services are provided to a special population; in this case, the state provides the funding for Medicaid recipients needing mental health services.

Supported employment
Programs that help clients get and keep long-term employment.

Utilization review
Examining the delivery of health care services for their appropriateness and medical necessity.

January 2002 saw the most recent closure—the Southgate Center for the developmentally disabled. The Northville Psychiatric Hospital is slated to close within three years. Hospital and center closures mean a decrease in the patient census at state mental health institutions: in FY 1992–93 the institutionalized population was 2,707; by FY 2000–01 the population had dropped to 1,328.

There also is a system of private hospital care, providing short-term care for the mentally ill, that people access through private health insurance or out-of-pocket payment. According to the MDCH, in 2001 there were 61 private psychiatric hospitals/units in Michigan, with the capacity to serve 2,038 adults and 394 minors. The number of private units is down, due mainly to financial considerations, from 72 in 1999, when there was capacity to serve 2,526 adults and 523 minors.

Funding
Exhibit 1 shows spending for community mental health, institutional care, and community residential services for the past five fiscal years plus the current year (FY 2001–02) appropriation. The data show that mental health expenditures increased the most in FY 1998–99—up 11.7 percent from the previous year. The current year appropriation is down slightly (0.3 percent) from last year's expenditures. Although the executive order of November 2001 reduced the MDCH budget by several million dollars, the majority of the cuts affected hospitals and nursing homes. Mental health funding did receive some cuts, but due to an increase in mental health services in FY 2001–02, the net effect was a freeze in funding.

DISCUSSION

Mental health advocates are concerned that (1) mental health resources in Michigan are insufficient, (2) the closure of so many state institutions means that some people with mental health needs are being deprived of a continuum of care, and (3) Michigan's new Medicaid prescription drug formulary (effective in February 2002) will deny Medicaid recipients access to certain mental-health drugs.

Hospital Closures
As stated, the state has closed 24 mental health institutions in the last two decades. Several reasons are cited: the belief that the mental health and developmentally disabled population should not be locked up but allowed to live freely and receive care in their community; growth of the community mental health system; development of psychotropic drugs that help manage mental illness; and last but not least, budget constraints.

Opponents of such extensive closures argue that the institutional beds being lost are not being replaced by enough beds in private general and psychiatric hospitals in the state. They contend that people in psychiatric hospitals are there because they cannot be properly treated in a community setting or in a regular hospital, where stays usually are short-term and unsuited for people with long-term mental illness. They further maintain that many patients who are displaced from institutions—for example, the Northville Psychiatric Hospital, where the beds are full and closure is expected by 2004—will end up in a homeless shelter or jail instead of in a community program or general hospital.

Parity
Observers generally argue that private insurance coverage for mental health services is inadequate. As may be seen in Exhibit 2, in recent years a large percentage of the state's mental health spending has gone to Medicaid recipients. But only about half of Michiganians with men-

EXHIBIT 1. Mental Health Spending, FY 1996–97 through FY 2001–02 ($ millions)

Expenditure Category	Actual Expenditures FY 1996–97	Actual Expenditures FY 1997–98	Adjusted Expenditures FY 1998–99	Adjusted Expenditures FY 1999–2000	Estimated Expenditures FY 2000–01	Appropriations FY 2001–02
Community mental health	$936.2	$1,173.4	$1,380.7	$1,380.2	$1,426.7	$1,417.0
Other CMH-related budget lines	7.2	0.0	0.0	6.9	7.2	7.2
Institutions, purchase of state services (POSS)	176.0	138.1	150.0	158.0	166.9	166.8
Institutions, other financing sources	67.8	54.1	57.0	61.0	63.1	67.4
Community residential services, POSS	101.3	32.8	0.0	0.0	0.0	0.0
Community residential services, other	93.0	28.7	6.7	0.6	1.0	0.9
TOTAL	$1,381.4	$1,427.0	$1,593.4	$1,606.6	$1,664.8	$1,659.3
Percentage change over previous year	−0.23%	3.30%	11.66%	0.83%	3.62%	−0.33%

SOURCE: Senate Fiscal Agency.

Sponsored by the Michigan Nonprofit Association and the Council of Michigan Foundations

tal health needs are eligible for Medicaid. Therefore, there is need for private insurers to cover mental health services for the non-Medicaid population.

In 1996 the federal Mental Health Parity Act was enacted, requiring insurers to provide the same aggregate lifetime and annual limits for mental health coverage as they do for medical and surgical coverage. The law, which expired in 2001, applied to treatment for mental illness, but it did not *require* insurers to cover mental health services (it said only that if they *do*, there must be parity in coverage). The law also did not prohibit insurers from imposing copayments, deductibles, and treatment time limits for mental health services that were different from those imposed for medical services. This meant, for example, that an insurer could require its members to pay cost-sharing amounts that were so high that mental health treatment still was inaccessible because of the out-of-pocket expense. Or the insurer could agree to cover only a certain number of days of mental health treatment.

In 2001 the Michigan Legislature introduced bills that address the parity issue. House Bills 5123 and 5128 and Senate Bills 101–02 would require health insurers in Michigan to ensure that their cost-sharing requirements

and benefit and service limitations for inpatient and outpatient mental health services are the same as those for inpatient and outpatient medical services. Like the expired federal law, these bills do not *mandate* mental health care coverage, but they differ from the federal law in that

- the Michigan bills would require commercial insurers, Blue Cross Blue Shield of Michigan, and HMOs to ensure that any cost-sharing amount or coverage limitation imposed on those requiring mental health services is no different from that imposed on those requiring medical services, and

- the bills do not exempt small businesses (those with 50 or fewer employees) from providing such coverage for their workers.

As of this writing, none of the bills has been reported out of committee. Parity opponents argue that it could be costly for health insurers and employers that provide insurance. Supporters counter that providing mental health coverage actually will lower the overall costs of treating mental illness because when it is treated early, the amount of care needed is far less than when it has become chronic due to a lack of care. Parity supporters also maintain that employers would receive a net benefit from paying the

EXHIBIT 2. Michigan Community Mental Health Expenditures, FY 1996–97 through FY 2001–02 ($ millions)

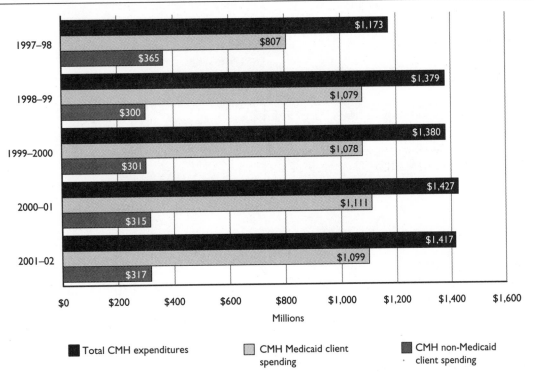

SOURCE: Senate Fiscal Agency.

Sponsored by the Michigan Nonprofit Association and the Council of Michigan Foundations

additional costs of mental health coverage because absenteeism from mental illness would be greatly reduced and job productivity increased.

Medicaid Prescription Drug Formulary

Several mental health organizations have joined the national Pharmaceutical Research and Manufacturing Association in its lawsuit against the state's new Medicaid prescription drug formulary, which limits the drugs that may be covered without preauthorization. Opponents of the formulary say that the state's new plan will deny patients access to some necessary psychotropic drugs. The MDCH argues that if a drug requiring prior authorization is medically necessary, the patient will receive that drug, but if a less costly drug will serve as well, Michigan taxpayers should not have to pay for the more expensive medication. Opponents counter that by requiring prior authorization for certain drugs, mental health patients, and their physicians, are forced to jump through too many hoops to get necessary medication.

The issue was addressed by the Senate Appropriations Committee in SB 1101, the FY 2002–03 funding bill for the MDCH. The committee added language allowing the state to negotiate rebates with pharmaceutical manufacturers. If the pharmaceuticals provide quarterly rebates on all their products, the products will not be subject to prior authorization except in the case of (1) drugs that required prior authorization during FY 2000–01 and (2) drugs dispensed to Medicaid recipients enrolled in health plans. At this writing, the bill has passed the Senate and awaits action in the House.

See also Aging; Health Care Access, Medicaid, and Medicare; Special Education.

Research on this policy topic was made possible by a grant from the Ethel and James Flinn Family Foundation.

FOR ADDITIONAL INFORMATION

Association for Children's Mental Health
941 Abbott Road
East Lansing, MI 48823
(517) 336-7222
(517) 336-8884 FAX

Center for Mental Health Services
Substance Abuse and Mental Health Services Administration
U.S. Department of Health and Human Services
5600 Fishers Lane, Room 17-99
Rockville, MD 20857
(301) 443-0001
(301) 443-1563 FAX
www.samhsa.gov

Mental Health Association in Michigan
15920 West 12 Mile Road
Southfield, MI 48076
(800) 482-9534
(248) 557-6777
(248) 557-5995 FAX
www.mha-mi.org

Michigan Association of Community Mental Health Boards
426 South Walnut Street
Lansing, MI 48933
(517) 374-6848
(517) 374-1053 FAX
www.macmhb.org

Michigan Psychiatric Society
271 Woodland Pass, Suite 125
East Lansing, MI 48823
(888) 810-6226
(517) 333-0220 FAX

Office of Mental Health and Substance Abuse Services
Michigan Department of Community Health
Lewis Cass Building
320 South Walnut Street
Lansing, MI 48913
(517) 335-0196
(517) 335-3090 FAX
www.michigan.gov/mdch

Privacy

BACKGROUND

For Americans, individual liberty includes a right to personal privacy, as manifested in the Fourth Amendment to the U.S. Constitution. The amendment was written in an age—long before the advent of computer databases and digital communications—when an invasion of privacy perforce was a physical, manual, focused, short-term, expensive, and relatively obtrusive act that might involve entering premises, intercepting and opening mail, questioning acquaintances, and, later, tapping a telephone line or taking photographs—all without the subject's permission or knowledge.

Today's invasion of privacy is more likely to be virtual, automated, unobtrusive, inexpensive, and lifelong. Others can find out what we buy and from whom, what we say and to whom, what we read, what turns us on, what turns us off, what ails us, where we go, and even whether we exceed the speed limit in getting there. Not only has the secluded and shuttered 18th century home held inviolable by the Fourth Amendment been replaced by a 21st century glass house, but technology also has given Peeping Tom much more powerful binoculars.

DISCUSSION

Michigan's first public act of the new millennium, P.A. 1 of 2000, was privacy legislation, and the state attorney general's office reports that Internet privacy is one of the main consumer concerns. But legislation may not be enough to halt the erosion of privacy in the Internet age. Human ingenuity, greed, and carelessness can overcome the best-intentioned legislation, and in the shrinking, borderless world of the Internet, state and local legislation can conflict with federal law, other nations' laws, and a growing body of international law.

Two key questions are emerging:

- Is privacy—among other democratically derived civil liberties—compatible with the privatization of America's critical information infrastructure and its governing functions?

- Does the rapid evolution of technology, relative to the necessary slowness of deliberative democracy, put privacy legislation in perpetual catch-up mode and thus render it ultimately ineffectual?

The view often is expressed that increasing our computer defenses should not come at the expense of civil liberties, that the very freedoms we seek to protect should not be undermined. Some point out that technology empowers both law enforcers and lawbreakers, and the latter cannot be stopped without impinging on personal privacy at least to some extent. Others say that lost in all the rhetoric is consideration of who has the right to own and control a citizen's private information.

But perhaps the bigger challenge is whether technology's rapid evolution renders privacy moot. For example, while a good deal of attention currently is being paid to the intrusive activities of large corporations, we may be overlooking smaller "spyware" operators and their hidden programs, sometimes bundled (unknown to the recipient) with

GLOSSARY

Carnivore
The code name of a software program developed for the FBI to monitor e-mail and other Internet traffic; it is installed on the premises of an Internet service provider.

Cookie
A record of a visit to a Web site; by itself, a cookie cannot identify the visitor.

Hotmail
A free Internet e-mail service owned by Microsoft. Hotmail does not check the validity of registrant identities, thus one may obtain an e-mail address without revealing one's true identity. Other companies, including Yahoo, offer similar, free e-mail accounts.

Magic Lantern
The code name of a virus-like software program developed for the FBI to capture the user's keystrokes as they are typed, defeating any encryption program the user relies on to protect the privacy of e-mail and other electronic communications; it can be surreptitiously installed, via e-mail or other means, on a user's computer.

Privacy
The state of being free from unsanctioned intrusion.

Screen saver
A computer program designed to prolong the useful life of computer monitors; many are offered free over the Internet.

Sponsored by the Michigan Nonprofit Association and the Council of Michigan Foundations

screen savers and other free computer programs. Much more intrusive than passive "cookies," spyware actively can track the Web sites and pages a user accesses, create a profile of the user's interests, deliver tailored pop-up ads, and even collect the personal and financial information people submit when they use the Internet to order goods or subscribe to services. In some cases, spyware operators hide behind essentially anonymous e-mail addresses (such as provided by Hotmail, Yahoo, and others) or a P.O. box number and may operate abroad as well. It is questionable whether legislation can protect Internet privacy at all, given the absence of borders on the Internet and the rapid evolution of spyware.

Substantial legislative activity, nationally and in Michigan, reflects public concerns about Internet, medical, financial, and genetic privacy. Exhibit 1 summarizes major privacy-related legislation enacted or introduced in Michigan since 1999. The fundamental issues underlying the concerns include ownership and control of personal data, national security, the expansion of personal data down to the genetic level, and identity theft.

We can distinguish between two principal privacy intruders: the private sector and the government. Private parties may seek to intrude not only for institutional security (e.g., monitoring employee e-mail) but also for sales, marketing, and promotional purposes. Intrusion of privacy by government is confined largely to record keeping and security concerns and bound by Constitutional guarantees to a standard of accountability higher than that which binds private parties.

Private-Sector Intrusion

Opt In versus Opt Out

Since we cannot survive in modern society without sometimes sharing our financial, medical, and other private information with strangers, the central issue becomes one of ownership and control: Who owns our private information, and should it be used by others with—or without—our explicit permission?

Many commercial Web site owners and advertisers that collect personal data from us use it for marketing or other purposes *unless* we take the initiative to ask that it not be so used; in other words, unless we specifically *opt out.* Businesses have been criticized and sued for not always making it clear that this is their policy and/or for making it difficult or tedious for customers to opt out. Under pressure from consumer groups and sometimes the threat of prosecution, some companies have switched to a policy of not using customer information for purposes other than the transaction at hand unless customers take the initia-

tive to authorize such use; in other words, unless they specifically *opt in.*

The Pew Internet and American Life Project finds that 86 percent of Internet users support an opt-in standard in regard to collection of personal information, which is at odds with the opt-out alternative favored by industry groups and endorsed by the Federal Trade Commission (FTC). The issue extends to telephone-user privacy: Telecommunication companies now are seeking permission to sell "customer proprietary network information," which includes names, addresses, calling records, and service options used. Consumer groups, citing the Pew data, are urging the FTC to insist on an opt-in standard for this proposal. In a case involving similar circumstances, however, a federal judge ruled that there was inadequate evidence that an opt-in standard would protect customer privacy interests, thus, in that instance it violated the First Amendment.

What happens when the stranger to whom you have entrusted personal information gets married and endows to the spouse all his/her worldly goods—including your data? The 1999 federal Gramm-Leach-Bliley Act allows banks, insurance companies, and brokerage companies to merge or affiliate and share consumers' personal information with one another. Supporters focus on the business efficiencies the act was intended to encourage. The act also requires financial institutions to offer individuals notice and an opportunity to opt out before selling their name, address, or Social Security number to an outside entity, but critics complain that most opt-out notices are not written in the plain language stipulated in the act and warn consumers to look carefully at the privacy notices.

The federal law does not extend the customer-notice provision to the insurance industry, however, and this led to P.A. 24 of 2001, which prohibits Michigan insurers from disclosing a customer's personal financial information to a third party unless the customer is notified and does not opt out. As with the federal mandate, the problem remains that people must read the fine print in notices, which, with all the appearance of being a solicitation, may be discarded unread.

Government Lists

Until 2000, private individuals, companies, and organizations could buy certain State of Michigan lists, but P.A. 192 of 2000 now prohibits the secretary of state from selling such information as driver's license and other agency records for the purpose of "surveys, marketing, or solicitations." (The act does not prohibit the sale of the lists for such other purposes as "motor-vehicle market-research activities," however.)

EXHIBIT 1. Selected Privacy-Related Legislation, Michigan, 1999–April 1, 2002

Act or Bill and Year of Enactment or Introduction	Legislation Summary
Medical Genetic Privacy	
P.A.s 26–28 (2000)	Prohibits insurers from using genetic tests for the purpose of denying coverage application or renewal.
P.A. 29 (2000)	Prohibits a genetic test from being ordered without the written, informed consent of the test subject.
P.A. 30 (2000)	Provides that if the State Police forensic laboratory determines after analysis that a sample has been submitted by an individual who has been eliminated as a suspect in the crime, the laboratory must dispose of the sample.
P.A. 31 (2000)	Specifies the destruction of genetic testing material following a court-ordered paternity test.
P.A. 33 (2000)	Provides for the retention and disposal of blood specimens taken from a newborn for the screening tests required by the act.
P.A. 32 (2000)	Prohibits an employer from requiring an individual to submit to a genetic test as a condition of employment or promotion.
P.A.s 86, 88–89, 91 (2001) HBs 4609–14, 4633 (2001)	The acts require DNA samples to be collected and maintained in certain felony crimes. The bills would extend the law to cover all felonies plus a number of misdemeanors and ordinance violations; included are fourth-degree criminal sexual conduct, enticing a child for immoral purposes, indecent exposure, window peeping, and various prostitution-related offenses. For juveniles, the requirements would apply to assault with intent to commit murder, manslaughter, and certain misdemeanor and ordinance violations. Collection would be required on conviction or, in the case of incarcerated offenders who had not previously been tested, prior to release.
HB 4936 (2001)	Would prohibit disclosure of individual patient health care information (except that specifically allowed by federal or state law, rule, regulation, or Medicaid policy) without the patient's (or authorized representative's) written consent. Separate written consent would be required for disclosure of genetic information.
Workplace/Employee Privacy	
HB 5481 (2001)	Would prohibit disclosure of public school employee records to for-profit businesses for the purpose of soliciting business from the employees.
HB 5527 (2001)	Would prohibit employer monitoring of employee communications unless the employer establishes an employee-monitoring policy and discloses the policy to employees.
Identity Theft	
P.A. 1 (2000)	Prohibits state and local government agencies from printing or writing Social Security, drivers license, or state identification numbers in such a way that they might be seen on or through envelopes or packages.
SB 955 (2001)	Would increase penalties for reproducing, altering, counterfeiting, forging, or duplicating a license photograph.
Telemarketing	
HB 4042 (2001)	Would require the Public Service Commission to establish or designate a do-not-call list and prohibit telephone solicitations to residential telephone subscribers on the list.
HB 4631 (2001)	Would require a residential telephone directory to include information about how a consumer may be included on the do-not-call list.
Financial Privacy	
P.A. 24 (2001)	Prohibits Michigan insurers from disclosing a customer's personal financial information to a third party unless the customer is notified and does not opt out.

▼

Sponsored by the Michigan Nonprofit Association and the Council of Michigan Foundations

Wiretap	
SB 497 (1999)	Would permit prosecutors to authorize, and judges to approve, applications by state and local law enforcement agencies to intercept communications if other investigative techniques have failed, are reasonably unlikely to succeed, or are too dangerous.
HB 5240 (2001)	Would authorize certain communication interceptions, the use of interception devices for certain offenses, and provide for and regulate the application, issuance, and execution of interception orders.

Consumer Privacy	
P.A. 192 (2000)	Amended P.A. 300 of 1949 to prohibit the sale by the Secretary of State of driver's license and other lists for purposes of "surveys, marketing, and solicitation."
SB 433 (2001)	Would allow the state to enter into a multistate sales and use tax agreement by which sales and use taxes on out-of-state purchases made via the Internet, telephone, and mail would be collected. Private-sector certified service providers (CSPs) would be contracted with to collect the taxes and distribute the revenue. The CSPs would be prohibited from retaining or disclosing personally identifying information except where a consumer claims exemption from tax liability; in such a case the consumer usually would have to be notified of that retention and afforded access to his/her own data, with a right to correct inaccuracies.

Internet Privacy	
HB 4680 (2001)	Would prohibit Internet service providers from (1) keeping any records of customers' browsing patterns or selling or distributing such information without first obtaining written permission or (2) divulging a customer's e-mail messages without the customer's written authorization. The bill also would prohibit a person or any other legal entity from placing an individual's "personal nonpublic information" (i.e., telephone or Social Security number, home/business/e-mail addresses, or medical information that the person has not given written authorization to disclose) on the Internet or otherwise distributing or using such information with the intent to cause the individual physical or financial harm.

SOURCE: Summarized from legislative texts and analyses available on the Michigan Legislature Web site www.michiganlegislature.org/mileg.asp?page=Bills

State facility and profession/occupation licensing and registration information is provided on the Michigan Department of Consumer and Industry Services Web site. Although presented to enable consumers to find service providers and check their credentials, the information may be used for whatever purpose the seeker wishes to put it, including telemarketing and other forms of solicitation.

Government Intrusion

National ID Card

Many people are concerned about direct government intrusion of privacy, and in particular over a move toward a national identification card, an idea made at least thinkable by the September 11, 2001, terrorist attacks. Michigan and federal legislation aiming to establish standardized medical records (see below) also evokes such fears. Databases, whether government, commercial, or both, could be integrated much more efficiently and cost effectively if everyone had a unique national identifier, but such databases carry the risk of being all-revealing to any person or institution that gains access to them. Some seek to overturn current law prohibiting the use of the Social Security number as a national identifier; others seek a new and unique identifier for specific purposes, such as an electronic medical record.

A related proposal would have every individual retaining some control over his/her personal data by storing it on an electronic "smart card." Several European and Asian countries have implemented limited smart card systems containing one's national identity number, driver's license information, and medical records.

National Security

Even before September 11 the need to protect defense, economic, and other key national information and transaction systems (including private-sector systems judged critical to national defense or the economy) from intruders and saboteurs was the basis of additional and strengthened government "cyber-security" measures that have significant privacy implications.

The Uniting and Strengthening America by Providing Appropriate Tools Required to Intercept and Obstruct Terrorism (USA PATRIOT) Act, enacted after the September 11 attacks, significantly expanded government surveillance authority, reduced judicial oversight, and criminalized as terrorism a wide range of activities, including computer hacking.

The act includes a sunset (expiration) date (December 31, 2005) on the enhanced electronic-surveillance provisions and an amendment providing judicial oversight of law enforcement's use of the FBI's Carnivore computer system. The latter enables the agency to eavesdrop on electronic communications, including e-mail. Nevertheless, the act vastly expands government investigative authority, especially with respect to the Internet. Exhibit 2 summarizes a selection of the expanded federal government powers.

Michigan's anti-terrorism package (P.A.s 112–137 and 140–143 of 2002) includes state-authorized wiretapping, a definition for terrorism in state criminal law, authority to seal affidavits used in issuing search warrants, and authority to search premises without notifying the resident. Objections to the laws center on their privacy-intrusive aspects, but proponents contend that the legislation not only combats terrorism but also strengthens state law enforcement officials' hand in investigating crimes involving drugs, gambling, racketeering, money laundering, computer-related crimes against children, and more.

Genetic Profiling

Since completion of the Human Genome Project, genetic profiling has taken center stage as the technology with the most immediate and substantial implications for privacy. In Michigan, for example, P.A. 250 of 1990 (DNA Identification Profiling System Act) requires a DNA sample from all felons and people convicted of certain sex-related misdemeanors, permitting investigators to compare DNA strands in hair, tissue, or bodily fluids found at a crime scene with the DNA of those previously convicted of a crime in Michigan. (Eight other states and the United Kingdom have similar laws.) Opponents say that there are scientific concerns about the reliability and validity of DNA tests and that the next step may be to collect DNA samples from anyone accused of a crime and, ultimately, from everyone. Supporters point out that DNA evidence is as important in protecting innocent people as it is in implicating the guilty and that the DNA database will be an invaluable investigation tool.

Medical Records

The 1996 federal Health Insurance Portability and Accountability Act (HIPAA) requires health care providers, health plans, and clearinghouses to adopt and use common data formats for sharing patient clinical and billing information electronically. The legislation includes strong privacy and data-security rules to which the industry must adhere by April 2004. The privacy rules require covered organizations to secure patient opt-in before releasing information to another entity, except in emergencies, and the information released has to be the minimum necessary to accomplish its purpose. Information that has been "de-identified" by removing name, address, and various other potential identifiers may be freely distributed. Pa-

---

EXHIBIT 2. Federal Government Powers Expanded by the USA PATRIOT Act, Selected Examples

Computer fraud

Government may wiretap anyone suspected of causing more than $5,000 worth of combined damage via a computer used in interstate commerce.

Definitions of terrorism

New and expanded definitions expose more people to electronic surveillance (and potential "harboring" and "material support" liability).

DNA database

Government may collect DNA samples not just from terrorists but from any violent criminal.

Hackers

Government may spy on suspected computer trespassers without a court order.

Intelligence sharing

Allows U.S. foreign intelligence agencies to share their findings with the FBI, thus circumventing limitations on domestic surveillance.

Internet surveillance

Government may spy on American Web surfers' activities, including the terms they enter into a search engine, on the basis that the surveillance may produce information relevant to an ongoing criminal investigation.

ISP customer information

Internet service providers may voluntarily hand over to law enforcement agencies all "non-content" information about their customers—i.e., a court order or subpoena is not needed. Government may now subpoena ISP records of users' session times and duration, temporarily assigned network (I.P.) addresses, and means and source of payments, including credit card or bank account numbers.

SOURCE: Selected and summarized from an Electronic Frontier Foundation analysis, available at http://www.eff.org/Privacy/Surveillance/Terrorism_militias/20011031_eff_usa_patriot_analysis.html

---

tients have the right to access and request changes to their health records. Supporters say the shared information will improve health care and reduce administrative costs, and they believe the privacy provisions are adequate. Opponents generally focus on the cost and complexity of implementing the requirements, but some fear that the privacy provisions may prove to be less adequate than thought, at the expense of patient privacy.

In Michigan, pending legislation (HB 4936) also aims to establish all Michigan residents' rights to medical privacy and to access their own medical information. All health care providers—not just physicians and hospitals/clinics, as is the case now—would be required to maintain the confidentiality of patients' medical records. The legislation complements HIPAA and would prohibit unauthorized disclosure, sale, or transfer of any information in any patient record, including electronic records stored on a computer, without first obtaining the written consent of the patient and would further require that any information disclosed be used only for the expressed purpose agreed to by the patient. The draft legislation has so far attracted little in the way of public debate.

Criminal Intrusion
ID Theft/Use
Identity theft occurs when someone uses someone else's identity (e.g., name, date of birth, Social Security number, driver's license number) to masquerade as that person. In the 18 months preceding the end of 2001, in metropolitan Detroit alone, the identity of some 3,000 residents was stolen and used for obtaining credit and other purposes. The high-tech crime unit of the Michigan Department of the Attorney General, working with federal, state, and local law-enforcement agencies, has taken action against counterfeit credit-card and check operations, and SB 955 would toughen penalties for forging driver's licenses, a common practice of identity thieves.

The federal government has mandated that states must collect Social Security numbers from motorists applying for or renewing a driver's license, and the Michigan secretary of state is preparing to comply. The federal intent is to help states track parents who are delinquent in making child-support payments. In Michigan, only about one parent in three pays required child support, and the total amount owed but not paid exceeds $7 billion. Supporters say collecting drivers' Social Security numbers will facilitate finding "deadbeat" parents and thereby help their children. Opponents argue that it is a step down the slippery slope toward creating a national identity system and an identity-theft risk as well.

Other
Space precludes a full discussion here of all the areas in which privacy is an issue. (See Exhibit 1 for a sampling of other areas.) The debate about privacy is intense and, as set out with regard to the matters discussed above, generally focuses, on the one hand, on providing efficiency and better tools to accomplish a purpose and, on the other hand, protecting individuals' private information from the consequences of its use by others.

See also Civil Rights and Liberties; Consumer Protection; Crime and Corrections; Emergency Preparedness and Response.

FOR ADDITIONAL INFORMATION

Electronic Frontier Foundation
454 Shotwell Street
San Francisco CA 94110
(415) 436-9333
(415) 436-9993 FAX
www.eff.org

Electronic Privacy Information Center
1718 Connecticut Avenue, N.W., Suite 200
Washington, DC 20009
(202) 483-1140
(202) 483-1248 FAX
www.epic.org

Federal Communications Commission
445 12th Street, S.W.
Washington, DC 20554
(888) 225-5322
(202) 418-0232 FAX
www.fcc.gov

Federal Trade Commission
CRC-240
Washington, D.C. 20580
(877) 382-4357
www.ftc.gov

Michigan Legislature
www.michiganlegislature.org
[Contains detailed and searchable records of Michigan laws and legislative activity]

Solid Waste and Recycling

BACKGROUND

Over the last few decades, the generation, recycling, and disposal of everyday garbage and trash—characterized by the U.S. Environmental Protection Agency (EPA) as municipal solid waste (MSW)—has changed dramatically.

Waste Generation

Currently, U.S. residents, businesses, and institutions produce about 230 million tons of MSW annually—approximately 4.6 pounds per person per day. Over the last 40 years the amount of waste generated annually has increased 161 percent and the amount generated per capita is up 70 percent (see Exhibit 1).

Because there are inadequate state data, the Michigan Department of Environmental Quality (MDEQ) uses national per capita estimates by the EPA to estimate the amount of MSW generated in Michigan: nearly 46 million tons annually. Waste generation would be even higher if not for such waste-prevention practices as composting, leaving grass clippings on the lawn, and reducing packaging.

Waste Disposal

Exhibit 2 shows that the amount of MSW disposed of nationally has doubled over the past 40 years, rising from about 83 million tons annually to 166 million. Fifteen percent is burned at combustion facilities, 57 percent is disposed of in landfills, and 28 percent is recycled.

EXHIBIT 1. Waste Generation, United States, 1960–1999

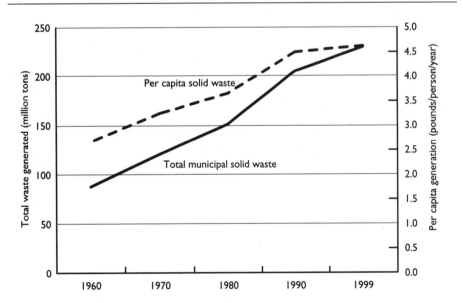

SOURCE: U.S. EPA (April 2000), Municipal Solid Waste in the United States: 1999 Facts and Figures.

Sponsored by the Michigan Nonprofit Association and the Council of Michigan Foundations

EXHIBIT 2. Waste Disposal and Recycling, United States, 1960–1999

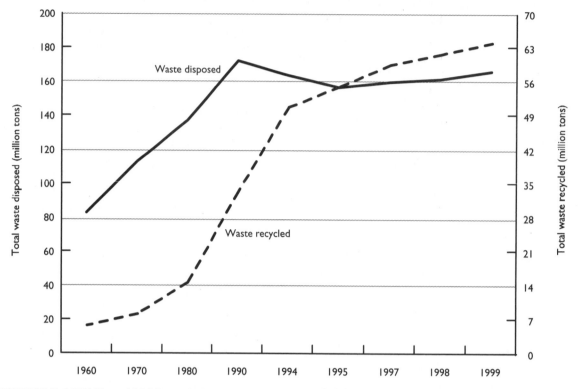

SOURCE: U.S. EPA (April 2000), Municipal Solid Waste in the United States: 1999 Facts and Figures..

Were it not for waste-prevention measures such as those mentioned above and other resource-recovery efforts, the problem would be much worse. In 1980, the year recycling began to "take off, " the amount of MSW that had to be disposed of nationally was 90 percent; today, at 72 percent, the figure is better.

Michigan MSW disposal-rate information has only recently been collected. In 1996 Public Act 359 amended the state Solid Waste Management Act and now requires landfills to report to the state the amount of waste received from all sources and geographic locations. Exhibit 3 shows that in 2001, 20 tons of MSW were disposed of in Michigan landfills; this is almost 43 percent more than in 1996, when data collection began.

State laws passed in the last decade have helped to reduce the amount of waste going into Michigan landfills, and, in some cases, the waste is put to good use. Examples of waste management include

■ barring yard waste from landfills and establishing composting sites—in some, humus is made from the waste for use as a soil conditioner;

EXHIBIT 3. Solid Waste Disposal, Michigan Landfills, 1996–2001

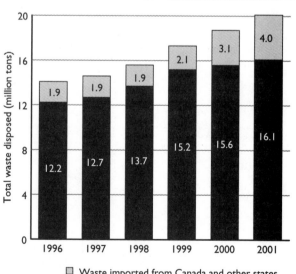

SOURCE: Michigan Department of Environmental Quality (April 2001), Report of Solid Waste Landfilled in Michigan.

- barring discarded tires from landfills and requiring that they be sent to and disposed of only in locations specifically set up for that purpose—in some, tires are prepared for recycling into other products; and

- barring from landfills products containing toxins and hazardous materials and requiring that they be disposed of in locations specifically established for that purpose—often a deposit is required on such products (e.g., refrigerators and wet-cell batteries) at purchase and refunded when they are returned for proper disposal.

Waste Management and Planning

The MDEQ's Waste Management Division administers the state's solid-waste program under part 115 of the state Natural Resources and Environmental Protection Act. The division

- reviews the construction permits and operating licenses for municipal and industrial nonhazardous solid-waste disposal facilities;

- inspects those facilities to ensure that they comply with operating requirements;

- manages the disposal-area financial-assurance program, which ensures that facility owners/operators have the funds necessary to meet the costs of (1) closure when capacity is reached, (2) post-closure maintenance and monitoring, and (3) corrective action if needed; and

- administers grants and loans related to waste-management planning and waste alternatives.

Among its other provisions, part 115 requires every Michigan county to develop and implement a solid-waste management plan. The plan must include input, through a local planning committee, from interested local organizations. A plan's purpose is to

- protect public health;

- assure adequate disposal capacity for all waste generated within county borders for 5- and 10-year periods of time;

- establish goals for waste prevention and recycling;

- control waste imported from or exported to other counties;

- define the roles of county and local governments in implementing and enforcing the plan; and

- assure that the county begins to investigate a new disposal site when a current site has less than five and a half years of capacity remaining.

Part 115 requires that the plans be updated every five years. The last round of updates occurred in 1997 and the next round was scheduled for 2002, but the MDEQ director has notified county boards of commissioners that the 2002 round will be delayed because of (1) state budget cuts, (2) pending revisions to the plan format and guidebook, and (3) the fact that many plans have been approved only recently.

Imported Waste

Among the states, Michigan is the third largest importer of MSW. Imported waste is not held to the same standards as in-state waste, and virtually all out-of-state MSW must be accepted because the U.S. Supreme Court has ruled that solid waste is an article of commerce subject to protection of the U.S. Constitution's Commerce Clause (*Philadelphia* v. *New Jersey*, 1978).

In 2001 Michigan imported four million tons from Canada, Illinois, Indiana, New Jersey, New York, Ohio, Pennsylvania, and Wisconsin—up 111 percent in the last five years (see Exhibit 3). Imported waste currently comprises 20 percent of all waste disposed of in Michigan, up from 12 percent in 1999. During the past two years, MSW imports from Canada have risen 156 percent and now constitute half of all imported waste received at Michigan landfills, the majority of it coming to Berrien, Monroe, Washtenaw, and Wayne counties.

Recycling

Nationally, recycling has increased from 10 percent of the MSW generated in 1980 to the current rate of 28 percent. In 1999 resource-recovery efforts prevented 64 million tons of materials from ending up in landfills and incinerators.

Michigan is one of eight states not collecting data about the amount of MSW recycled and/or composted annually. The Michigan Recycling Coalition (MRC) estimates that in 1999 Michigan recycled 2.5 million tons of MSW—about 16 percent of the state's discarded glass, metal, organic matter, paper, plastic, and other products. This is considerably lower than the average (26 percent) of all Great Lakes states. Recycling in Michigan includes curbside collection in 345 locales and drop-off collection in 413 others.

DISCUSSION

Bottle Bill

Legislation has been introduced to expand Michigan's so-called bottle bill (passed in 1976) to "new age" drinks, effective January 1, 2003. House Bill 4096 would require deposits on single-serving containers of bottled water, juice, and iced tea; SB 223 would extend the deposit re-

Sponsored by the Michigan Nonprofit Association and the Council of Michigan Foundations

quirement only to single-serving juice containers. Proponents cite the well-known recycling and environmental benefits that have resulted from the current law, which covers containers for beer, soft drinks, carbonated and mineral water, wine coolers, and canned cocktails.

Opponents claim that expanded coverage will impose a huge burden on retailers, who would have to take the additional returns. Storeowners say that the presence of dirty containers in a store where food is sold poses health risks, which expanding the practice would exacerbate, especially in view of recent changes in the state health code. They also point to the costs (including personnel) of collecting, processing, and storing the empties.

At this writing, a compromise seems possible whereby stores would receive incentives to buy bottle-return machines that are operated by customers, which would reduce retailers' health risks and personnel costs.

Waste Imports

As mentioned, Michigan is the nation's third largest trash importer. MDEQ officials estimate that Michigan's current major landfills will not fill up for another 15 years, but if garbage imports keep increasing at their current rate—up 47 percent in FY 1999–2000—the state could run out of room in a decade, accelerating the need for new sites.

At the federal level, the proposed Solid Waste International Transportation Act would authorize states to prohibit or limit the receipt and disposal of MSW generated outside the country. A similar bill, the Solid Waste Interstate Transport Act, also under consideration, would ban garbage generated outside a state unless a local government has agreed to accept it or the state specifically permits it. In Michigan, numerous bills are pending to address imported trash.

- In the Senate, SB 46 would hold out-of-state MSW to the same standards as in-state waste—that is, certain types of waste would be prohibited (e.g., wet-cell batteries, tires, and anything containing harmful toxins). Senate Bill 222 would prohibit any imported waste.

- In the House, HBs 5598–99 would require the MDEQ to inspect, at the border, every solid-waste unit transporting trash from Canada to Michigan. HB 5573 would hold waste ash generated out of state to the same standards as that generated in state. HB 5602 would prohibit trash from being imported from Canada unless it is in hermetically sealed containers to prevent it from entering the environment during

transport. HB 5561 would permit a county to ban solid waste or ash from its disposal areas if it was generated in a county that does not have a recycling rate comparable to its own. HB 4317 would prohibit solid waste or ash from being imported from states and countries that do not have a solid waste or disposal regulatory system at least as stringent as Michigan's.

Environmentalists strongly support legislation to restrict or ban the amount of waste being imported into Michigan. Waste-disposal companies fear that such a move would pose economic problems for their business and could harm many landfill-hosting communities as well. For example, Berrien County's Bertrand Township, population 2,300, earns about $50,000 a year from landfill fees, half from trash trucked in from Indiana and Illinois; the money goes mostly to road improvements.

Michigan may be attracting outside waste in part because it has done a better job of planning. Chicago and South Bend suburbs are among the out-of-state cities that find it less expensive to haul waste to Michigan than to plan, construct, and monitor sites in their own state.

The MDEQ opposes importation of waste from Canada but believes that banning or even limiting it would violate the U.S. Constitution or the North American Free Trade Agreement.

Scrap Tires

Michigan generates nine million scrap tires annually, which end up in stockpiles across the state that pose such health and safety hazards as breeding disease-carrying mosquitoes and rodents and catching fire from arson, accident, or lightning. Recycling methods developed to reduce the tire stockpiles include chipping the tires for use in gardens, playgrounds, parks, and road resurfacing material and also recycling them into new tires.

One recycling alternative—burning scrap tires to create power—garners considerable controversy. Citizens and environmentalists are concerned about the health implications of emissions from tire-burning power plants, which may contain human carcinogens and components of acid rain. Plant operators and the MDEQ claim that the public is safe as long as air-emissions standards are met. They say that no more pollutants result from burning tires than from burning such common fuel sources as wood and coal. Michigan has eight tire-burning power plants, and permits are being sought for two more.

Deep-Injection Wells

Deep-injection wells are very controversial. These wells are 4,000 to 5,000 feet deep and injected with liquid waste, most commonly leachate (liquidized garbage mixed with rainwater). There currently are 21 in Michigan; of the 15 that are active, five are used for hazardous waste. Another well, proposed for Romulus, recently was approved and is awaiting MDEQ licensure.

Opponents to deep-injection wells claim that they pollute the groundwater and pose other environmental hazards as well. Supporters say that the groundwater is safe because the waste is deposited below the water table.

FOR ADDITIONAL INFORMATION

Michigan Environmental Council
119 Pere Marquette Street
Lansing, MI 48912
(517) 487-9539
(517) 487-9541 FAX
www.mecprotects.org

Michigan Recycle Coalition
1609 East Kalamazoo Street, Suite One
P.O. Box 10240
Lansing, MI 48901
(517) 371-7073
(517) 371-1509 FAX
www.michiganrecycles.org

Office of Solid Waste
U.S. Environmental Protection Agency
Ariel Rios Building
1200 Pennsylvania Avenue, N.W.
Washington, DC 20460
(703) 308-8895
(703) 308-0513 FAX
www.epa.gov/osw

Waste Management Division
Michigan Department of Environmental Quality
Constitution Hall, Lower Level
525 West Allegan Street
P.O. Box 30241
Lansing MI 48909
(517) 373-2730
(517) 373-4797 FAX
www.michigan.gov/mdeq

Sponsored by the Michigan Nonprofit Association and the Council of Michigan Foundations

Special Education

BACKGROUND

Special education in Michigan is subject to federal laws that dictate the minimum standards with which states must comply. The major federal law relating to special education is the Individuals with Disabilities Education Act (IDEA) of 1974, which requires that all children with disabilities receive a "free, appropriate education" that meets their individual needs. To this end, each special-education student is assigned an individualized educational planning team (IEPT) consisting of educators, specialists, and the child's parents. The IEPT identifies each special-education pupil's academic needs and specifies the best way to educate him/her.

The federal act requires that special education be provided in the least restrictive environment possible, to ensure that special-education students are not unnecessarily segregated or treated in a way that is not equal to that of general-education pupils. IDEA also requires that children with disabilities be educated in the regular classroom unless the nature or severity of the disability is such that education in regular classes with the use of supplementary aids and services cannot be achieved "satisfactorily."

Michigan has its own special-education regulations that set a higher standard than the federal requirements. For example, certain services (particularly for children who are severely mentally or physically impaired) must be provided for 230 days a year, 50 more than required by federal law. The state also requires schools to educate students in some disability categories from birth to age 26, compared to birth through age 21 as required by federal law.

Currently, Michigan has about 228,000 students who receive some type of special-education service. The amount of time these students receive special-education instruction ranges from as little as an hour a day to all day. If calculated on a full-time equivalent (FTE) basis, the number of special-education students is 75,000.

The total number of special-education students has increased 17 percent in the last five years (since FY 1996–97) and 30 percent in the last decade. The FTE number is up 23 percent since FY 1996–97 (compared to a 3.4 percent increase in the general-education enrollment). The FTE special-education number currently comprises 4.4 percent of the total student population.

Disabilities as defined in Michigan range from severe multiple impairments to learning disability (LD); the latter—by far the largest disability category—refers to several conditions that impair one's ability to learn, including attention deficit disorder. Forty-two percent of the state's special-education pupils are classified as LD (see the exhibit), exactly the same percentage as five years ago.

Mainstreaming/Inclusion

In the 1980s, a few years after IDEA passed, *mainstreaming* (putting special-education students in regular classrooms) began to emerge as a common practice, but students with more severe disabilities still were educated in separate classrooms and included in a regular classroom for only a few hours a day. During the last several years, more parents of special-education students have been advocating having their children placed full

Michigan Special-Education Enrollment, by Disability, FY 2000–01

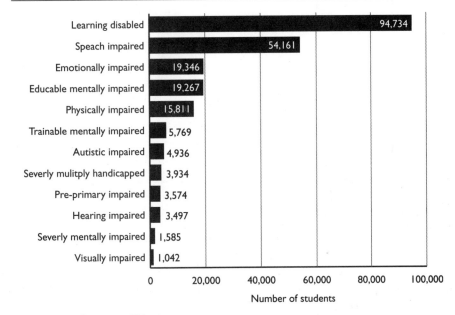

Learning disabled	94,734
Speach impaired	54,161
Emotionally impaired	19,346
Educable mentally impaired	19,267
Physically impaired	15,811
Trainable mentally impaired	5,769
Autistic impaired	4,936
Severly mulitply handicapped	3,934
Pre-primary impaired	3,574
Hearing impaired	3,497
Severly mentally impaired	1,585
Visually impaired	1,042

Number of students

SOURCE: Michigan Department of Education.

Least restrictive environment (LRE)
Federal law requires schools to educate special-education students in the least restrictive environment possible: "To the maximum extent appropriate, students with disabilities [should be] educated with children who are not disabled."

Mainstreaming/inclusion
Placing special-education students in general-education classrooms for all or part of the day; the latter generally is referred to as "inclusion."

Special education
Schooling of students with such disabilities as blindness, speech impairment, emotional disability, learning disability, or physical handicap.

time in general-education classrooms and, as a result, more IEPTs have been requiring it. Even students with very severe disabilities more frequently are being educated in regular classrooms for the full school day. Teacher's aides often are assigned to help the disabled students, or special-education teachers work with the student for part of the day in the regular classroom.

In 1997 IDEA was revised to strengthen the mainstreaming requirements. The IEPTs now must more clearly relate to the general-education curriculum, children with disabilities must be included in state and district assessments, and regular progress reports must be made to parents. Michigan and all states are revising their administrative rules to comply with the new federal guidelines; the result will accelerate the already strong trend toward educating special- and general-education students side by side.

Cost

The United States can boast that its education system is among the most equitable in the world because it makes a genuine effort to meet all students' needs. The trade-off for this equity is a higher education cost per student. Combined with the fact that more children are being classified as needing special education each year, per student special-education costs have been rising for many districts, and they constitute more of total school funding every year.

In Michigan (as elsewhere) there is insufficient good data to accurately measure annual, per capita, special-education costs. However, data reported by local districts to the state on the allowable special-education costs for state reimbursement permit a rough estimate: in total, more than $1.7 billion in FY 2000–01—an average of about $18,000 per FTE special-education pupil. The average for a general-education student was about $6,200, which means it costs nearly three times as much to educate a special-education pupil as it does a general-education student.

Special education's higher cost is due to several factors.

- Special-education class sizes must be small, to meet state and federal regulations and students' needs. Michigan administrative rules for special education specify, for example, that class size must not exceed 15 pupils for educable mentally impaired students and three for autistic students.

- Teacher aides are required in many instances as well. For example, when the class size for educable mentally impaired students reaches 12, schools must assign an aide to the class.

- Districts are having to pay growing staffing costs each year, partially due to a shortage of qualified special-education teachers in Michigan and nationwide and the need to have aides in regular classrooms to help mainstreamed special-education students.

Local school districts repeatedly have sued the state for requiring districts to provide special-education services without giving the districts the money to pay for them. Specifically, in *Durant v. State of Michigan,* a group of school districts claimed that the state, in violation of the state constitution, had imposed "unfunded mandates" on them for special education (and other) programs, forcing them to use general operations money for special-education purposes.

After 17 years of litigation, the Michigan Supreme Court agreed with the plaintiffs and ordered the state to pay the districts $212 million in retribution. Subsequently, to avoid future lawsuits, the state changed how it funds special education. The districts, however, took exception to the funding changes, arguing that the state simply shifted general operating funds into special education without increasing the overall amount of funding. As a result, there have been additional lawsuits: "Durant II" resulted in a change in the legal description of how special-education funds are paid, and "Durant III" currently is being litigated and could cost the state more than $400 million.

State policymakers point out that the federal government has imposed on the states an unfunded mandate for special-education services: While IDEA requires states to comply with numerous special-education requirements, the federal government does not provide the resources to pay for them. When IDEA initially was enacted, in 1974, it committed the federal government to reimbursing states for 40 percent of national average per pupil expenditures for educating disabled students, but the funds never were appropriated. In 2001 a battle was fought to finally pay the 40 percent—putting approximately $17.1 billion into state hands for special education—but the effort failed,

and the federal contribution in Michigan currently is about 20 percent.

DISCUSSION

As mentioned, more than 40 percent of the state's special-education pupils are classified as learning disabled. No one is certain why there are so many LD students in Michigan (and elsewhere as well). Some postulate that it reflects societal troubles, such as poor parenting, drug and alcohol use by expectant mothers, inadequate child nutrition, or children watching too much television. Others believe that more students are classified with learning or other disabilities than is warranted; they claim, for example, that some teachers classify students as "learning disabled" when it may be that they simply learn more slowly than others, which demands more of a teacher's time. These critics call for a stricter definition of what constitutes a "special-education" student or for schools to provide disincentives for teachers to classify students as needing special education.

Mainstreaming/Inclusion

Opponents to mainstreaming/inclusion argue that general-education teachers usually have had little, if any, special-education training and are unprepared to educate students with such disabilities as Down's Syndrome, blindness, deafness, or severe hearing loss. Some critics of full-time mainstreaming say that having certain special-education pupils in the same classroom as general-education pupils is detrimental to the latter, because teachers must devote too much time to the special needs of the disabled students. They point out that special-education children with emotional or other impairments often disrupt the classroom, taking time and attention away from general-student instruction. Finally, inclusion opponents fear that general-education academic standards will be lowered or the learning pace slowed to accommodate special-education students' needs.

Critics also maintain that mainstream schooling frequently is not in the best interest of the special-education student. They point out that general-education classes are a good deal larger than special-education classes, and pupils with special needs receive less personal attention than in center programs (facilities that serve special-education students from several districts) or special-education classrooms. They also contend that mainstreaming/inclusion means that students with disabilities have less contact with teachers specially suited and trained to teaching them. They point out that some parents who switch their children from center programs to mainstream classrooms end up returning them to the centers because they need the special facilities or the specially trained staff.

Mainstreaming advocates assert that being in a regular classroom is highly beneficial to special-education students. They say that these pupils suffer a stigma and lowered self-esteem when they are segregated in separate classrooms or buildings. They believe that students with disabilities have a need to "fit in" and to socialize with their peer group, and they are deprived of this when they are segregated. Advocates also point to studies that find that special-education pupils who are mainstreamed tend to have higher academic achievement, higher self-esteem, a greater probability of attending college, and better physical health than those who are not.

Many mainstreaming advocates also believe that mainstreaming benefits general-education students as well as special-education students; they believe that mainstreaming/inclusion promotes diversity in schools and helps all students to learn to accept others who are different from themselves. To counter the charge that general-education teachers are not adequately trained to educate children with special needs, mainstreaming/inclusion supporters point out that teachers sometimes have an aide or special-education teacher in the classroom with them. Many dispute the argument that disabled students slow the learning rate for the rest of the class, while others say it is irrelevant whether or not mainstreaming/inclusion slows the academic pace in classrooms, arguing that it is a civil right.

Despite the controversy over mainstreaming/inclusion, federal law requires it when possible. Schools must follow a child's IEPT decisions, and if the committee believes that a child should (or should not) be placed in a general-education classroom, federal law requires that the decision be carried out. The courts have reinforced federal law, finding that mainstreaming/inclusion is a right, not just a privilege, of disabled students.

Special-Education Costs

Although the state still is paying its Durant settlement, the special-education cost issue is not yet put to rest. As mentioned, the districts that sued the state in the Durant case claim that the state simply has shifted operating funds into special education and schools still have to sacrifice part of their general operating monies to pay special-education costs. The state believes it is in full compliance with the Durant ruling.

Not only have the Durant lawsuits focused further attention on special-education costs, but including disabled students in the regular classroom has made special education more visible to all. Some educators, lawmakers, and others say that special education requires an unacceptably high proportion of the state's school funds, and per student costs should be reduced. They say that the fact that state requirements in some cases exceed federal requirements means that the state could reduce costs by lowering these requirements. Among the changes they suggest are allowing larger class sizes for special-education students, reducing from 230 to 180 the number of days of instruction required, lowering from 26 to 21 years the age to which some special-education students must receive schooling, and easing some regulations pertaining to training special-education teachers.

The state recently undertook just such an effort when it began to revise the administrative rules for special education to comply with the 1997 IDEA revisions. The rules, established 25 years ago, set out the specific requirements that districts must follow to provide special education. One draft of the proposed changes included measures to ease state requirements for special education, including allowing larger class sizes and reducing the number of instruction days required. In public hearings, opponents of the changes protested vigorously that the quality of education for disabled students would be damaged, and the proposals to relax these requirements were dropped.

One less controversial policy option to reduce special-education enrollment (as well as to improve the performance of general-education students) is to use preschool education to help identify and intervene with children at risk of academic problems. In Michigan, the Michigan School Readiness Program (MSRP) has funding of more than $70 million annually to help serve four-year-olds. Also, in 2000, when the state had a large surplus in the state School Aid Fund, it created a $45 million program to help parents of children aged under five prepare their children for school and a $20 million program to expand the MSRP program to serve children for a longer period each day. While due to budget cuts these programs are not included in the governor's FY 2002–03 budget recommendations, the fact that they were created in the first place underscores the growing support for preschool as a way to help at-risk children at a younger age.

See also Children's Early Education and Care; K–12 Funding.

FOR ADDITIONAL INFORMATION

Citizens Alliance to Uphold Special Education
2365 Woodlake Drive, Suite 100
Okemos, MI 48864
(800) 221-9105
(517) 347-1004 FAX
www.causeonline.org

Sponsored by the Michigan Nonprofit Association and the Council of Michigan Foundations

SPECIAL EDUCATION

Michigan Association of School Administrators
1001 Centennial Way, Suite 300
Lansing, MI 48917
(517) 327-5910
(517) 327-0771 FAX
www.gomasa.org

National Center for Learning Disabilities
381 Park Avenue South, Suite 1401
New York, NY 10016
(212) 888-7373
(212) 545-9665 FAX
http://ncld.org

National Information Center for Children and Youth
 with Disabilities
P.O. Box 1492
Washington, DC 20013
(800) 695-0285
www.nichcy.org

Office of Special Education and Early Intervention Services
Michigan Department of Education
608 West Allegan Street
P.O. Box 30008
Lansing, MI 48909
(517) 373-3324
www.michigan.gov/mde/off/sped

Office of Special Education and Rehabilitative Services
U.S. Department of Education
400 Maryland Avenue, S.W.
Washington, DC 20202
(202) 205-5465
www.ed.gov/offices/OSERS

Substance Abuse

BACKGROUND

Problems associated with using alcohol, tobacco, and other drugs (ATOD) affect millions of Americans and have enormous financial and human costs. In financial terms, each year ATOD-related problems—including absenteeism, health and welfare expenses, property damage, accidents, and medical expenses—conservatively cost Michiganians more than $2 billion; lost productivity alone costs business and industry around $700 million. Nationally,

- alcohol and other drug use is a key factor in many violent crimes: domestic violence (as many as 87 percent of cases), manslaughter (as many as 68 percent), parental child abuse (64 percent), assault (62 percent), murder/attempted murder (54 percent), robbery (48 percent), and rape (42 percent);

- about 45 percent of traffic fatalities are caused by alcohol-related crashes;

- annually, 20–35 percent of the nation's nearly 30,000 suicide victims had a history of alcohol abuse or were drinking shortly before they died;

- among college students, 4.4 million are binge drinkers and another 1.9 million are heavy drinkers;

- almost half of all new HIV/AIDS cases are related to drug use; and

- 23 percent of Americans are smokers.

Alcohol and Tobacco

By a substantial margin, alcohol is the most widely abused drug in every age group—including children. The 2001 Michigan Youth Risk Behavior Survey (MYRBS) reveals that many Michigan youth use alcohol at a very young age. Underaged drinkers are more likely than others to engage in the dangerous behavior of binge drinking. The survey of 9–12th graders reveals that

- 77 percent have had one or more alcoholic drinks;

- 29 percent have had five or more alcoholic drinks in a row; and

- 32 percent have ridden in a vehicle driven by someone who had been drinking.

Alcohol use is also substantial among Michigan's adult population. Studies reveal that

- 94 percent have consumed alcohol;

- in the month preceding the survey, 59 percent had consumed alcohol; and

- an estimated 5.7 percent are chronic drinkers and another 19 percent are binge drinkers.

Tobacco is the second most commonly used drug among adolescents. According to the 2001 risk behavior surveys,

- 64 percent of 9–12th graders have smoked cigarettes;

Sponsored by the Michigan Nonprofit Association and the Council of Michigan Foundations

- 26 percent of 9–12th graders had smoked cigarettes in the 30 days preceding the survey;

- just under 18 percent of high school students smoke every day; and

- 24 percent of adults smoke.

Illicit Drugs

Marijuana is the most widely used illicit substance among all age groups, but "club" drug use is increasing. The 2001 MYRBS finds that among Michigan high schoolers,

- 44 percent have used marijuana, and in the month preceding the survey, 24 percent had used it;

- 8 percent have used cocaine (powder, crack, or freebase); and

- in the preceding year, 36 percent had been offered, sold, or given an illegal drug on school property.

The 1999 National Household Survey on Drug Abuse shows that among Michigan adults,

- in the month preceding the survey, about 5 percent had used marijuana;

- almost 7 percent had used an illicit drug in the preceding month; and

- nearly 2 percent had used cocaine during the preceding year.

Financial Burden

The National Center on Addiction and Substance Abuse (Columbia University) reports that in 1998 (the latest year for which comparable data are available) all states spent a total of $81 billion—more than 13 percent of their collective budget—on problems related to substance abuse and addiction. Michigan spent $2.7 billion, just over 12 percent of its budget. Michigan's per capita spending related to the burden of substance abuse on public programs is 12th highest in the nation. (Michigan is third from the bottom in spending on substance-abuse prevention, treatment, and research.)

Of every substance-abuse dollar spent by the state, one cent was for prevention and treatment programs and 99 cents was to pay for the burden the problem imposes on public programs—e.g., criminal justice, Medicaid, child welfare, and mental health. Of the $1.3 billion spent on justice-related programs in Michigan, $1.1 billion was linked to substance abuse.

According to the Tobacco-Free Michigan Action Coalition, tobacco use indirectly costs Michigan taxpayers $2.5 billion annually for health care, lost productivity, and absenteeism. The coalition says that Medicaid payments related to smoking totaled $350 million in Michigan in 2000. The national Centers for Disease Control and Prevention reports that nationally, every pack of cigarettes sold costs $7 in medical care and lost productivity.

Combating ATOD Use

Surveys reveal that almost 10 percent of Michigan's population—more than one million people—either are dependent on or abuse one or more substances. From 1995 to 1997, more than 3,500 state residents died because of their substance abuse/dependence problem. Major state initiatives to combat substance abuse fall into three categories: prevention, treatment, and law enforcement.

The Michigan Department of Education is responsible for one of the state's most comprehensive ATOD-use prevention efforts: the Michigan Model for Comprehensive School Health Education (the Michigan Model), which currently is being taught in 90 percent of Michigan's public schools and many private schools.

The Division of Substance Abuse Quality and Planning in the Michigan Department of Community Health (MDCH) is responsible for carrying out state and federal substance-abuse mandates. The division's key responsibility is to develop, administer, and coordinate public and private funding and other resources for substance-abuse prevention and treatment services. The division contracts with 15 regional coordinating agencies, which, in turn, identify local needs and priorities and subcontract with local programs that provide necessary services.

The Office of Drug Control Policy, also in the MDCH, focuses mainly on enforcing drug laws and monitoring the state's Safe and Drug-Free Schools and Communities initiative—a state and federal government effort to curb drug use among teens. The office also oversees the Drug Abuse Resistance Education (DARE) program, which entails uniformed law-enforcement personnel teaching substance-abuse and violence prevention to children.

DISCUSSION

Although most people agree that ATOD use has enormous economic and social consequences, they are uncertain about the best policy for alleviating the problem. As with any government program, the financial and other resources available to address substance abuse are limited. Thus policymakers must determine how those resources will be balanced among the three methods to combat the problem—prevention, treatment, and law enforcement.

Prevention

Many people believe that significant resources should be targeted toward prevention because such initiatives often are the least expensive, reach the most people, and, in the long run, yield savings. Yet a recent report by the Michigan Association of Substance Abuse Coordinating Agencies finds that Michigan's contribution to substance-abuse prevention and treatment has not increased in more than ten years.

The State of Michigan currently spends about $15.6 million annually to fund community-based prevention programs. This money is distributed to the 15 substance-abuse coordinating agencies throughout the state, which allocate the funds to programs in their regions. In addition, about $3.2 million is appropriated annually for the Michigan Model program, with 30 percent of these funds used to train teachers on substance-abuse prevention curriculum and to purchase prevention materials.

Many argue that spending for prevention is insufficient, especially in view of its long-term benefits. Some point to funds from the tobacco settlement as a possible source of prevention funding, but even among these advocates, there is greater support for using settlement monies to cover the costs of treating people with smoking-related illnesses.

Treatment and Law Enforcement

Currently, the larger debate centers on how spending should be divided between treatment and law enforcement. Some argue for more resources to be spent on treating people who currently have ATOD problems because (1) their problems are contributing to law-enforcement and corrections costs, health care costs, and other social problems, and (2) treatment is shown to be effective in reducing these problems and costs. Others contend that the funding priority should be law enforcement because the rest of society deserves to be protected from those who engage in ATOD abuse and drug trafficking.

Currently, state spending is directed more to law enforcement than the other methods, although efforts are underway to change drug and alcohol violation laws in ways that may dramatically change future spending. Initiatives to make changes in mandatory minimum sentencing, to divert more low-level drug and alcohol offenders into treatment, and to make treatment more readily available to anyone who needs it are among the primary efforts being proposed.

Mandatory Minimum Sentencing

While three prisons recently closed in Michigan, the state's prison population is growing at a rate of 120 prisoners a month. Of the almost 10,000 drug cases in Michigan courts

in 1999, almost 4,000 resulted in incarceration in a state prison or county jail. Michigan drug laws remain among the most stringent in the nation despite reform of Michigan's "650 lifer" law, which required a mandatory sentence of life without parole for individuals convicted of delivering 650 grams or more of cocaine or heroin (these offenders now are eligible for parole at 15, 17½, or 20 years, based on their prior record and cooperation).

Two bills currently before the legislature (HBs 5394–95) would require judges, in setting sentences for major drug crimes, to follow guidelines that take into account such variables as whether there were prior offenses and whether there was physical injury caused to the victim, even if it would mean imposing a sentence that is less than the mandatory minimum. In addition, the use of mandatory consecutive sentencing ("stacked sentences") would be limited to major drug dealers. The bills also would repeal "lifetime probation" for the lowest-level drug offenders.

Supporters of these bills point to the problems caused by limiting a judge's discretion in sentencing. When judges are not allowed to consider additional factors, they may be forced to send someone to prison for a much longer period of time than his/her crime merits; this may be more harsh than necessary and also contribute to prison overcrowding.

Opponents argue that the threat of harsh sentences is a deterrent to drug dealers and traffickers. They also believe that drug dealers of any level should receive stiff penalties to keep them from providing harmful substances to children, which proliferates the already considerable problems of substance abuse and addiction.

Treating Offenders

According to several studies, treatment reduces drug use by 40–60 percent and significantly decreases criminal activity during and after treatment. The Campaign for New Drug Policies currently is working on a Michigan ballot initiative that would divert nonviolent offenders convicted of drug possession from prison to treatment; similar initiatives have passed in 17 states, including Arizona and California. If passed, the Michigan initiative would

- require a 20-year mandatory minimum sentence for drug kingpins (defined by the individual's role in organizing and profiting from the crime) and major drug traffickers;

- establish a Drug Sentencing Commission to construct sentencing guidelines for mid- and low-level drug dealers that are based on the offender's role in the crime; and

Sponsored by the Michigan Nonprofit Association and the Council of Michigan Foundations

■ provide court-ordered treatment instead of jail for certain nonviolent drug users.

The program would allocate $18 million to treatment programs above and beyond current funding for treatment. The state also would be required to restore FY 2000–01 funding levels for drug treatment, prevention, and related rehabilitation programs, effectively reversing budget cuts of 2002.

Proponents of this initiative—or similar programming if the initiative fails—believe that treating rather than jailing low-level, nonviolent, drug offenders will reduce the burden on over-crowded prisons, and they point out that the cost of long-term residential treatment (the most expensive treatment option) is significantly less than the cost of incarceration ($30,400 a year). They argue that treatment through any means—court-ordered or self-referred—will reduce the prison population and result in significant savings to state and local corrections agencies.

Opponents note that such changes will not solve prison crowding, as Michigan already diverts many low-level drug offenders into treatment. In fact, fewer than 5,000 of the state's 47,000 inmates are serving time for drug crimes. Some also worry that this initiative will create a "soft" stance on drug use and encourage future efforts to legalize illegal substances.

Insurance Parity

Senate Bills 101–02 (similar to HBs 5123 and 5128) would require that group or nongroup coverage provided by Blue Cross Blue Shield of Michigan, policies issued by insurers, and contracts issued by health maintenance organizations provide *parity* for both substance-abuse and mental-health treatment. Parity would mean that deductibles, co-pays, and benefit or service limitations for substance-abuse and mental-health treatment may not be more restrictive than they are for other treatment.

Many see insurance parity as a key public policy issue. Because more than 70 percent of people who currently use illicit drugs, as well as 75 percent of individuals who are alcoholics, are employed and may have health insurance, parity would improve many people's access to appropriate and adequate treatment. Others point out that if substance-abuse insurance parity is mandated, insurance premiums surely will rise, and they worry that this would force some people to elect to go without coverage or lead some employers to drop coverage.

Counter to these fears, studies find that the effect of substance-abuse parity on premiums is so small that there is minimal likelihood that individuals would lose coverage. Numerous studies conclude that parity will increase premiums by less than one percent, or less than $1 per family member per month.

These bills' supporters further point to the cost of leaving addiction untreated: Nationally, according to a 1996 federal Center for Substance Abuse Treatment study, alcohol and illicit drug use in the workplace costs $140 billion a year in lost productivity, medical claims, and accidents.

Treatment Effectiveness

Because not all addicts remain abstinent after treatment, it may appear that treating substance abuse and addiction is ineffective, and this has been a primary argument against both diverting low-level offenders from incarceration to treatment and providing insurance parity for treatment. Many believe that substance abuse is a matter of choice and, if they wish, addicts can choose to stop using alcohol and other drugs. Treatment proponents point to research showing that (1) substance abuse is an illness characterized by complex biological, psychological, and social causes and effects, and (2) appropriate treatment much improves the chances of successful recovery.

Through the years, the predominant view has been that abuse and dependency are diseases or manifestations of disease, and the success rates associated with addiction treatment are equivalent to those of such chronic diseases as diabetes, hypertension, and asthma. Several conservative estimates find that every $1 invested in addiction treatment yields a savings of $4–7 in reduced drug-related crime, criminal justice costs, and theft. A Chevron Corporation study (1990) found that the company saved $10 for every $1 it spent to treat employees with substance-abuse problems.

See also Communicable Diseases and Public Health; Crime and Corrections; Highway Funding and Safety; Mental Health Funding and Services; Tobacco Settlement; Youth at Risk.

FOR ADDITIONAL INFORMATION

Division of Substance Abuse Quality and Planning
Michigan Department of Community Health
Lewis Cass Building, 2d Floor
320 South Walnut Street
Lansing, MI 48913
(517) 335-0278
(517) 241-2611 FAX
www.michigan.gov/mdch

Sponsored by the Michigan Nonprofit Association and the Council of Michigan Foundations

East Coast Office
Campaign for New Drug Policies
[Michigan office expected to open soon]
Michigan@drugreform.org
(617) 330-8777
(617) 330-8774 FAX
www.drugreform.org

Learning Support Unit
Office of School Excellence
Michigan Department of Education
608 West Allegan Street
P.O. Box 30008
Lansing, MI 48909
(517) 241-4284
(517) 373-1233 FAX
www.michigan.gov/mde

Michigan Association of Substance Abuse
   Coordinating Agencies
2875 Northwind Drive, Suite 215
East Lansing, MI 48823
(517) 337-4406
(517) 337-8578 FAX

Office of Drug Control Policy
Michigan Department of Community Health
Lewis Cass Building, 2d Floor
320 South Walnut Street
Lansing, MI 48913
(517) 373-4700
(517) 373-2963 FAX
www.michigan.gov/mdch

Sponsored by the Michigan Nonprofit Association and the Council of Michigan Foundations

Taxes on Businesses

BACKGROUND

According to a 1995 study (latest available data) by the Institute on Taxation and Economic Policy (Washington), 42 percent of Michigan's state and local taxes are collected from business, slightly more than the national average of roughly 41 percent; Michigan ranks 34th highest among the 50 states. The major levies affecting Michigan businesses are

- the single business tax (SBT),
- real and personal property taxes (state and local),
- the unemployment insurance (UI) tax,
- vehicle fuel and registration taxes,
- the sales tax (although this is a consumer rather than a business levy, an estimated 25–30 percent is paid by business), and
- workers' disability compensation insurance (although this is not a tax, it is a major business cost imposed by government).

It is unlikely that the final incidence of these costs falls on business: A large share is passed on to consumers, employees, or shareholders in the form of higher prices, lower salaries, or lower profit.

Since 1991 business taxes in Michigan have been reduced significantly. The Senate Fiscal Agency estimates that in fiscal year 2000–01, tax savings to business will total about $1.5 billion, including $850 million in SBT relief. The next most likely candidate for major reduction is the personal property tax on machinery and equipment.

All the levies are discussed below except the sales tax and vehicle fuel/registration taxes, which are discussed elsewhere in this book.

Single Business Tax

The SBT, easily Michigan's most important business tax, is a levy on the value a business adds to its product during production, whether the product is automobiles or legal services. The main components of the added value are labor, interest paid, depreciation, and profit. An SBT deduction is allowed for capital investment, and special relief is provided for firms that are labor intensive or have gross receipts below a certain level; complete exemption is allowed for very small businesses.

The current rate (tax year 2002) is 1.9 percent. The original rate was 2.35 percent, which was reduced to 2.3 percent in 1994. In 1999 legislation was enacted that reduces the rate 0.1 percent each year until the tax is eliminated.

The SBT took effect in 1976 as a replacement for seven business taxes, of which the largest three were the corporate income tax, personal property tax on inventory, and corporate franchise tax. Not only has the SBT added stability to the Michigan tax structure, but it has exhibited reasonably good growth potential: Collections rose from about $800 million in the levy's first full year (FY 1976–77) to about $2.2 billion in FY 2000–

01. The latter figure is down from about $2.5 billion in the prior year due to the 0.1 percent rate reduction and the weak Michigan economy.

Single business tax receipts comprised about 9 percent of all state tax revenue when the levy went into effect, rose to a high of 17.5 percent in 1988, and now are back to 9 percent. The exhibit shows the distribution of SBT revenue by industry class for FY 1997–98 (latest data available). Manufacturing provides the largest part of SBT revenue, roughly 39 percent, but in the last decade its share has declined from about 55 percent. In comparison, the services sector's share rose from about 10 percent to 18 percent.

In theory, a value-added tax should extract a contribution from all firms, regardless of organization, size, or business type. In practice, however, more than half the businesses in Michigan do not have an SBT liability largely because of an exemption for small firms and the deduction for capital investment; about 75 percent of the tax is paid by 5 percent of the firms. The SBT's actual effective rate (after credits, exemptions, and deductions are applied) is 1.57 percent; it rises from 0.2 percent for the smallest firms to 1.98 percent for businesses with a tax base exceeding $100 million. (These calculations are based on FY 1997–98 data

Distribution of Single Business Tax Collections, by Industry (quarterly payments only), FY 1997–98

Industry	Tax Liability (thousands)	Percentage of Total
Forestry, fishing, and agriculture	$8,552	0.4%
Mining	9,740	0.4
Construction	102,725	4.4
Manufacturing	913,136	39.4
Nondurable goods	208,111	0.9
Transportation equipment	295,436	12.8
Other durable goods	409,588	17.6
Transportation	46,297	2.0
Communication and utilities	168,688	7.3
Wholesale trade	109,191	4.7
Retail trade	312,384	13.5
Finance, insurance, and real estate	176,524	7.6
Services	425,279	18.4
Other	42,701	1.8
TOTAL	$2,315,219	100.0%

SOURCE: Michigan Department of Treasury (July 2001), The Michigan Single Business Tax, 1997–98.
NOTE: 1997–98 data are the latest available.

and do not reflect subsequent revisions to the SBT, but the changes probably have not substantially altered the tax's effective rate.)

Over the years there have been many important revisions to the SBT. One concerns the capital acquisition deduction (CAD)—the SBT deduction allowed for purchase of real and personal property—and is being challenged in court. To make the CAD more fair to firms doing business in Michigan but headquartered in other states, multistate SBT payers are permitted to apportion their deduction using the same formula they use to apportion their tax base. This is a three-factor formula involving the portions of a firm's payroll, property, and sales that are located in Michigan. For tax years after 1998, the in-state sales factor increased to 90 percent (up from 80 percent) and the Michigan payroll and property factors each fell to 5 percent (down from 10 percent). The change has been challenged by an Illinois corporation that contends that the Michigan CAD burdens out-of-state businesses and discriminates against interstate commerce. The state court of claims agreed, but the appeals court ruled in 2001 that the CAD is not designed to punish multistate taxpayers and it has not harmed those who choose to increase their Michigan presence. The case is expected to be appealed to the Michigan Supreme Court. If ruled unconstitutional, the tax will revert to the old CAD calculation and the sales-payroll-property apportionment formula will return to 70-15-15 percent.

The most recent and far-reaching SBT change was enacted in 1999, reducing the rate 0.1 percent each year until 2021, when the tax is completely eliminated. The legislation does include a provision that suspends the phaseout if the balance in the Budget Stabilization Fund falls below $250 million, which may be the case by the end of FY 2002–03.

Property Tax

The property tax is Michigan's oldest form of taxation, dating back to 1893. State government and all local governments levy taxes on the value of real and personal property owned by commercial operations; in addition, the state levies a tax on utility property, which equates to the statewide average property tax rate for commercial, industrial, and utility property (50.82 mills in 2000). All other business property, classified as commercial or industrial, is taxed at varying rates by local government units.

In 2000, for all jurisdictions, taxes on real property will generate about $8 billion and on personal property about $1.7 billion. Of total business property taxes, about two-thirds are levied on real property and one-third on personal property.

Sponsored by the Michigan Nonprofit Association and the Council of Michigan Foundations

Real Property

The school finance reform legislation of 1993 and 1994 (Proposal A) changed the manner in which residential and business properties are taxed. Prior to the reforms, both were taxed in the same way, but at varying rates, by local government units. Under the new system,

■ a 6-mill statewide education tax on all property is levied for the state School Aid Fund, and

■ an 18-mill school operating levy on business property is levied for local school districts.

As a result of the reform, the average tax rate for all property in 2000 was 39.32 mills, down from 56.64 mills in 1993, the last year under the old system. The average tax rate on business property in 2000 was 50.82 mills; on non-business property the average was 32.8 mills. In 2000 business paid just under $4 billion in property taxes—roughly 42 percent of all property tax paid in the state. In 1993 business had paid about 28 percent of all property taxes.

All property, other than utility, is assessed by its local government and equalized by the county and the state. The annual assessment increase on each parcel is limited to the inflation rate or 5 percent, whichever is less (in 2001, assessments were limited to a 3.2 percent increase). When property is sold, it is reassessed at current market value. Local governments thus must keep track of two values for each parcel: the taxable value and the assessed value. The assessment cap is more beneficial to residential than business property, because the former generally increases more in value.

Personal Property

Personal property generally is defined as property not permanently affixed to land: e.g., equipment, furniture, tools, computers. In Michigan, only businesses pay the personal property tax (PPT). From 1985 to 2000, personal property taxes grew from $668 million to about $1.7 billion—an increase of over 150 percent (about 57 percent when adjusted for inflation).

The state levies 6 mills on personal property, the same as Proposal A established for real property. There are state and local taxes that are tied to the PPT (i.e., state utilities tax and industrial facilities tax). The local levy varies from place to place, depending on what has been approved by local voters. Thus, if in City A, 12 mills are levied on real property, 12 mills also are levied on the personal property of those who must pay it.

Reliance on PPT collections varies across the state. In some rural counties, less than $10 million is raised annually from it, while in some more populous counties the figure exceeds $3 billion. In some counties the PPT represents less than 5 percent of total taxable property value; in others it is significant—in Midland and Kalkaska counties, 35 percent and 22 percent, respectively (2001). The statewide average is about 12 percent.

Although Proposal A substantially reduced the PPT (the average nonhomestead, which includes business property, rate fell from 56.6 to 48.17 mills, about a 15 percent decline), most statewide business associations still list PPT repeal as a major legislative goal.

Thirty-five states levy a PPT and in most, the levy is similar to Michigan's. Ten, including Illinois, New York, and Pennsylvania, have no PPT. The remaining five levy a PPT but allow specific exemptions (e.g., for manufacturing equipment).

Workers' Disability and Unemployment Compensation

In early 2002 the governor signed an executive order (1) combining the Unemployment Agency and the Bureau of Workers' Compensation into a new Bureau of Workers' and Unemployment Compensation and (2) moving the new bureau—along with the Wage and Hour Division—into the Michigan Department of Consumer and Industry Services. The objective is to combine functions with a similar purpose into a single agency: Workers' compensation and unemployment assistance benefits exist to replace wages lost by workers, and the Wage and Hour Division collects wages and fringe benefits owed to workers.

Workers' Disability Compensation

Although workers' compensation is a major business cost, it is not a tax. The law requires that every employer subject to the federal Workers' Disability Compensation Act provide a way to assure that it can pay benefits to its workers injured on the job. Most companies buy insurance to protect them from workers' injury claims. With state permission, some financially sound employers are permitted to self-insure for this coverage by paying into a regulated pool.

The state's assigned-risk pool (a state-managed entity from which hard-to-insure companies may purchase coverage) cut its rates every year from 1996 to 2000, but in 2001 rates increased for the first time in several years largely because (1) a major insurance writer went out of business, (2) reinsurance rates increased sharply after the September 11 terrorist attacks, and (3) rates had been artificially low in the past few years due in part to recent rate cuts.

According to the Workers' Compensation Research Institute (Cambridge), Michigan's workers' compensation system is improving, as indicated by three measures.

Sponsored by the Michigan Nonprofit Association and the Council of Michigan Foundations

- From 1992 to 2000, the annual average total benefits per worker fell more than 5 percent (adjusted for inflation).

- From 1992 to 2000, the number of lost-time claims per 100 workers (the claim rate) fell from 2.5 to about 1.5 percent.

- From 1991 to 2001, the interval from the time a dispute is filed to when a decision is handed down following a formal hearing fell from 18.1 to 12.6 months.

There are many ways to compare workers' compensation state by state. The National Academy of Social Insurance (Washington) has published 1999 state data showing that indemnity and medical benefits paid in Michigan amount to 0.9 percent of covered payroll. The national average is 1.05 percent, and Michigan ranks roughly in the middle of the pack: 28th among the 50 states.

Unemployment Compensation
Unemployment insurance (UI) is a form of social insurance, administered in Michigan by the state Unemployment Agency (UA). It is designed to provide money to help workers replace some of their lost wages after becoming unemployed. Unemployment insurance taxes are paid by almost all businesses that (1) employ one or more employees in any 20 given weeks in a calendar year or (2) in a calendar year paid $41,000 or more in payroll to employees covered by unemployment insurance.

Michigan's average weekly UI benefit in the 2d quarter of 2001 was $262, about 37 percent of the $710 statewide average weekly wage. Nationally, the average weekly benefit was $229 a week in 2000. Michigan ranks 8th in average wage and 31st in wage replacement.

Employers pay two unemployment taxes: federal and state. The Federal Unemployment Trust Account (FUTA) assesses an effective rate of 0.8 percent against the first $7,000 of each employee's wage. This money goes into the federal fund, which doesn't directly pay benefits to former workers but does assist the state with administrative and other costs associated with the program.

The state tax is levied on the first $9,500 of each covered employee's wages paid each calendar year, and the rate paid on that $9,500 is phased in over a business's first five years in operation. The taxes are deposited in the state Unemployment Insurance Trust Fund, which makes payments to workers who have become unemployed. Each employer has an "account"—that is, a record is kept on how much the firm has paid in and how much the trust fund has paid out in benefits to the firm's former workers.

- Generally, in the first four years of a business's liability, the tax rate varies according to the type of business it is and how much in benefits has been paid out in the firm's behalf (for further detail, readers are directed to *Michigan in Brief, 6th Edition*, at *www.michiganinbrief.org*).

- In the fifth and subsequent years, the firm's tax rate is based on the full amount of any unemployment benefits paid out and whether it has built any reserve in its account. For 2001 tax rates may range from 0.1 percent (for businesses that have had no layoffs in the last seven years and an adequate reserve in their account) to 8.1 percent (for firms with high layoffs and little or no reserve).

Public Act 25 of 1995 made several important changes in unemployment taxes and the changes resulted in UI taxes being reduced every year since. Although Michigan's jobless tax sometimes goes as high as 10 percent, rates normally range from 0.1–8.1 percent. In 2002 some 161,000 employers will receive a 10 percent across-the-board cut in their unemployment taxes and about 105,000 will qualify for reductions in the account-building component of their tax rate; each tax cut will save employers a total of about $100 million. The reductions will apply to employers who are "fully experience rated"—typically those who have been in business for at least five years. They will be incorporated into the 2002 tax rate notices that the UA will issue to employers in December.

The average employer tax rate as a percentage of taxable wages fell from a recent high of 4.46 percent in 1994 and an all-time high of 5.71 percent in 1985 to 2.78 percent in 1998 (latest data available). The balance in the UI Trust Fund, which needs to be substantial as a cushion against recession, was $2.9 billion as of June 30, 2001.

DISCUSSION

Single Business Tax
The SBT generates controversy mainly for two reasons: It (1) substantially increased the tax burden of many businesses that had been paying little or no tax, and (2) requires a tax payment even when no profit is earned. Some have argued that the SBT hurts small firms and that a business should not pay a tax unless it earns a profit. Others contend that because all firms use government services, all should make a contribution (as with the local property tax) regardless of whether a profit is reported, that a two-tier tax structure would be unfair, that moving to a profits tax would make the SBT more unstable, and that the tax burden on most small businesses is too minor to have a negative effect on them.

Sponsored by the Michigan Nonprofit Association and the Council of Michigan Foundations

Many observers believe the complete phaseout of the tax was an overreaction to claims that the tax is too complex, unfair to small business, and not based on ability to pay. They believe that many SBT critics lost sight of the levy's original purposes: to (1) simplify the tax system, (2) increase its stability, (3) provide a more neutral tax treatment for businesses, and (4) improve the investment climate.

Supporters of the tax point out that in large part the goals have been achieved, but they were compromised over the years by numerous changes in the tax. Currently, the major concerns are (1) the revenue loss due to the phase-out—about $130 million annually—and (2) the fact that when the tax is completely phased out, there will be no major state tax on business, which will shift the burden to the individual taxpayer.

Phase-out supporters argue that business taxes are passed on to the consumer, result in businesses paying lower wages, and result in owners earning lower profits. Some observers believe that a case can be made to simplify the tax and return it to its original purpose by eliminating most special provisions and lowering the rate rather than phasing the levy out.

Property Tax

Prior to passage of school finance reform and the reduction in property tax rates, Michigan's property tax burden was about one-third above the national average and 50 percent above the burden in the adjoining states of Ohio and Indiana, which caused many to view the tax as detrimental to economic development, particularly in southeast Michigan, where tax rates are higher than in most other regions of the state. Since the reforms, Michigan is at about the national average, although the tax on business still is modestly higher.

While real property tax is of less concern since the reforms, the business community still views the personal property tax on machinery and equipment as a large negative for the business climate.

Opponents of the PPT argue that it is a major reason that the cost to locate or expand a business in Michigan is higher than elsewhere, and business leaders see the tax as one of the top five anti-competitive provisions of Michigan law. Some analysts argue that since the nontax costs of production sometimes are higher in Michigan than elsewhere (labor costs usually are mentioned), to attract new jobs the tax burden for business actually should be lower than in competing states.

Opponents also argue that administrating the PPT is burdensome and unfair. Unlike the tax on real property, personal property is self-reported by each firm. Each year, every business must provide the local assessor with a form itemizing each piece of personal property and its age. The assessor then assigns a value, using depreciation schedules published by the state, to each item. This self-reporting, opponents argue, is time-consuming for businesses and leads to substantial underreporting.

The Michigan Chamber of Commerce's goal is to eliminate the PPT, and to that end, it supports

- enacting legislation to (1) annually exempt the first $25,000 in assessed and taxable value per jurisdiction, (2) remove such intangible costs as sales tax, freight, labor, and engineering charges from the tax base, (3) define buildings on leased land and certain leasehold improvements as "unsecured" real property, and (4) adequately fund the annual updating of all tangible PPT depreciation tables promulgated by the State Tax Commission;

- revising P.A. 328 of 1998 to allow all communities, not just distressed areas, to abate all new personal property taxes so as to spur economic development;

- providing relief for any taxpayer assessed in lieu of the general ad valorem (value-added) tax regime, either through higher or new SBT credits; and

- enacting legislation to end the discriminatory nature of the assessment and taxation of intangible property owned by telecommunication and railroad companies (only the tangible personal property of other property taxpayers is assessed and taxed).

Some analysts believe that eliminating, reducing, or reforming the PPT is easier said than done, and they point out that

- reducing or eliminating the tax would affect the revenue stream to Michigan government at all levels: city, county, township, school, and state;

- since the PPT base varies widely across the state, the effect of reducing or eliminating the tax would be much greater in some places than others;

- the tax is in large part a local tax that could be changed or eliminated by state law;

- it is very difficult to quantify the economic effect of reducing the PPT; and

- there is a long list of technical questions involved in reform.

Both opponents and proponents of changing or eliminating the PPT agree that it negatively affects economic development, but they disagree on how much and in what circumstances. Opponents do not believe that reducing/eliminating the PPT will increase economic activity enough to offset the direct revenue loss.

Among the technical problems that would arise in PPT reform is the fact that personal property never has been tightly defined in state law. Although some categories of personal property are mentioned in statute, personal property generally is defined as all property that is "not real." Since in Michigan the tax rates on real and personal property always have been identical, this vagueness has not been too troublesome, but the statutory distinction between the two will become very important if personal property comes to be taxed at a lower rate than real property.

Currently, there are no specific proposals to reduce or modify the PPT. The state did revise the depreciation schedules in 1999, the first major revision since 1964, but some jurisdictions still are not using them for utility property. Based on the property's age and useful life, these schedules determine depreciation factors that then are multiplied by the property's original cost; this calculation establishes the item's taxable value. Many observers argue that the state's use of only a few schedules results in the actual value of personal property being misrepresented for many businesses.

A number of reform proposals have been offered in the past, and one or more of these could reemerge. Readers are directed to *Michigan in Brief, 6th edition,* at *www.michiganinbrief.org* for a list of these options.

Workers' Disability Compensation Costs

Despite recent cost declines, the business community still believes legislation is needed to reduce fraudulent and unwarranted claims. The Michigan Manufacturers Association reports that its membership surveys show that workers' compensation costs rank among the matters that most concern manufacturers.

Unemployment Compensation Tax

Unemployment insurance costs long have been viewed by the business community as a burden and a deterrent to economic development. Others see UI benefits as essential to keeping unemployed workers and their families from quickly falling into poverty. In 1998 UI taxes paid by Michigan businesses amounted to $103 per capita, 30 percent above the U.S. average of $79. Since 1996 unemployment taxes have been cut every year, for a total savings of about $1.2 billion, which has brought Michigan more in line with other states and reduced the negative effect that UI taxes have on the state's business climate.

These taxes pay for benefits: In 2001 the *average* weekly benefit paid in Michigan was $262 per capita, about 14 percent above the national average (down from 18 percent in 1995) and the highest in the Great Lakes region. Michigan's *maximum* weekly benefit of $300 is the lowest in the Great Lakes states, however, and 21st lowest among all the states.

The governor has recommended that UI benefits be increased for the first time since 1996. There is general agreement that the maximum weekly benefit should be increased from $300 to $415, but there is serious disagreement on one issue: Republicans want to establish a "waiting week," meaning that unemployed workers would not get benefits for the first week they are out of work. The waiting week, which 38 other states have, would reduce the amount Michigan businesses have to pay into the UI fund. Democrats and organized labor oppose the provision, arguing that a waiting week unnecessarily penalizes the unemployed. At this writing, a conference committee is working to resolve differences in legislation passed by the House and Senate to raise the weekly benefit.

See also K–12 Funding; Highway Funding and Safety; Taxes on Consumers.

FOR ADDITIONAL INFORMATION

Citizens Research Council of Michigan
38777 Six Mile Road, Suite 201A
Livonia, MI 48152
(734) 542-8001
(734) 542-8004 FAX
www.crcmich.org

Michigan Chamber of Commerce
600 South Walnut Street
Lansing, Ml 48933
(517) 371-2100
(517) 371-7224 FAX
www.michamber.com

Michigan Economic Development Corporation
300 North Washington Square
Lansing, MI 48913
(517) 373-9808
(517) 335-0198 FAX
http://medc.michigan.org

Michigan Manufacturers Association
620 South Capitol Avenue.
Lansing, MI 48933
(517) 372-5900
(517) 372-3322 FAX
www.mma-net.org

Sponsored by the Michigan Nonprofit Association and the Council of Michigan Foundations

TAXES ON BUSINESSES

Office of Revenue and Tax Analysis
Michigan Department of Treasury
430 West Allegan Street
Lansing, MI 48922
(517) 373-2697
(517) 373-3298 FAX
www.michigan.gov.treasury

Workers' Compensation Center
Michigan State University
207 South Kedzie Hall
East Lansing, MI 48824-1032
(517) 432-7721
(517) 432-7723 FAX
www.lir.msu.edu/wcc

Workers' Compensation Research Institute
955 Massachusetts Avenue
Cambridge, MA 02139
(617) 661-9274
(617) 661-9284 FAX
www.wcrinet.org

Taxes on Consumers

BACKGROUND

Sales and Use Taxes

Article IX, section 8, of the Michigan Constitution provides for a *sales tax* on retailers of no more than 6 percent of their gross tangible sales of personal property. The constitution also requires that at least 73 percent of the revenue generated by the levy be dedicated to funding K–12 education. Any hike in the sales tax rate must be accomplished through a constitutional amendment.

The sales tax base consists of most final retail transactions of goods in the state. The major exceptions are

- prescription drugs;

- food for human consumption except that for immediate consumption (i.e., most food bought at a grocery store is exempt, but food bought at a restaurant is not);

- business purchases used for resale;

- most services;

- residential heating fuel, which is taxed at only 4 percent; and

- purchases by government agencies and eligible nonprofit organizations.

Michigan also levies a *use tax* based on use or storage of certain property in the state—that is, goods bought outside the state but used in Michigan are exempt from the sales tax but subject to an identical 6 percent use tax. Use taxes were devised by states to offset the loss of sales tax revenue when goods are purchased out of state and also to remove the disadvantage to local businesses of competing with out-of-state firms. Some services, such as hotel room rentals and telephone service payments, also are subject to the use tax and so are private used-car transactions.

In FY 2000–01 the state sales tax generated about $6.4 billion, while the use tax raised another $1.3 billion for a total of $7.7 billion. Of sales tax collections,

- 73 percent are deposited in the School Aid Fund, to be used for K–12 education;

- 24 percent go to local units of government, through revenue sharing; and

- 3 percent go to the state's general and transportation funds.

Of use tax collections,

- 33 percent are deposited in the School Aid Fund; and

- 67 percent are deposited in the General Fund.

Exhibit 1 shows the changes in sales and use tax revenue for three representative years. In 1984 they generated $2.2 billion, more than 17 percent of total state revenue. By 1997 revenue had risen to $6.5 million and the percentage to 22 percent. The reason for the

GLOSSARY

Base
In taxation, the dollar value on which a tax is levied.

Consumption tax
A levy on consumer goods.

Intangible property
A financial asset having no intrinsic value but representing value—e.g., securities, accounts receivable, notes.

Nexus
The minimum physical presence or link to a state that would subject a business to a state's tax system and require the business to collect and remit taxes.

Remote sales
Usually, catalog and Internet purchases.

Sales tax
A flat percentage levy on an item's selling price: in Michigan, 6 percent.

Tangible property
Any property other than real estate or money that has physical substance and can be touched—e.g., furniture, cars, jewelry.

Use tax
A levy on a good's initial use (as opposed to one levied on its sale). In Michigan the use tax applies to (1) items purchased out of state, and (2) items used or stored in the state; it also applies to private used-car transactions.

EXHIBIT 1. Michigan Sales and Use Tax Collections, Selected Fiscal Years

Fiscal Year	Sales and Use Tax Revenue (billions)	Percentage of Total State Revenue
1983–84	$2.2	17.3%
1996–97	6.5	22.2
2000–01	7.7	21.2

SOURCES: Michigan Department of Treasury and Senate Fiscal Agency.

increased collections, both in absolute terms and as a percentage of total revenue, is the 1994 rate increase, from 4 percent to 6 percent, brought about by the school-finance reform package known as Proposal A; this raised the sales/use tax rate for the first time in more than 30 years, and all the additional revenue is dedicated to K–12 education. In 2001 collections were down as a share of total state revenue, in part because of an economic slowdown.

Exhibit 2 presents FY 1985–2001 actual and inflation-adjusted annual collection data. Tax collections rose every year but one (1991), but after adjusting for inflation, they essentially were flat from 1986 to 1993. Tax collections rose sharply following the rate increase, then slowed slightly, increasing at an annual rate of 2.8 percent (adjusted for inflation), then in FY 2001 fell about 2 percent.

All but five states levy a sales tax, most in the 3–7 percent range. Unlike Michigan, many allow some local governments (usually counties or high-population cities) to levy a separate sales tax in addition to the state levy.

Taxes on Remote Sales

Sales/use tax revenues are being eroded by remote (mail order and Internet) sales, and the revenue lost is becoming a serious fiscal problem for state and local governments. The Michigan Department of Treasury estimates that in FY 1999–2000 the state loss was $187 million and by FY 2004–05 will be about $350 million.

There are a number of legal and practical issues that keep states from collecting taxes on remote sales, among them the U.S. Supreme Court ruling that mail-order and Internet firms that do not have *nexus* (the minimum physical presence or link that requires them to collect taxes or be subject to a state's tax system) in a state are not required to collect taxes from buyers living in that state.

Resolving the issues related to taxing remote sales will require either voluntary compliance by remote retailers

EXHIBIT 2. Michigan Sales and Use Tax Collections, FYs 1985–2001 ($ billions)

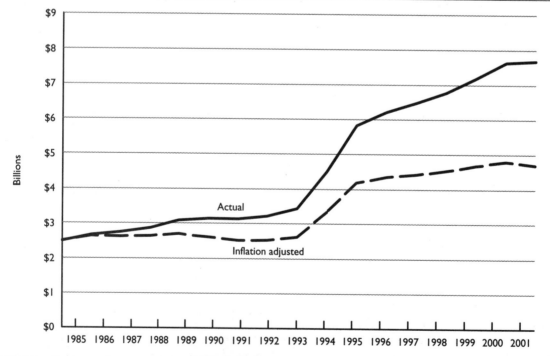

SOURCE: Michigan Department of Treasury. Calculations by Public Sector Consultants, Inc.

Sponsored by the Michigan Nonprofit Association and the Council of Michigan Foundations

or congressional action. To help increase compliance by Michigan residents, the state has taken the unique approach of adding a line on the personal income tax form for calculating the amount of tax owed on remote purchases. This has met with some, but limited, success: For tax year 2000, the state collected about $3.1 million from 80,150 filers.

To address the tax collection and related issues, the Streamlined Sales Tax Project, a cooperative effort among retailers, remote-sales retailers, state and local governments, and national organizations, has been initiated. Its purpose is to simplify state sales-tax laws and rates and provide incentives for remote firms to voluntarily collect and remit the tax.

Other Consumption Taxes
On Tobacco Products
Michigan, like most states, imposes a tax, which is collected from wholesalers on all tobacco products: cigarettes, cigars, non-cigarette smoking tobacco, and smokeless tobacco. The current tax was adopted in 1994, replacing the original cigarette tax, which was adopted in 1947. The rate is

- 37.5 mills per cigarette, or 75¢ a pack; and

- 16 percent of the wholesale price on all other tobacco products.

The U.S. median per pack cigarette tax rate is 34¢ (January 1, 2002), ranging from $1.425 in Washington to 3¢ in Kentucky. Michigan's is the second highest rate in the Great Lakes region (Wisconsin's is 77¢); in Indiana and Ohio, which adjoin Michigan, the rates are 15.5¢ and 24¢, respectively.

Tobacco taxes generated about $596 million for Michigan in FY 2000–01. Of the *cigarette tax* collections,

- 63.4 percent are deposited in the School Aid Fund;

- 25.3 percent go to General Fund;

- 6 percent go to the Healthy Michigan Fund; and

- 5.3 percent are deposited in the Health and Safety Fund.

Of the *non-cigarette tobacco tax* collections,

- 94 percent go to the School Aid Fund; and

- 6 percent go to Healthy Michigan Fund.

Cigarette smuggling, both organized and casual, of cigarettes from Canada and other lower-tax states has been a problem. Not only does Michigan's high tax rate contribute to the problem, but until 1998, so did the absence on cigarette packs of any physical evidence that the tax had been paid.

In 1998 the state began to require a tax stamp on each pack of cigarettes, and experience is showing a benefit to enforcement and revenue. Smuggling is significantly down and tax-collection revenue is up. Taking into account the long-term decline in tobacco consumption that likely occurred, the cigarette stamp program saved the state an estimated $90–95 million over the first two years of the program. From FY 1998–99 to FY 2000–01, collections fell about 3 percent, about that expected from reduced cigarette consumption, indicating that little smuggling now is occurring.

On Beer
Michigan's beer and other alcoholic-beverage taxes originally were levied in separate statutes that were repealed and replaced by Public Act 58 of 1998.

Michigan has taxed beer since 1933 and currently imposes a levy on beer manufactured or sold in the state. A credit is allowed for beer shipped out of state or sold to a military installation or Indian reservation.

A tax of $6.30 per barrel is imposed, with a $2 per barrel credit for brewers producing less than 20,000 barrels annually. The rate has not changed since 1966, when it was reduced from $6.61 per barrel. Nationwide, rates range from 63¢ per barrel (Wyoming) to $29.30 (Hawaii). In the Great Lakes region, Michigan's rate is highest, and Wisconsin's, at $2.05, is lowest.

The Michigan beer tax generated about $45 million in FY 2000–01. The proceeds go to the General Fund.

On Wine
Michigan first imposed a wine levy in 1933. The tax is levied per liter, a credit is allowed for that shipped out of state or sold to military installations or Indian reservations, and the rates are

- 13.5¢ per liter for wines made from imported grapes and having 16 percent or less alcohol;

- 20¢ for wines made from imported grapes and having more than 16 percent alcohol;

- 1¢ for wines made in Michigan from domestic grapes or fruit; and

Sponsored by the Michigan Nonprofit Association and the Council of Michigan Foundations

■ 48¢ for mixed spirit drinks (e.g., "wine coolers").

Per gallon, the Michigan tax equates to 51¢, second highest in the Great Lakes region. Only Illinois, at 73¢ a gallon, is higher.

The Michigan wine tax generated about $6 million in FY 2000–01, and the proceeds go to the General Fund.

On Liquor

Michigan has taxed the retail price of spirits since 1959. Currently, a rate of 12 percent is levied on spirits sold for on-premise consumption and a rate of 13.85 percent on spirits sold for off-premise consumption.

The tax generated about $87 million in FY 2000–01. Of the collections,

■ 29 percent go to the General Fund;

■ 29 percent go to the School Aid Fund;

■ 29 percent go to the Convention Facility Development Fund; and

■ the remainder goes to the Liquor Purchase Revolving Fund.

Other

The property tax, which affects virtually all adults because it is paid directly by all landowners and indirectly by all renters, is not a consumption tax and is not discussed here. Readers interested in the property tax are referred to "K–12 Funding" and "Taxes on Businesses," elsewhere in this book.

Motor-vehicle fuel taxes also affect virtually everyone, either directly, at the pump, or indirectly through the taxes' effect on the cost of goods and services. Motor-vehicle fuel taxes are discussed in "Highway Funding and Safety."

DISCUSSION

Sales and Use Taxes

Debate about sales/use taxes in Michigan centers primarily on three issues.

■ Should the taxes be extended to services?

■ Do the taxes disproportionately affect the poor?

■ Should the state rely on levies that taxpayers cannot avoid but cannot deduct from their federal income tax liability?

First, the current sales/use tax base is shrinking relative to the economy as a whole. These taxes historically have been levied on the sales/use of tangible goods. Most services—ranging from professional business services to dry cleaning—have been exempt. However, as the state has changed, the proportion of the economy subject to the taxes has diminished. For example, in 1977 only 12.3 percent of the Michigan economy (private-sector gross state product) was attributed to service industries (and, therefore, in large part exempt from consumption taxes), but by 1999 that percentage had risen to 21.8 percent. This trend will continue, which means that Michigan is relying on a consumption tax base that is shrinking each year relative to the economy as a whole. If Michigan were to extend the consumption taxes to services (the fastest growing sector of the economy), estimates are that state revenue would be boosted by more than $2 billion annually. Others assert that taxing services would dampen growth of the state's most dynamic economic sector.

Second, Michigan's sales tax exemptions for most food and medicine are intended to ease the tax's hardship on lower-income families, but some observers believe the hardship should be further reduced and the revenue loss offset by an increase in the state income tax. In the past, most analysts thought consumption taxes to be slightly regressive, meaning that their burden (relative to available income) is reduced as one earns more income. In recent years, however, tax fairness is beginning to be judged by its lifetime, rather than annual, burden on income. Analysts using the new measure conclude that the relative burden of consumption taxes is roughly equal for all income groups.

Third, since the mid-1980s sales/use taxes may not be deducted against one's federal income tax liability. Some analysts argue that this change has raised the total burden of the sales/use taxes compared to other state levies. For example, if Ms. X itemizes on her federal return, the after-tax cost of $100 in local property taxes is $100 minus her marginal federal tax rate—on average, about $75. But since consumption taxes may not be itemized, the after-tax cost of $100 in sales/use taxes is $100. While not disputing this point, some analysts downplay federal deductibility's importance. They point out that deductibility is irrelevant for the majority of taxpayers, since most do not itemize on their federal return (in a typical year, only one-third of Michigan taxpayers itemize at the federal level, and those who do tend to be at the higher end of the income scale).

Some analysts point out that sales/use taxes have certain advantages.

■ Some portion of the tax burden may be exported to non-Michigan residents who travel into this state. An

Sponsored by the Michigan Nonprofit Association and the Council of Michigan Foundations

estimated 5–15 percent of all Michigan sales/use tax revenue comes from sales to nonresidents.

■ Some point out that the public finds sales/use taxes more palatable than other levies because purchases are made at the consumer's discretion. A family may forgo, delay, or accelerate buying items subject to the sales tax, depending on current circumstances.

■ Some believe an important criterion of a good state tax system is "balance"—having roughly the same reliance on all revenue sources. In Michigan, since the 1994 sales/use tax increase, the state annually generates roughly about the same amount from both consumption taxes and income taxes.

Taxes on Remote Sales

The most serious problems in collecting taxes on remote sales are the wide differences in (1) rates levied by state and local governments and (2) how the thousands of taxing jurisdictions define what is taxable and what is not. If the states can simplify and standardize tax law and collection procedures, the undue burden that the multitude of rates/definitions imposes on remote-sales merchants would be eliminated, weakening the position that the Commerce Clause of the U.S. Constitution excuses firms without nexus from collecting the purchaser's state tax.

The most recent remote-sales action in Michigan is P.A. 122 of 2001, which makes Michigan a partner with 19 other states in the Streamlined Sales Tax Project, which has as its objective developing a way to collect state taxes on Internet, catalog, and telephone sales. The law's provisions

■ allow the state to enter into a multistate sales/use tax agreement;

■ create a board of governors that can represent the state in relevant meetings with other states;

■ provide for registering Internet and catalog sellers, who would have to select a way to collect and remit sales/use taxes;

■ allow Internet and catalog sellers to contract with certified service providers for collecting and storing the taxes;

■ permit use of an automated system to calculate each jurisdiction's tax on a transaction;

■ limit Internet/catalog sellers' liability for taxes on transactions made before a seller registers; and

■ provide for consumer privacy.

Supporters of taxing remote sales point to the revenue it would bring in, which is especially important because three-quarters of state sales tax revenue goes to K–12 schools and about one-third to local units of government. They also assert that there are fairness issues: Taxing remote sales would assure fairness to (1) Michigan merchants who must compete against remote merchants and (2) people who cannot afford computers to do their shopping.

Opponents also cite fairness issues: They say that (1) Internet and catalog vendors with no physical presence in a state receive none of the benefits of the taxes they would have to collect and remit at some expense to themselves, and (2) consumers who buy from home are not using the roads or many other state services they use when they go to a store. Opponents also are concerned about privacy. They say one of the advantages of the sales tax over other taxes is anonymity—in a store, shoppers do not have to give their name or address, and their buying habits are not tracked; a national, third-party tax-collection system may require such individual information.

Tobacco and Alcohol Taxes

Current public policy debate in Michigan about tobacco taxation revolves primarily around how the revenue is spent. Some wish to see more go directly into tobacco-use prevention and cessation programs. Others believe that state prevention and cessation spending is adequate, pointing out that in addition to specific programs, the state addresses tobacco use through school and health programs.

There currently is no public policy debate in Michigan on the subject of alcohol taxes.

See also Highway Funding and Safety; K–12 Funding; Local Government Organization and Issues; Taxes on Businesses; Tobacco Settlement.

FOR ADDITIONAL INFORMATION

Citizens Research Council
Michigan National Tower, Suite 1502
124 West Allegan Street
Lansing, MI 48933
(517) 485-9444
(517) 485-0423 FAX
www.crcmich.org
        and
3877 Six Mile Road, Suite 201A
Livonia, MI 48152
(734) 542-8001
(734) 542-8004 FAX
www.crcmich.org

Sponsored by the Michigan Nonprofit Association and the Council of Michigan Foundations

TAXES ON CONSUMERS

Michigan Chamber of Commerce
600 South Walnut Street
Lansing, MI 48933
(517) 371-2100
(517) 371-7224 FAX
www.michamber.com

Michigan Department of Treasury
430 West Allegan Street
Lansing, MI 48922
(517) 373-3200
www.michigan.gov/treasury

Senate Fiscal Agency
Victor Center, Suite 800
201 North Washington Square
P.O. Box 30036
Lansing, MI 48909
(517) 373-2768
(517) 373-1986 FAX
www.senate.state.mi.us/sfa

Streamlined Sales Tax System for the 21st Century
www.geocities.com/streamlined2000

Sponsored by the Michigan Nonprofit Association and the Council of Michigan Foundations

Telecommunications

BACKGROUND

Given how many Michiganians use and see others use computers, access the Internet, pick up a traditional telephone, and reach for a cellular phone in modern life, it is hard to remember how much has changed in the last 20 years. In 1982,

GLOSSARY

Broadband
A high-speed Internet connection. In Michigan law, "broadband" is defined as transmission of at least 144 Kbps in at least one direction by any means (a typical modem operates at 56 Kbps). Current broadband services include cable modems, digital subscriber lines (DSLs), T-1 and fractional T-1 lines, and high-speed satellite services. A broadband connection to the Internet allows more information to be transmitted per minute than with a standard modem connection. In most cases, the primary benefit to the user is that a set amount of information is transferred faster; also, being able to transit more information makes possible certain activities (e.g., videoconferencing) that are impossible or impractical with lower capacity connections.

Competitive local-exchange carrier (CLEC)
A telephone company that offers local telephone service (home or business dial tone) in direct competition to the local service provided by an incumbent local-exchange carrier (ILEC). TDS Metrocom is an example of a CLEC.

Incumbent local-exchange carrier (ILEC)
An exchange carrier that was in the local market before competition was permitted. Ameritech and GTE/Verizon are ILECs in their respective areas, which include most Michigan residents.

- IBM celebrated the first birthday of its first personal computer (PC), Compaq Computer manufactured the first IBM-compatible computer, and there were about 5.5 million PCs in use nationwide;

- the building block of what would become the Internet was approved, but invention of the World Wide Web was nine years away;

- AT&T had just been notified that as part of a settlement with the U.S. Department of Justice, it would be split in 1984 into separate components: long-distance (AT&T) and local (the seven "baby Bells"—the regional Bell operating companies). Michigan Bell, Michigan's AT&T subsidiary, would join with several other Midwestern states to form Ameritech; and

- the first commercial cellular telephone service began, in Chicago.

Fast forward 20 years. In 2002,

- just over half (53 percent) of Michigan residents report having at least one computer in their home, and worldwide, an estimated 34 million computers were sold in the last quarter of 2001;

- there are more than 32 million Web sites on the Internet, and nearly two-thirds of Michiganians have used the Internet at least once;

- Ameritech is now a subsidiary of SBC Communications, which itself is a combination of other baby Bell companies (Southwestern Bell and Pacific Bell) and a majority owner of Cingular Wireless; and

- communication by telephone never was easier—in 2000 Michigan had more than 3 million cellular subscribers and nearly 5.4 million traditional telephone lines.

Telephone Service

The Michigan telephone industry dates back to 1877, when an Ontonagon businessman installed a line between the Lake Superior port and his inland office. When other business owners requested a similar arrangement, the Ontonagon Telephone Company was created. Other local telephone companies were established around the state during the same year, and in 1913 Michigan legislators gave the Michigan Public Service Commission (MPSC) power to regulate the industry.

Currently, more than 94 percent of all Michigan households have a telephone, with service available from myriad companies offering either local or long-distance service. For the most part, neither the federal Telecommunications Act of 1996 nor the Michigan Telecommunications Act of 2000 has resulted in major telephone companies being able to offer customers both local *and* long-distance service. Although many Michigan

Sponsored by the Michigan Nonprofit Association and the Council of Michigan Foundations

consumers and businesses receive a single bill for their local and long-distance calls, separate companies still provide the services.

The exhibit shows that for local telephone service, Ameritech is still Michigan's largest incumbent local-exchange carrier (ILEC). Competitive local-exchange carriers (CLECs) operate only about 6 percent of all local telephone lines. For residential long-distance service, AT&T remains the dominant provider with more than half of all presubscribed long-distance telephone lines. (The presubscribed carrier is the one to which the consumer has subscribed for long-distance service from that telephone number.)

In 2000, changes to the Michigan Telecommunications Act were enacted, including a three-year freeze on local telephone rates, elimination of a line charge that Ameritech and Verizon had been allowed to impose on their customers, and a provision that local calling areas must include all adjacent telephone exchanges—even if the exchange is in a different area code.[1] The removal of the user line charge ($3.28/line for Ameritech customers and $3.50/line for GTE/Verizon customers) has been challenged in federal court by both Ameritech and Verizon; a stay allows both companies to continue charging the fee pending the litigation outcome. Much of the revised act will expire in 2005, requiring the legislature once again to update the law.

Also in 2000, Ameritech was faced with a host of complaints, predominately about installation and repair delays. The Public Service Commission received nearly 21,000 complaints from Ameritech customers, a 28 percent increase over the prior year. By mid-year Ameritech admitted to taking too long to respond to the average nonemergency repair request, and by year-end had committed additional financial resources, hired additional line-repair staff, and entered into a settlement with the MPSC that includes awarding financial credits to customers for installation and repair services not provided within a specified period. By mid-2001 Ameritech reported almost 24,000 fewer outstanding installation and repair orders than in mid-2000 and had cut the average wait for repairs from 66 hours to 31 hours.

Readers interested in a fuller discussion of local telephone service are referred to *Michigan in Brief, 6th Edition*, which may be found on line at *www.michiganinbrief.org*.

[1]Since 1998 Michigan has been assigned three new area codes (*231, 586,* and *989*) and is slated for two more (*269* and *947*) in 2002. When fully operational, Michigan will have 12 area codes (10 discrete regions and two that overlay others).

Local and Long-Distance Market Shares, Michigan, Selected Years

Provider	Year and Percentage of All Lines	
Local Service	2000	1997
Ameritech	78.2%	82.4%
GTE/Verizon	11.7	10.9
Independent companies[a]	3.6	3.5
Competitive local-exchange carriers[b]	6.5	3.1
Long-Distance Service	1999	1996
AT&T	65.4%	62.7%
MCI/Worldcom	14.7	16.8
Sprint	5.6	6.2
All others	14.4	14.2

SOURCES: Michigan Public Service Commission (for information on local service); FCC Common Carrier Bureau (for long distance).
[a]Some areas in Michigan are served by an incumbent local telephone company other than Ameritech or GTE/Verizon; these are independent telephone companies.
[b]Competitive local-exchange carriers compete against the incumbent local carrier, whether that carrier is Ameritech, GTE/Verizon, or an independent.

Internet Access

People are accessing the Internet in increasing numbers. In a 2001 survey conducted for Cyber-state.org, a Michigan-focused information-technology advocate, almost two-thirds of respondents (63 percent) reported that they had used the Internet at some point; this was an 11 percent increase from 1998.

Statewide, however, the Internet is neither equally accessible nor equally accessed. Wide variations in computer ownership and Internet use exist by region, age, race, education level, and income—this is the so-called *digital divide*.

■ Of those younger than 25 years, 91 percent report having been on line; of those aged 65 and older, just 22 percent.

■ In the City of Detroit and northern lower Michigan, fewer than half of the residents have a computer in their home.

■ As education increases, so does PC ownership: Among residents with less than a high school education, 19 percent own at least one computer; among those with a college education, 51 percent own at least one. And the difference in Internet access between the least and most educated Michiganians is vast: Among those not graduating from high school, only 35 percent re-

Sponsored by the Michigan Nonprofit Association and the Council of Michigan Foundations

port having been on line; of those with a college degree, 88 percent have been.

In late 2001 the governor announced a plan to speed deployment of high-speed Internet access statewide. He believes that high-speed Internet access (that is, faster and with more capacity than is possible with a traditional modem) is necessary to the state's continued economic growth. In support, the Michigan Economic Development Corporation released an analysis of what a statewide, high-speed Internet infrastructure would mean for Michigan: According to the Gartner Group, implementing the governor's plan to create a system for high-speed Internet access will, by 2010, (1) generate nearly a half-million additional jobs over and above the normal job growth rate, (2) increase high-speed Internet use from the expected 20 percent to 50 percent, and (3) increase gross state product by $440 billion, reflecting the value of additional goods and services that are made possible by the advanced infrastructure.

DISCUSSION

Michigan policymakers operate under several constraints in influencing public policy surrounding both telephones and the Internet. A great deal of telephone policy is in the hands of

- the federal government (via the federal Telecommunications Act of 1996);

- the Federal Communications Commission (FCC); or

- state and federal court rulings on lawsuits that have arisen from both the 1996 act and the FCC's subsequent rules and regulations to implement it.

Much of Internet policy is in the hands of

- major corporations that provide either content (e.g., AOL Time Warner) or infrastructure (e.g., WorldCom);

- international commissions/consortiums (e.g., the Internet Engineering Task Force and the Internet Corporation for Assigned Names and Numbers); and

- Internet users themselves (in the choices they make).

In addition to government and legal constraints, policymakers at all levels are faced with the rapid pace of technological change. In the 18 years from 1982 to 2000, for example, the United States went from a handful to 101 million cellular telephones; 22 million were added from 1999 to 2000 alone.

Policymakers also face the phenomenon of *convergence*—that is, when, over time, separate devices begin integrating features of other devices. Today, for example, one can make a long-distance call from a computer, receive e-mail on a cellular phone, and browse the Web using a handheld computer or PalmPilot.™ Policymakers are faced with deciding which—or all—of these devices is a computer (or a telephone), to say nothing of whether the rules should be different if the computer is used to make a local versus a long-distance phone call.

Telephone Service: Creating Competition

One arena where Michigan policymakers do have influence is in creating a competitive environment for local telephone service in the state. Ameritech continues to dominate local service, and its competitors sometimes complain that Ameritech is not timely in responding to their requests for installation of equipment and lines or access to the Ameritech network. In early 2002 the MPSC agreed, finding that Ameritech was violating several provisions of the Michigan Telecommunications Act that require the company to give competitive local providers full access to the company's network. The case is pending before the commission. In addition, Ameritech's parent company, SBC Communications, has been fined $6 million by the FCC for not meeting conditions set forth in the regulatory approval to merge with Ameritech in 1999. To date, SBC Communications has been fined more than $59 million by the federal government and, for violations similar to that found by the MPSC, assessed more than $43 million in penalties by the five Ameritech home states.

Work continues at both the state and federal level to enforce, interpret, or rewrite the guiding telecommunications laws. In Michigan, HB 4764 has been introduced to separate the local telephone operations of any phone company having more than 250,000 lines (currently only Ameritech and Verizon) into *wholesale* and *retail* divisions. The wholesale division would provide and maintain the physical network, while the retail division would sell directly to consumers and businesses. The intent of "structurally separating" the operations of incumbent telephone providers is to remove an incumbent provider's incentive to resist competition: If a wholesale entity receives its revenue from a number of companies that deal directly with consumers, it is in the wholesaler's best interest to treat all retail companies the same. Proponents of structural separation also believe that it would be easier to monitor and analyze separate business entities.

Critics of structural separation point out that it is hard enough to monitor incumbent providers when these functions are combined, and they fear that having separate wholesale and retail functions would allow incumbent

Sponsored by the Michigan Nonprofit Association and the Council of Michigan Foundations

providers to become less "transparent" by hiding transactions in both divisions. In addition, HB 4764 would require that at least 20 percent of the retail company's stock be traded separately from the wholesale company's stock, meaning that 80 percent still could be held by the incumbent provider. Despite legislative intent, incentives would remain for the wholesale company to treat its largest retail customers favorably, which means that competitive local providers still could have unequal access to the telephone network. Finally, in the long run, structural separation may not matter for Michigan consumers or businesses because of the growth of alternative local telephone service provided by cable television and cellular telephone companies.

Creating a High-Speed Internet Infrastructure

As mentioned, in late 2001 the governor introduced a plan to speed deployment of Michigan's broadband infrastructure. The governor noted that (1) in the growth rate of broadband lines, Michigan ranked 24th in the nation in 2001, and (2) in per line investment by incumbent local-exchange carriers, the state was dead last in both 2000 and 2001. The governor's plans are set out in Public Acts 48–50 of 2002.

■ A new office—the Michigan Broadband Development Authority, housed in the Department of Treasury—is created to issue tax-exempt bonds to telecommunications companies. The authority is patterned after the Michigan State Housing Development Authority, which offers incentives to developers to create affordable housing in Michigan.

■ The new authority may issue bonds for all facilities, telecommunications hardware and software, and intellectual property necessary to deploy broadband Internet access throughout the state.

■ A statewide policy on municipal rights-of-way is to be established and oversight provided through a new, separate authority (Metropolitan Extension Telecommunications Rights-of-Way Oversight Authority), housed in the Michigan Department of Consumer and Industry Services.

■ Telecommunications providers are required to obtain a right-of-way access license for a one-time $500 fee and to pay the rights-of-way authority an annual fee of 2¢ per foot until March 31, 2003, and 5¢ per foot thereafter. The fee is 1¢ per foot for cable television providers.

■ Companies are permitted to claim a tax credit equal to 6 percent of eligible expenditures for placing new broadband lines into service that operate at speeds of at least 200 Kbps in both directions (sending and receiving).

Proponents of these measures believe that the slow pace of broadband rollout in Michigan was a growing liability for attracting and retaining new businesses in the state. Major state initiatives—e.g., the $1 billion life-sciences corridor and a statewide economic-development focus on advanced manufacturing—rely on businesses having widespread access to high-speed Internet services. Supporters point out that if broadband access in the state were to continue to be sporadic, with adjoining townships unable to receive high-speed service at all or at affordable rates, then businesses would face a huge hurdle in selecting sites that will enable them to expand.

The legislation's opponents believe that the governor's statistics are flawed. While granting that Michigan's broadband *growth* rate is in the middle of all states in the nation, several telecommunications companies also point out that Michigan is 11th in the United States in the total number of providers of high-speed lines. In addition, some opponents argue that given the high quality of the existing public-telephone network, the low per line investments by incumbent local-exchange carriers shows the economies of scale in Michigan—the per line cost to wire a home in Michigan, one of the more densely populated states, simply is less than it is in the more rural states. Critics also question whether broadband deployment has been as slow as the governor believes. The Telecommunications Association of Michigan, for example, notes that one-third of all rural telephone exchanges had broadband access at year-end 2001, and nearly two-thirds (58 percent) expect it by year-end 2002.

Consumer Internet Demand and Concerns

Others who are skeptical of the broadband initiative ask whether Michigan consumers and businesses need high-speed Internet access at all. A survey conducted in January 2002 by the Cyber-state.org policy group finds that 70 percent of Michigan residents understand little about broadband, even in southeast Michigan where it is widely available. Telecommunications providers have made similar observations, noting that even where they offer high-speed Internet service, few customers sign up.

While supporters agree that high-speed Internet is not well understood today, they believe this will change in the next few years as new services emerge. For example, today many consumers are able to send an e-mail to a health care provider's office, but their simple modem will not permit them to have an on-line consultation with the provider that includes sending or receiving diagnostic materials (e.g., EKGs, x-rays). Supporters believe that if broadband access cannot be speeded to all locations in the state, Michigan will lag behind the nation in the proportion of residents and businesses that can take full advantage of future Internet-based services.

Bridging the Digital Divide

As mentioned, there is considerable variation in the extent to which Michiganians have access to and use computers and the Internet. As new and expanded services and devices are introduced into the marketplace, either through invention or convergence, Michigan policymakers will be asked to figure out how to make sure all citizens have access to these devices.

Part of the problem in addressing the digital divide is that the divide itself may be characterized in many ways—by age, employment, education, and so on. For example, it has been proposed that computers be provided to libraries to help give Internet access to low-income residents, but this does little unless there also is money to (1) train people to use the computers and (2) maintain and regularly upgrade the equipment and software. Similarly, policies to increase computer use in K–12 classrooms does not help older Michigan residents who have lost their jobs due to technological change or are timid about using new technology and devices.

In some cases, however, the rapid pace of technological change can work to the advantage of policymakers. As Internet access via cellular telephones increases, the Internet will reach a segment of the Michigan population that currently does not have a computer at home. In addition, as cable television and satellite providers deploy broadband Internet access, consumers and businesses will not be as reliant for access on the incumbent telephone carriers.

See also Consumer Protection.

FOR ADDITIONAL INFORMATION

Cyber-state.org
3520 Green Court, Suite 300
Ann Arbor, MI 48105
(734) 302-4755
(734) 302-4996 FAX
www.cyber-state.org

Federal Communications Commission
445 12th Street S.W.
Washington, DC 20554
(888) 225-5322
(202) 418-0232 FAX
www.fcc.gov

Michigan Cable Telecommunications Association
412 West Ionia Street
Lansing, MI 48933
(517) 482-2622
(517) 482-1819 FAX
www.michcable.org

Michigan Competitive Telecommunications
    Providers Association
P.O. Box 20064
Lansing, MI 48901
(517) 372-4400
(517) 372-4045 FAX
www.mctpa.com

Michigan Economic Development Corporation
300 North Washington Square
Lansing, MI 48913
(517) 373-9808
(517) 335-0198 FAX
http://medc.michigan.org

Michigan Public Service Commission
P.O. Box 30221
Lansing, MI 48909
(517) 241-6180
(517) 241-6181 FAX
www.cis.state.mi.us/mpsc

Telecommunication Association of Michigan
124 West Allegan Street, Suite 1400
Lansing, MI 48933
(517) 482-4166
(517) 482-3548 FAX
www.telecommich.org

Sponsored by the Michigan Nonprofit Association and the Council of Michigan Foundations

Tobacco Settlement

BACKGROUND

In the mid-1990s, to secure compensation for health care expenditures for ailments arising from tobacco use, 46 states and two jurisdictions filed lawsuits in their state courts against the tobacco industry. In June 1997 a group of state attorneys general presented an agreement reached between the states and the tobacco industry that purported to settle all current and pending class action lawsuits brought against the industry by states and other government entities.

To make the settlement binding on all 50 states, Congressional action would be necessary. A number of bills—including the bipartisan effort sponsored by senators McCain, Gorton, Breaux, and Hollings—were introduced for this purpose. Among its other provisions, the McCain bill would have (1) required the tobacco industry to pay considerably more than the amount agreed to by the states and the industry; (2) raised cigarette taxes by $1.10 a pack over five years; (3) preserved the Food and Drug Administration's ability to regulate the tobacco industry in ways that the agreement did not; and (4) drastically restricted cigarette marketing, advertising, and promotion.

Following the bill's introduction, several major players in the tobacco industry withdrew support of the Congressional process for developing comprehensive tobacco legislation, citing Congress's deviation from the terms of the June 20 agreement, and launched a successful advertising campaign to kill the bill.

Meanwhile, four states reached individual settlements with the tobacco industry, yielding total payments of at least $35 billion over the next 25 years. In 1998 an agreement—known as the master settlement agreement—between the remaining states, including Michigan, and the industry resulted in a deal to settle pending state cases and defuse potential claims in the remaining states. The industry committed to paying these states $206 billion over the next 25 years for recovery of their tobacco-related health care costs. In addition, $5 billion would be paid to 14 states to compensate them for potential harm to their tobacco industry. The new deal did not require Congressional approval because it did not include provisions pertaining to federal jurisdiction over the nicotine contained in tobacco products. It also did not grant the industry's major wish: a limit on future lawsuits.

The agreement did not specify how the states would spend the money they received in the tobacco settlement, but it generally was seen as a unique opportunity for the states to reduce the financial and health burden that tobacco use imposes on American families and government.

Michigan's Settlement Monies

Michigan's initial payment from the tobacco industry was $104.5 million, to be followed by $279–365 million annually for 24 years. The federal Centers for Disease Control and Prevention (CDC) issued guidelines recommending how much money should be spent annually in each state to implement an effective, comprehensive tobacco-use prevention program; for Michigan, the amount is $53–149 million. Michigan, however, allocates none of its settlement money directly to tobacco-use prevention and cessation; it is one of only three states to take this approach.

Sponsored by the Michigan Nonprofit Association and the Council of Michigan Foundations

Michigan policymakers enacted legislation allocating 75 percent of the tobacco-settlement funds to support the Michigan Merit Award program, a fund providing college scholarships to high school students who do well on the Michigan Educational Assessment Program test. The remaining 25 percent goes into the Tobacco Settlement Trust Fund, which supports a variety of programs, including a prescription-drug program for seniors and various health programs and research efforts.

Tobacco Use in Michigan

In Michigan in 2000, according to the state Behavioral Risk Factor Survey, 24 percent of the population—about 2.4 million adults—were smokers; this is down from 27.5 percent in 1998. The national average is 23.2 percent.

Teen smoking in Michigan also has dropped: Preliminary figures from the state Youth Tobacco Survey show that 27.6 percent of 9–12th graders smoked in 2001, down 10 percent from 1997. This puts Michigan youth just below the national average, which is 28 percent.

According to the Tobacco-Free Michigan Action Coalition, tobacco use indirectly costs Michigan taxpayers $2.5 billion annually for health care, lost work productivity, and work absenteeism. The coalition also says that Medicaid payments related to smoking totaled $350 million in Michigan in 2000.

DISCUSSION

The state's decision to spend the majority of Michigan's tobacco settlement on education rather than health programs engendered forceful debate that continues. Many interested parties believe that much of the settlement properly should be spent on tobacco-use prevention and cessation programs and/or to cover health care costs, stating that (1) this was the intent with which the lawsuits were brought against the industry, and (2) polls indicate that there is (a) strong support for spending the money on tobacco-use prevention and health care matters and (b) little support for spending it on the Michigan Merit Award program.

Among Michigan's current programs to prevent and reduce tobacco use are a health-education, promotion, and research program; a smoking-prevention program aimed at youth; and a school-based HIV/AIDS, risk-behavior, and health-education program. The recent drop in teen smoking is attributed by Michigan Department of Community Health officials to an assertive and expanded K–12 component on tobacco-use prevention. In the 2001–02 school year, more than 100 Michigan middle and high schools implemented a teen smoking-cessation program developed by the American Lung Association.

In 2001 the House Fiscal Agency reported that since the settlement payments began in 1999, the state is spending about $8 million annually, less than 2 percent of the amount of the settlement revenue, on general anti-smoking projects. Proponents of maintaining the current spending level contend that funding for anti-tobacco programming is closer to $75 million if one takes into account the portion of the $5 billion in Medicaid spending that includes anti-tobacco programs and the relevant portion of the $170 million spent for programs to prevent smoking, teen pregnancy, and AIDS. As evidence of the effectiveness of these programs, they point to the drop in smoking among both adults and teens, and data from Michigan's Health Risk Behaviors 2000 give some credence to this position: The percentage of smokers tends to decrease as education and income level increase.

Proponents of upholding current policy with regard to the tobacco settlement believe that because there already is in place strong and sufficiently funded tobacco-use prevention programming, the state will be doing more to help its youth be healthy and successful by spending the money on the scholarship program. Those in favor of using the settlement mainly for health care believe that doing so would free some of the money currently spent for health care and allow it to be spent on other state programs.

Supporters of spending the majority of the money on anti-tobacco programs believe that health care costs resulting from smoking will not drop without significant efforts to reduce tobacco use. Although smoking in Michigan appears to be declining, those who would have the settlement money spent in line with the CDC recommendations point out that the percentage of smokers in Michigan still exceeds the national average.

Of the six states where tobacco-prevention spending is within the CDC guidelines, only one—Indiana—still has a smoking rate higher than Michigan's. In Massachusetts and California, two states that have had programs in place for quite some time, smoking rates (19.9 percent and 17.2 percent, respectively) are significantly lower than in Michigan.

The Citizens for a Healthy Michigan coalition has launched a petition drive to put a question on the November 2002 ballot asking voters if they wish to amend the state constitution to redirect the settlement funds now being used in the Michigan Merit Award program to

Sponsored by the Michigan Nonprofit Association and the Council of Michigan Foundations

- a Tobacco Illness Care Fund (46 percent of total settlement funds),

- a Tobacco Settlement Research and Education Fund (31 percent),

- a prescription-drug assistance program for senior citizens (13 percent), and

- the state General Fund (10 percent).

Opponents of the ballot question say that its passage would kill the Michigan Merit Award program, and although initial polling revealed little support for spending the settlement funds on the program, it has gained popularity as more than 91,000 scholarships have been awarded since its implementation.

Supporters of the ballot question point to the success with which other states have used tobacco settlement funds to reduce smoking rates. Florida has seen a considerable drop in smoking among middle-school and high school students (reductions of 47 percent and 30 percent, respectively). They say that lawmakers will find another way to fund the scholarship program if it is a priority.

See also K–12 Quality and Testing; Substance Abuse; Taxes on Consumers; Youth at Risk.

FOR ADDITIONAL INFORMATION

Citizens for a Healthy Michigan
P.O. Box 16087
Lansing, MI 48901
(800) 235-1910
www.mha.org/tobacco/index.htm

House Fiscal Agency
Michigan House of Representatives
124 North Capitol Avenue
P.O. Box 30014
Lansing, MI 48909
(517) 373-8080
www.house.state.mi.us/hfa

Michigan Department of Community Health
Lewis Cass Building, 6th Floor
320 South Walnut Street
Lansing, MI 48913
(517) 373-3500
www.michigan.gov/mdch

National Center for Tobacco-Free Kids
1400 I Street, Suite 1200
Washington, DC 20005
(202) 296-5469
www.tobaccofreekids.org

Tobacco Control Resource Center
Northeastern University School of Law
400 Huntington Avenue
Boston, MA 02115
(617) 373-2026
www.tobacco.neu.edu

Tobacco Free Michigan Action Coalition
617 Seymour Street
Lansing, MI 48933
(517) 827-0020
www.tobaccofreemichigan.org

Water Quality

BACKGROUND

Water covers approximately 40 percent of Michigan's nearly 97,000 square miles of surface area and includes more than 35,000 lakes and ponds, 36,000 miles of rivers and streams, and nearly 25 million acres in the four Great Lakes (Erie, Huron, Michigan, Superior) bordering the state. Because of its unique geographic configuration—two large peninsulas—all rivers and streams in the state eventually flow into one of the four Great Lakes or their connecting waters (St. Marie's River, St. Clair River, Detroit River, or Lake St. Clair).

Michigan protects both surface water and groundwater from pollution that would impair certain uses of the water. These "protected" uses are defined by state law and include (1) recreation, (2) support of fish, wildlife, and aquatic organisms, and (3) domestic, agricultural, and industrial water withdrawals. Under state law and delegated federal authority, Michigan's primary regulatory mechanism is a permit system that limits waste that may be discharged into Michigan waters. The state law is Public Act 451 of 1994, the Michigan Natural Resources and Environmental Protection Act (NREPA), and the federal authority is derived from the U.S. Environmental Protection Agency (EPA) under the federal Clean Water Act.

Traditionally, water-pollution control has focused on regulating *point*, or discrete, sources of discharges, such as those from municipal and industrial waste-treatment systems. Over the last 30 years such regulation significantly improved water quality in Michigan, but in the last decade it has become evident that additional pollution sources need to be controlled. For example, stormwater runoff has been found to be a major point source of pollution, particularly in urban areas, and recent federal court decisions require delegated-authority states, such as Michigan, to regulate, under the pollution-control permit system, certain municipal and private stormwater-management systems.

Certain *nonpoint*, or diffuse, sources also can significantly impair water quality. These include runoff from urban and agricultural lands, contaminated rain/snow, and leachate from contaminated land and water-bottom sediments. Control and remediation (cleanup) of these nonpoint sources often fall outside of the permit system, necessitating alternative approaches, such as preventing pollution by use of "best management practices" and, in some cases, removing or containing the source or the contaminants.

Surface Water

Michigan's surface-water quality improvements over the last three decades are due in large measure to the investment of billions of public and private funds for treating and/or properly disposing of industrial and sanitary waste that once polluted state waters. In general, the water quality in lakes and streams in the northern two-thirds of the state is high, with the few exceptions being in and around highly urbanized areas or adjacent to old mining or industrial sites. In the southern third, a number of rivers, streams, and lakes, while improving, still do not meet water-quality standards; this is due to agricultural, industrial, commercial, and residential land uses and the resulting point and nonpoint pollution.

GLOSSARY

Animal feedlot operation (AFO)
An operation where farm animals are held in a confined space for an extended period, creating the need for waste management so as to prevent water pollution. A concentrated animal feeding operation (CAFO), as defined by the EPA, must have a water-discharge permit.

Combined sewer overflow (CSO)
Occurs when the capacity of a combined sewer, which carries storm water, domestic sewage, and industrial waste to a wastewater treatment facility in a single pipe, is exceeded (usually during wet weather); such systems originally were designed to discharge the excess untreated waste into the nearest water body (that is, to overflow into it).

Generally accepted agricultural and management practices (GAAMPs)
Pollution-prevention practices recognized and/or established by the Michigan Department of Agriculture under the Right to Farm Act.

Groundwater
Water found underground in (1) shallow silt, sand, and gravel deposits or (2) deep, fractured, or porous rock.

Nonpoint-source pollution
A diffuse discharge containing pollutants that does not have a single point of discharge; examples are rain, runoff from adjacent lands, or air deposition.

Sponsored by the Michigan Nonprofit Association and the Council of Michigan Foundations

Many inland lakes and streams still have pollution problems caused by the presence of such persistent toxic chemicals as polychlorinated biphenyls (PCBs), certain pesticides, and heavy metals, such as mercury, that increase in concentration as they move through the food chain (that is, they *bioaccumulate*). Mercury is the most pervasive toxic substance found in fish in Michigan, and the Michigan Department of Community Health's annual fish-consumption advisories (warnings) due to high mercury levels apply virtually throughout the state for many species.

The federal Clean Water Act (section 305[b] of the federal Water Pollution Control Act) requires that each state with delegated pollution-control authority biennially report to the EPA. This so-called section 305(b) report, among its other elements, must (1) identify lakes and river segments where pollution-control efforts have not attained state standards and (2) under certain circumstances, establish the limit for various pollutants that cannot be exceeded (the total maximum daily load [TMDL]) if attainment with water-quality standards is to be achieved.

The Michigan Department of Environmental Quality (MDEQ) has TMDLs established or planned in numerous locations for a variety of pollutants, including phosphorus, a nutrient responsible for nuisance algal growths and other negative affects resulting from excessive enrichment, and *Escherichia coli (E. coli)*, a bacteria indicative of the presence of untreated human waste, which is a threat to public health. For *E. coli* alone, the MDEQ is developing TMDLs on 69 lakes and river segments.

In 2001 the MDEQ and the Michigan Department of Natural Resources jointly published *State of Michigan's Environment 2001—First Biennial Report* under a 1999 statute requiring the departments to biennially prepare a comprehensive status report on the state's environment. The report tracks various physical, biological, and chemical indicators of environmental quality, describes monitoring programs, and presents information on water-quality measures (including indices for measuring the quality of the Great Lakes). The departments acknowledge that there are gaps in the data and analysis in the 2001 report but expect that over time, the reports will be an important tool in tracking the performance of programs addressing water quality and other environmental issues.

Combined Sewer Overflow (CSO)

Historically, older urban areas built sewers in which so-called sanitary waste (domestic sewage), industrial waste, and stormwater are combined and carried in a single pipe. Under normal conditions, all the wastewater goes to, and is treated at, a municipal wastewater facility before being discharged to lakes or rivers. But when there is a storm (or excessive snowmelt), and flow exceeds pipe capacity, a problem arises because the combined systems were designed to overflow and discharge the untreated waste directly into surface waters. Because more than 50 cities still have combined systems, CSOs are a serious water-quality problem in many areas of Michigan. In the last decade, local governments have expended approximately $1.0 billion to build CSO holding/treatment basins or new, separated sanitary sewers. This has helped to substantially reduce the number of untreated CSOs, but an estimated $1.7 billion more is needed over the next 10 years to address remaining problems.

Sanitary Sewer Overflow (SSO)

Even when the sanitary sewer system is separate from the stormwater system, overflows (sanitary sewer overflows, or SSOs) may occur. Although there are various causes, persistent SSOs usually result from stormwater entering the separate sanitary sewer from a pipe failure, from infiltration through pipe connections, or from roof drains and basement footing drains that are connected directly to the sanitary system. SSOs also occur,

---

On-site disposal system (OSDS)
A system designed to treat and discharge waste near its source; commonly, a septic tank and drain field.

Point-source pollution
A single, identifiable source of pollutants; examples are discharges from wastewater-treatment facilities or storm-water pipes.

Protected water uses
Purposes (e.g., domestic consumption, fish habitat, recreation) for which water is protected under state and federal law.

Sanitary sewer overflow (SSO)
Unplanned discharge, when pipe capacity is exceeded, of untreated waste from separate sanitary sewers into a water body.

Surface water
Water found above ground, in lakes, streams, rivers, bogs, wetlands, and other visible water bodies.

Total maximum daily load (TMDL)
A regulatory term describing the limit imposed, to achieve water-quality standards, on the combined discharges of a particular pollutant into a river segment or lake.

usually following a major storm, if a local government responds to basement sewage backups by using a relief pump to temporarily discharge the excess wastewater, which is untreated, into the nearest lake or stream. Although this violates the law, the MDEQ has exercised enforcement discretion in such instances.

Recently, the EPA has targeted SSOs, and, in 2000, the MDEQ adopted new SSO reporting requirements that have been incorporated into state law. The number of SSOs reported under the new state requirement is expected to exceed several hundred. Completely eliminating SSOs may be impractical given the design and capacity of sewers already in place, but many communities already have corrected or have plans underway to address SSO problems. Correction of SSOs statewide will be very costly and could take years.

Basement flooding associated with SSOs has prompted numerous homeowner lawsuits to recover damages from their local government. A lower court ruled in 2000 that local governments cannot assert government immunity in the case of SSOs and, under a strict liability standard, could be held liable for economic as well as noneconomic damages. Local governments fear that being held to a strict liability standard will result in very high judgments and, in response, the legislature enacted P.A. 222 of 2001, which limits local government liability in such instances. At this writing, a consolidated basement-flood-damage case, involving the cities of Farmington Hills and Allen Park, is before the Michigan Supreme Court. The decision could result in substantially different compensation between those with basements flooded before and those flooded after the effective date of this new state law.

Stormwater Management

The federal Clean Water Act requires that stormwater discharges be regulated, and the EPA established a phased approach. Phase I regulations mandate that all municipalities having a separated sewer system serving a population of 100,000 or more must obtain a permit to discharge their stormwater into surface waters, Michigan, using its delegated authority (see above), promulgated general stormwater-discharge regulations in 1995. Phase I affects five Michigan cities: Ann Arbor, Flint, Grand Rapids, Lansing, and Warren. The costs of complying vary, but the average expenditure just to meet the application requirements was estimated to be $600,000. The costs of implementing the stormwater plan will be in addition.

Phase II regulations require virtually all public agencies (i.e., cities, townships, villages, counties, the Michigan Department of Transportation, and colleges and universities) in the urbanized areas of southern Michigan that have stormwater facilities to obtain a stormwater-discharge permit by 2003. In 1997 the MDEQ established a voluntary, alternative, *watershed*-based general permit. Forty-three communities and cooperating public agencies in the Rouge River watershed, in southeast Michigan, volunteered to be trailblazers for this innovative approach. They have developed seven subwatershed plans that lay the foundation on which each public agency has prepared its stormwater pollution-prevention initiative. Based on the success in the Rouge River watershed and with the MDEQ's encouragement, several other areas are considering the watershed alternative, which now has received EPA approval for meeting Phase II requirements.

Cost of Needed Infrastructure

A statewide assessment of Michigan's sewer infrastructure needs (*Managing the Cost of Clean Water—An Assessment of Michigan's Sewer Infrastructure Needs*) was completed in 2000 by Clean Water Michigan, a coalition of representatives of local government, county drain commissioners, local health agencies, regional governments, environment groups, and business organizations. This assessment determined that it may cost as much as $6 billion in the next 20 years for locals to correct combined-sewer problems, replace/repair/expand existing sanitary sewers, and/or improve existing wastewater treatment plants. In 2001 the Southeast Michigan Council of Governments produced a more comprehensive evaluation of new sewer infrastructure and maintenance costs, estimating that an additional $14–26 billion will be needed by 2030 in just that seven-county area.

The high costs projected for meeting the sewer infrastructure needs of the state relate in part to the relatively new requirements for CSO and SSO remediation, but the major costs arise from the fact that 60–70 percent of the existing sanitary sewer systems and treatment plants were built more than 30 years ago and need or soon will need major repair or replacement. Many of these facilities were built with federal and state grant dollars that no longer are available. The Michigan State Revolving Loan Fund (SRF) currently is the largest source of financial help to local governments that must improve their sewer infrastructure. Annually, about $200 million is available, but it is estimated that over the next five years, $350 million a year will be needed to meet the demand for these state-subsidized loans. The older urban areas are the most likely to have CSOs, SSOs, and aging wastewater-treatment plants and sewers. In most, the population and tax base are decreasing, and, in many, the average household income is below the statewide average, which increases the financial burden on the residents.

Sponsored by the Michigan Nonprofit Association and the Council of Michigan Foundations

To address this need, a measure recently enacted (P.A. 220 of 2001) will increase state capitalization of the SRF. The new law authorizes a transfer from the Budget Stabilization Fund (providing that its balance exceeds $250 million) of up to $25 million a year for the next five years to match any increase in federal dollars. While not providing immediate new dollars for loans to local communities, the authorization does bolster growing support in Congress for increasing the federal allocation for such programs nationwide.

Groundwater

Nearly half of Michigan's population relies on groundwater for its domestic water. In addition, near-surface groundwater is the primary source of many of Michigan's rivers and lakes.

Protecting the Water Supply

In the last decade, the MDEQ has identified more than 10,000 sites where groundwater has been polluted, and it estimates that 560 water supplies were affected by polluted groundwater in 2001. Most of those problems relate to seepage into groundwater from old landfills, manufacturing spills, waste-disposal practices, mining operations, bulk-chemical storage, and underground oil- and gasoline-storage tanks. The latter problem was diminished considerably by a correction program and the requirement that substandard underground tanks be upgraded/replaced by December 1998; in 2001 there were fewer than 300 substandard storage tanks in use.

Much of the 1998 Michigan Environmental Bond monies were expended by the MDEQ to protect or replace public water supplies or restore other natural resources impaired by groundwater contamination. A portion of the $335 million Clean Michigan Initiative Fund also is being used to help clean up contaminated sites and assist local governments in addressing serious problems.

Despite the positive effect of new requirements for solid-waste disposal, new underground storage-tank standards, and a series of laws enacted in the past 20 years addressing the handling, storage, and disposal of hazardous materials, the legacy of past practices leaves the state with hundreds, if not thousands, of places where the groundwater no longer is suitable as a drinking water supply. The MDEQ Environmental Response Division maintains a catalog of contaminated sites (currently about 3,000) that are suspected to have polluted groundwater and also provides information on the status of cleanup and what is known about the source and extent of the contamination.

Septic Systems

Under Michigan law, disposing of any liquid waste from any source into the waters of the state, including groundwater, requires a permit. On-site disposal systems (OSDSs), frequently referred to as septic systems, that discharge waste into the ground are subject to MDEQ regulation. Under MDEQ rules, residential OSDSs are subject to review and approval by local (county, city, or district) health departments using state guidelines. If a septic system is designed, installed, and maintained properly, in a suitable location, it will provide cost-effective and environmentally safe waste disposal. But if any one of these essential factors is ignored, the system can fail and release harmful contaminants to the groundwater and, potentially, to surface waters.

There are more than 1.2 million septic systems in Michigan, serving approximately 3.7 million people, and the number is increasing by more than 10,000 a year. State law does not require that septic systems be properly maintained, and the local governments are responsible for addressing failures. Only seven counties (Benzie, Grand Traverse, Macomb, Ottawa, Shiawassee, Washtenaw, and Wayne) require that a septic system be inspected when a property is sold. Results from such inspections in Wayne and Washtenaw counties indicate that the failure rate for older systems is 20 percent or higher.

Pollution Prevention

Preventing water pollution at its source is much less expensive than having to remove it at a treatment facility or remediate environmental impairments resulting from inadequate treatment. The state has both regulatory programs and voluntary education programs intended to reduce or eliminate waste generation. Pre-treatment of waste, to remove or reduce certain chemicals, particularly toxics, is required of industries that discharge into municipal treatment systems. One of the major foci for stormwater and nonpoint-source water-pollution control is education that encourages homeowners, businesses, industry, and farmers to use "best management practices" in storing, handling, and using potentially polluting materials. For many of the more toxic, persistent, and bioaccumulative chemical compounds, the most effective form of pollution control is recycling and reuse, or, if less toxic substitutes are available, elimination. State and federal prohibitions on the use of certain pesticides (e.g., DDT) and industrial compounds (e.g., PCBs) and restrictions on the use of chemicals (e.g., mercury) have been effective in reducing the levels of these harmful chemicals in water, fish, and fish-eating animals.

DISCUSSION

No one wants to be identified as advocating for polluted water, but the cost of maintaining clean water and the high price of correcting the remaining problems has engendered strong advocacy for less expensive approaches, fewer government mandates, more emphasis on risk-based remediation, and nonregulatory alternatives. On the other side, advocates for cleaner water, including those directly affected by potential and present pollution, urge stringent enforcement of existing requirements and full cleanup of the sources of water pollution. Compounding the debate is the fact that many of the remaining water-quality problems are more complex than those previously faced; in many cases, they also are much more expensive to correct and yield much lower direct benefit for every dollar spent. The arguments on both sides are well known and are not repeated here. The following pertains to pending water-quality actions and likely state or federal policy changes.

On-Site Disposal Systems (Septic Tanks and Tile Fields)

Legislation introduced in 2001 (SB 107) would establish standards for residential on-site disposal systems, require that they be inspected before a home may be sold, and mandate that local governments provide educational materials to OSDS owners. Local governments' concern about paying for such a program and developers' and real estate firms' concern about the effect on home sales have stalled the bill. The bill's supporters point to the success of programs in the seven counties that have time-of-sale inspection and the need to prevent significant surface and groundwater contamination from failing systems.

A related bill, SB 108, would (1) require monitoring to assess the effects on state waters of discharges of untreated or partially treated sanitary waste from CSOs, SSOs, and failing OSDSs and (2) provide Clean Water Fund grants to local agencies to assess such discharges and train local OSDS inspectors. The full fiscal implications of the bill are not known, and some argue that existing monitoring programs are adequate. Supporters argue that better information is needed to accurately assess the extent of the problem and the costs of responding.

Agriculture Practices

Michigan farm waste generally is regulated under nonpoint-pollution-prevention programs developed under the state Right to Farm Act. Animal feedlot operations (AFOs) that meet the EPA definition of a concentrated animal feeding operation (CAFO), generally those with more than 1,000 animals, are regulated through a point-source permit. Agricultural nonpoint-pollution-prevention programs in Michigan emphasize the use of the generally accepted agricultural and management practices (GAAMPs) identified by the Michigan Department of Agriculture and endorsed by the MDEQ in 1997 in a joint memorandum.

In early 2001 the EPA proposed to modify the federal regulations governing CAFO permits by requiring more agricultural operations to obtain such a permit and eliminating certain current exemptions. The rules are pending while the EPA considers comments and tries to resolve concerns expressed by the U.S. Department of Agriculture. Advocates of the proposed changes argue that the growing number of AFOs and their animal-waste management practices have generated water-pollution problems and should be regulated. Opponents argue that expanding the permit requirements to include more farming operations will be too costly and that current state pollution-prevention programs are adequate to address water-pollution concerns.

NOTE: In May, just before this edition went to print, the legislature voted to put a $1 billion general-obligation bond issue on the November ballot; the bonds' proceeds would be used to help finance sewer construction and renovation.

See also Air Quality; Great Lakes Concerns; Solid Waste and Recycling.

Research on this policy topic was made possible by a grant from the Frey Foundation.

FOR ADDITIONAL INFORMATION

CSO/SSO searchable data base
Michigan Department of Environmental Quality,
www.deq.state.mi.us/csosso

Investing in Southeast Michigan's Quality of Life: Sewer Infrastructure Needs
Southeast Michigan Council of Governments (2001),
www.semcog.org/products/pdfs/sewerneeds2.pdf

Managing the Cost of Clean Water—An Assessment of Michigan's Sewer Needs
Public Sector Consultants (2000), *www.pscinc.com/underground/index.html*

Michigan Fish Advisory
Michigan Department of Community Health (2002),
www.michigan.gov/mdch

Michigan Environmental Council
119 Pere Marquette Drive, Suite 2A
Lansing, MI 48912
(517) 487-9539
(517) 487-9541 FAX
www.mecprotects.org

Michigan Manufacturers Association
P.O. Box 14247
Lansing, MI 48901
(517) 372-5900
(517) 372-3322 FAX
www.mma-net.org

Michigan Municipal League
1675 Green Road
Ann Arbor, MI 48105
(800) 653-2483
(734) 662-8083 FAX
www.mml.org

Michigan United Conservation Clubs
2102 Wood Street
P.O. Box 30235
Lansing, MI 48909
(517) 371-1041
(517) 371-1505 FAX
www.mucc.org

Michigan Water Quality Report (Year 2002 305[b] Report)
Michigan Department of Environmental Quality (2002),
www.michigan.gov/deq

Rouge River stormwater program
www.wcdoe.org/rougeriver/stormwater/status.html

State of Michigan's Environment 2001—First Biennial Report
Michigan Department of Environmental Quality (2001),
www.michigan.gov/deq

Stormwater rules
Michigan Department of Environmental Quality (2002),
www.michigan.gov/deq

Surface Water Quality Division
Michigan Department of Environmental Quality
P.O. Box 30273
Lansing, MI 48909
(517) 373-1949
(517) 373-2040 FAX
www.michigan.gov/deq

U. S. Environmental Protection Agency
www.epa.gov/epahome/resource.htm

Wayne County Department of Environment
415 Clifford Street, 7th Floor
Detroit, MI 48226
(313) 224-3630
(313) 224-0045 FAX
www.wcdoe.org

Welfare Reform: TANF Reauthorization

GLOSSARY

Child Care and Development Block Grant (CCDBG)
Federal funding to the states for child-care assistance to low-income families. Along with Temporary Assistance for Needy Families (TANF) allocations, the CCDBG has become a primary source of additional funding for state child-care subsidies and is part of the TANF reauthorization debate.

Family Independence Program (FIP)
Michigan's Temporary Assistance for Needy Families (TANF) program.

Food Stamp Program (FSP)
Federal U.S. Department of Agriculture program that provides funding to help low-income people purchase food, often through ATM-like debit cards rather than paper coupons or stamps. Current funding for the FSP expires in September 2002 at the same time as Temporary Assistance for Needy Families (TANF) appropriations.

Michigan Family Independence Agency (FIA)
The state agency that administers the Family Independence Program (FIP) and related programs, including child daycare, food stamps, and child welfare; also determines eligibility for Medicaid.

BACKGROUND

In 1996, with the passage of the federal Personal Responsibility and Work Opportunity Reconciliation Act (PRWORA), the system of public assistance for poor people living in the United States underwent dramatic change. Welfare reform marked a shift in public policy from federal programs administered under strict guidelines (notably Aid to Families with Dependent Children) to block grants that give states funding and authority to develop and administer their own programs with limited federal oversight.

Welfare reform at the state level is funded through the Temporary Assistance for Needy Families (TANF) block grant. TANF funding and provisions must receive federal reauthorization prior to September 30, 2002.

The overall goal of federal welfare reform was to move those dependent on public assistance into the work force, establish limits for most benefits, and end "entitlement" programs that guaranteed cash assistance to all eligible adults and children. TANF funding makes it possible for each state to create and manage programs with far less federal involvement than before. Flexibility, even if it meant reduced federal funding, was advocated by most governors. To gain more flexibility and authority, a few states obtained federal waivers to change their welfare system prior to enactment of federal reform.

Michigan was a forerunner in this arena. As early as 1992 the state began moving benefit recipients toward more work participation and greater personal responsibility for ending their dependence on public assistance. To Strengthen Michigan Families (TSMF), Michigan's 1992 welfare-reform initiative, tied eligibility for benefits to working, attending school or job training, or performing community service. The TSMF program became the basis for the state TANF program, and Michigan was among the first states to receive federal approval to implement its TANF plan following PRWORA's passage.

Welfare Reform in Michigan

In Michigan, as elsewhere across the country, the number of people receiving welfare assistance since 1996 has decreased by roughly half.

- In January 1997 Michigan had approximately 155,000 cases in the Family Independence Program (FIP), its TANF program.

- By February 2002 the caseload was 77,207 (comprising 214,436 recipients).

Despite the reduction, the number of applications for cash assistance (about 160,000 a year) has not changed much since 1992, when Michigan first began to tie work requirements to benefits. Applications for child-care subsidies, however, have increased 10-fold: In 1992 there were about 1,200 applications a month; today the monthly average approaches 10,500.

Sponsored by the Michigan Nonprofit Association and the Council of Michigan Foundations

Work participation, measured by the earned-income rate among FIP participants, currently stands at just under 28 percent. Almost 46,000 cases are deferred from work requirements and work-related activities, either because they are child-only cases or the clients are disabled or otherwise limited in their ability to meet program requirements. Michigan has no established time limits for FIP benefits, a distinct feature of the state's welfare program. While PRWORA limits federal funding of assistance to a lifetime maximum of five years, Michigan has not set a limit for state funding.

Applications for FIP and associated programs must be made at local Family Independence Agency (FIA) offices. FIP participants may be eligible for child care and food stamps (administered by the FIA), and Medicaid (administered by the Michigan Department of Community Health).

Personal Responsibility and Work Opportunity Reconciliation Act (PRWORA)
The federal law signed in 1996 that overhauled the nation's welfare system and established the Temporary Assistance for Needy Families (TANF) block grant.

■ Since 1996 Michigan's annual child-care funding has more than tripled—from $128 million to more than $450 million, and the child-care caseload has increased accordingly. Child care for FIP participants is fully subsidized. When a family leaves welfare, the state helps to pay for child care while the family income is below a certain level, but a co-payment is required.

■ FIP participants also are eligible to receive food stamps. The number of Michigan families receiving them had decreased about 24 percent since welfare reform was implemented, but the FIA reports that in December 2000 the caseload began to increase rapidly and is up 30 percent since then.

Temporary Assistance for Needy Families (TANF)
The block-grant program created by the federal government in 1996 to replace existing welfare funding and give states more administrative/program flexibility to move people from welfare to work. The funding goes to states in the form of block grants, which they use to provide cash grants to eligible recipients and fund related state programs.

■ Medicaid, which provides health care coverage for eligible low-income people, is another benefit that most FIP participants use. Although the FIA qualifies FIP participants for Medicaid coverage, the program is administered through the Michigan Department of Community Health.

Work First, Michigan's TANF work program, is administered by the Michigan Department of Career Development. Work First funding is allocated to the 25 regional workforce development boards that contract with local organizations to deliver services. Although Michigan work-requirement policies do allow for training and education, Work First focuses primarily on job search and employment. FIP participants attend a Work First session when they first qualify for benefits, to learn the rules and regulations that govern cash assistance. If FIP participants do not meet Work First requirements, they are subject to sanctions that can terminate cash benefits and reduce food stamps. In the first five months of 2000, for example, more than 4,000 FIP cases were closed for non-compliance. Policies that will be implemented in April 2002 make it possible for recipients and their families to be terminated from FIP in as few as 20 days for not complying with Work First requirements.

To Strengthen Michigan Families (TSMF)
The Michigan welfare-reform initiative, started in 1992, to encourage employment, give financial support to families, and require welfare recipients to assume personal responsibility for ending their dependence on welfare. After 1996 it evolved into the state plan required under PRWORA.

FIA Perspective on TANF Reauthorization
The Michigan FIA director has testified in Washington on issues related to TANF reauthorization. Based on Michigan's experience with welfare reform, he calls for

Work First
The work component of Michigan's TANF program; it is administered by the state Department of Career Development. Services are delivered through contract with local organizations, including nonprofit groups, for-profit companies, and public educational institutions.

■ funding to remain at the same level, to pay benefits and provide support services;

■ more flexibility, to allow states to be more innovative;

■ simplifying programs related to welfare, such as food stamps, to reduce the administrative burden on the states; and

■ addressing broader issues related to welfare reform, especially family formation and poverty reduction.

DISCUSSION

In 1996 federal welfare reform sparked heated debate across the political spectrum—about society's obligation to the poor, the excesses of "welfare queens," the disintegration of the family, the cycle of poverty, and the economic limitations of government. More than five years later, the political heat has largely cooled. Caseloads have declined nationwide, federal expenditures for cash assistance have declined, and overall poverty rates have fallen. Parties on both sides of the debate disagree about which force deserves credit—welfare policy changes or the economic boom of the late 1990s. But even those who opposed welfare reform and continue to oppose its limitations and the burdens it places on poor people admit that their worst fears for families and children in the immediate aftermath of welfare reform were not fully realized.

TANF Reauthorization Issues

Despite the apparent short-term success of welfare reform, there are many questions about the long-term effects, and TANF reauthorization is providing a platform for raising its more complicated dimensions. These questions pertain not only to federal reauthorization but also to state policies about how, what, and to what end public assistance shall be provided.

■ Many people have left welfare only to join the ranks of the working poor. If, in leaving welfare, one can get only a minimum-wage paycheck, it puts health care coverage, child care, and transportation beyond reach. Many former recipients are working in low-wage jobs and have no opportunity to acquire the skills they need to move beyond transient or entry-level employment. To what extent should government provide the support that low-income families need to become economically self-sufficient? How closely should federal TANF funding be tied to how well a state performs in reducing poverty as opposed to reducing caseload? Debate on such questions will affect matters such as the time limits imposed on public assistance, programs to help the working poor, and the extent to which states' flexibility should be increased to allow them to meet their population's specific needs.

■ As caseloads have fallen, welfare-reform critics charge that access to welfare-related services (e.g., food stamps, child care, health care) has plummeted, often due to how states, including Michigan, implement welfare programs. In some cases, policy changes have been confusing to recipients with the result that otherwise eligible people unnecessarily lost food stamps and Medicaid coverage. In some states, TANF funds are being used in place of state funding to support existing programs and balance the state budget. In states facing budget shortfalls, program administrators may have little incentive to spend more TANF funds on lowering barriers to access. Some observers see shrinking federal oversight and the focus on flexibility as leading to insufficient accountability, making access problems more probable.

■ The proportion of births to unmarried women, including teens, remains high. Many believe that the authorization should continue TANF's family-building provisions with the object of reducing long-term demand for public assistance, and a likely subject of the reauthorization debate will be "family formation" issues. This raises the question of the extent to which state welfare programs may be required to use their federal funds to promote marriage and other value-related objectives.

Conclusion

The TANF reauthorization process is prompting an examination of welfare reform and its effects on people and the state human-services infrastructure. The most controversial elements of welfare reform—work requirements and time limits on benefits—now are firmly established in public policy. Thus, most analysts believe the current reauthorization debate will center on funding for work-support programs and giving states the flexibility they wish to set related program requirements.

See also Career Development; Child Care; Health Care Access, Medicaid, and Medicare; Immigrants: Human Services Benefits; Youth at Risk.

FOR ADDITIONAL INFORMATION

The Brookings Institution
1775 Massachusetts Avenue, N.W.
Washington, DC 20036
(202) 797-6000
(202) 797-6004
www.brookings.org

Michigan Department of Career Development
201 North Washington Square
Lansing, MI 48933
(517) 241-4000
(517) 373-0314 FAX
www.michigan.gov/mdcd

Sponsored by the Michigan Nonprofit Association and the Council of Michigan Foundations

Michigan Family Independence Agency
235 South Grand Avenue
P.O. Box 30037
Lansing, MI 48909
(517) 373-2000
(517) 335-6101 FAX
www.michigan.gov/fia

Michigan League for Human Services
1115 South Pennsylvania Avenue, Suite 202
Lansing, MI 48912
(517) 487-5436
(517) 371-4546 FAX
www.milhs.org

National Governors' Association
Hall of the States
444 North Capitol Street
Washington, DC 20001
(202) 624-5300
(202) 624-5313 FAX
www.nga.org

The Urban Institute
2100 M Street, N.W.
Washington, DC 20037
(202) 833-7200
(202) 331-9747 FAX
www.urban.org

Youth at Risk

BACKGROUND

Research identifies a multitude of *risk factors*—that is, circumstances, influences, or behaviors in a youth's life that put him/her at risk of not growing into a well-adapted adult. The sources of risk for youth may be simplistically categorized as *external* or *internal*.

- External factors include growing up impoverished, having inadequate health care, being abused or neglected, or residing in an unsafe neighborhood.

- Internal factors relate to lifestyle decisions made by a young person and include deciding to smoke, abuse substances, become sexually active at an early age, or engage in violent or criminal activities.

Despite this distinction, internal and external risk factors are linked. Positive and negative external factors affect young children greatly and can influence the rest of their life, including their later lifestyle decisions. Poverty, for example, is found by numerous studies to be associated with youth being abused or neglected and with their experiencing such difficulties as reduced school readiness, dropping out of school, teen pregnancy, and behavior problems.

Advances in the fields of child development, brain science, and social science are changing how risk among youth is studied and understood. First, risk now is understood to be complex—that is, it involves environmental, neurological, *and* social factors rather than single or separable factors, behaviors, and outcomes. Moreover, there is growing consensus that identifying, preventing, and ameliorating risk must begin in early childhood rather than waiting until later, when the results manifest themselves.

Adolescent-behavior research supports focusing on the importance of youth having "assets" in their life—that is, protective factors (e.g., a caring and stable family, a safe school, positive peer influences) that increase their resiliency and reduce the likelihood that they will engage in high-risk behavior. The Search Institute (Minneapolis) has surveyed more than one million youth nationwide and is at the forefront of this approach. Many Michigan communities are making efforts to measure the existence or absence of assets in the lives of their young people.

The risk factors presented here are those of current public policy concern in Michigan: poverty, infant and child mortality, access to health care, abuse and neglect, teenage parenthood, crime and delinquency, and tobacco use. Another, substance abuse, is addressed elsewhere in this book.

DISCUSSION

Youth Poverty

Compared to others, youngsters living in poverty are at higher risk than others of dying in infancy, being in poorer health, having lower academic achievement, and, as adults, earning less income. The U.S. Census Bureau estimates that more than 350,000 Michigan children and youth live in households with income below the poverty level. This is 14 percent of all children, down from 19 percent in 1990 and lower than the national

GLOSSARY

Asset
In reference to youth, a factor considered essential to good growth and development—e.g., caring family, safe school, positive peer influence.

Juvenile delinquency
Illegal behavior by a minor; includes both "status" offenses (pertain only to minors, e.g., truancy) and "index" offenses (pertain regardless of age, e.g., breaking and entering).

Medicaid
A federal/state program that pays for health care services delivered mainly to eligible low-income people.

Poverty threshold
The amount of household income below which it is believed a family cannot meet basic food, shelter, clothing, and other needs; the level is adjusted annually by the federal government and varies by family size. In 2002 for a family of four, the amount is $18,100.

Risk
In reference to youth, a circumstance, influence, or behavior that mitigates against a young person's growing up with the cognitive, social, emotional, and physical ability to be a well-adapted adult.

Youth, young people
In this article, persons aged 0–18. The definition of adolescence varies by program and study.

Sponsored by the Michigan Nonprofit Association and the Council of Michigan Foundations

figure of 17 percent. Exhibit 1 displays the household distribution of childhood poverty. Despite the fact that the number of poor children has dropped, the Children's Defense Fund indicates that a child is more likely to be poor today than was the case 20 or 30 years ago.

Poor children are most likely to be living in a female-only headed household, but many live in two-parent homes; the lowest incidence is in male-only headed households. Although the risk factors discussed below may exist independently of a youth's financial circumstances, it is widely agreed that poverty often is a significant factor.

Infant and Youth Mortality

In Michigan from 1990 to 2000, the infant mortality rate (i.e., deaths among children under age one) fell from 10.7 to 8.2 deaths per 1,000 live births. The overall decline belies the fact that most of it occurred in the first half of the decade, and the rate actually increased slightly in 2000 (from 8.0 in 1999). From age one to adolescence, the leading cause of death is unintentional injury. Among adolescents, the three leading causes are motor-vehicle accidents, homicide, and suicide. Actions proposed to address infant and youth mortality in Michigan include

- establishing a MIFamily health insurance plan that would extend coverage to 200,000 more people and increase low-income women's access to pre- and

post-natal care, which would reduce risk of infant mortality;

- enacting legislation that holds gun owners responsible if a child or youth gains access to an improperly or unsafely stored firearm; and

- standardizing laws governing firearm safety features such as trigger locks.

Access to Health Care

Inadequate access to health care means that youngsters do not receive regular checkups, immunizations, treatment, and early intervention for health or development problems. Adequate access can help prevent developmental delays and other long-term effects of undetected or untreated health and development problems. Michigan's efforts at providing health insurance for all children have been quite effective: According to the Census Bureau, only 6 percent of all Michigan children are not covered by health insurance.

Among poor Michigan children—for this purpose, defined by the state as those living in households at or below 200 percent of the poverty level—about 129,000 (more than 4 percent of all Michigan children) are believed to be uninsured. In Michigan, there are two main sources of insurance for low-income children: MIChild and Medicaid. MIChild was created in 1998 as a safety net for children aged 1–18 who were ineligible for public assistance

EXHIBIT 1. Child Poverty, by Type of Household, Michigan and the United States, 2000

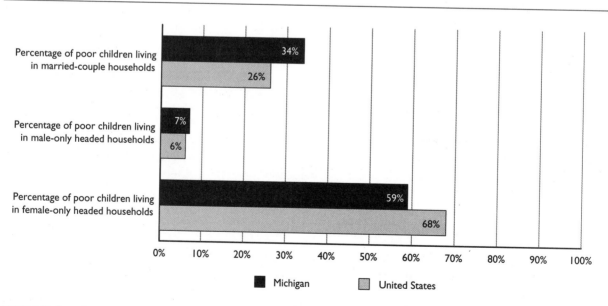

SOURCE: Public Sector Consultants, Inc., using U.S. Census data.
NOTE: Children living below the poverty level comprise 14 percent of all Michigan children and 17 percent of all U.S. children.

Sponsored by the Michigan Nonprofit Association and the Council of Michigan Foundations

and Medicaid. Modeled after private insurance, families pay a monthly premium ($5) for coverage. An indirect effect of MIChild has been to increase children's Medicaid enrollment because a high percentage of adults applying for MIChild coverage for their children are eligible for Medicaid.

One major aspect of Medicaid coverage for children and youth is preventive health care focused on developmental assessment and identifying health problems, which is accomplished through the Early and Periodic Screening, Diagnostic and Treatment (EPSDT) program. Critics assert that the state's effort in ensuring this care has been uneven. For example, a review of 1999 data from the Michigan Department of Community Health (MDCH) reveals that despite the high incidence of insurance, older youth are less likely than infants to receive basic preventive care such as physical examinations, immunization review, vision and hearing tests, and developmental assessment (see Exhibit 2).

Federal targets for EPSDT screenings are set at 80 percent. Michigan has not reported a screening rate that exceeds 51 percent. To respond to the state's need to address participation in screening programs, some advocate for

- providing incentives to parents and providers to obtain/provide the screenings;

- establishing service-delivery and data-collection standards consistent with EPSDT standards;

- changing the name of the program to something more engaging and compelling; and

- making the program mobile, so that screenings can occur where children and youth are gathered.

Abuse and Neglect

A great deal of research links abuse and neglect suffered as a youth with later delinquent and criminal behavior. The National Institute of Justice finds that childhood abuse/neglect increases the odds of future delinquency or criminal behavior by almost 30 percent.

In FY 1999–2000, nearly 129,000 allegations of abuse/neglect were made, and, after investigation, the state removed 3,750 children from their home to protect them from continued abuse/neglect. In each case the child is assessed for future risk, and if deemed to be of high or intensive risk, on-going services to deal with the risk must be offered. Participation in services may be voluntary or court ordered.

Michigan's Child Protection Law requires a number of professionals to report suspected abuse/neglect; failure to report results in a fine (the maximum was increased by Public Act 14 of 2002) and possible imprisonment. Most reports are made by law-enforcement personnel, school counselors and administrators, and hospital/clinic and FIA social workers. Of those not required to report suspected child abuse/neglect, most reports come from an anonymous source or a relative, friend/neighbor, or a parent/caretaker outside the home.

Public policy options currently under consideration to address the neglect/abuse risk factor include

- improving accountability of the child-protection system through annual audits of the Michigan Family Independence Agency's (FIA) child-protection and foster-care services;

- extending whistle-blower protection to FIA child-protection and foster-care workers;

- standardizing training for professionals mandated by law to report abuse/neglect;

- ensuring better continuity of legislative oversight; and

- providing and expanding early-childhood programs to include parenting classes.

EXHIBIT 2. Percentage of Medicaid-Enrolled Michigan Children Receiving EPSDT Preventive Services, by Service Category, 1999

Age	Immunization Review	Vision Screening	Hearing Screening	Developmental Assessment	Physical Examination
0 – 2	85%	49%	49%	65%	70%
3 – 6	71	45	50	47	60
7 – 12	48	37	49	35	45
13 – 21	58	29	52	30	39

SOURCE: Michigan Department of Community Health (1999), "EPSDT Review."

Sponsored by the Michigan Nonprofit Association and the Council of Michigan Foundations

Crime and Delinquency

Juvenile justice and delinquency services are the concern of both the Michigan Department of Corrections (MDOC) and the FIA Bureau of Juvenile Justice (BJJ).

The MDOC handles juvenile offenders who have been waived into the adult corrections system—in July 2000, about 519 youths—mostly in "boot camps." In 1999 the MDOC opened the Michigan Youth Correctional Facility, a 450-bed prison for males aged under 19 who are convicted of a violent or assault crime. The facility is run by contract with a private corrections corporation, which has evoked some controversy. A legislative committee investigated numerous complaints, including understaffing, inadequate officer training (95 percent had no previous corrections experience), a high number of suicide attempts, and the absence of certified special-education teachers. Public Act 41 of 2001 requires the MDOC to report quarterly to the legislature on such matters as offender-control incidents, suicides, attempted suicides, assaults, fights, weapons use, and various staffing and program matters.

The BJJ provides services to youths aged 12–20 who are named by the courts as state wards or who are court wards and assigned to the FIA for care and supervision. At any point in time, there usually are about 5,000 wards in a variety of living arrangements, including six medium-to-high security facilities and four community-based, low-security residential care centers; because of space constraints and other considerations, some youth are sent to out-of-state facilities. In 2001 the Office of Auditor General released a performance audit of BJJ services citing several matters that the department has agreed to address.

- The intake/placement processes of the courts and the FIA need improvement to ensure that proper background information on youths is collected.

- Assessments are not always conducted in accordance with department policies.

- There is insufficient oversight of the out-of-state facilities where some youths are sent.

- Caseloads of probation officers and caseworkers often are too high.

- Youth have insufficient access to prevention services.

- Evaluation of prevention services often is insufficient.

A report by Michigan's Children notes that while youth violence is declining, the state lacks an overall, coordinated prevention strategy. Most state funding directed at youth violence is aimed at punishing delinquents. Youth-violence prevention monies are dispersed through several state agencies and are significantly smaller than the amount going to delinquency services. To address the state's problems of youth delinquency and violence, advocacy groups propose

- establishing a statewide, coordinated effort at violence prevention;

- providing local communities with flexible funding to meet local needs;

- providing more opportunities for adult supervision through before- and after-school programs and other youth programs;

- permitting judges to review cases when a juvenile turns 21, to determine whether s/he requires further intervention; and

- encouraging conflict-resolution strategies, such as peer-mediation programs in local schools.

Teenage Pregnancy

The birth rate among Michigan teenagers has been falling. In 1990, births to women aged 19 and younger comprised 13 percent of all births in the state; by 2000 the percentage had been reduced to 10 percent. Children born of teenaged parents are at risk because they are much more likely than children of others to have low birth weight (a health risk), grow up in poverty, have inadequate health care, develop behavioral problems, and experience physical and developmental problems. A large of body of research finds a correlation between poverty and teenage pregnancy.

Public policy options are somewhat divided on how best to prevent or alleviate the ill effects of teenage pregnancy and parenthood.

- Some advocate for greater use of abstinence-only education in schools; others advocate for more education about contraception and abortion.

- Some believe that sex education needs to be brought up to date and made more relevant to today's youth; others believe that sex education should not be a part of any school curriculum, but left to parents.

Furthermore, funding for services that include contraception and other reproductive health care services are tenuous at best. For example, House Bill 4655 proposes to give priority for state funding to family-planning providers who provide few or no abortion services. This bill stands to cut $1.8 million dollars in state funding to Planned Parenthood of Michigan, a major provider of family-planning services in the state.

Tobacco Use

According to the 2001 Michigan Youth Risk Behavior Survey, the biennial poll of high school students,

- 30 percent have used a tobacco product at some time,

- 64 percent have smoked at some time, and

- 26 percent had smoked in the month preceding the survey.

These numbers are lower than those found in previous surveys. The Michigan departments of Community Health and Education credit the decline to intensive health education, including the Michigan Model for Comprehensive School Health Education, a state-developed model curriculum that addresses health issues and helps young people to build risk-avoidance skills. More than 90 percent of Michigan school districts use the model.

Since 1998 the state has received approximately $600 million from the national tobacco settlement. Most of that money has been directed to programs other than tobacco-use prevention and treatment. This is decried by those who believe that the money rightfully should be spent for anti-tobacco purposes and possibly other health-related programs, but it is supported by those who believe that state spending (about $8 million, according to the MDCH) for this purpose from other sources is adequate. The Michigan Health and Hospital Association is developing a ballot question for November 2002 that if passed would redirect settlement spending from scholarships to health care.

See also Abortion; Children's Early Education and Care; Child Support; Communicable Diseases and Public Health; Crime and Corrections; Domestic Violence; Firearms Regulation; Foster Care and Adoption; Health Care Access, Medicaid, and Medicare; Immigrants: Human Resources Benefits; K–12 Quality and Testing; Substance Abuse; Tobacco Settlement; Welfare Reform: TANF Reauthorization.

Research on this policy topic was made possible by a grant from The Skillman Foundation.

FOR ADDITIONAL INFORMATION

Bureau of Juvenile Justice
Michigan Family Independence Agency
Grand Tower, Suite 401
235 Grand Avenue
Lansing, MI 48909
(517) 335-3489
www.michigan.gov/fia

Michigan's Children
428 Lenawee Street
Lansing, MI 48933
(517) 485-3500
(800) 485-3650 FAX
www.michiganschildren.org

Michigan Department of Community Health
Lewis Cass Building
320 South Walnut Street
Lansing, MI 48913
(517) 373-3740
(517) 335-3090 FAX
www.michigan.gov/mdch

Michigan Department of Corrections
P.O. Box 30003
Lansing, MI 48909
(517) 335-1426
(517) 375-2628 FAX
www.michigan.gov/corrections

Office of Children's Protective Services and Foster Care
Michigan Family Independence Agency
Grand Tower, Suite 510
235 Grand Avenue
Lansing, MI 48909
(517) 373-2083
www.michigan.gov/fia

Search Institute
Banks Building
615 First Avenue N.E., Suite 125
Minneapolis, MN 55413
(800) 888-7828
(612) 376-8955
(612) 376-8956 FAX
www.search-institute.org

Sponsored by the Michigan Nonprofit Association and the Council of Michigan Foundations

Appendix A
Census 2000

BACKGROUND

Unless otherwise noted, the data presented are from the 2000 Census or the Census 2000 Supplementary Survey (C2SS).

The U.S. Constitution, Article I, requires that every ten years the federal government conduct a census of the nation's population. The census serves several purposes, one of which is to allocate the 435 seats of the U.S. House of Representatives among the 50 states. Another is to establish the basis for distributing funding for many federal programs (more than $100 billion annually) as well as state programs. Census figures also are used for planning; for example, new highways are built and fire protection districts established on the basis of current and projected population. In addition, there are numerous provisions in law pertaining to the population of local jurisdictions.

Because the census has a significant effect on federal funding to the states, there is great concern that the count be as accurate as possible. In 1990 more than five million people are believed to have been missed, many the traditionally underserved minority and homeless populations. To correct this in 2000, the Census Bureau proposed to statistically sample areas with lower-than-average response rates, but the proposal was denied by Congress and ruled out by the U.S. Supreme Court. To try to improve the count in 2000, the bureau, for the first time, used a professional advertising campaign, spending $167 million to encourage participation. Although the precise over- and undercounts are not yet known, the census is thought to have been successful. Michigan's response rate was 71 percent, down slightly from 72 percent in 1990. Nationwide, the response rate was 67 percent, up from 61 percent in 1990. The counting errors that occurred in 2000 are not expected to be problematic for either Michigan or the nation.

The 2000 Census found significant change in the Michigan population since the 1990 count, and there are many implications for residents and both public- and private-sector policymakers. Presented here are the changes we believe to be among the most relevant. Implications are discussed elsewhere in this book, in the pieces addressing specific topics.

POPULATION

According to Census 2000, Michigan's population is 9,938,444, up 6.9 percent since 1990. This growth is significantly higher than the 0.4 percent growth in the 1980s and the 4.3 percent growth in the 1970s, yet far under the current national growth estimate of 13.2 percent.

- The median Michigan household income is $43,448, ranking it 17th in the country; the national median is $41,343.

- Fifty-one percent of Michigan's population are female; 49 percent are male.

GLOSSARY

Group quarters
The living arrangement for people not living in a household. The census divides group quarters into two types: **institutional** *(e.g., corrections facilities, nursing homes, and mental hospitals) and* **noninstitutional** *(e.g., college dormitories, military barracks, group homes, missions, and shelters).*

Household
The living arrangement whereby one or more persons live in a given housing unit. The census divides households into two types: **family** *(consisting of two people related by blood, marriage, or adoption and perhaps children) and* **nonfamily** *(consisting of one person or two or more unrelated people).*

Median
The middle value in a distribution that divides the distribution exactly in half; for example, the median age in Michigan is 35.5 years, which means that one-half of the population is younger and one-half is older.

Exhibits 1 and 2 present data on Michigan age and racial/ethnic distribution, respectively. The largest age group consists of 35–44-year-olds, and the largest racial group comprises Caucasians.

The Center for Urban Studies at Wayne State University reports that nine of Michigan's 83 counties lost population. All but one of the nine, Iosco, are central urban counties (Bay, Saginaw, Ingham, Wayne) and rural western Upper Peninsula counties (Gogebic, Iron, Marquette, Ontonogan). The population loss in Iosco, a northeastern lower peninsula county, is attributable to closure of a military base. The largest gains in population are seen in southern Michigan, particularly the Detroit suburban ring, and Kent County.

- Livingston County led all Michigan counties in percentage of growth, expanding by more than 35 percent since the 1990 count.

- Oakland County led all counties in the number of people gained—more than 110,000 (10.2 percent growth).

- Among metropolitan counties that lost population, Wayne County suffered most, losing 50,000 people (a 2.4 percent decrease).

- Detroit, with 951,270 residents, lost 7.5 percent of its population; this is the smallest decline since the city began shrinking in the 1950s, but it brings the city below one million, the threshold for several funding and taxing-authority laws.

EXHIBIT 1. Age Distribution, Number and Percentage of Total Population, Michigan, 2000

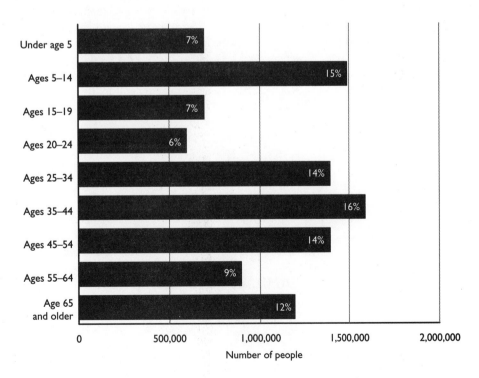

SOURCE: U.S. Bureau of Census.

Sponsored by the Michigan Nonprofit Association and the Council of Michigan Foundations

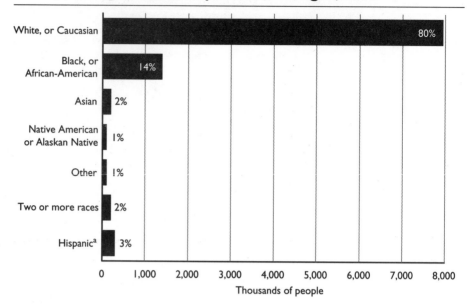

EXHIBIT 2. Racial and Ethnic Groups, Number (thousands) and Percentage of Total Population, Michigan, 2000

SOURCE: U.S. Bureau of Census.

[a]Persons of Hispanic descent may be of any race, therefore this table adds up to more than 100 percent.

REAPPORTIONMENT

One reason for the decennial census is to reapportion the 435 seats in the U.S. House of Representatives. Because Michigan's population grew less than was the case in some other states, Michigan has lost one seat in the House. Each of four other Great Lakes States—Illinois, Indiana, Ohio, and Wisconsin—also lost one seat (only Minnesota retained all its seats). This reflects the larger population shift away from the Midwest and Northeast to the West and South. This reduced congressional representation means reduced influence over the federal matters and money that affect Michigan and the region.

The census also is the basis for reapportioning the Michigan Legislature and state appeals court. Thirty of the 110 Michigan House districts were redrawn; most affected are districts representing Detroit and Wayne, Macomb, and Oakland counties. Representation follows population: As people move from core cities to the suburbs, representation—and political power—follows. All but one of the Michigan Senate districts were redrawn, but because these districts are much larger than the House districts, the political effect of reapportionment is not as significant. The boundaries of all four state court of appeals districts also were redrawn, to equalize the population among them.

FAMILIES AND CHILDREN

Michigan has more than three million households, of which 68 percent are family households. Of the family households,

- 33 percent have dependent children present;

- 51 percent are headed by married couples, and 45 percent of these households (1.2 million) have dependent children present; and

- 13 percent are headed by females, and 60 percent of these (roughly 284,000) have dependent children present.

In looking at Michigan youth (under age 18), we see that

- in the 1990s the youth population grew by 5.6 percent, to upwards of 2.5 million;

- due to the declining birth rate in the 1990s, there was a 4.3 percent drop in the number of children aged under five; and

- in the 1990s the number of Michigan children living below the poverty level dropped slightly, from 19 percent in 1990 to 14 percent (an estimated 350,000) in 2000.

According to a report by Kids Count in Michigan, Census 2000 data reveal important changes in the living arrangements of Michigan's children during the 1990s. As Exhibit 3 shows, the biggest change is in the proportion of children who live with their single

EXHIBIT 3. Children's Living Situation, Percentage Changes, Michigan, 1990 to 2000

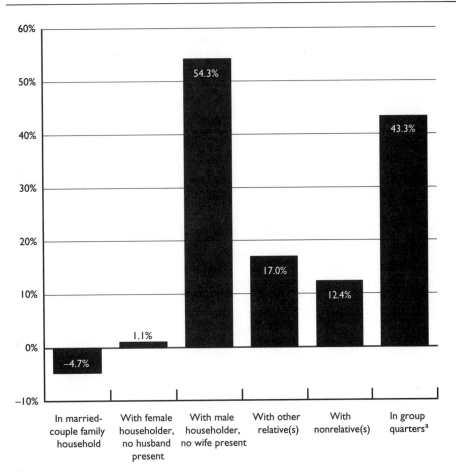

SOURCE: Michigan's Children (November 2001), Children in Michigan: An Early Look at the Census 2000 Data.
[a]Non-household arrangements, either institutional (e.g., corrections facilities, nursing homes) or noninstitutional (e.g., dormitories, barracks, shelters, group homes).

Sponsored by the Michigan Nonprofit Association and the Council of Michigan Foundations

father. The proportion of children living with their single mother increased the least, and the proportion of children living with two married parents decreased.

SENIOR CITIZENS

Michigan's population is aging.

- In 1990 Michigan's median age was 32.6 years; now it is 35.5, and by 2020 it is expected to be 37.9.

- More than one million people (12.3 percent of the total population) are aged 65 and older in Michigan; this is a 10 percent increase from 1990.

- The oldest Michiganians (85 and older) are growing in number as well and at a faster rate than other age groups. There now are nearly 142,500 in this age group (1.4 percent of the total population), a 33.3 percent increase from 1990.

CORRECTIONS

In 2000, according to census figures, there were 65,330 adults and youth in Michigan jails and prisons (about two-thirds in state prisons); this is a 53 percent increase over 10 years ago. This far outpaces the growth rate (6.9 percent) of the general population.

LOCAL GOVERNMENT

According to a 2001 report prepared by the Legislative Service Bureau, there are 340 sections of law, encompassing 58 major subject areas, in Michigan statute that classify and grant authority to local governments *based on the unit's population*. These statutes are tied to 129 different population figures, which means that census 2000 results are greatly affecting the applicability of certain laws. Of particular concern are laws relating to the allocation of funds (e.g., revenue sharing, highway monies) and the authority to levy or raise taxes and fees.

As mentioned above, Detroit's population has fallen below one million, which is the authority threshold in certain tax laws. Whether this will negate the city's authority to levy certain taxes and fees is unclear and could be decided in the courts or by legislative action.

FOR ADDITIONAL INFORMATION

Center for Urban Studies
Wayne State University
656 West Kirby, 3040 F/AB
Detroit, MI 48202
(313) 577-2208
(313) 577-1274 FAX
www.cus.wayne.edu

Citizen's Research Council of Michigan
38777 Six Mile Road, Suite 201A
Livonia, MI 48152
(734) 542-8001
(734) 542-8004 FAX
        and
1502 Michigan National Tower
Lansing, MI 48933
(517) 485-9444
(517) 485-0423 FAX
www.crcmich.org

Michigan Information Center
Romney Building, 10th Floor
111 South Capitol Avenue
P.O. Box 30026
Lansing, MI 48909
(517) 373-7910
(517) 373-2939 FAX
www.michigan.gov/dmb/mic

U.S. Census Bureau
www.census.gov

APPENDIX B
Economic Base of Michigan

These ten exhibits display key statistics pertaining to Michigan's economic base—wage and salary employment, unemployment, nonfarm employment, consumer price index, per capita income, personal income, motor-vehicle sales, motor-vehicle production, agricultural income, and tourism spending—with comparisons to the nation as a whole; the latest comparable data are used. Sources are the U.S. Bureau of Labor Statistics; Michigan Department of Career Development; Michigan Employment Service Agency; *Automotive News Market Data Book*, Crain Communications, Inc.; Michigan Senate Fiscal Agency; U.S. Department of Commerce, U.S. Bureau of Economic Analysis; and Michigan State University Department of Park, Tourism, and Recreational Resources.

EXHIBIT 1. Wage and Salary Employment, Percentage Change from Previous Year, United States and Michigan, 1980–2001

Because of Michigan's reliance on the motor-vehicle industry, the state economy traditionally has been more volatile than the national economy. This exhibit shows that during the upswing of the 1980s, wage and salary job growth in Michigan exceeded that of the nation as a whole, but during the recession that followed (in the early 1990s), so did the state's job declines. Since 1996 employment growth in Michigan has trailed national employment growth, in part because Michigan did not benefit as much from the technology boom as the nation as a whole.

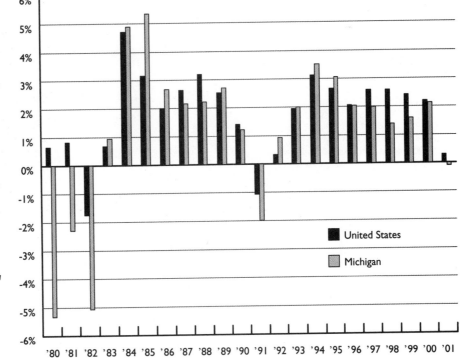

Sponsored by the Michigan Nonprofit Association and the Council of Michigan Foundations

EXHIBIT 2. Unemployment Rate, United States and Michigan, 1970–2001

The unemployment rate measures the percentage of the total work force actively looking for work. During economic downturns, the rate tends to underestimate the number of unemployed because people become discouraged and stop looking. Michigan's reliance on the heavy-manufacturing sector is a primary reason that except for a dramatic reversal from 1994 to 2001, the unemployment rate in Michigan historically has been higher than the U.S. rate.

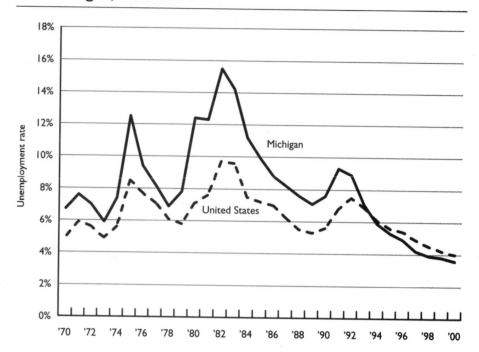

EXHIBIT 3. Nonfarm Employment Distribution, by Industry, United States and Michigan, 2001

The distribution of employment by industry in Michigan is similar to that of the United States with one notable exception: Michigan has a larger share of manufacturing than the rest of the country, due in large part to the concentration of the motor-vehicle industry in the state. In 2000, motor-vehicle jobs accounted for 6.1 percent of Michigan wage and salary employment and about 20 percent of all manufacturing jobs. (The percentages would be higher if related jobs in such other industries as metalworking and rubber and plastic were included.)

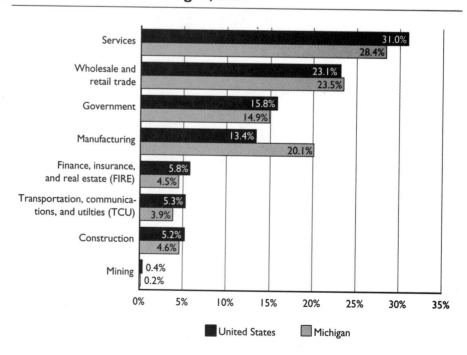

Sponsored by the Michigan Nonprofit Association and the Council of Michigan Foundations

EXHIBIT 4. Consumer Price Index, United States and Michigan, 2000

A consumer price index is an indicator of cost-of-living changes. The Detroit–Ann Arbor index is used here because it is the only one available for Michigan, and it approximates the price level for the state as a whole. The base period against which price increases are measured is 1982–84 for all categories except recreation and education/communications, which are measured from 1997. As may be seen in the "all items" figures, prices in Michigan generally have not risen quite as much they have nationwide. The exceptions are (1) transportation, in which Michigan prices have increased 62.5 percent since the base period, while U.S. prices are up 53.3 percent and (2) the relatively new categories of recreation and education/ communications. In 2001 the U.S. CPI increased 2.0 percent and the Michigan (Detroit–Ann Arbor) CPI increased 2.7 percent.

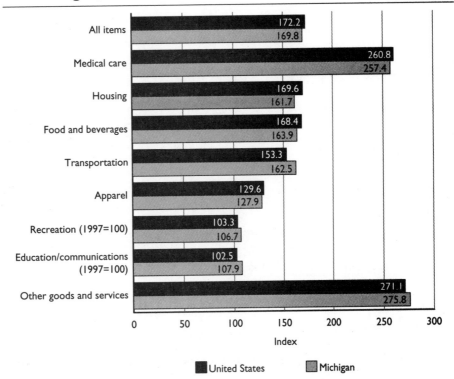

EXHIBIT 5. Michigan per Capita Income as Percentage of U.S. per Capita Income, 1950–2000

Michigan's per capita income exceeded that of the United States during the 1950s, 1960s, and 1970s. However, in the 1980s, when the automobile industry began experiencing serious problems and engaged in extensive layoffs and cost-cutting measures, the state's per capita income fell below the national average. The initial dip occurred in 1981 (although the falloff had began in 1977) and since then, Michigan's per capita income has see-sawed around the national rate, exceeding it in only seven of the last 20 years.

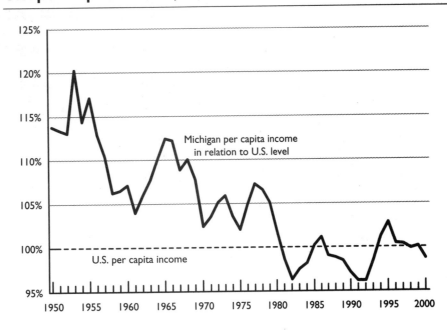

Sponsored by the Michigan Nonprofit Association and the Council of Michigan Foundations

EXHIBIT 6. U.S. and Michigan Personal Income, Total and per Capita, 1976–2000

Year	Michigan per Capita	U.S. per Capita	Michigan as % of U.S.	Michigan Personal Income (millions)	Percentage Change	U.S. Personal Income (millions)	Percentage Change	Real Michigan Personal Income (millions)	Percentage Change	Real U.S. Personal Income (millions)	Percentage Change
1976	$7,084	$6,756	104.9%	$64,588	12.9%	$1,469,752	10.8%	$64,588	7.2%	$1,469,752	4.8%
1977	7,957	7,421	107.2	72,863	12.8	1,630,901	11.0	68,182	5.6	1,531,325	4.2
1978	8,834	8,291	106.5	81,287	11.6	1,841,340	12.9	70,706	3.7	1,606,936	4.9
1979	9,701	9,230	105.1	89,727	10.4	2,072,839	12.6	69,246	−2.1	1,624,580	1.1
1980	10,369	10,183	101.8	95,967	7.0	2,313,921	11.6	63,903	−7.7	1,597,841	−1.6
1981	11,125	11,280	98.6	102,455	6.8	2,588,335	11.9	62,440	−2.3	1,620,201	1.4
1982	11,462	11,901	96.3	104,477	2.0	2,759,954	6.6	61,178	−2.0	1,627,372	0.4
1983	12,243	12,554	97.5	110,771	6.0	2,935,040	6.3	63,044	3.0	1,676,745	3.0
1984	13,576	13,824	98.2	122,857	10.9	3,260,064	11.1	67,619	7.3	1,785,348	6.5
1985	14,734	14,705	100.2	133,728	8.8	3,498,662	7.3	71,121	5.2	1,850,129	3.6
1986	15,573	15,397	101.1	142,146	6.3	3,677,359	5.1	74,551	4.8	1,909,140	3.2
1987	16,130	16,284	99.1	148,191	4.3	3,945,515	7.3	75,356	1.1	1,976,231	3.5
1988	17,198	17,403	98.8	158,529	7.0	4,255,000	7.8	77,558	2.9	2,046,572	3.6
1989	18,276	18,566	98.4	169,163	6.7	4,582,429	7.7	78,565	1.3	2,102,744	2.7
1990	19,022	19,584	97.1	177,103	4.7	4,885,525	6.6	78,223	−0.4	2,126,904	1.1
1991	19,311	20,039	96.4	181,495	2.5	5,065,416	3.7	77,452	−1.0	2,116,169	−0.5
1992	20,263	20,979	96.6	192,038	5.8	5,376,662	6.1	80,263	3.6	2,180,556	3.0
1993	21,366	21,557	99.1	203,828	6.1	5,598,446	4.1	82,933	3.3	2,204,509	1.1
1994	22,829	22,358	102.1	219,121	7.5	5,878,362	5.0	86,431	4.2	2,256,942	2.4
1995	23,931	23,272	102.8	231,594	5.7	6,192,235	5.3	88,523	2.4	2,311,930	2.4
1996	24,394	24,286	100.4	238,095	2.8	6,528,103	5.4	88,681	0.2	2,367,425	2.4
1997	25,505	25,427	100.3	250,216	5.1	6,928,545	6.1	90,929	2.5	2,456,288	3.8
1998	26,870	26,909	99.9	264,645	5.8	7,418,754	7.1	94,067	3.5	2,589,737	5.4
1999	27,886	27,859	100.1	275,963	4.3	7,769,648	4.7	95,636	1.7	2,653,619	2.5
2000	29,071	29,451	98.7	289,390	4.9	8,312,312	7.0	96,804	1.2	2,746,635	3.5

This exhibit includes several measures of personal income: total, real (adjusted for inflation), and per capita.

In 2000 total Michigan personal income (MPI) was $289.4 billion, about 3.5 percent of total U.S. personal income. Michigan personal income growth historically lags behind national growth: From 1995 to 2000, MPI increased only 25.0 percent while the national rate rose 34.2 percent. The picture is similar for the last 20 years: From 1980 to 2000, MPI increased 201.6 percent compared with national growth of 259.2; the average annual growth rates were 5.7 percent and 6.6 percent, respectively.

Adjusted for inflation, the real 20-year average annual growth rates for Michigan and the nation were 2.0 percent and 2.7 percent, respectively.

One reason that Michigan historically has lagged behind the nation is that the Midwest is growing more slowly than the South and West. More recently, the state did not benefit as much as other states from the explosive growth of the technology sector in the 1990s.

Sponsored by the Michigan Nonprofit Association and the Council of Michigan Foundations

EXHIBIT 7. U.S. Light Motor-Vehicle Sales, 1970–2001

Sales of light motor vehicles (vehicles weighing less than 10,000 pounds—includes cars, SUVs, vans, and some pickups) historically have been volatile, as may be seen in the steep peaks and valleys shown here. After the roller coaster ride of the 1970s, light motor-vehicle sales increased consistently in the 1980s but, although the increase parallels income and population growth, the entire increase was in light trucks. The move from passenger cars to trucks accelerated in the 1990s. Passenger car sales averaged almost 1.3 million units less annually than in the 1980s, and light-truck sales averaged about 2.3 million units more. In 2001 total sales surpassed 17 million, an all-time high, but over half (50.5 percent) of the units sold were light trucks; many were minivans and SUVs that replaced station wagons and large sedans for family transportation.

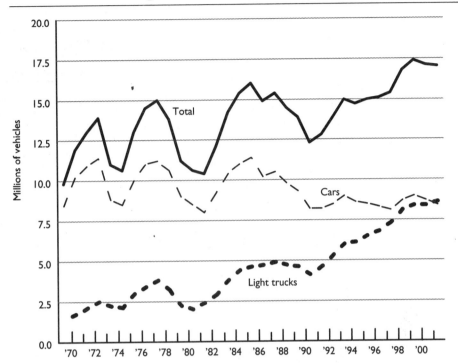

EXHIBIT 8. Michigan Motor-Vehicle Production as a Percentage of U.S. Production, 1970–2001

Michigan's share of U.S. motor-vehicle production has declined over the past 30 years. The decline is due to more foreign competition, which has caused plant closures in Michigan, and the movement of some motor-vehicle production to lower-cost states and nations. Another factor is that while Michigan produces fully a third of all cars built in the country, it produces only 17.5 percent of the light trucks. In number of units, Michigan motor-vehicle production peaked at nearly 4.3 million units in 1973. In 2001 Michigan production was about 3.1 million units, almost 28.0 percent below the 1973 level.

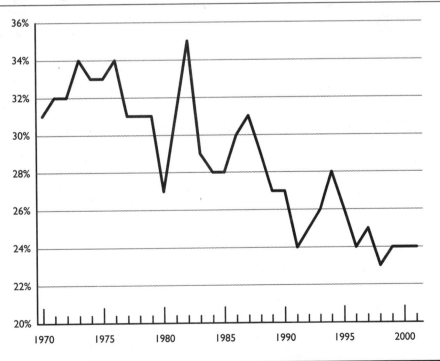

Sponsored by the Michigan Nonprofit Association and the Council of Michigan Foundations

EXHIBIT 9. Farm Income as a Percentage of Personal Income, Michigan and Selected States, 2000

Agriculture is an important Michigan industry but relatively small in terms of income generated, and it is less important than in many other states: Nationwide, farm income in 2000 was 0.6 percent of total personal income, but in Michigan it was only 0.2 percent. Michigan ranks below other states in the Great Lakes region in terms of agriculture's contribution to the economy.

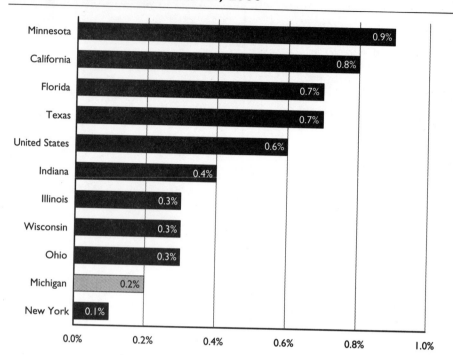

EXHIBIT 10. Estimated Tourism Spending, Michigan, 1996–2000 ($ billions)

Tourism is a major industry in Michigan, generating nearly 164,000 direct jobs and about $2.2 billion in tax revenue (1999 estimates). When spillover or multiplier effects is considered, the industry is responsible for about 215,000 jobs.

Year	Spending on Trips of 100 Miles or More	Tourism Payroll	Direct Tourist Jobs	State-Local Tax Receipts
1996	$9.6	$2.4	$143,000	$1.5
1997	10.0	3.0	157,000	1.8
1998	10.6	3.2	157,000	2.0
1999	11.5	3.5	163,500	2.2
2000 (preliminary)	12.5	NA	NA	NA

NA = Not available.

Sponsored by the Michigan Nonprofit Association and the Council of Michigan Foundations

INDEX

Primary title listings are in boldface.

Sponsored by the Michigan Nonprofit Association and the Council of Michigan Foundations

INDEX

Sponsored by the Michigan Nonprofit Association and the Council of Michigan Foundations

Sponsored by the Michigan Nonprofit Association and the Council of Michigan Foundations

Sponsored by the Michigan Nonprofit Association and the Council of Michigan Foundations

Sponsored by the Michigan Nonprofit Association and the Council of Michigan Foundations

PREVIOUS EDITIONS: TOPICS

Excerpts from previous editions may be obtained by contacting the Production Division, Public Sector Consultants, Inc., 600 West St. Joseph Street, Suite 10, Lansing, Michigan, 48933-2267; 517/484-4954 (telephone) or 517/484-6549 (FAX).

1998–99 (6th) EDITION

1992–93 (5th) EDITION

1990–91 (4th) EDITION

Abortion
Adolescent Health Care
Aeronautics
Agriculture
AIDS and HIV Infection
Air Pollution Regulation
Automobile Insurance Rates
Beverage Containers: Unclaimed Deposits
Bibliography (Appendix)
Business Climate
Campaign Financing
Camp Grayling Modifications
Child and Family Services
Child Care
Court Administration
Crime
Demographics (Appendix)
Domestic Violence
Economic and Political History of Michigan
    (Chapter 1)
Economic Development: Michigan Strategic Fund
Economic Outlook (Appendix)
Education: Community College Funding
Education: Early Childhood
Education: K–12 Education/School Finance Reform
Education: K–12 Quality
Education: University Funding
Facts about Michigan (Appendix)
Financial Institutions

Firearms Regulation
Gambling
Generic Prescription Drugs
Genetic Mapping
Great Lakes Concerns
Groundwater Contamination
Hazardous Waste Disposal
Health Care Access
Health Care Costs
Health Care Regulation
Health Promotion
Holidays (Appendix)
Homeless, The
Hospital Finances
Housing Affordability
Income Tax: State Rates, Credits, and Deductions
Indian Treaty Rights
Infant Mortality
Inheritance Tax
Intergovernmental Cooperation
Job Training
Key Economic Statistics (Appendix)
Legislative Review of Government Programs
Liability: Medical
Liability: Products
Long-Term Care Alternatives
Medicaid
Medical Treatment Decisions
Mental Health: Funding and Services

Nursing Home Care
Off-Road Vehicles
Organ and Tissue Transplants
Part-Time Legislature, A
Pornography and Obscenity
Prison Alternatives
Prison Construction
Property Taxes
Radioactive Waste Disposal
Reapportionment
Regional Economies in Michigan (Appendix)
Single Business Tax
Solid Waste Management
State Budget (Chapter 3)
Structure of State Government (Chapter 2)
Substance Abuse: Law Enforcement
Substance Abuse: Prevention and Treatment
Surface Water Quality
Taxes on Services and Mail Order Sales
Telecommunication: Local Telephone Regulation
Transportation Funding
Trucking Regulation
Unemployment
Unemployment Insurance
User Fees
Welfare
Wetlands
Workers' Disability Compensation

1988–89 (3d) EDITION

Abortions: Medicaid Funding
Acid Rain
AIDS
Air Pollution Regulation
Alzheimer's Disease
Automobile Emissions Testing
Automobile Safety
Bibliography (Appendix)
Biennial State Budget
Boating
Bonding/State Debt
Blue Cross and Blue Shield of Michigan
Business Climate
Campaign Financing
Capital Punishment
Casino Gaming
Child Care
Civil Rights
Consumer Protection
Court Funding
Crime
Demographics (Appendix)
Detroit People Mover
Detroit Strategic Plan
Divestiture of Michigan Pension Fund Investment
    in South Africa
Domestic Violence
Drug Testing in the Workplace
Economic and Political History of Michigan
    (Chapter 1)
Economic Development: Agriculture and Forestry
    Products
Economic Development: Michigan Strategic Fund
Economic Development: Promoting Michigan
Economic Development: Regulatory Relief
Economic Development: Urban Enterprise Zones
Economic Outlook (Appendix)
Education: Community College Funding
Education: Dropout Prevention
Education: Funding for Public Universities
Education: Michigan Education Trust

Education: Preschool
Education: Spending for K–12 Education/School
    Finance Reform
Education: State Support and Regulation of Private
    Schools
Educational Competence
Energy Needs
Environmental Regulation: Reorganization
Facts about Michigan (Appendix)
Farm Debt
Farmland Protection
Firearms Regulation
Foster Care
Great Lakes Water Diversion
Great Lakes Water Levels
Great Lakes Water Quality
Groundwater Contamination
Hazardous Substances in the Community
Hazardous Substances in the Workplace
Hazardous Waste Disposal
Health Care Access for the Poor
Health Care Costs
Health Care Regulation
Health Promotion
Holidays (Appendix)
Homeless, The
Housing: Low-Income
Income Tax: State Rates, Credits, and Deductions
Indian Treaty Fishing
Infant Mortality
Job Training
Juvenile Offenders
Key Economic Statistics (Appendix)
Labor Unions
Land Use and Zoning
Liability: Bars and Restaurants
Liability: Medical
Liability: Products
Long-Term Care Alternatives
Lottery: Where the Money Goes
Medicaid

Medical Treatment Decisions
Mental Health: Community Services
Mental Health: Institutions
Migrant Workers
Minimum Wage, The
Mortgage Reform
Natural Resources Trust Fund
No-Fault Automobile Insurance
Nursing Home Care
Organ Transplants
Part-Time Legislature
Prison Alternatives
Prison Overcrowding
Prison Sentencing Guidelines
Privatization
Property Taxes
Radioactive Waste Disposal
Radon Gas
Regional Economies in Michigan (Appendix)
Revenue Sharing
Sex Education
Single Business Tax
Smoking in Public Places
Solid Waste Management
State Budget (Chapter 3)
Structure of State Government (Chapter 2)
Substance Abuse
Suicide Among Teenagers
Surrogate Parenting
Transportation Funding
Trucking Safety
Unclaimed Beverage Container Deposits
Unemployment
Unemployment Insurance
United States/Canada Free Trade Agreement
Utility Regulation
Water Quality
Welfare
Wetlands
Workers' Disability Compensation
Youth Corps

Sponsored by the Michigan Nonprofit Association and the Council of Michigan Foundations

1987–88 (2d) EDITION

Abortion
Abortions: Medicaid Funding
Acid Rain
Administrative Rules
AIDS
Air Pollution Regulation
Alzheimer's Disease
Annexation
Arts: State Funding
Auto Theft
Balanced Budget Amendment
Banking Law Reform
Beverage Container Deposits: Unclaimed
Bibliography (Appendix)
Biennial State Budget
Blue Cross and Blue Shield Reorganization
Budget Stabilization Fund (BSF)
Business Climate
Campaign Financing
Capital Punishment
Child Abuse
Child Care
Civil Rights
Comparable Worth
Court Funding
Crime Rates
Crime Victims' Rights
Demographics (Appendix)
Detroit People Mover
Divestiture of Michigan Pension Fund Investment
    in South Africa
Drug Testing in the Workplace
Drunk Driving
Economic and Political History of Michigan
    (Chapter 1)
Economic Development: Michigan Strategic Fund
Economic Development: Regulatory Relief
Economic Development: Urban Enterprise Zones
Economic Outlook (Appendix)
Education: Community College Funding
Education: Dropout Prevention
Education: Funding for Public Four-Year Colleges
    and Universities

Education: Guaranteed Tuition Program
Education: State Spending on K–12
Education: State Support for Private Schools
Education: Vandalism and Violence in Schools
Educational Competence
Facts about Michigan (Appendix)
Farm Debt
Farmland Protection
Federal Budget: Effect on Michigan
Federal Tax Reform
Firearms Regulation
Food Stamps
Foster Care
Great Lakes Water Diversion
Great Lakes Water Levels
Great Lakes Water Quality
Groundwater Contamination
Hazardous Substances in the Workplace
Hazardous Waste Disposal
Health Care Cost Containment
Health Care Regulation
Health Promotion
Holidays (Appendix)
Homeless, The
Income tax: Graduated vs. Flat Rate
Income Tax: Local
Income Tax: State Rates, Credits, and Deductions
Indian Treaty Fishing
Infant Mortality
Infrastructure Replacement
Job Training
Key Economic Statistics (Appendix)
Liability Insurance: Bars and Restaurants
Liability Insurance: Directors and Officers
Liability Insurance: Governments
Liability Insurance: Products
Lottery: Where the Money Goes
Medicaid
Medical Malpractice Insurance: Availability and
    Tort Reform
Medical Treatment Decisions
Mental Health Institutions
Mental Health Programming

Mortgage Reform
National Guard Federalization
Natural Resources Trust Fund
No-Fault Auto Insurance
Nonpoint Pollution
Nursing Home Care
Organ Transplants
Part-Time Legislature
Prison Overcrowding
Prison Sentencing Guidelines
Privatization
Promoting Michigan
Promoting Michigan Food Products
Property Taxes
Radioactive Waste Disposal
Radon Gas
Regional Economies in Michigan (Appendix)
Revenue Sharing: Federal/State Assistance to Local
    Units of Government
Seat Belt Law
Single Business Tax
Smoking in Public Places
Solid Waste Management
State Budget (Chapter 3)
State Debt
Structure of State Government (Chapter 2)
Substance Abuse
Suicide Among Teenagers
Surrogate Mothering
Teenage Pregnancies, Sex Education, and Birth
    Control
Tobacco Products: Taxation
Transportation Funding
Transportation: High-Speed Rail
Unemployment
Unemployment Insurance
Utility Regulation
Vehicle Emissions Testing
Water Quality
Welfare: Caseloads and Expenditures
Welfare Reform
Workers' Compensation
Youth Corps

1986 (1st) EDITION

Abortion
Abortions: Medicaid Funding
Acid Rain
AIDS
Air Pollution Regulation
Auto Theft
Balanced Budget Amendment
Banking Law Reform
Biennial State Budget
Blue Cross/Blue Shield Mutualization
Bottle Deposits on Wine Coolers
Bottle Deposits: Unclaimed
Budget Stabilization Fund (BSF)
Business Climate
Campaign Financing
Capital Punishment
Child Abuse
Civil Rights
Comparable Worth
Crime Rates
Crime Victim's Rights
Detroit People Mover
Divestiture of Michigan Pension Fund: Investment
    in South Africa
Dramshop Liability Law Reform
Drunk Driving

Economic and Political History of Michigan
    (Chapter 1)
Economic Development: Regulatory Relief
Education: Community College Funding
Education: Higher Education Funding
Education: State Spending on K–12
Education: State Support for Private Schools
Education: Vandalism and Violence in Schools
Equal Rights Amendment
Facts about Michigan (Appendix)
Farm Debt
Farmland Protection
Firearms Regulation
Food Stamps
Foster Care
Governmental Liability
Gramm-Rudman-Hollings Deficit Reduction Act
Great Lakes Water Diversion
Great Lakes Water Levels
Great Lakes Water Quality
Groundwater Contamination
Hazardous Substances in the Workplace
Hazardous Waste Disposal
Health Care Cost Containment
Health Care Regulation
Income Tax: Graduated vs. Fixed

Income Tax: Local
Indian Treaty Fishing
Infant Mortality
Infrastructure Replacement
Insurance: Essential Insurance Reform
Lottery: Where the Money Goes
Medicaid
Medical Malpractice Insurance: Availability and
    Tort Reform
Medical Treatment Decisions
Mental Health Institutions
Mental Health Programming
Natural Resources Trust Fund
Non-Point Pollution
Nursing Home Care
Part-Time Legislature
Prison Overcrowding
Privatization
Promoting Michigan
Promoting Michigan Food Products
Property Taxes
Radioactive Waste Disposal
Revenue Limitation: The Headlee Amendment
Revenue Sharing: Federal/State Assistance to Local
    Government
Seat Belt Law

Sponsored by the Michigan Nonprofit Association and the Council of Michigan Foundations

Sponsored by the Michigan Nonprofit Association and the Council of Michigan Foundations

Michigan *in* Brief
2002–03

Sponsored by the Michigan Nonprofit Association and the Council of Michigan Foundations
Produced and published by Public Sector Consultants, Inc.

Objective discussion of more than forty Michigan public policy issues, presenting background information, points of contention and consensus, and sources of additional information ❧ A summary of the state's political, cultural, and economic history ❧ Descriptions of the three branches of state government ❧ An explanation of the state budget process ❧ A description of Michigan's nonprofit sector ❧

Michigan *in* Brief **Order Form**

Please print or type

NAME _____ TITLE _____

ORGANIZATION _____

ADDRESS _____

CITY _____ STATE _____ ZIP _____

TELEPHONE _____ FACSIMILE _____

E-MAIL ADDRESS _____

Make check payable to Michigan Nonprofit Association and mail to
Michigan Nonprofit Association
1048 Pierpont Drive, Suite 3
Lansing, MI 48911-5976

Please indicate the number of copies you are purchasing.

Michigan in Brief Handbook
$30 each x Qty. _____ = $_____
Shipping and handling included

Michigan sales tax (6%)
If applicable + $_____

TOTAL ENCLOSED $_____

Payment must accompany order

Sponsored by the Michigan Nonprofit Association and the Council of Michigan Foundations